California

Everyday

Mathematics

The University of Chicago School Mathematics Project

Math Masters

Grade 4

McGraw Hill **Wright Group**

The University of Chicago School Mathematics Project (UCSMP)

Max Bell, Director, UCSMP Elementary Materials Component; Director, *Everyday Mathematics* First Edition
James McBride, Director, *Everyday Mathematics* Second Edition
Andy Isaacs, Director, *Everyday Mathematics* Third Edition
Amy Dillard, Associate Director, *Everyday Mathematics* Third Edition

Authors

Max Bell, John Bretzlauf, Amy Dillard, Robert Hartfield, Andy Isaacs, James McBride, Kathleen Pitvorec, Peter Saecker, Robert Balfanz*, William Carroll*, Sheila Sconiers*

First Edition only

Technical Art	**Teachers in Residence**	**Editorial Assistant**
Diana Barrie	Carla L. LaRochelle	Laurie K. Thrasher
	Rebecca W. Maxcy	

Contributors

Martha Ayala, Virginia J. Bates, Randee Blair, Donna R. Clay, Vanessa Day, Jean Faszholz, James Flanders, Patti Haney, Margaret Phillips Holm, Nancy Kay Hubert, Sybil Johnson, Judith Kiehm, Deborah Arron Leslie, Laura Ann Luczak, Mary O'Boyle, William D. Pattison, Beverly Pilchman, Denise Porter, Judith Ann Robb, Mary Seymour, Laura A. Sunseri-Driscoll

Photo Credits

©Corbis, p. 114 *top right;* ©Gregory Adams/Getty Images, cover, *top right;* ©Getty Images, cover, *center,* pp. v, 68, 346 *top left, center right, bottom right;* ©Tony Hamblin; Frank Lane Picture Agency/Corbis, cover, *bottom left;* ©Ken O'Donoghue, pp. 57, 293; ©Vladimir Pcholkin/Getty Images, pp. 93 *right,* 101; ©PhotoEdit, Inc., p. 346 top *right;* ©Shutterstock, p. 346 *center left, bottom left;* ©Roger Wood/Corbis, p. 93 *left.*

This material is based upon work supported by the National Science Foundation under Grant No. ESI-9252984. Any opinions, findings, conclusions, or recommendations expressed in this material are those of the authors and do not necessarily reflect the views of the National Science Foundation.

www.WrightGroup.com

Send all inquiries to:
Wright Group/McGraw-Hill
P.O. Box 812960
Chicago, IL 60681

ISBN 978-0-07-612895-2
MHID 0-07-612895-4

2 3 4 5 6 7 8 9 MAL 13 12 11 10 09 08

The *McGraw-Hill* Companies

Contents

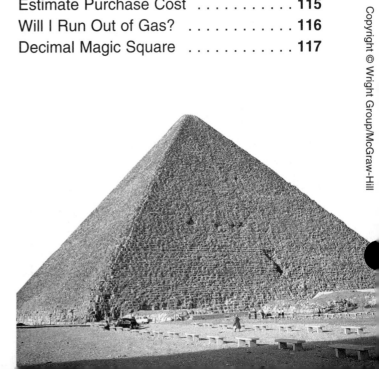

iv   Contents

Unit 5

Unit 6

Contents   **v**

Contents   **vii**

Teaching Aid Masters

Game Masters

Family Letter

California Mathematics Content Standards

Welcome to *Everyday Mathematics!* Throughout the year, your child will be given assignments and activities to do at home. These assignments, called Study Links, are correlated to the California Mathematics Content Standards which describe what every student in California can and needs to learn in mathematics. The standards are identified at the bottom of the Study Link pages and are listed here for your reference.

Study Link	California Content Standard
1•2	**Measurement and Geometry 3.0** Students demonstrate an understanding of plane and solid geometric objects and use this knowledge to show relationships and solve problems.
1•3	**Measurement and Geometry 3.8** Know the definition of different quadrilaterals (e.g., rhombus, square, rectangle, parallelogram, trapezoid).
1•3	**Measurement and Geometry 3.5** Know the definitions of a right angle, an acute angle, and an obtuse angle. Understand that 90°, 180°, 270°, and 360° are associated, respectively, with $\frac{1}{4}$, $\frac{1}{2}$, $\frac{3}{4}$, and full turns.
1•4	**Measurement and Geometry 3.8** Know the definition of different quadrilaterals (e.g., rhombus, square, rectangle, parallelogram, trapezoid).
1•5	**Measurement and Geometry 3.8** Know the definition of different quadrilaterals (e.g., rhombus, square, rectangle, parallelogram, trapezoid).
1•5	**Measurement and Geometry 3.0** Students demonstrate an understanding of plane and solid geometric objects and use this knowledge to show relationships and solve problems.
1•5	**Measurement and Geometry 3.7** Know the definitions of different triangles (e.g., equilateral, isosceles, scalene) and identify their attributes.
1•5	**Number Sense 3.1** Demonstrate an understanding of, and the ability to use, standard algorithms for the addition and subtraction of multidigit numbers.
1•6	**Measurement and Geometry 3.0** Students demonstrate an understanding of plane and solid geometric objects and use this knowledge to show relationships and solve problems.
1•7	**Measurement and Geometry 3.2** Identify the radius and diameter of a circle.
1•7	**Number Sense 3.1** Demonstrate an understanding of, and the ability to use, standard algorithms for the addition and subtraction of multidigit numbers.

Study Link	California Content Standard
1•8	**Measurement and Geometry 3.0** Students demonstrate an understanding of plane and solid geometric objects and use this knowledge to show relationships and solve problems.
2•1	**Number Sense 1.1** Read and write whole numbers in the millions.
2•2	**Number Sense 3.0** Students solve problems involving addition, subtraction, multiplication, and division of whole numbers and understand the relationships among the operations.
2•2	**Number Sense 4.1** Understand that many whole numbers break down in different ways (e.g., $12 \times 4 \times 3 = 2 \times 6 = 2 \times 2 \times 3$).
2•3	**Number Sense 1.0** Students understand the place value of whole numbers and decimals to two decimal places and how whole numbers and decimals relate to simple fractions. Students use the concepts of negative numbers.
2•3	**Number Sense 1.1** Read and write whole numbers in the millions.
2•4	**Number Sense 1.0** Students understand the place value of whole numbers and decimals to two decimal places and how whole numbers and decimals relate to simple fractions. Students use the concepts of negative numbers.
2•4	**Number Sense 1.1** Read and write whole numbers in the millions.
2•5	**Statistics, Data Analysis, and Probability 1.0** Students organize, represent, and interpret numerical and categorical data and clearly communicate their findings.
2•5	**Statistics, Data Analysis, and Probability 1.1** Formulate survey questions; systematically collect and represent data on a number line; and coordinate graphs, tables, and charts.
2•5	**Statistics, Data Analysis, and Probability 1.2** Identify the mode(s) for sets of categorical data and the mode(s), median, and any apparent outliers for numerical data sets.

Study Link	California Content Standard
2•6	**Statistics, Data Analysis, and Probability 1.1** Formulate survey questions; systematically collect and represent data on a number line; and coordinate graphs, tables, and charts.
2•6	**Statistics, Data Analysis, and Probability 1.2** Identify the mode(s) for sets of categorical data and the mode(s), median, and any apparent outliers for numerical data sets.
2•6	**Statistics, Data Analysis, and Probability 1.3** Interpret one- and two-variable data graphs to answer questions about a situation.
2•7	**Number Sense 2.1** Estimate and compute the sum or difference of whole numbers and positive decimals to two places.
2•7	**Number Sense 3.1** Demonstrate an understanding of, and the ability to use, standard algorithms for the addition and subtraction of multidigit numbers.
2•7	**Mathematical Reasoning 2.1** Use estimation to verify the reasonableness of calculated results.
2•8	**Statistics, Data Analysis, and Probability 1.2** Identify the mode(s) for sets of categorical data and the mode(s), median, and any apparent outliers for numerical data sets.
2•9	**Number Sense 2.1** Estimate and compute the sum or difference of whole numbers and positive decimals to two places.
2•9	**Number Sense 3.1** Demonstrate an understanding of, and the ability to use, standard algorithms for the addition and subtraction of multidigit numbers.
3•1	**Number Sense 3.0** Students solve problems involving addition, subtraction, multiplication, and division of whole numbers and understand the relationships among the operations
3•1	**Mathematical Reasoning 1.1** Analyze problems by identifying relationships, distinguishing relevant from irrelevant information, sequencing and prioritizing information, and observing patterns.
3•1	**Algebra and Functions 1.4** Use and interpret formulas (e.g., area = length × width or A = lw) to answer questions about quantities and their relationships.
3•2	**Number Sense 3.0** Students solve problems involving addition, subtraction, multiplication, and division of whole numbers and understand the relationships among the operations.
3•2	**Number Sense 4.0** Students know how to factor small whole numbers.
3•2	**Number Sense 4.1** Understand that many whole numbers break down in different ways (e.g., 12 = 4 × 3 = 2 × 6 = 2 × 2 × 3).

Study Link	California Content Standard
3•3	**Number Sense 3.0** Students solve problems involving addition, subtraction, multiplication, and division of whole numbers and understand the relationships among the operations.
3•3	**Number Sense 4.0** Students know how to factor small whole numbers.
3•4	**Mathematical Reasoning 2.0** Students use strategies, skills, and concepts in finding solutions.
3•4	**Number Sense 3.0** Students solve problems involving addition, subtraction, multiplication, and division of whole numbers and understand the relationships among the operations.
3•4	**Number Sense 4.0** Students know how to factor small whole numbers.
3•5	**Algebra and Functions 1.0** Students use and interpret variables, mathematical symbols, and properties to write and simplify expressions and sentences.
3•5	**Number Sense 3.0** Students solve problems involving addition, subtraction, multiplication, and division of whole numbers and understand the relationships among the operations.
3•6	**Number Sense 3.0** Students solve problems involving addition, subtraction, multiplication, and division of whole numbers and understand the relationships among the operations.
3•6	**Mathematical Reasoning 2.3** Use a variety of methods, such as words, numbers, symbols, charts, graphs, tables, diagrams, and models, to explain mathematical reasoning.
3•6	**Number Sense 4.0** Students know how to factor small whole numbers.
3•7	**Number Sense 3.1** Demonstrate an understanding of, and the ability to use, standard algorithms for the addition and subtraction of multidigit numbers.
3•8	**Number Sense 3.0** Students solve problems involving addition, subtraction, multiplication, and division of whole numbers and understand the relationships among the operations.
3•8	**Number Sense 2.1** Estimate and compute the sum or difference of whole numbers and positive decimals to two places.
3•8	**Mathematical Reasoning 1.0** Students make decisions about how to approach problems.
3•8	**Mathematical Reasoning 2.3** Use a variety of methods, such as words, numbers, symbols, charts, graphs, tables, diagrams, and models, to explain mathematical reasoning.

CA2 California Content Standards

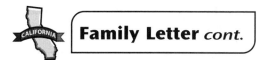

Study Link	California Content Standard
3♦9	**Algebra and Functions 1.0** Students use and interpret variables, mathematical symbols, and properties to write and simplify expressions and sentences.
3♦10	**Number Sense 3.0** Students solve problems involving addition, subtraction, multiplication, and division of whole numbers and understand the relationships among the operations.
3♦10	**Algebra and Functions 1.0** Students use and interpret variables, mathematical symbols, and properties to write and simplify expressions and sentences.
3♦10	**Algebra and Functions 1.2** Interpret and evaluate mathematical expressions that now use parentheses.
3♦10	**Algebra and Functions 1.3** Use parentheses to indicate which operation to perform first when writing expressions containing more than two terms and different operations.
3♦11	**Algebra and Functions 1.0** Students use and interpret variables, mathematical symbols, and properties to write and simplify expressions and sentences.
3♦11	**Algebra and Functions 1.1** Use letters, boxes, or other symbols to stand for any number in simple expressions or equations (e.g., demonstrate an understanding and the use of the concept of a variable).
3♦11	**Algebra and Functions 2.0** Students know how to manipulate equations.
4♦1	**Number Sense 1.0** Students understand the place value of whole numbers and decimals to two decimal places and how whole numbers and decimals relate to simple fractions. Students use the concepts of negative numbers.
4♦2	**Number Sense 2.1** Estimate and compute the sum or difference of whole numbers and positive decimals to two places.
4♦3	**Number Sense 1.2** Order and compare whole numbers and decimals to two decimal places.
4♦3	**Number Sense 1.9** Identify on a number line the relative position of positive fractions, positive mixed numbers, and positive decimals to two decimal places.
4♦4	**Number Sense 2.0** Students extend their use and understanding of whole numbers to the addition and subtraction of simple decimals.
4♦4	**Number Sense 2.1** Estimate and compute the sum or difference of whole numbers and positive decimals to two places.
4♦4	**Number Sense 2.2** Round two-place decimals to one decimal or to the nearest whole number and judge the reasonableness of the rounded answer.

Study Link	California Content Standard
4♦5	**Number Sense 2.0** Students extend their use and understanding of whole numbers to the addition and subtraction of simple decimals.
4♦5	**Number Sense 2.1** Estimate and compute the sum or difference of whole numbers and positive decimals to two places.
4♦6	**Number Sense 2.0** Students extend their use and understanding of whole numbers to the addition and subtraction of simple decimals.
4♦6	**Number Sense 2.1** Estimate and compute the sum or difference of whole numbers and positive decimals to two places.
4♦7	**Number Sense 1.0** Students understand the place value of whole numbers and decimals to two decimal places and how whole numbers and decimals relate to simple fractions. Students use the concepts of negative numbers.
4♦7	**Number Sense 1.2** Order and compare whole numbers and decimals to two decimal places.
4♦7	**Number Sense 1.6** Write tenths and hundredths in decimal and fraction notations and know the fraction and decimal equivalents for halves and fourths (e.g., $\frac{1}{2}$ = 0.5 or .50; $\frac{7}{4}$ = $1\frac{3}{4}$ = 1.75).
4♦8	**Number Sense 2.1** Estimate and compute the sum or difference of whole numbers and positive decimals to two places.
4♦9	**Number Sense 1.2** Order and compare whole numbers and decimals to two decimal places.
4♦10	**Number Sense 4.0** Students know how to factor small whole numbers.
5♦1	**Number Sense 3.0** Students solve problems involving addition, subtraction, multiplication, and division of whole numbers and understand the relationships among the operations.
5♦1	**Number Sense 2.1** Estimate and compute the sum or difference of whole numbers and positive decimals to two places.
5♦2	**Number Sense 3.0** Students solve problems involving addition, subtraction, multiplication, and division of whole numbers and understand the relationships among the operations.
5♦2	**Algebra and Functions 1.1** Use letters, boxes, or other symbols to stand for any number in simple expressions or equations (e.g., demonstrate an understanding and the use of the concept of a variable).
5♦2	**Mathematical Reasoning 1.1** Analyze problems by identifying relationships, distinguishing relevant from irrelevant information, sequencing and prioritizing information, and observing patterns.

Family Letter *cont.*

Study Link	California Content Standard
5•3	**Number Sense 1.4** Decide when a rounded solution is called for and explain why such a solution may be appropriate.
5•3	**Number Sense 2.1** Estimate and compute the sum or difference of whole numbers and positive decimals to two places.
5•4	**Number Sense 1.4** Decide when a rounded solution is called for and explain why such a solution may be appropriate.
5•4	**Number Sense 3.3** Solve problems involving multiplication of multidigit numbers by two-digit numbers.
5•5	**Number Sense 3.0** Students solve problems involving addition, subtraction, multiplication, and division of whole numbers and understand the relationships among the operations.
5•5	**Number Sense 3.2** Demonstrate an understanding of, and the ability to use, standard algorithms for multiplying a multidigit number by a two-digit number and for dividing a multidigit number by a one-digit number; use relationships between them to simplify computations and to check results.
5•5	**Number Sense 3.3** Solve problems involving multiplication of multidigit numbers by two-digit numbers.
5•6	**Number Sense 3.2** Demonstrate an understanding of, and the ability to use, standard algorithms for multiplying a multidigit number by a two-digit number and for dividing a multidigit number by a one-digit number; use relationships between them to simplify computations and to check results.
5•6	**Number Sense 3.3** Solve problems involving multiplication of multidigit numbers by two-digit numbers.
5•7	**Number Sense 3.2** Demonstrate an understanding of, and the ability to use, standard algorithms for multiplying a multidigit number by a two-digit number and for dividing a multidigit number by a one-digit number; use relationships between them to simplify computations and to check results.
5•8	**Number Sense 1.0** Students understand the place value of whole numbers and decimals to two decimal places and how whole numbers and decimals relate to simple fractions. Students use the concepts of negative numbers.
5•8	**Number Sense 1.1** Read and write whole numbers in the millions.
5•8	**Number Sense 3.0** Students solve problems involving addition, subtraction, multiplication, and division of whole numbers and understand the relationships among the operations.
5•8	**Mathematical Reasoning 2.0** Students use strategies, skills, and concepts in finding solutions.

Study Link	California Content Standard
5•9	**Number Sense 1.1** Read and write whole numbers in the millions.
5•9	**Number Sense 1.0** Students understand the place value of whole numbers and decimals to two decimal places and how whole numbers and decimals relate to simple fractions. Students use the concepts of negative numbers.
5•10	**Number Sense 1.1** Read and write whole numbers in the millions.
5•10	**Number Sense 1.3** Round whole numbers through the millions to the nearest ten, hundred, thousand, ten thousand, or hundred thousand.
5•11	**Statistics, Data Analysis, and Probability 1.0** Students organize, represent, and interpret numerical and categorical data and clearly communicate their findings.
5•11	**Number Sense 1.2** Order and compare whole numbers and decimals to two decimal places.
5•11	**Number Sense 2.1** Estimate and compute the sum or difference of whole numbers and positive decimals to two places.
6•1	**Number Sense 3.0** Students solve problems involving addition, subtraction, multiplication, and division of whole numbers and understand the relationships among the operations.
6•1	**Number Sense 3.4** Solve problems involving division of multidigit numbers by one-digit numbers.
6•1	**Mathematical Reasoning 2.3** Use a variety of methods, such as words, numbers, symbols, charts, graphs, tables, diagrams, and models, to explain mathematical reasoning.
6•2	**Number Sense 3.4** Solve problems involving division of multidigit numbers by one-digit numbers.
6•2	**Mathematical Reasoning 1.2** Determine when and how to break a problem into simpler parts.
6•3	**Number Sense 3.2** Demonstrate an understanding of, and the ability to use, standard algorithms for multiplying a multidigit number by a two-digit number and for dividing a multidigit number by a one-digit number; use relationships between them to simplify computations and to check results.
6•3	**Number Sense 3.4** Solve problems involving division of multidigit numbers by one-digit numbers.
6•4	**Number Sense 1.4** Decide when a rounded solution is called for and explain why such a solution may be appropriate.
6•4	**Number Sense 3.4** Solve problems involving division of multidigit numbers by one-digit numbers.

CA4   California Content Standards

Study Link	California Content Standard
6◆4	**Mathematical Reasoning 2.3** Use a variety of methods, such as words, numbers, symbols, charts, graphs, tables, diagrams, and models, to explain mathematical reasoning.
6◆5	**Measurement and Geometry 2.0** Students use two-dimensional coordinate grids to represent points and graph lines and simple figures.
6◆5	**Measurement and Geometry 2.2** Understand that the length of a horizontal line segment equals the difference of the x-coordinates.
6◆5	**Measurement and Geometry 2.3** Understand that the length of a vertical line segment equals the difference of the y-coordinates.
6◆5	**Measurement and Geometry 3.5** Know the definitions of a right angle, an acute angle, and an obtuse angle. Understand that 90°, 180°, 270°, and 360° are associated, respectively, with $\frac{1}{4}$, $\frac{1}{2}$, $\frac{3}{4}$, and full turns.
6◆6	**Measurement and Geometry 3.5** Know the definitions of a right angle, an acute angle, and an obtuse angle. Understand that 90°, 180°, 270°, and 360° are associated, respectively, with $\frac{1}{4}$, $\frac{1}{2}$, $\frac{3}{4}$, and full turns.
6◆6	**Number Sense 3.2** Demonstrate an understanding of, and the ability to use, standard algorithms for multiplying a multidigit number by a two-digit number and for dividing a multidigit number by a one-digit number; use relationships between them to simplify computations and to check results.
6◆7	**Measurement and Geometry 3.5** Know the definitions of a right angle, an acute angle, and an obtuse angle. Understand that 90°, 180°, 270°, and 360° are associated, respectively, with $\frac{1}{4}$, $\frac{1}{2}$, $\frac{3}{4}$, and full turns.
6◆8	**Measurement and Geometry 2.0** Students use two-dimensional coordinate grids to represent points and graph lines and simple figures.
6◆9	**Measurement and Geometry 2.0** Students use two-dimensional coordinate grids to represent points and graph lines and simple figures.
6◆10	**Number Sense 3.0** Students solve problems involving addition, subtraction, multiplication, and division of whole numbers and understand the relationships among the operations.
6◆10	**Number Sense 3.2** Demonstrate an understanding of, and the ability to use, standard algorithms for multiplying a multidigit number by a two-digit number and for dividing a multidigit number by a one-digit number; use relationships between them to simplify computations and to check results.

Study Link	California Content Standard
6◆10	**Number Sense 3.4** Solve problems involving division of multidigit numbers by one-digit numbers.
7◆1	**Number Sense 1.5** Explain different interpretations of fractions, for example, parts of a whole, parts of a set, and division of whole numbers by whole numbers; explain equivalents of fractions (see Standard 4.0).
7◆1	**Number Sense 1.7** Write the fraction represented by a drawing of parts of a figure; represent a given fraction by using drawings; and relate a fraction to a simple decimal on a number line.
7◆1	**Number Sense 1.9** Identify on a number line the relative position of positive fractions, positive mixed numbers, and positive decimals to two decimal places.
7◆1	**Number Sense 3.1** Demonstrate an understanding of, and the ability to use, standard algorithms for the addition and subtraction of multidigit numbers.
7◆2	**Number Sense 1.5** Explain different interpretations of fractions, for example, parts of a whole, parts of a set, and division of whole numbers by whole numbers; explain equivalents of fractions (see Standard 4.0).
7◆3	**Statistics, Data Analysis, and Probability 2.0** Students make predictions for simple probability situations.
7◆3	**Statistics, Data Analysis, and Probability 2.2** Express outcomes of experimental probability situations verbally and numerically (e.g., 3 out of 4; $\frac{3}{4}$).
7◆4	**Number Sense 1.5** Explain different interpretations of fractions, for example, parts of a whole, parts of a set, and division of whole numbers by whole numbers; explain equivalents of fractions (see Standard 4.0).
7◆4	**Number Sense 1.7** Write the fraction represented by a drawing of parts of a figure; represent a given fraction by using drawings; and relate a fraction to a simple decimal on a number line.
7◆5	**Number Sense 1.5** Explain different interpretations of fractions, for example, parts of a whole, parts of a set, and division of whole numbers by whole numbers; explain equivalents of fractions (see Standard 4.0).
7◆5	**Number Sense 1.7** Write the fraction represented by a drawing of parts of a figure; represent a given fraction by using drawings; and relate a fraction to a simple decimal on a number line.
7◆5	**Mathematical Reasoning 2.3** Use a variety of methods, such as words, numbers, symbols, charts, graphs, tables, diagrams, and models, to explain mathematical reasoning.

Study Link	California Content Standard
7◆5	**Measurement and Geometry 3.0** Students demonstrate an understanding of plane and solid geometric objects and use this knowledge to show relationships and solve problems.
7◆6	**Number Sense 1.5** Explain different interpretations of fractions, for example, parts of a whole, parts of a set, and division of whole numbers by whole numbers; explain equivalents of fractions (see Standard 4.0).
7◆6	**Number Sense 1.7** Write the fraction represented by a drawing of parts of a figure; represent a given fraction by using drawings; and relate a fraction to a simple decimal on a number line.
7◆7	**Number Sense 1.5** Explain different interpretations of fractions, for example, parts of a whole, parts of a set, and division of whole numbers by whole numbers; explain equivalents of fractions (see Standard 4.0).
7◆8	**Number Sense 1.6** Write tenths and hundredths in decimal and fraction notations and know the fraction and decimal equivalents for halves and fourths (e.g., $\frac{1}{2}$ = 0.5 or .50; $\frac{7}{4}$ = $1\frac{3}{4}$ = 1.75).
7◆8	**Number Sense 1.7** Write the fraction represented by a drawing of parts of a figure; represent a given fraction by using drawings; and relate a fraction to a simple decimal on a number line.
7◆9	**Number Sense 1.9** Identify on a number line the relative position of positive fractions, positive mixed numbers, and positive decimals to two decimal places.
7◆9	**Mathematical Reasoning 2.3** Use a variety of methods, such as words, numbers, symbols, charts, graphs, tables, diagrams, and models, to explain mathematical reasoning.
7◆10	**Number Sense 1.5** Explain different interpretations of fractions, for example, parts of a whole, parts of a set, and division of whole numbers by whole numbers; explain equivalents of fractions (see Standard 4.0).
7◆10	**Number Sense 1.7** Write the fraction represented by a drawing of parts of a figure; represent a given fraction by using drawings; and relate a fraction to a simple decimal on a number line.
7◆11	**Statistics, Data Analysis, and Probability 1.1** Formulate survey questions; systematically collect and represent data on a number line; and coordinate graphs, tables, and charts.
7◆12	**Statistics, Data Analysis, and Probability 2.0** Students make predictions for simple probability situations.

Study Link	California Content Standard
7◆12	**Statistics, Data Analysis, and Probability 2.1** Represent all possible outcomes for a simple probability situation in an organized way (e.g., tables, grids, tree diagrams).
7◆12	**Statistics, Data Analysis, and Probability 2.2** Express outcomes of experimental probability situations verbally and numerically (e.g., 3 out of 4; $\frac{3}{4}$).
8◆1	**Measurement and Geometry 1.0** Students understand perimeter and area.
8◆1	**Measurement and Geometry 1.3** Understand that rectangles that have the same perimeter can have different areas.
8◆1	**Measurement and Geometry 1.4** Understand and use formulas to solve problems involving perimeters and areas of rectangles and squares. Use those formulas to find the areas of more complex figures by dividing the figures into basic shapes.
8◆2	**Measurement and Geometry 1.0** Students understand perimeter and area.
8◆3	**Measurement and Geometry 1.0** Students understand perimeter and area.
8◆3	**Measurement and Geometry 1.1** Measure the area of rectangular shapes by using appropriate units, such as square centimeter, (cm2), square meter (m2), square kilometer (km2), square inch (in.2), square yard (yd.2), or square mile (mi.2).
8◆3	**Measurement and Geometry 1.4** Understand and use formulas to solve problems involving perimeters and areas of rectangles and squares. Use those formulas to find the areas of more complex figures by dividing the figures into basic shapes.
8◆4	**Measurement and Geometry 1.0** Students understand perimeter and area.
8◆5	**Algebra and Functions 1.1** Use letters, boxes, or other symbols to stand for any number in simple expressions or equations (e.g., demonstrate an understanding and the use of the concept of a variable).
8◆5	**Algebra and Functions 1.4** Use and interpret formulas (e.g., area = length × width or A = lw) to answer questions about quantities and their relationships.
8◆5	**Measurement and Geometry 1.1** Measure the area of rectangular shapes by using appropriate units, such as square centimeter, (cm2), square meter (m2), square kilometer (km2), square inch (in.2), square yard (yd.2), or square mile (mi.2).
8◆5	**Measurement and Geometry 1.4** Understand and use formulas to solve problems involving perimeters and areas of rectangles and squares. Use those formulas to find the areas of more complex figures by dividing the figures into basic shapes.

Study Link	California Content Standard
8◆6	**Measurement and Geometry 1.0** Students understand perimeter and area.
8◆6	**Algebra and Functions 1.1** Use letters, boxes, or other symbols to stand for any number in simple expressions or equations (e.g., demonstrate an understanding and the use of the concept of a variable).
8◆6	**Algebra and Functions 1.4** Use and interpret formulas (e.g., area = length × width or A = lw) to answer questions about quantities and their relationships.
8◆6	**Measurement and Geometry 1.4** Understand and use formulas to solve problems involving perimeters and areas of rectangles and squares. Use those formulas to find the areas of more complex figures by dividing the figures into basic shapes.
8◆7	**Algebra and Functions 1.1** Use letters, boxes, or other symbols to stand for any number in simple expressions or equations (e.g., demonstrate an understanding and the use of the concept of a variable).
8◆7	**Algebra and Functions 1.2** Interpret and evaluate mathematical expressions that now use parentheses.
8◆7	**Algebra and Functions 1.4** Use and interpret formulas (e.g., area = length × width or A = lw) to answer questions about quantities and their relationships.
8◆7	**Measurement and Geometry 1.0** Students understand perimeter and area.
8◆7	**Measurement and Geometry 1.4** Understand and use formulas to solve problems involving perimeters and areas of rectangles and squares. Use those formulas to find the areas of more complex figures by dividing the figures into basic shapes.
8◆8	**Statistics, Data Analysis, and Probability 1.0** Students organize, represent, and interpret numerical and categorical data and clearly communicate their findings.
9◆1	**Number Sense 1.6** Write tenths and hundredths in decimal and fraction notations and know the fraction and decimal equivalents for halves and fourths (e.g., $\frac{1}{2}$ = 0.5 or .50; $\frac{7}{4}$ = $1\frac{3}{4}$ = 1.75).
9◆2	**Number Sense 1.6** Write tenths and hundredths in decimal and fraction notations and know the fraction and decimal equivalents for halves and fourths (e.g., $\frac{1}{2}$ = 0.5 or .50; $\frac{7}{4}$ = $1\frac{3}{4}$ = 1.75).
9◆3	**Number Sense 1.6** Write tenths and hundredths in decimal and fraction notations and know the fraction and decimal equivalents for halves and fourths (e.g., $\frac{1}{2}$ = 0.5 or .50; $\frac{7}{4}$ = $1\frac{3}{4}$ = 1.75).

Study Link	California Content Standard
9◆4	**Number Sense 1.6** Write tenths and hundredths in decimal and fraction notations and know the fraction and decimal equivalents for halves and fourths (e.g., $\frac{1}{2}$ = 0.5 or .50; $\frac{7}{4}$ = $1\frac{3}{4}$ = 1.75).
9◆5	**Number Sense 1.6** Write tenths and hundredths in decimal and fraction notations and know the fraction and decimal equivalents for halves and fourths (e.g., $\frac{1}{2}$ = 0.5 or .50; $\frac{7}{4}$ = $1\frac{3}{4}$ = 1.75).
9◆6	**Number Sense 3.0** Students solve problems involving addition, subtraction, multiplication, and division of whole numbers and understand the relationships among the operations.
9◆6	**Mathematical Reasoning 2.3** Use a variety of methods, such as words, numbers, symbols, charts, graphs, tables, diagrams, and models, to explain mathematical reasoning.
9◆6	**Mathematical Reasoning 3.1** Evaluate the reasonableness of the solution in the context of the original situation.
9◆7	**Statistics, Data Analysis, and Probability 1.0** Students organize, represent, and interpret numerical and categorical data and clearly communicate their findings.
9◆7	**Number Sense 3.2** Demonstrate an understanding of, and the ability to use, standard algorithms for multiplying a multidigit number by a two-digit number and for dividing a multidigit number by a one-digit number; use relationships between them to simplify computations and to check results.
9◆8	**Number Sense 3.3** Solve problems involving multiplication of multidigit numbers by two-digit numbers.
9◆8	**Mathematical Reasoning 2.1** Use estimation to verify the reasonableness of calculated results.
9◆8	**Mathematical Reasoning 2.3** Use a variety of methods, such as words, numbers, symbols, charts, graphs, tables, diagrams, and models, to explain mathematical reasoning.
9◆9	**Number Sense 3.4** Solve problems involving division of multidigit numbers by one-digit numbers.
9◆9	**Number Sense 3.2** Demonstrate an understanding of, and the ability to use, standard algorithms for multiplying a multidigit number by a two-digit number and for dividing a multidigit number by a one-digit number; use relationships between them to simplify computations and to check results.
9◆9	**Mathematical Reasoning 2.3** Use a variety of methods, such as words, numbers, symbols, charts, graphs, tables, diagrams, and models, to explain mathematical reasoning.

California Content Standards   **CA7**

Study Link	California Content Standard
10•1	**Measurement and Geometry 3.4** Identify figures that have bilateral and rotational symmetry.
10•2	**Measurement and Geometry 3.4** Identify figures that have bilateral and rotational symmetry.
10•3	**Measurement and Geometry 3.4** Identify figures that have bilateral and rotational symmetry.
10•3	**Number Sense 3.2** Demonstrate an understanding of, and the ability to use, standard algorithms for multiplying a multidigit number by a two-digit number and for dividing a multidigit number by a one-digit number; use relationships between them to simplify computations and to check results.
10•4	**Measurement and Geometry 3.4** Identify figures that have bilateral and rotational symmetry.
10•5	**Measurement and Geometry 3.4** Identify figures that have bilateral and rotational symmetry.
10•6	**Number Sense 1.8** Use concepts of negative numbers (e.g., on a number line, in counting, in temperature, in "owing").
11•1	**Statistics, Data Analysis, and Probability 1.0** Students organize, represent, and interpret numerical and categorical data and clearly communicate their findings.
11•2	**Measurement and Geometry 3.0** Students demonstrate an understanding of plane and solid geometric objects and use this knowledge to show relationships and solve problems.
11•2	**Measurement and Geometry 3.6** Visualize, describe, and make models of geometric solids (e.g., prisms, pyramids) in terms of the number and shape of faces, edges, and vertices; interpret two-dimensional representations of three-dimensional objects; and draw patterns (of faces) for a solid that, when cut and folded, will make a model of the solid.
11•3	**Measurement and Geometry 3.0** Students demonstrate an understanding of plane and solid geometric objects and use this knowledge to show relationships and solve problems.
11•3	**Measurement and Geometry 3.6** Visualize, describe, and make models of geometric solids (e.g., prisms, pyramids) in terms of the number and shape of faces, edges, and vertices; interpret two-dimensional representations of three-dimensional objects; and draw patterns (of faces) for a solid that, when cut and folded, will make a model of the solid.

Study Link	California Content Standard
11•4	**Measurement and Geometry 3.6** Visualize, describe, and make models of geometric solids (e.g., prisms, pyramids) in terms of the number and shape of faces, edges, and vertices; interpret two-dimensional representations of three-dimensional objects; and draw patterns (of faces) for a solid that, when cut and folded, will make a model of the solid.
11•4	**Number Sense 3.2** Demonstrate an understanding of, and the ability to use, standard algorithms for multiplying a multidigit number by a two-digit number and for dividing a multidigit number by a one-digit number; use relationships between them to simplify computations and to check results.
11•5	**Mathematical Reasoning 3.2** Note the method of deriving the solution and demonstrate a conceptual understanding of the derivation by solving similar problems.
11•6	**Number Sense 1.8** Use concepts of negative numbers (e.g., on a number line, in counting, in temperature, in "owing").
11•6	**Number Sense 3.2** Demonstrate an understanding of, and the ability to use, standard algorithms for multiplying a multidigit number by a two-digit number and for dividing a multidigit number by a one-digit number; use relationships between them to simplify computations and to check results.
12•2	**Mathematical Reasoning 1.1** Analyze problems by identifying relationships, distinguishing relevant from irrelevant information, sequencing and prioritizing information, and observing patterns.
12•2	**Number Sense 3.2** Demonstrate an understanding of, and the ability to use, standard algorithms for multiplying a multidigit number by a two-digit number and for dividing a multidigit number by a one-digit number; use relationships between them to simplify computations and to check results.
12•3	**Mathematical Reasoning 1.1** Analyze problems by identifying relationships, distinguishing relevant from irrelevant information, sequencing and prioritizing information, and observing patterns.
12•3	**Number Sense 3.3** Solve problems involving multiplication of multidigit numbers by two-digit numbers.
12•3	**Number Sense 3.4** Solve problems involving division of multidigit numbers by one-digit numbers.
12•4	**Number Sense 3.3** Solve problems involving multiplication of multidigit numbers by two-digit numbers.

Family Letter *cont.*

Study Link	California Content Standard
12◆4	**Number Sense 3.4** Solve problems involving division of multidigit numbers by one-digit numbers.
12◆4	**Mathematical Reasoning 1.1** Analyze problems by identifying relationships, distinguishing relevant from irrelevant information, sequencing and prioritizing information, and observing patterns.
12◆5	**Mathematical Reasoning 1.1** Analyze problems by identifying relationships, distinguishing relevant from irrelevant information, sequencing and prioritizing information, and observing patterns.

Study Link	California Content Standard
12◆5	**Mathematical Reasoning 2.3** Use a variety of methods, such as words, numbers, symbols, charts, graphs, tables, diagrams, and models, to explain mathematical reasoning.
12◆6	**Number Sense 3.0** Students solve problems involving addition, subtraction, multiplication, and division of whole numbers and understand the relationships among the operations.
12◆6	**Statistics, Data Analysis, and Probability 1.2** Identify the mode(s) for sets of categorical data and the mode(s), median, and any apparent outliers for numerical data sets.

Teaching Masters
and
Study Link Masters

Name   Date   Time

LESSON 1·2   Collinear-Points Puzzle

Three or more points on the same line are called **collinear points.**

Example: Points A, B, and C are collinear points on the line below. ABC means that A, B, and C are collinear points, and point B is between points A and C.

$$\overleftrightarrow{A \quad B \quad C}$$

1. The following are true statements about $\overleftrightarrow{EH}$:
   EFH and FGH
   The following are false statements about $\overleftrightarrow{EH}$:
   FEH and FHG

   $$\overleftrightarrow{E \quad F \quad\quad G \quad H}$$

   a. Name two more true statements about line EH. _____

   b. Name two more false statements about line EH. _____

2. Place collinear points J, K, L, M, N, and O on the line below using these clues:

   ◆ J and O are not between any points.
   ◆ MKL
   ◆ NLJ
   ◆ MKN

3. Show a different solution to the puzzle in Problem 2.

4. Create a collinear-points puzzle on the back of this page. Be sure to give enough clues. Record your solution on the line below. Ask someone to solve your puzzle. Can the problem solver find more than one solution to your puzzle?

10

Name   Date   Time

STUDY LINK 1·3   Angles and Quadrangles

Use a straightedge to draw the geometric figures.

1. Draw 2 examples of a rectangle.

2. Draw 2 examples of a trapezoid.

3. How are the polygons in Problems 1 and 2 similar? How are they different?

4. a. Draw right angle DEF.

5. Draw an angle that is larger than a right angle. Label the vertex K.

   b. What is the vertex of the angle? Point _____

   c. What is another name for ∠DEF? ∠ _____

   Practice

6. 9 + 8 = _____   7. 7 + 8 = _____   8. 30 + 80 = _____

9. _____ = 50 + 40   10. _____ = 17 + 94   11. 158 + 93 = _____

11

STUDY LINK 1·1 Unit 1: Family Letter

Introduction to *Fourth Grade Everyday Mathematics*®

Welcome to *Fourth Grade Everyday Mathematics.* It is part of an elementary school mathematics curriculum developed by the University of Chicago School Mathematics Project (UCSMP).

Everyday Mathematics offers students a broad background in mathematics. Some approaches may differ from those you used as a student, but the approaches used are based on research, field test results, and the mathematics students will need in this century.

Fourth Grade Everyday Mathematics emphasizes the following content:

Algebra and Uses of Variables Reading, writing, and solving number sentences

Algorithms and Procedures Exploring addition, subtraction, multiplication, and division methods; inventing individual procedures and algorithms; and experimenting with calculator procedures

Coordinate Systems and Other Reference Frames Using numbers in reference frames: number lines, coordinates, times, dates, and latitude and longitude

Exploring Data Collecting, organizing, displaying, and interpreting numerical data

Functions, Patterns, and Sequences Designing, exploring, and using geometric and number patterns

Geometry and Spatial Sense Developing an intuitive sense about 2- and 3-dimensional objects, their properties, uses, and relationships

Measures and Measurement Exploring metric and U.S. customary measures: linear, area, volume, weight; and exploring geographical measures

Numbers, Numeration, and Order Relations Reading, writing, and using whole numbers, fractions, decimals, percents, negative numbers; and exploring scientific notation

Operations, Number Facts, and Number Systems Practicing addition and subtraction to proficiency; and developing multiplication and division skills

Problem Solving and Mathematical Modeling Investigating methods for solving problems using mathematics in everyday situations

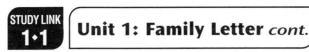

Naming and Constructing Geometric Figures

During the next few weeks, the class will study the geometry of 2-dimensional shapes. Students will examine definitions and properties of shapes and the relationships among them. Students will use compasses to construct shapes and to create their own geometric designs.

Please keep this Family Letter for reference as your child works through Unit 1.

Vocabulary

Important terms in Unit 1:

concave (nonconvex) polygon A polygon in which at least one vertex is "pushed in."

concave polygon

convex polygon A polygon in which all vertices are "pushed outward."

convex polygon

endpoint A point at the end of a line segment or a ray.

line Informally, a straight path that extends infinitely in opposite directions.

line segment A straight path joining two points. The two points are called the endpoints of the segment.

parallelogram A quadrilateral that has two pairs of parallel sides. Opposite sides of a parallelogram have equal lengths. Opposite angles of a parallelogram have the same measure.

polygon A 2-dimensional figure that is made up of three or more line segments joined end to end to make one closed path. The line segments of a polygon may not cross.

quadrangle (quadrilateral) A polygon that has four sides and four angles.

ray A straight path that extends infinitely from a point called its endpoint.

rhombus A quadrilateral whose sides are all the same length. All rhombuses are parallelograms. Every square is a rhombus, but not all rhombuses are squares.

trapezoid In *Everyday Mathematics*, a quadrilateral that has exactly one pair of parallel sides.

vertex The point where the rays of an angle, the sides of a polygon, or the edges of a polyhedron meet.

Do-Anytime Activities

To work with your child on concepts taught in this unit, try these interesting and rewarding activities:

1. Help your child discover everyday uses of geometry as found in art, architecture, jewelry, toys, and so on.

2. See how many words your child can think of that have Greek/Latin prefixes such as *tri-, quad-, penta-, hexa-,* and *octa-.*

3. Help your child think of different ways to draw or make figures without the use of a compass, protractor, or straightedge. For example, you can trace the bottom of a can to make a circle, bend a straw to form a triangle, or make different shapes with toothpicks.

4. Challenge your child to draw or build something, such as a toothpick bridge, using triangular and square shapes. Or show pictures of bridges and point out the triangles used in bridges to provide support.

Building Skills through Games

In Unit 1, your child will play the following games.

Addition Top-It See *Student Reference Book,* page 263. This game provides practice with addition facts.

Polygon Pair-Up See *Student Reference Book,* page 258. This game provides practice identifying properties of polygons.

Sprouts See *Student Reference Book,* page 313. This game provides practice with simple vertex-edge graphs and developing game strategies.

Subtraction Top-It See *Student Reference Book,* pages 263 and 264. This is a variation of *Addition Top-It* and provides practice with subtraction facts.

Sz'kwa See *Student Reference Book,* page 310. This game provides practice with intersecting line segments and developing game strategies.

As You Help Your Child with Homework

As your child brings assignments home, you may want to go over the instructions together, clarifying them as necessary. The answers listed below will guide you through this unit's Study Links.

Study Link 1·2

2. a.

b.

   c. The line has arrows on both ends, but the line segment does not.

3. a.

   b. No. A ray's endpoint must be listed first when naming a ray.

4. A ruler has markings on it, so it can be used to measure.

Study Link 1·3

Sample answers:

1.

2.

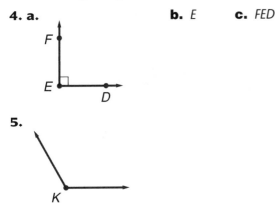

3. The polygons in Problems 1 and 2 have 4 sides and at least 1 pair of parallel sides. The Problem 1 polygons have 2 pairs of equal, parallel sides and all right angles.

4. a.   **b.** *E*   **c.** *FED*

5.

Study Link 1·4

1. Sample answer:

2. a. yes   **b.** yes   **c.** yes   **d.** no

3. Sample answer: **4.** kite

Study Link 1·5

1. rectangle   **2.** Equilateral triangle

3. rhombus

Study Link 1·6

1. A, B, C, E, F, G, I   **2.** B, C

3. C, E, F, I   **4.** A

5. A, B, D, F, G, H, I   **6.** D, G, H

7. 2

Study Link 1·8

1. Sample answers:

   a. square   **c.** hexagon

2. Sample answer: Sides are all the same length, and interior angles are all the same measure.

LESSON 1·1   **Relation-Symbol *Top-It***

1. Cut out the relation symbol cards at the bottom of the page.

2. Shuffle 4 each of the number cards 0–9 and place the deck facedown on the table.

3. Each student turns over 2 cards and makes the largest 2-digit number possible.

4. Students take turns placing the correct relation symbol (>, <, or =) between the cards and reading the number sentence.

Example:

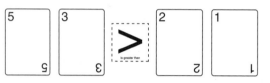

53 is greater than 21.

5. The student with the larger number takes the cards.

6. Play ends when not enough cards are left for each student to have another turn. The student with the most cards wins.

7. Record number sentences for several rounds of play.

53 > 21 _____   _____

_____   _____

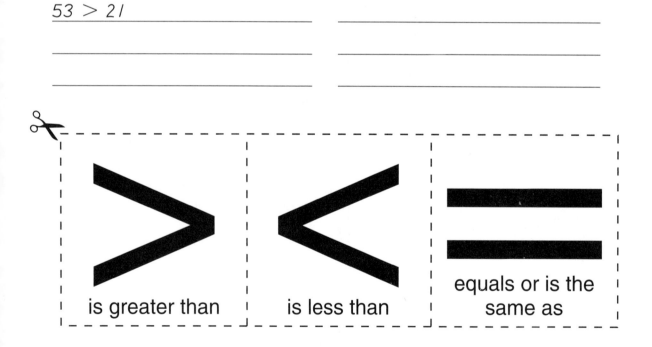

is greater than   is less than   equals or is the same as

**LESSON
1·1** | **Symbols Scavenger Hunt**

Mathematicians use symbols instead of writing out words such as *is greater than, is less than,* and *equals.* Search the *Student Reference Book* to find as many symbols as you can. Record the symbols and the words they stand for in the table below.

Symbol	Meaning
>	*is greater than*

✂ ---

Name _____ Date _____ Time _____

**LESSON
1·1** | **Symbols Scavenger Hunt**

Mathematicians use symbols instead of writing out words such as *is greater than, is less than,* and *equals.* Search the *Student Reference Book* to find as many symbols as you can. Record the symbols and the words they stand for in the table below.

Symbol	Meaning
>	*is greater than*

Copyright © Wright Group/McGraw-Hill

STUDY LINK 1·2

Line Segments, Lines, and Rays

SRB
90 91

1. List at least 5 things in your home that remind you of line segments.

_____

_____

_____

Use a straightedge to complete Problems 2 and 3.

2. a. Draw and label line *AB*.

   b. Draw and label line segment *AB*.

   c. Explain how your drawings of $\overleftrightarrow{AB}$ and $\overline{AB}$ are different.

_____

_____

3. a. Draw and label ray *CD*.

   b. Anita says $\overrightarrow{CD}$ can also be called $\overrightarrow{DC}$. Do you agree? Explain.

_____

_____

4. Explain how a ruler is different from a straightedge.

_____

_____

Practice

5. $13 - 7 =$ _____

6. $15 - 8 =$ _____

7. _____ $= 90 - 50$

8. $140 - 60 =$ _____

9. _____ $= 57 - 39$

10. $115 - 86 =$ _____

Measurement and Geometry 3.0

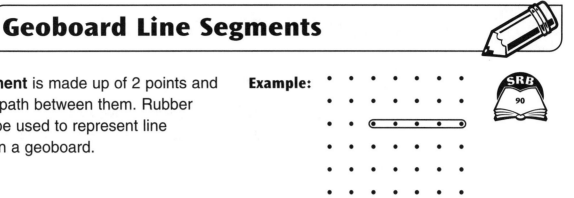

LESSON 1·2 Geoboard Line Segments

A **line segment** is made up of 2 points and the straight path between them. Rubber bands can be used to represent line segments on a geoboard.

Example:

This line segment touches 5 pins.

Practice making line segments, and then follow the directions below. Record your work.

1. Make a line segment that touches 4 pins.

2. Make a line segment that touches 4 different pins.

3. Make the shortest line segment possible.

4. Make the longest line segment possible.

5. Cami says she cannot make a **line** on her geoboard. Do you agree? Explain why or why not. (*Hint:* Look up **line** in the glossary of your *Student Reference Book.*)

_____

_____

LESSON 1·2   Collinear-Points Puzzle

Three or more points on the same line are called **collinear points.**

Example: Points *A, B,* and *C* are collinear points on the line below. *ABC* means that *A, B,* and *C* are collinear points, and point *B* is between points *A* and *C*.

$$\longleftrightarrow \overset{\textstyle A}{\bullet} \quad \overset{\textstyle B}{\bullet} \quad \overset{\textstyle C}{\bullet} \longleftrightarrow$$

1. The following are true statements about $\overleftrightarrow{EH}$:
   EFH and *FGH*
   The following are false statements about $\overleftrightarrow{EH}$:
   FEH and *FHG*

   $$\longleftrightarrow \overset{E}{\bullet}\; \overset{F}{\bullet} \qquad \overset{G}{\bullet}\,\overset{H}{\bullet} \longrightarrow$$

   a. Name two more true statements about line *EH.* _____

   _____

   b. Name two more false statements about line *EH.* _____

   _____

2. Place collinear points *J, K, L, M, N,* and *O* on the line below using these clues:

   ◆ *J* and *O* are not between any points.

   ◆ *MKL*

   ◆ *NLJ*

   ◆ *MKN*

   $$\longleftrightarrow \bullet \quad \bullet \qquad \bullet \qquad \bullet \quad \bullet \qquad \bullet \longrightarrow$$

3. Show a different solution to the puzzle in Problem 2.

   $$\longleftrightarrow \bullet \quad \bullet \qquad \bullet \qquad \bullet \quad \bullet \qquad \bullet \longrightarrow$$

4. Create a collinear-points puzzle on the back of this page. Be sure to give enough clues. Record your solution on the line below. Ask someone to solve your puzzle. Can the problem solver find more than one solution to your puzzle?

   $$\longleftrightarrow \longrightarrow$$

10

Name _____ Date _____ Time _____

STUDY LINK 1·3 **Angles and Quadrangles**

SRB
92 99
100

Use a straightedge to draw the geometric figures.

1. Draw 2 examples of a rectangle.

2. Draw 2 examples of a trapezoid.

3. How are the polygons in Problems 1 and 2 similar? How are they different?

_____

_____

_____

4. a. Draw right angle *DEF*.

5. Draw an angle that is larger than a right angle. Label the vertex *K*.

b. What is the vertex of the angle? Point _____

c. What is another name for ∠*DEF*? ∠ _____

| Practice |

6. 9 + 8 = _____   **7.** 7 + 8 = _____   **8.** 30 + 80 = _____

9. _____ = 50 + 40   **10.** _____ = 17 + 94   **11.** 158 + 93 = _____

Measurement and Geometry 3.8; Measurement and Geometry 3.5

11

LESSON 1·3 Pattern-Block Sort

Label one sheet of paper: **These fit the rule.**
Label another sheet of paper: **These do NOT fit the rule.**

Sort the pattern blocks (hexagon, trapezoid, square, triangle, 2 rhombuses) according to the rules given below. Then use the shapes marked "PB" on your Geometry Template to record the results of your sort.

1. Exactly 4 sides		**2.** All sides the same length	
These fit the rule.	These do NOT fit the rule.	These fit the rule.	These do NOT fit the rule.

3. 4 sides *and* all sides the same length		**4.** All angles the same measure, *and* all sides the same length	
These fit the rule.	These do NOT fit the rule.	These fit the rule.	These do NOT fit the rule.

5. Make up your own rule. Sort the pattern blocks according to your rule. Record your rule and the pattern blocks that fit your rule on the back of this page.

LESSON 1·3 **Polygon Search**

1. Study the figure at the right.

   a. How many triangles do you see?

   _____

   b. How many triangles have a right angle?

   _____

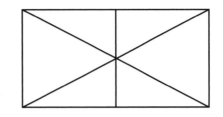

2. Study the figure at the right.

   a. How many squares do you see?

   _____

   b. How many triangles?

   _____

   c. How many rectangles that are *not* squares?

   _____

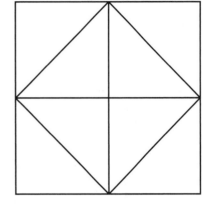

3. Make up a geometry puzzle like the one in Problem 2. Use a straightedge to draw line segments to connect some of the dots in the array. Write the answers on the back of this page. Then ask someone to count the number of different polygons in your puzzle.

```
    •     •     •     •

    •     •     •     •

    •     •     •     •

    •     •     •     •
```

LESSON 1·4 | **Math Message: Properties of Polygons**

All of these have something in common.

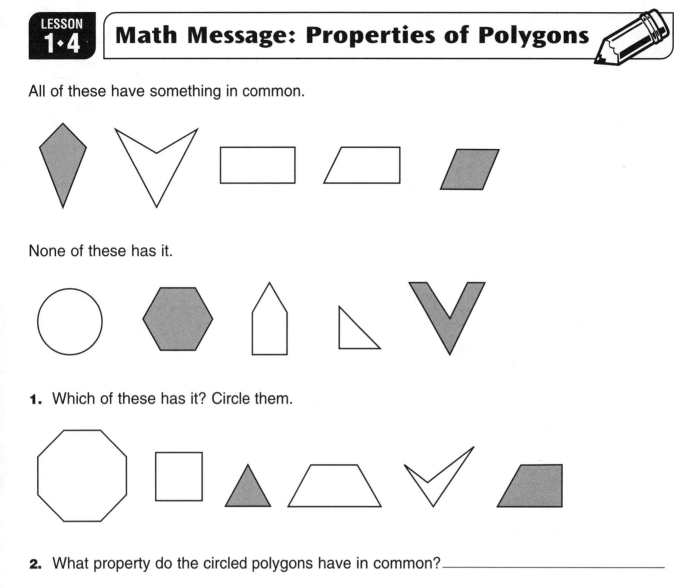

None of these has it.

1. Which of these has it? Circle them.

2. What property do the circled polygons have in common? _____

_____

_____

3. Use your straightedge to draw a polygon that has this property.

STUDY LINK 1·4   **Classifying Quadrangles**

SRB
99 100

1. A parallelogram is a quadrangle (quadrilateral) that has 2 pairs of parallel sides.

   Draw a parallelogram.

2. Answer *yes* or *no*. Explain your answer.

   a. Is a rectangle a parallelogram? _____

   _____

   b. Is a square a parallelogram? _____

   _____

   c. Is a square a rhombus? _____

   _____

   d. Is a trapezoid a parallelogram? _____

   _____

3. Draw a quadrangle that has at least 1 right angle.

4. Draw a quadrangle that has 2 pairs of equal sides but is NOT a parallelogram.

   This is called a _____.

Practice

5. $12 - 6 =$ _____

6. $16 - 7 =$ _____

7. $210 - 150 =$ _____

8. _____ $= 140 - 80$

9. _____ $= 93 - 58$

10. $123 - 76 =$ _____

LESSON 1·4 | **Parallel Line Segments**

1. All of these are **parallel** line segments. Make each pair on your geoboard.

2. None of these are parallel line segments. Make each pair on your geoboard.

3. Some of these are parallel line segments. Make each pair on your geoboard. Circle the parallel line segments.

4. How would you describe parallel line segments to a friend?

_____

_____

_____

_____

5. Practice making other parallel line segments on your geoboard.

16

Straw-Squares Puzzle

LESSON 1·4

1. Gather 17 straws of the same length. Arrange them as shown to the right.

The arrangement of straws forms a rectangle. The object of this puzzle is to remove straws from the arrangement so that only 2 squares remain.

- ◆ You must remove *exactly 6* straws from the arrangement.

- ◆ You may not move any of the other straws.

2. Record your work on the picture above by marking an X on the straws you removed. Trace over the remaining straws that form the 2 squares.

✂ -

Name   Date   Time

Straw-Squares Puzzle

LESSON 1·4

1. Gather 17 straws of the same length. Arrange them as shown to the right.

The arrangement of straws forms a rectangle. The object of this puzzle is to remove straws from the arrangement so that only 2 squares remain.

- ◆ You must remove *exactly 6* straws from the arrangement.

- ◆ You may not move any of the other straws.

2. Record your work on the picture above by marking an X on the straws you removed. Trace over the remaining straws that form the 2 squares.

STUDY LINK 1·5 | Polygon Riddles

Answer each riddle. Then use a straightedge to draw a picture
of the shape in the space to the right.

SRB
96–100

1. I am a quadrangle.
I have 2 pairs of parallel sides.
All of my angles are right angles.
I am not a square.

What am I? _____

2. I am a polygon.
All of my sides have the same measure.
All of my angles have the same measure.
I have 3 sides.

What am I? _____

3. I am a polygon.
I am a quadrangle.
All of my sides are the same length.
None of my angles are right angles.

What am I? _____

Try This

4. On the back of this page, make up your own polygon riddle using 4 clues.
Make 2 of the clues hard and 2 of the clues easy. Check your riddle by using a
straightedge to draw a picture of the polygon. Ask a friend or someone at
home to solve your polygon riddle.

Practice

5. $8 + 9 =$ _____

6. $7 + 8 =$ _____

7. $90 + 70 =$ _____

8. _____ $= 60 + 50$

9. _____ $= 54 + 59$

10. $185 + 366 =$ _____

Measurement and Geometry 3.0, 3.7, 3.8; Number Sense 3.1

LESSON 1·5 | # Polygons on a Geoboard

Practice using rubber bands to make polygons on a geoboard, then follow the directions below. Use a straightedge to record your work.

SRB 96

1. Make a triangle in which each side touches at least 4 pins.

2. Make a square in which each side touches at least 3 pins.

3. Make a trapezoid.

4. Make a hexagon that only touches 8 pins.

5. Compare your polygons with those of a partner. In the space below, make a list of how the polygons are alike and how they are different.

LESSON 1·5 *The Greedy Triangle*

1. Make an equilateral triangle using your straws. Use a straightedge to draw the shape you made in the table below.

2. With the straws, continue adding one side and one angle to show all the changes that the triangle went through.

3. Complete the table below while making the shapes.

Shape	Drawing of Shape	Number of Sides	Number of Angles
equilateral triangle		3	3
quadrilateral		4	
pentagon		5	
hexagon		6	
heptagon		7	
octagon		8	
nonagon		9	
decagon		10	

What Is a Kite?

These are kites.

These are NOT kites.

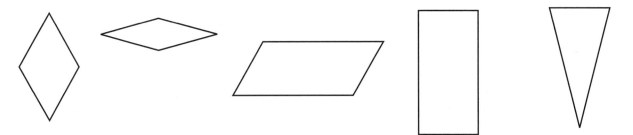

If you had to explain what a kite is, what would you say?

_____

_____

_____

_____

_____

Name _____ Date _____ Time _____

LESSON 1·5

What Is a Rhombus?

These are rhombuses.

These are NOT rhombuses.

   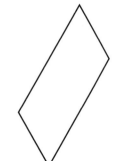

If you had to explain what a rhombus is, what would you say?

_____

_____

_____

_____

_____

_____

STUDY LINK 1·6   Properties of Geometric Figures

SRB
96–100

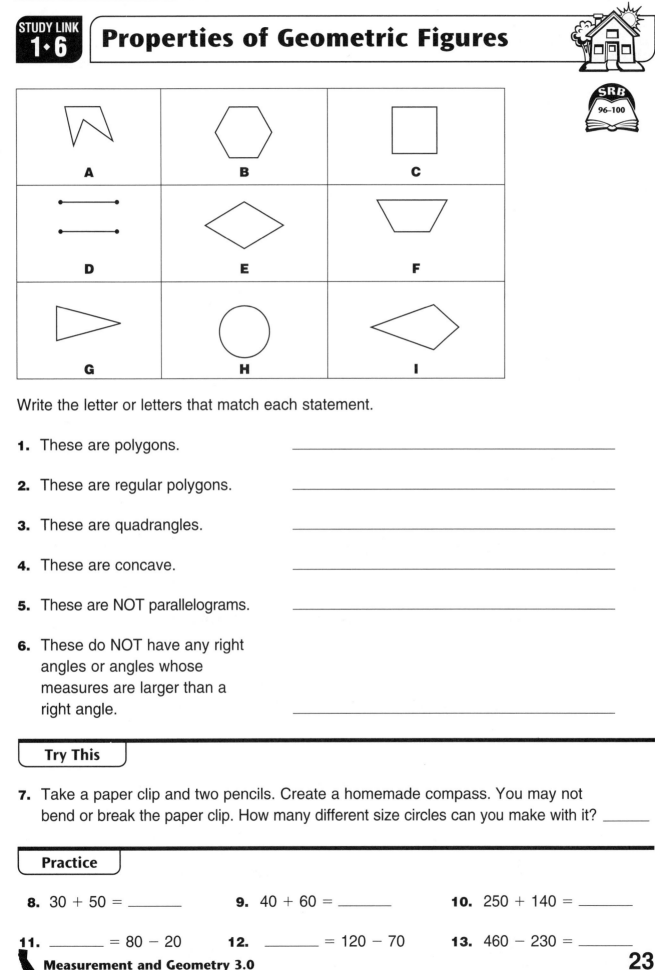

A	B	C
D	E	F
G	H	I

Write the letter or letters that match each statement.

1. These are polygons. _____

2. These are regular polygons. _____

3. These are quadrangles. _____

4. These are concave. _____

5. These are NOT parallelograms. _____

6. These do NOT have any right angles or angles whose measures are larger than a right angle. _____

Try This

7. Take a paper clip and two pencils. Create a homemade compass. You may not bend or break the paper clip. How many different size circles can you make with it? _____

Practice

8. $30 + 50 =$ _____   **9.** $40 + 60 =$ _____   **10.** $250 + 140 =$ _____

11. _____ $= 80 - 20$ **12.** _____ $= 120 - 70$ **13.** $460 - 230 =$ _____

Measurement and Geometry 3.0

23

LESSON 1·6   A Crowded-Points Puzzle

Nine points are crowded together in a large, square room.
The points do not like crowds.

1. Use a straightedge to draw 2 squares so that each point will have
a room of its own.

2. Explain what you did to solve this puzzle.

   ◆ Describe the squares you drew using vocabulary words you learned in class.

   ◆ Tell how you know that the 2 polygons you drew are squares.

_____

_____

_____

_____

LESSON 1·7

Math Message

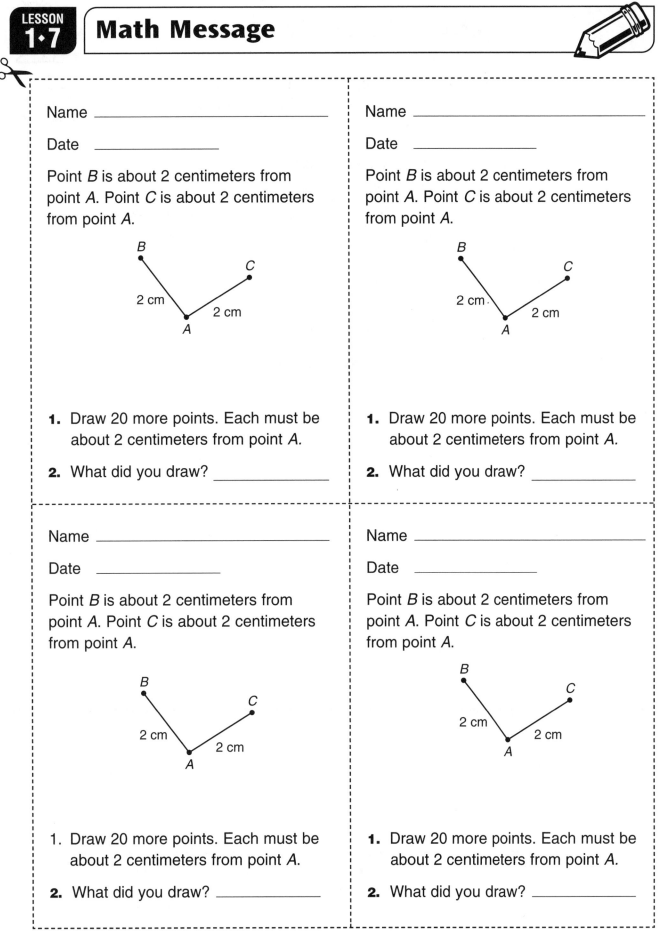

Name _____

Date _____

Point *B* is about 2 centimeters from point *A*. Point *C* is about 2 centimeters from point *A*.

2 cm   2 cm

1. Draw 20 more points. Each must be about 2 centimeters from point *A*.

2. What did you draw? _____

Name _____

Date _____

Point *B* is about 2 centimeters from point *A*. Point *C* is about 2 centimeters from point *A*.

2 cm   2 cm

1. Draw 20 more points. Each must be about 2 centimeters from point *A*.

2. What did you draw? _____

Name _____

Date _____

Point *B* is about 2 centimeters from point *A*. Point *C* is about 2 centimeters from point *A*.

2 cm   2 cm

1. Draw 20 more points. Each must be about 2 centimeters from point *A*.

2. What did you draw? _____

Name _____

Date _____

Point *B* is about 2 centimeters from point *A*. Point *C* is about 2 centimeters from point *A*.

2 cm   2 cm

1. Draw 20 more points. Each must be about 2 centimeters from point *A*.

2. What did you draw? _____

STUDY LINK 1·7 | # The Radius of a Circle

1. Find 3 circular objects. Trace around them to make 3 circles in the space below or on the back of this page. For each circle, do the following:

   a. Draw a point to mark the approximate center of the circle. Then draw a point on the circle.

   b. Use a straightedge to connect these points. This line segment is a **radius** of the circle.

   c. Use a ruler to measure the radius to the nearest centimeter. If you do not have a ruler at home, cut out the one at the bottom of this page.

   d. Record the measure of the radius next to the circle.

Example:

SRB
104

| Practice |

2. _____ = 80 + 20   **3.** _____ = 30 + 90   **4.** 580 + 370 = _____

5. 120 − 30 = _____   **6.** 160 − 70 = _____   **7.** 650 − 280 = _____

Measurement and Geometry 3.2; Number Sense 3.1

LESSON 1·7 | Tangent Circles

Two circles that "barely touch" (touch at just one point) are said to be **tangent** to each other.

On a separate sheet of paper, draw two congruent circles that are tangent to each other. Then draw a third congruent circle that is tangent to each of the other two circles.

Here is one way.

1. Draw a circle. Afterward, do not change the opening of the compass.

2. Use a straightedge to draw a line segment from the center of the circle. Make the segment at least twice as long as the radius of the circle.

3. On this segment, mark a point that is outside of the circle. Make the distance from the circle to the point equal to the radius of the circle. Use your compass.

4. Draw a second circle, using the point you marked for the center of the circle.

Directions continue on *Math Masters,* page 28.

LESSON 1·7 **Tangent Circles** *continued*

5. Open the compass so that the anchor is on the center of one circle and the pencil point is on the center of the other circle.

6. Swing the compass and make a mark (an arc) above the two circles.

7. Move the anchor to the center of the other circle and make an arc through the first arc.

8. Close the compass to the original opening (the radius of the original circles).

9. Put the anchor on the point where the two arcs intersect. Draw a third circle.

LESSON 1·7 **Radius, Chord, and Diameter**

A **radius** is a line segment that connects the center of a circle with any point on the circle.

A **chord** is a line segment that connects 2 points on a circle.

A **diameter** is a special chord. It is special because it is the chord with the largest possible length for that circle.

Use your straightedge to inscribe the polygons described in Problems 1–4.

1. Draw 4 chords to make a rectangle.

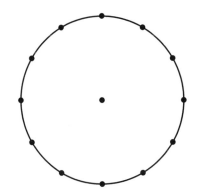

2. Draw a diameter and 3 chords to make a trapezoid.

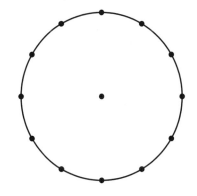

3. Draw 3 chords to make an isosceles triangle.

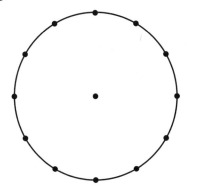

4. Draw 4 chords to make a kite.

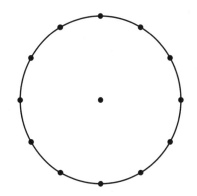

29

STUDY LINK 1·8 | Inscribed Polygons

1. Use a straightedge to inscribe a different polygon in each of the circles below. Write the name of each polygon.

Example:

SRB
96 97
115

kite

a. _____

b. _____

c. _____

d. _____

2. Are any of the polygons that you drew *regular polygons?* Explain how you know.

_____

_____

_____

Practice

3. 41 + 27 = _____

4. _____ = 263 + 59

5. 461 + 398 = _____

6. _____ = 72 − 36

7. 158 − 71 = _____

8. 742 − 349 = _____

Measurement and Geometry 3.0

LESSON 1·8

A Hexagon Design

1. Outline the regular hexagon in the design to the right
   using a red crayon or pencil. Use your crayons
   or pencils to color the design in an interesting way.

2. How do you know the polygon you outlined is a regular hexagon? _____

   _____

   _____

   _____

✂ --

Name   Date   Time

Copyright © Wright Group/McGraw-Hill

LESSON 1·8

A Hexagon Design

1. Outline the regular hexagon in the design to the right
   using a red crayon or pencil. Use your crayons
   or pencils to color the design in an interesting way.

2. How do you know the polygon you outlined is a regular hexagon? _____

   _____

   _____

   _____

Creating 6-Point Designs

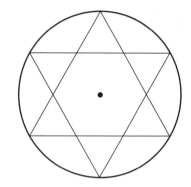

1. This 6-pointed star is called a **hexagram.** Use your compass and straightedge to construct a hexagram on a separate sheet of paper.

2. Construct another large hexagram on a separate sheet of paper. Draw a second hexagram inside the first, and then a third hexagram inside the second. Make a hexagram design by coloring your construction.

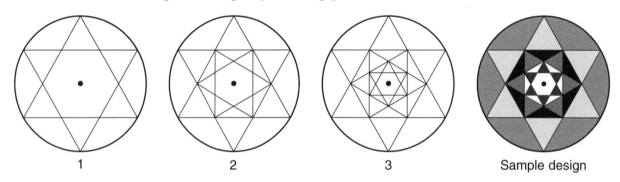

1   2   3   Sample design

3. Construct the hexagram pattern several more times. Color each one in a different way to create a new design.

4. Construct the following pattern several times on separate sheets of paper. Color each one in a different way.

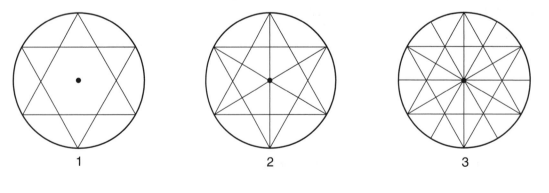

1   2   3

| Try This |

5. Create and color your own 6-point designs on separate sheets of paper.

LESSON 1·8   An Inscribed Equilateral Triangle

Follow each step below. Draw on a separate sheet of paper. Repeat these steps several times. Then cut out your best work and tape it to the bottom of this page.

Step 1   Draw a circle. (Keep the same compass opening for Steps 2 and 3.) Draw a dot on the circle. Place the anchor of your compass on the dot and draw a mark on the circle.

Step 2   Place the anchor of your compass on the mark you just made and draw another mark on the circle.

Step 3   Do this 4 more times to divide the circle into 6 equal parts. The 6th mark should be on the dot you started with or very close to it.

Step 4   With your straightedge, connect 3 alternating marks (every other mark) on the circle to form an equilateral triangle. Use your compass to check that the sides of the equilateral triangle are about the same length.

STUDY LINK 1·9 | # Unit 2: Family Letter

Using Numbers and Organizing Data

Your child is about to begin this year's work with numbers. The class will examine what numbers mean and how they are used in everyday life.

In today's world, numbers are all around us—in newspapers and magazines and on TV. We use them

◆ to count things *(How many people are in the room?)*

◆ to measure things *(How tall are you?)*

◆ to create codes *(What is your Social Security number?)*

◆ to locate things in reference frames *(What time is it?)*

◆ to express rates, scales, and percents *(How many miles per gallon does your car get? What percent voted for Jamie?)*

Sometimes students will need to interpret a collection of numbers. The class will learn to organize such collections of numbers in tables and graphs and to draw conclusions about them.

Computation is an important part of problem solving. Fortunately, we are no longer restricted to paper-and-pencil methods of computation. We can use calculators or computer programs to solve lengthy or complex problems. Your child will practice mental and paper-and-pencil methods of computation, use a calculator, and have opportunities to decide which is most appropriate for solving a particular problem.

Many of us were taught that there is just one way to do computations. For example, we may have learned to subtract by "borrowing." We may not have realized that there are other ways of subtracting numbers. While students will not be expected to learn more than one method, they will examine several different methods and realize that there are often several ways to arrive at the same result. They will have the option of using the methods with which they are comfortable or even inventing one of their own.

Mathematics games will be used throughout the school year to practice various arithmetic skills. Through games, practice becomes a thinking activity to be enjoyed. The games your child will play in this unit will provide practice with renaming numbers, with addition, and with subtraction. They require very little in the way of materials, so you may play them at home as well.

Please keep this Family Letter for reference as your child works through Unit 2.

STUDY LINK 1·9 | **Unit 2: Family Letter** *cont.*

Vocabulary

Important terms in Unit 2:

algorithm A set of step-by-step instructions for doing something, such as carrying out a computation or solving a problem.

base 10 Our number system in which each place in a number has a value 10 times the place to its right and $\frac{1}{10}$ the place to its left.

column-addition A method for adding numbers in which the addends' digits are first added in each place-value column separately, and then 10-for-1 trades are made until each column has only one digit. Lines are drawn to separate the place-value columns.

	100s	10s	1s
	2	4	8
+	1	8	7
Add the columns:	3	12	15
Adjust the 1s and 10s:	3	13	5
Adjust the 10s and 100s:	4	3	5

equivalent names Different names for the same number. For example, 2 + 6, 4 + 4, 12 − 4, 18 − 10, 100 − 92, 5 + 1 + 2, eight, VIII, and ⊮⊮ /// are equivalent names for 8.

line plot A sketch of data in which check marks, Xs, or other marks above a labeled line show the frequency of each value.

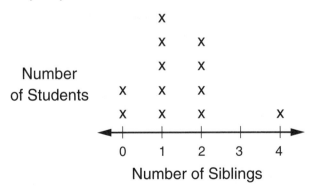

Number of Students

Number of Siblings

mean The sum of a set of numbers divided by the number of numbers in the set. The mean is often referred to simply as the "average."

median The middle value in a set of data when the data are listed in order from least to greatest. If there is an even number of data points, the median is the *mean* of the two middle values.

mode The value or values that occur most often in a set of data.

name-collection box A diagram that is used for writing *equivalent names* for a number. The box to the right shows names for 8.

8
2 + 6
4 + 4
VIII
eight

partial-differences subtraction A way to subtract in which differences are computed separately for each place (ones, tens, hundreds, and so on). The partial differences are then added to give the final answer.

			932
		−	356
Subtract the hundreds:	900 − 300	→	600
Subtract the tens:	30 − 50	→ − 20
Subtract the ones:	2 − 6	→ − 4
Find the total:	600 − 20 − 4	→	576

partial-sums addition A way to add in which sums are computed for each place (ones, tens, hundreds, and so on) separately. The partial sums are then added to give the final answer.

			496
			229
		+	347
Add the hundreds:	400 + 200 + 300	→	900
Add the tens:	90 + 20 + 40	→	150
Add the ones:	6 + 9 + 7	→ +	22
Find the total:	900 + 150 + 22	→	1,072

range The difference between the maximum and the minimum in a set of data.

trade-first subtraction A subtraction method in which all trades are done before any subtractions are carried out.

whole numbers The numbers 0, 1, 2, 3, 4, and so on.

35

Do-Anytime Activities

To work with your child on the concepts taught in this unit, try these interesting and rewarding activities:

1. Have your child see how many numbers he or she can identify in newspapers, magazines, advertisements, or news broadcasts.

2. Have your child collect and compare the measurements (height and weight) or accomplishments of favorite professional athletes.

3. Look up the different time zones of the United States and the world, quizzing your child on what time it would be at that moment at a particular location.

4. Have your child look for different representations of the same number. For example, he or she may see the same money amounts expressed in different ways, such as 50¢, $0.50, or 50 cents.

Building Skills through Games

In Unit 2, your child will play the following games. For detailed instructions, see the *Student Reference Book.*

Addition Top-It See *Student Reference Book*, page 263. This game provides practice with addition facts.

Fishing for Digits See *Student Reference Book*, page 242. This game provides practice identifying digits and the values of the digits, and adding and subtracting.

High-Number Toss See *Student Reference Book*, page 252. This game provides practice reading, writing, and comparing numbers.

Name That Number See *Student Reference Book*, page 254. This game reinforces skills in using all four operations.

Polygon Pair-Up See *Student Reference Book*, page 258. This game provides practice identifying properties of polygons.

Subtraction Target Practice See *Student Reference Book*, page 262. This game provides practice with subtraction and estimation.

Subtraction Top-It See *Student Reference Book*, pages 263 and 264. This is a variation of *Addition Top-It* and provides practice with subtraction facts.

As You Help Your Child with Homework

As your child brings assignments home, you may want to go over the instructions together, clarifying them as necessary. The answers listed below will guide you through this unit's Study Links.

Study Link 2·2

1. Sample answers: 8×8; 32×2; $10 + 54$

2. Sample answers: 2×66; 11×12; $66 + 66$; $30 + 30 + 30 + 30 + 12$; $(50 \times 2) + 32$

3. Sample answers: $20 + 20$; $80 \div 2$; $\frac{1}{2} \times 80$

4. Sample answers: 9×4; $72 \div 2$; $(12 \times 4) - 12$

Study Link 2·3

1. 876,504,000   2. 23,170,080

3. 876,504,000

4. **a.** thousand; 400,000

   b. million; 80,000,000

   c. million; 500,000,000

   d. thousand; 30,000

5. **b.** 596,708   **d.** 1,045,620

6. **b.** 13,877,000   **d.** 150,691,688

Study Link 2·4

2. 581,970,000   3. 97,654,320

5. **a.** 487,000,063   **b.** 15,000,297

6. 97,308,080

Study Link 2·5

2. 27   3. 8   4. 2   5. 6   6. 5

Study Link 2·6

1. **Student Data on Television Time**

   [graph with vertical axis "Number of Students" and horizontal axis labeled 16 17 18 19 20 21 22 23]

   Number of Hours Spent
   Watching Television Each Week

2. **a.** 23   **b.** 16   **c.** 7   **d.** 20   **e.** 20

4. 19.7

Study Link 2·7

1. 152   2. 510   3. 613

4. 1,432   5. 2,520   6. 5,747

11. 136   12. 720   13. 225

14. 720   15. 1,573   16. 2,356

Study Link 2·8

1. **a.** 645   **b.** 19   **c.** 626   **d.** 151

2. Giraffe, Asian elephant, and rhinoceros

3. 90   4. dog   5. mouse

Study Link 2·9

1. 68   11. 29

2. 382   12. 57

3. 367   13. 406

4. 3,746   14. 224

5. 2,889   15. 4,479

6. 2,322   16. 2,538

LESSON 2·1

Uses of Numbers

Answer the following questions:

SRB 2

1. How many students are in your class? _____ students

2. What is your mailing address? _____

3. In what year were you born? _____

4. About how long do you have to eat lunch at school? _____ minutes

5. What time does school start? _____

6. About how many times older than you is your principal? _____

7. Write and answer a question that has a number for an answer.

_____

_____

- ✂

LESSON 2·1

Uses of Numbers

Answer the following questions:

SRB 2

1. How many students are in your class? _____ students

2. What is your mailing address? _____

3. In what year were you born? _____

4. About how long do you have to eat lunch at school? _____ minutes

5. What time does school start? _____

6. About how many times older than you is your principal? _____

7. Write and answer a question that has a number for an answer.

STUDY LINK 2·1 | Numbers Everywhere

Find examples of numbers—all kinds of numbers. Look in newspapers and magazines. Look in books. Look on food packages. Ask people in your family for examples.

Write your numbers below. If an adult says you may, cut out the numbers and tape them onto the back of this page.

Be sure you write what the numbers mean.

Example: Mount Everest is 29,028 feet high. It is the world's tallest mountain.

_____

_____

_____

_____

_____

_____

_____

_____

_____

_____

_____

_____

_____

_____

_____

_____

_____

_____

_____

_____

Practice

1. $5 \times 3 =$ _____
2. _____ $= 4 \times 3$
3. _____ $= 10 \div 2$
4. $8 \div 4 =$ _____

Number Sense 🔢

LESSON 2·1 | **Solving Frames-and-Arrows Problems**

1. On the number line below, count by 3s starting with 0. Circle every number that is part of the count.

SRB
160 161

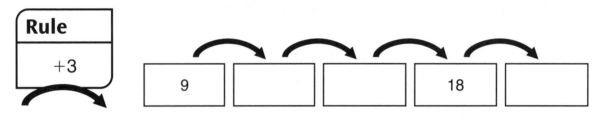

0 1 2 3 4 5 6 7 8 9 10 11 12 13 14 15 16 17 18 19 20 21 22

2. Use the rule to fill in the missing numbers.

Rule

+3

```
[  9  ] → [     ] → [     ] → [  18  ] → [     ]
```

3. Find the rule and fill in the missing numbers.

a. **Rule**

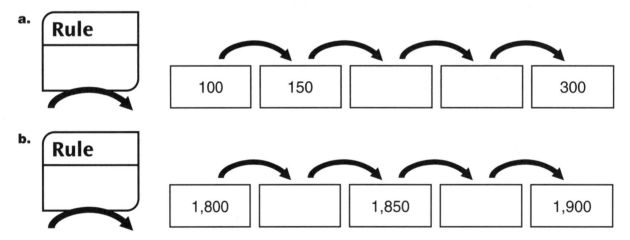

```
[ 100 ] → [ 150 ] → [     ] → [     ] → [ 300 ]
```

b. **Rule**

```
[ 1,800 ] → [     ] → [ 1,850 ] → [     ] → [ 1,900 ]
```

4. Explain how you figured out the rule for Problem 3b.

_____

_____

Try This

5. Find the missing numbers.

350 ____ ____ ____ 550

LESSON 2·1 | Missing Numbers on a Number Line

Mrs. Gonzalez told her students that there is a strategy they can always use to find missing numbers on a number line when the missing numbers are the same distance apart.

Solve the problems.

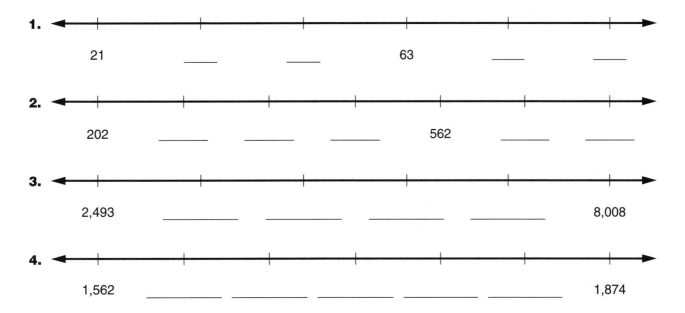

1. 21 _____ _____ 63 _____ _____

2. 202 _____ _____ _____ 562 _____ _____

3. 2,493 _____ _____ _____ _____ 8,008

4. 1,562 _____ _____ _____ _____ _____ 1,874

5. Describe a strategy that the students in Mrs. Gonzalez's class might have used to solve all of the problems on this page.

_____

_____

_____

_____

_____

6. Create a number-line problem like the ones above. Ask a partner to solve it.

STUDY LINK 2·2 | **Many Names for Numbers**

1. Write five names for 64.

64

2. Write five names for 132.

132

3. Pretend that the 4-key on your calculator is broken. Write six ways to display the number 40 on the calculator without using the 4-key. Try to use different numbers and operations.

    Example: $2 \times 2 \times 10$

_____   _____   _____

_____   _____   _____

Try This

4. Now pretend that all the keys on your calculator work except for the 3-key and the 6-key. Write six ways to display the number 36 without using these keys.

_____   _____   _____

_____   _____   _____

Practice

5. $20 + 60 =$ _____

6. _____ $= 60 + 90$

7. _____ $= 80 - 30$

8. $110 - 40 =$ _____

Number Sense **3.0**; Number Sense 4.1

LESSON 2·2 | Domino Sums

Materials   ☐ 1 or 2 sets of double-9 dominoes or *Math Masters,*
                    pages 394–396

SRB
149

☐ number cards 0–18 (1 each; from the Everything Math Deck, if available)

Directions

1. Lay out the number cards in order from 0 through 18.

2. Place each domino above the number card that shows the sum of the domino's dots. In the example below, the sum of 4 and 1 is 5, and the sum of 2 and 3 is 5.

   2 + 3 and 4 + 1 are **equivalent names** for the number 5.

   Example:

3. In the space below, list the addition facts shown by the dominoes. Before you begin, decide how you will organize the facts.

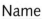

LESSON 2·2 Pan-Balance Problems

A **pan balance** is used to weigh objects. When the weight of the objects in one pan is the same as the weight of the objects in the other pan, the pans are in perfect balance.

In each figure below, the pans hold **equivalent names** for a number. The pans are in perfect balance. Fill in the missing numbers. Write the name for the pan balance.

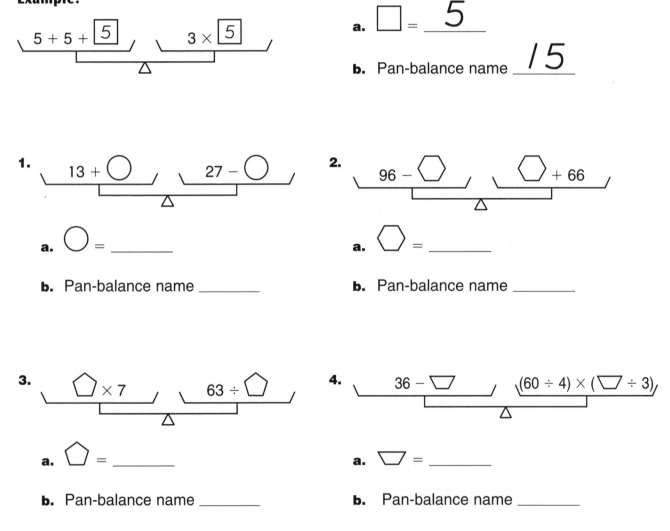

Example:

$5 + 5 + \boxed{5}$ $3 \times \boxed{5}$

a. $\square =$ _5_

b. Pan-balance name _15_

1. $13 + \bigcirc$ $27 - \bigcirc$

a. $\bigcirc =$ _____

b. Pan-balance name _____

2. $96 - \hexagon$ $\hexagon + 66$

a. $\hexagon =$ _____

b. Pan-balance name _____

3. $\pentagon \times 7$ $63 \div \pentagon$

a. $\pentagon =$ _____

b. Pan-balance name _____

4. $36 - \bigtriangledown$ $(60 \div 4) \times (\bigtriangledown \div 3)$

a. $\bigtriangledown =$ _____

b. Pan-balance name _____

STUDY LINK 2·3 | **Place Value in Whole Numbers**

1. Write the number that has

   6 in the millions place,
   4 in the thousands place,
   7 in the ten-millions place,
   5 in the hundred-thousands place,
   8 in the hundred-millions place, and
   0 in the remaining places.

   __ __ _6_, __ __ __, __ __ __

2. Write the number that has

   7 in the ten-thousands place,
   3 in the millions place,
   1 in the hundred-thousands place,
   8 in the tens place,
   2 in the ten-millions place, and
   0 in the remaining places.

   __ __, __ __ __, __ __ __

3. Compare the two numbers you wrote in Problems 1 and 2.

   Which is greater? _____

4. The 6 in 46,711,304 stands for 6 _*million*_, or _6,000,000_.

   a. The 4 in 508,433,529 stands for 400 _____, or _____.

   b. The 8 in 182,945,777 stands for 80 _____, or _____.

   c. The 5 in 509,822,119 stands for 500 _____, or _____.

   d. The 3 in 450,037,111 stands for 30 _____, or _____.

Try This

5. Write the number that is 1 hundred thousand more.

   a. 210,366 _*310,366*_   b. 496,708 _____

   c. 321,589 _____   d. 945,620 _____

6. Write the number that is 1 million more.

   a. 3,499,702 _*4,499,702*_   b. 12,877,000 _____

   c. 29,457,300 _____   d. 149,691,688 _____

Practice

7. 32, 45, 58, ____, ____, ____   8. ____, ____, ____, 89, 115, 141

   Rule: _____   Rule: _____

LESSON 2·3   **Number-Grid Puzzles**

1. Find the missing numbers.

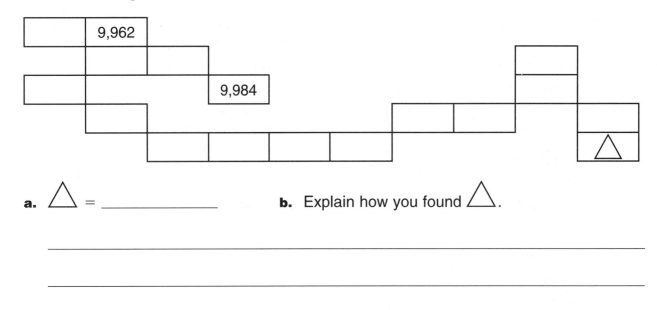

a. △ = _____

b. Explain how you found △.

_____

_____

_____

2. Below is a number-grid puzzle cut from a different number grid. Figure out the pattern, and use it to fill in the missing numbers.

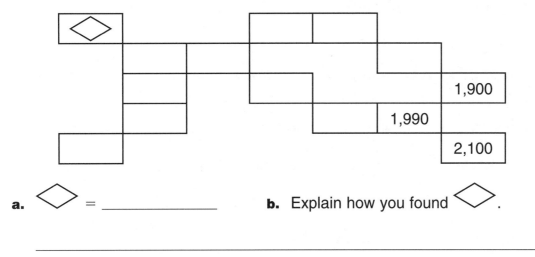

a. ◇ = _____

b. Explain how you found ◇.

_____

_____

_____

c. Describe how this number grid is different from number grids you have used before.

_____

_____

Name _____ Date _____ Time _____

LESSON 2·4 | Calculator "Change" Problems

Use this page with *Math Journal 1,* page 36, Problem 1.

	Start with	Place of Digit	Change to	Operation	New Number
a.	570	Tens			
b.	409	Hundreds			
c.	54,463	Thousands			
d.	760,837	Tens			
e.	52,036,458	Ones			
f.		Ten Thousands			
g.		Millions			

Make up your own calculator "change" problems.

	Start with	Place of Digit	Change to	Operation	New Number
a.					
b.					
c.					
d.					
e.					
f.					
g.					
h.					
i.					

Place Values in Whole Numbers

1. Write the numbers in order from smallest to largest.

15,964   1,509,460   150,094,400
1,400,960   15,094,600

_____

_____

_____

_____

_____

2. Write the number that has

5 in the hundred-millions place,
7 in the ten-thousands place,
1 in the millions place,
9 in the hundred-thousands place,
8 in the ten-millions place, and
0 in all other places.

___ ___ ___, ___ ___ ___, ___ ___ ___

3. Write the largest number you can. Use each digit just once.

3 5 0 7 9 2 6 4 _____

4. Write the value of the digit 8 in each numeral below.

a. 80,007,941 _____

b. 835,099,714 _____

c. 8,714,366 _____

d. 860,490 _____

5. Write each number using digits.

a. four hundred eighty-seven million, sixty-three _____

b. fifteen million, two hundred ninety-seven _____

Try This

6. I am an 8-digit number.
- The digit in the thousands place is the result of dividing 64 by 8.
- The digit in the millions place is the result of dividing 63 by 9.
- The digit in the ten-millions place is the result of dividing 54 by 6.
- The digit in the tens place is the result of dividing 40 by 5.
- The digit in the hundred-thousands place is the result of dividing 33 by 11.
- All the other digits are the result of subtracting any number from itself.

What number am I? ___ ___, ___ ___ ___, ___ ___ ___

Number Sense 1.0; Number Sense 1.1

LESSON 2·4 | Use a Place-Value Tool

1. Display each number below in your place-value flip book. Then display, read, and record the numbers that are 10 more, 100 more, and 1,000 more. Circle the digit that changed.

Number	10 more	100 more	1,000 more
146	1⑤6	②46	①,146
508			
2,368			
4,571			
15,682			

2. Display each number below in your place-value flip book. Then display, read, and record the numbers that are 10 less, 100 less, and 1,000 less. Circle the digit that changed.

Number	10 less	100 less	1,000 less
2,345	2,3③5	2,②45	①,345
3,491			
6,839			
12,367			
45,130			

3. Use your place-value flip book to help you answer the following questions.

   a. What number is 50 more than 329? _____

   b. What number is 300 more than 517? _____

   c. What number is 60 less than 685? _____

   d. What number is 400 less than 932? _____

49

LESSON 2·4 Crack the Muffin Code

Daniel takes orders at the Marvelous Muffin Bakery. The muffins are packed into boxes that hold 1, 3, 9, or 27 muffins. When a customer asks for muffins, Daniel fills out an order slip.

- If a customer orders 5 muffins, Daniel writes CODE 12 on the order slip.
- If a customer orders 19 muffins, Daniel writes CODE 201 on the order slip.
- If a customer orders 34 muffins, Daniel writes CODE 1021 on the order slip.

1. What would Daniel write on the order slip if a customer asked for 47 muffins? Explain.

CODE _____

_____

_____

_____

_____

2. If the Marvelous Muffin Bakery always packs its muffins into the fewest number of boxes possible, what is a code Daniel would never write on an order slip? Explain.

CODE _____

_____

_____

_____

_____

3. The largest box used by the bakery holds 27 muffins. Daniel thinks the bakery should have a box one size larger. How many muffins would the new box hold? Explain.

_____ muffins

_____

_____

_____

_____

STUDY LINK 2·5 | **Collecting Data**

1. Make a list of all the people in your family. Include all the people living at home now. Also include any brothers or sisters who live somewhere else. The people who live at home do not have to be related to you. Do not forget to write your name in the list.

   You will need this information to learn about the sizes of families in your class.

   _____ _____ _____

   _____ _____ _____

   _____ _____ _____

   How many people are in your family? _____ people

The tally chart at the right shows the number of books that some students read over the summer. Use the information to answer the questions below.

Number of Books Reported	Number of Students
2	///
3	̶H̶H̶
4	
5	̶H̶H̶ //
6	̶H̶H̶ /
7	//
8	////

2. How many students reported the number of books they read? _____

3. What is the **maximum** (the largest number of books reported)? _____

4. What is the **minimum** (the smallest number of books reported)? _____

5. What is the **range?** _____

6. What is the **mode** (the most frequent number of books reported)? _____

Practice

7. 30 + 50 = _____

8. _____ = 70 + 70 + 70

9. _____ = 90 + 80 + 60

10. 100 + 40 + 70 = _____

Statistics, Data Analysis, and Probability 1.0, 1.1, 1.2 **51**

LESSON 2·5 Dice-Roll Tally Chart

Tally marks are vertical marks used to keep track of a count.
The fifth tally mark crosses the first four.

Examples:

/	//	///	////	̸/̸/̸/̸/
one	two	three	four	five
̸/̸/̸/̸/ /	̸/̸/̸/̸/ //	̸/̸/̸/̸/ ///	̸/̸/̸/̸/ ////	̸/̸/̸/̸/ ̸/̸/̸/̸/
six	seven	eight	nine	ten

1. Roll a pair of dice and find the sum.

2. Make a tally mark next to the sum in the chart below.

3. Set a timer for 3 minutes. Roll the dice and make a tally mark for each sum until the timer goes off.

Sum	Tallies
2	
3	
4	
5	
6	
7	
8	
9	
10	
11	
12	

4. Answer the questions below.

   a. How many times did you roll a sum of

      4? _____ times

      7? _____ times

      11? _____ times

   b. Which sum was rolled the most number of

      times? _____

   c. Which sum was rolled the least number of

      times? _____

   d. How many times did you roll the dice in all?

      _____ times

   e. On the back of this page, write two more things that you notice about the data you collected.

52

Name   Date   Time

LESSON 2·5 Making a Prediction Based on a Sample

Sometimes large numbers of people or things are impossible to count
or take too much time to count. A smaller **sample** of data is often used
to make predictions about a larger group or **population.**

You and your class collected, recorded, and analyzed data about
the number of raisins found in $\frac{1}{2}$-ounce boxes of raisins.

Use the raisin data you collected on journal page 38 to answer the
following questions.

1. Without opening it, how many raisins do you think are in a large box
   (12 or 15 ounces) of raisins?

   About _____ raisins are in a _____-ounce box.

2. Explain the strategy you used to make your prediction.

   _____

   _____

   _____

3. Suppose you only knew the number of raisins in a single $\frac{1}{2}$-ounce box of
   raisins. Would that affect your prediction about the number of raisins in the
   large box? Why or why not?

   _____

   _____

   _____

   _____

STUDY LINK 2·6 Line Plots

The students in Sylvia's class estimated how much time they spend watching television each week. The tally chart below shows the data they collected.

1. Construct a line plot for the data.

Number of Hours per Week Spent Watching TV	Number of Students
16	///
17	///
18	
19	//// /
20	//// ////
21	/
22	////
23	//

Student Data on Television Time

Number of Students

16 17 18 19 20 21 22 23

Number of Hours Spent
Watching Television Each Week

2. Find the following landmarks for the data:

  a. The maximum number of hours spent watching television each week. _____ hours

  b. minimum _____ hours   **c.** range _____ hours

  d. mode _____ hours   **e.** median _____ hours

3. Estimate the amount of time that you watch television each week. _____ hours

---

Try This

4. Calculate the mean number of hours Sylvia and her classmates spent

watching TV each week. _____ hours

Practice

5. $80 + 30 =$ _____

6. _____ $= 90 + 90$

7. _____ $= 70 + 60$

8. $120 + 30 =$ _____

Statistics, Data Analysis, and Probability 1.1, 1.2, 1.3

LESSON 2·6 | Find the Median Number

The number in the middle of an ordered set of data is called the **middle value,** or **median.**

SRB
73

For Problems 1–3,

◆ Draw nine cards from a deck of number cards.

◆ Arrange the cards in order from smallest to largest.

◆ Record the numbers in the boxes below.

◆ Circle the number in the middle.

Example:

0 2 5 5 (7) 8 9 13 18
smallest   largest

1.

⬚⬚⬚⬚⬚⬚⬚⬚⬚
smallest   largest

The median of my nine cards is _____.

2.

⬚⬚⬚⬚⬚⬚⬚⬚⬚
smallest   largest

The median of my nine cards is _____.

3.

⬚⬚⬚⬚⬚⬚⬚⬚⬚
smallest   largest

The median of my nine cards is _____.

4. Describe how you found the middle number in the problems above.

_____

_____

_____

5. If you arranged the cards in Problem 1 in order from *largest* to *smallest,* would the middle number stay the same? _____ Explain.

_____

_____

55

LESSON 2·6

Comparing Family-Size Data

1. Create a display that compares the family-size data from your class with those of other fourth-grade classes.

SRB 70-75

2. Compare the maximum, minimum, range, mode, and median for family size for each class. Write about the similarities and differences. Use the back of this page if you need more space.

_____

_____

_____

_____

_____

_____

_____

Combine and organize the data from all of the classes. Then answer the following questions.

3. What is the *median* family size for all of the classes? _____ people

4. How does your class median compare with the larger sample?

_____

_____

5. What is the *mean* family size for all of the classes? _____ people

6. If you had to predict the family size of a student from your school that you did not know, what would you predict? Explain your answer.

_____

_____

_____

STUDY LINK 2·7 | Multidigit Addition

Make a ballpark estimate. Use the **partial-sums method** to add. Compare your answer with your estimate to see if your answer makes sense.

1. 67 + 85	**2.** 439 + 71	**3.** 227 + 386
Ballpark estimate: _____	Ballpark estimate: _____	Ballpark estimate: _____
4. 493 + 939	**5.** 732 + 1,788	**6.** 4,239 + 1,508
Ballpark estimate: _____	Ballpark estimate: _____	Ballpark estimate: _____

Practice

7. $8 \times 7 =$ _____

8. $9 \times 9 =$ _____

9. _____ $\div 6 = 9$

10. _____ $\div 4 = 8$

Number Sense 2.1; Number Sense 3.1; Mathematical Reasoning 2.1

Multidigit Addition *continued*

Make a ballpark estimate. Use the **column-addition method** to add.
Compare your answer with your estimate to see if your answer makes sense.

SRB
11

11. 89 + 47	**12.** 634 + 86	**13.** 148 + 77
Ballpark estimate: _____	Ballpark estimate: _____	Ballpark estimate: _____
14. 481 + 239	**15.** 746 + 827	**16.** 508 + 1,848
Ballpark estimate: _____	Ballpark estimate: _____	Ballpark estimate: _____

Practice

17. 16, 21, 26, _____, _____, _____   Rule: _____

18. _____, 52, _____, 104, 130, _____   Rule: _____

Number Sense 2.1; Number Sense 3.1; Mathematical Reasoning 2.1

LESSON 2·7

Addition Number Stories

Use *Math Masters,* page 405 and base-10 blocks to solve the number stories.
Record what you did in the parts-and-total diagrams.

Example:

The class had 43 blue crayons and 15 red crayons.

How many crayons did they have in all?

_58_ crayons

Total	
58	
Part	**Part**
43	15

1. Auntie May had 24 fish and 11 hamsters. How many pets did she have altogether?

   _____ pets

Total	
Part	**Part**

2. Jordan made a flower basket for his mother that had 23 daisies and 8 roses. How many flowers were in the basket?

   _____ flowers

Total	
Part	**Part**

3. Lucia had 38 cents and Madison had 29 cents. If they put their money together, how much money would they have?

   _____ cents

Total	
Part	**Part**

4. Miguel has 54 baseball cards. Janet gave him 47 more baseball cards. How many baseball cards does he have now?

   _____ baseball cards

Total	
Part	**Part**

59

LESSON 2·8

Measuring and Drawing Line Segments

Measure the following line segments to the nearest $\frac{1}{2}$ centimeter.

SRB 128

1. ————————————

About _____ cm

2. ——————————————————

About _____ cm

3. ——————————————

About _____ cm

4. ————————————————————

About _____ cm

Draw line segments having the following lengths:

5. 8 centimeters

6. 10 centimeters

7. 3.5 centimeters

Try This

8. Draw a line segment having the following length: 46 millimeters

STUDY LINK 2·8 | **Gestation Period**

The period between the time an animal becomes pregnant and the time its baby is born is called the **gestation period.** The table below shows the number of days in the average gestation period for some animals.

1. For the gestation periods listed in the table ...

   a. what is the maximum number of days?

   _____ days

   b. what is the minimum number of days?

   _____ days

   c. what is the range (the difference between the maximum and the minimum)?

   _____ days

   d. what is the median (middle) number of days?

   _____ days

Average Gestation Period (in days)	
Animal	**Number of Days**
dog	61
giraffe	457
goat	151
human	266
Asian elephant	645
mouse	19
squirrel	44
rhinoceros	480
rabbit	31

Source: World Almanac

2. Which animals have an average gestation period that is longer than 1 year?

   _____

3. How much longer is the average gestation period for a goat than for a dog? _____ days

4. Which animal has an average gestation period that is about twice as long

   as a rabbit's? _____

5. Which animal has an average gestation period that is about half as long

   as a squirrel's? _____

Practice

6. 56 + 33 = _____   7. _____ = 167 + 96

8. _____ = 78 − 32   9. 271 − 89 = _____

Statistics, Data Analysis, and Probability 1.2

61

LESSON 2·8 Construct a "Real" Graph

Do this activity with a partner.

Materials ☐ set of pattern blocks from your teacher

☐ graph mat (4 copies of *Math Masters,* page 406 taped together)

SRB
76

1. Display the pattern blocks on the graph mat so that you can easily count and compare the number of hexagons, trapezoids, triangles, squares, blue rhombi, and tan rhombi.

hexagon   trapezoid   triangle   square   blue rhombus   tan rhombus

2. Use your display to answer the following questions.

   a. Which pattern block appears the most? _____ The least? _____

   b. How many hexagons and triangles are there altogether? _____

   c. How many more trapezoids are there than squares? _____

3. Use your display to complete the following statements.

   a. There are fewer _____ than _____.

   b. There are more _____ than _____.

   c. There is the same number of _____ as _____.

4. Write a question that can be answered by looking at your display. Answer your question.

   a. Question _____

   _____

   b. Answer _____

Try This

5. How many more quadrangles are there than nonquadrangles? _____

LESSON 2·8 "One Size Fits All" Claim

Makers of adjustable baseball caps claim that "one size fits all." Do you think this is a true statement? Use the head-size data you collected on journal pages 46 and 47 to help you decide.

1. Select a baseball cap and adjust the headband to the smallest size. Measure and record the distance around the inside of the baseball cap to the nearest half centimeter.

   Smallest size: _____ cm

2. Now adjust the headband to the largest size. Measure and record.

   Largest size: _____ cm

3. Compare the measurements above with the head-size data you and your class collected. Could this baseball cap be worn by everyone in the class? Explain your answer.

   _____

   _____

   _____

   _____

4. Do you think you have enough information to decide whether or not the claim "one size fits all" is true? _____ Explain.

   _____

   _____

   _____

   _____

STUDY LINK 2·9 Multidigit Subtraction

Make a ballpark estimate. Use the **trade-first subtraction method** to subtract. Compare your answer with your estimate to see if your answer makes sense.

SRB
12

1.	2.	3.
96 − 28	469 − 87	732 − 365
Ballpark estimate: _____	Ballpark estimate: _____	Ballpark estimate: _____
4.	5.	6.
4,321 − 575	5,613 − 2,724	6,600 − 4,278
Ballpark estimate: _____	Ballpark estimate: _____	Ballpark estimate: _____

Practice

7. 8 × _____ = 64   **8.** 9 × _____ = 72   **9.** 56 = _____ × 8   **10.** 42 = _____ × 7

Number Sense 2.1; Number Sense 3.1

STUDY LINK 2·9 **Multidigit Subtraction** *continued*

Make a ballpark estimate. Use the **partial-differences method** to subtract.
Compare your answer with your estimate to see if your answer makes sense.

11. 84 − 55	**12.** 136 − 79	**13.** 573 − 167
Ballpark estimate: _____	Ballpark estimate: _____	Ballpark estimate: _____
14. 506 − 282	**15.** 5,673 − 1,194	**16.** 3,601 − 1,063
Ballpark estimate: _____	Ballpark estimate: _____	Ballpark estimate: _____

Practice

17. _____, _____, 55, 44, _____, 22   Rule: _____

18. _____, _____, _____, _____, 72, 81   Rule: _____

LESSON 2·9

Subtraction by Counting Up

Use the **counting-up method** to solve these problems. Use the number lines if they are helpful.

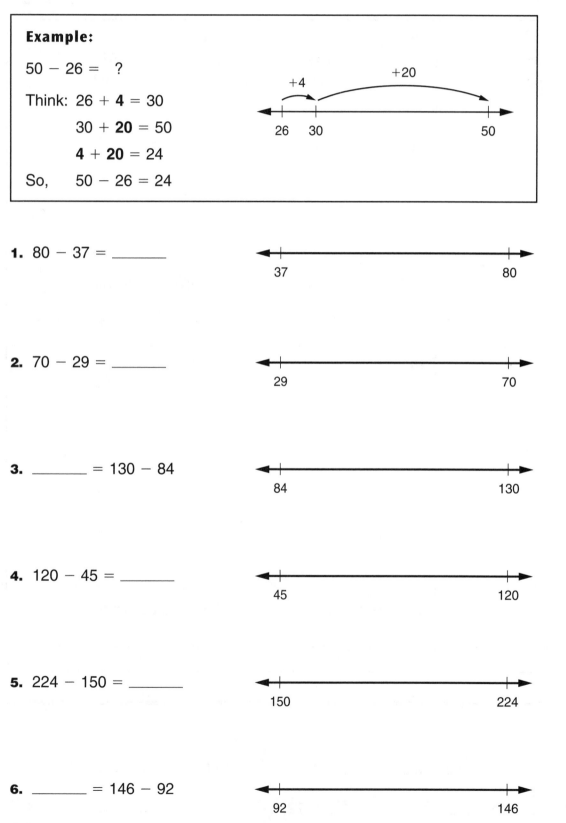

Example:

50 − 26 =   ?

Think: 26 + **4** = 30

30 + **20** = 50

4 + **20** = 24

So,   50 − 26 = 24

```
      +4          +20
   ╭──╮   ╭──────────────╮
◄──┼───┼──────────────────┼──►
   26  30                 50
```

1. 80 − 37 = _____

```
◄──┼──────────────────────┼──►
   37                      80
```

2. 70 − 29 = _____

```
◄──┼──────────────────────┼──►
   29                      70
```

3. _____ = 130 − 84

```
◄──┼──────────────────────┼──►
   84                     130
```

4. 120 − 45 = _____

```
◄──┼──────────────────────┼──►
   45                     120
```

5. 224 − 150 = _____

```
◄──┼──────────────────────┼──►
   150                    224
```

6. _____ = 146 − 92

```
◄──┼──────────────────────┼──►
   92                     146
```

LESSON 2·9

Number-Tile Problems

Cut out the 20 number tiles at the bottom of the page. Use them to help you solve the problems.

1. Use five odd-numbered tiles to make the smallest possible difference.

2. Use five even-numbered tiles (that includes 0) to make the largest possible difference. Do not use 0 as the first digit.

3. Use one set of the number tiles 0–9. Find the missing digits in these addition and subtraction problems.

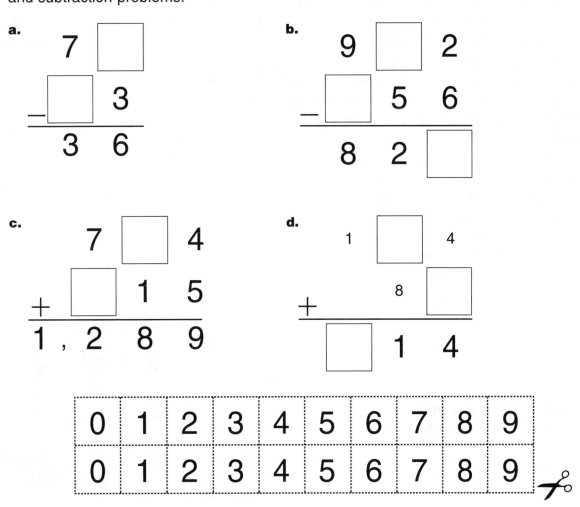

a.

```
   7 ☐
 − ☐ 3
 ─────
   3 6
```

b.

```
  9 ☐ 2
− ☐ 5 6
 ───────
  8 2 ☐
```

c.

```
    7 ☐ 4
  + ☐ 1 5
  ────────
  1 , 2 8 9
```

d.

```
  1 ☐   4
  +   8 ☐
  ─────────
  ☐   1 4
```

0	1	2	3	4	5	6	7	8	9
0	1	2	3	4	5	6	7	8	9

67

Unit 3: Family Letter

Multiplication and Division; Number Sentences and Algebra

One of our goals in the coming weeks is to finish memorizing the multiplication facts for single-digit numbers. To help students master the facts, they will play several math games. Ask your child to teach you one of the games described in the *Student Reference Book,* and play a few rounds together.

The class will also take a series of 50-facts tests for multiplication. Because correct answers are counted only up to the first mistake (and not counted thereafter), your child may at first receive a low score. If this happens, don't be alarmed. Before long, scores will improve dramatically. Help your child set a realistic goal for the next test, and discuss what can be done to meet that goal.

Your child will use Multiplication/Division Fact Triangles to review the relationship between multiplication and division. (For example, $4 \times 5 = 20$, so $20 \div 5 = 4$ and $20 \div 4 = 5$.) You can use the triangles to quiz your child on the basic facts and test your child's progress.

In this unit, alternative symbols for multiplication and division are introduced. An asterisk ($*$) may be substituted for the traditional $\times$ symbol, as in $4 * 5 = 20$. A slash ($/$) may be used in place of the traditional $\div$ symbol, as in $20/4 = 5$.

In Unit 3, the class will continue the World Tour, a yearlong project in which the students travel to a number of different countries. Their first flight will take them to Cairo, Egypt. These travels serve as background for many interesting activities in which students look up numerical information, analyze this information, and solve problems.

Finally, the class will have its first formal introduction to solving equations in algebra. (Informal activities with missing numbers in number stories have been built into the program since first grade.) Formal introduction to algebra in fourth grade may surprise you, because algebra is usually regarded as a high school subject. However, an early start in algebra is integral to the *Everyday Mathematics* philosophy.

Please keep this Family Letter for reference as your child works through Unit 3.

Vocabulary

Important terms in Unit 3:

dividend In division, the number that is being divided. For example, in 35 ÷ 5 = 7, the dividend is 35.

divisor In division, the number that divides another number. For example, in 35 ÷ 5 = 7, the divisor is 5.

Fact family A set of related arithmetic facts linking two inverse operations. For example, 4 + 8 = 12, 8 + 4 = 12, 12 − 4 = 8, and 12 − 8 = 4 is an addition/subtraction fact family, and 4 * 8 = 32, 8 * 4 = 32, 32/4 = 8, and 32/8 = 4 is a multiplication/ division fact family.

Fact Triangle A triangular flash card labeled with the numbers of a *fact family* that students can use to practice addition/subtraction or multiplication/ division facts.

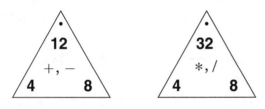

factor One of two or more numbers that are multiplied to give a product. For example, 4 * 1.5 = 6; so 6 is the product, and 4 and 1.5 are the factors. See also *factor of a counting number* n.

factor of a counting number *n* A counting number whose product with some other counting number equals *n*. For example, 2 and 3 are factors of 6 because 2 * 3 = 6. But 4 is not a factor of 6 because 4 * 1.5 = 6 and 1.5 is not a counting number.

multiple of a number *n* A product of *n* and a counting number. The multiples of 7, for example, are 7, 14, 21, 28, and so on.

number sentence Two numbers or expressions separated by a relation symbol (=, >, <, ≥, ≤, or ≠). Most number sentences also contain at least one operation symbol (+, −, ×, *, ·, ÷, /). Number sentences may also have grouping symbols, such as parentheses.

open sentence A *number sentence* in which one or more *variables* hold the places of missing numbers. For example, 5 + *x* = 13 is an open sentence.

percent (%) Per hundred, or out of a hundred. For example, "48% of the students in the school are boys" means that, on average, 48 out of every 100 students in the school are boys; 48% = $\frac{48}{100}$ = 0.48

product The result of multiplying two numbers called *factors*. For example, in 4 * 3 = 12, the product is 12.

quotient The result of dividing one number by another number. For example, in 35 ÷ 5 = 7, the quotient is 7.

square number A number that is the product of a counting number and itself. For example, 25 is a square number because 25 = 5 * 5. The square numbers are 1, 4, 9, 16, 25, and so on.

variable A letter or other symbol that represents a number. A variable can represent one specific number. For example, in the number sentence 5 + *n* = 9, only *n* makes the sentence true. A variable may also stand for many different numbers. For example, *x* + 2 < 10 is true if *x* is any number less than 8. And in the equation *a* + 3 = 3 + *a*, *a* stands for all numbers.

"What's My Rule?" problem A type of problem that asks for a rule for relating two sets of numbers. Also, a type of problem that asks for one of the sets of numbers, given a rule and the other set of numbers.

Rule	in	out
×8	6	48
	10	80
	3	
		56
		64

69

Do-Anytime Activities

To work with your child on the concepts taught in this unit, try these interesting and rewarding activities:

1. Continue to work on multiplication and division facts by using Fact Triangles and fact families and by playing games described in the *Student Reference Book.*

2. As the class proceeds through the unit, give your child multidigit addition and subtraction problems related to the lessons covered, such as 348 + 29, 427 + 234, 72 − 35, and 815 − 377.

3. Help your child recognize and identify real-world examples of right angles, such as the corner of a book, and examples of parallel lines, such as railroad tracks.

Building Skills through Games

In Unit 3, your child will play the following games.

Baseball Multiplication See *Student Reference Book,* pages 231 and 232.

Two players will need 4 regular dice, 4 pennies, and a calculator to play this game. Practicing the multiplication facts for 1–12 and strengthening mental arithmetic skills are the goals of *Baseball Multiplication.*

Beat the Calculator See *Student Reference Book,* page 233.

This game involves 3 players and requires a calculator and a deck of number cards, four each of the numbers 1 through 10. Playing *Beat the Calculator* helps your child review basic multiplication facts.

Division Arrays See *Student Reference Book,* page 240.

Materials for this game include number cards, 1 each of the numbers 6 through 18; a regular (6-sided) die; 18 counters; and paper and pencil. This game, involving 2 to 4 players, reinforces the idea of dividing objects into equal groups.

Multiplication Top-It See *Student Reference Book,* page 264.

The game can be played with 2 to 4 players and requires a deck of cards, four each of the numbers 1 through 10. This game helps your child review basic multiplication facts.

Name That Number See *Student Reference Book,* page 254.

Played with 2 or 3 players, this game requires a complete deck of number cards and paper and pencil. Your child tries to name a target number by adding, subtracting, multiplying, and dividing the numbers on as many of the cards as possible.

As You Help Your Child with Homework

As your child brings assignments home, you may want to go over the instructions together, clarifying them as necessary. The answers listed below will guide you through some of the Study Links in this unit.

Study Link 3·1

1. 60, 230, 110, 280, 370

2. 110, 80, 310, 240, 390

3. 34, 675, 54; +46   **4.** 9, 50, 420; ×7

5. 2, 400, 2,000   **6.** Answers vary.

7. 115   **8.** 612   **9.** 1,440

Study Link 3·2

2. 1, 2, 3, 4, 6, 9, 12, 18, 36   **3.** 1, 16; 2, 8; 4, 4

4. 56   **5.** Sample answer: 4, 8, 12, 16   **6.** 53

7. 388   **8.** 765

Study Link 3·3

1. 24   **2.** 54   **3.** 28   **4.** 16

5. 45   **6.** 18   **7.** 40   **8.** 25

9. 48   **11.** 1, 2, 3, 6, 9, 18

Study Link 3·4

1. 6   **2.** 8   **3.** 6   **4.** 3

6. 20; 5   **7.** 18; 6   **8.** 49; 7   **9.** 9; 2

10. 7; 5   **11.** 7; 4

12. Sample answer: 10, 15, 20, 25

13. 1, 2, 3, 4, 6, 8, 12, 24

Study Link 3·5

1. 5   **2.** 7   **3.** 72   **4.** 10

5. 32   **15.** 1,646   **16.** 5,033

17. 289   **18.** 1,288

Study Link 3·6

3. a. T

4. about 128,921 miles;
132,000 − 3,079 = 128,921

5. a. 4

6. 1, 2, 3, 4, 6, 12

7. Sample answers: 16, 24, 32, 40

Study Link 3·7

	Cities	Measurement on Map (inches)	Real Distance (miles)
1.	Cape Town and Durban	4	800
2.	Durban and Pretoria	$1\frac{3}{4}$	350
3.	Cape Town and Johannesburg	4	800
4.	Johannesburg and Queenstown	2	400
5.	East London and Upington	$2\frac{1}{2}$	500
6.	____ and ____	Answers vary.	

Study Link 3·8

1. 659 − 457 = 202; 202

2. 1,545 + 2,489 = 4,034; 4034

3. 700 − 227 = 473; 473

4. 1,552 − 1,018 = 534; 534

5. 624 + 470 + 336 = 1,430; 1,430   **6.** 9

7. 6, 12, 18, 24, 30, 36, 42, 48, 54, 60

Study Link 3·9

1. F   **2.** F   **3.** T   **4.** T

5. F   **6.** T   **7.** T   **8.** ?

11. b. 7 * 8 = 56   **12.** 36, 60, 84; +12

13. 54, 216, 324; +54

Study Link 3·10

1. 27   **2.** 33   **3.** 1   **4.** 24

5. 37   **6.** 8   **7.** 3 * (6 + 4) = 30

8. 15 = (20/4) + 10   **9.** 7 + (7 * 3) = 4 * 7

10. 9 * 6 = (20 + 7) * 2

11. 72 ÷ 9 = (2 * 3) + (18 ÷ 9)

12. 35 ÷ (42 ÷ 6) = (10 − 6) + 1   **13.** ?

14. ?   **15.** F   **16.** T   **17.** F   **18.** T

71

STUDY LINK
3·1

"What's My Rule?"

SRB
162–166

Complete the "What's My Rule?" tables and state the rules.

1.

Rule
Add 40

in	out
20	
190	
70	
240	
330	

2.

Rule
−60

in	out
	50
	20
	250
	180
	330

3. Rule: _____

in	out
131	177
	80
104	150
629	
	100

4. Rule: _____

in	out
70	490
	63
	350
20	140
60	

Try This

5. Rule: There are 20 nickels in $1.00.

dollars	nickels
3	60
	40
5	100
20	
100	

6. Create your own.

Rule: _____

in	out

Practice

7. _____ = 47 + 68   **8.** 359 + 253 = _____   **9.** 787 + 653 = _____

Number Sense **3.0**; Mathematical Reasoning 1.1; Algebra and Functions 1.4

LESSON 3·1 "What's My Rule?" Polygon Sides

1. Use square pattern blocks to help you complete the table.

Number of Squares	Number of Sides
1	4
2	8
3	
5	
7	
8	

2. Suppose there are 12 squares. Explain how to find the number of sides without counting.

_____

_____

3. Use triangle pattern blocks to help you complete the table.

Number of Triangles	Number of Sides
1	3
2	6
	15
	12
	9
	18

4. Suppose there are 30 sides. Explain how to find the number of triangles without counting.

_____

_____

73

Name _____ Date _____ Time _____

LESSON 3·1 | **"What's My Rule?" Perimeter**

The distance around a shape is called its **perimeter.** The perimeter of a square pattern block is 4 inches.

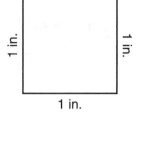

1 in.

1 in.   1 in.

1 in.

$$1 + 1 + 1 + 1 = 4$$

1. Place 2 square pattern blocks side by side. What is the perimeter of the shape?

   _____ inches

2. Complete the "What's My Rule?" table. Use square pattern blocks to create the shapes.

3. Explain the rule for finding the perimeter of the shapes.

   _____

   _____

   _____

Number of Square Pattern Blocks	Perimeter of Shape (inches)
1	4
2	
3	
4	
5	
6	
7	
8	

4. Use your rule to complete the following: 214 square pattern blocks are placed side by side. What is the perimeter of the shape? _____ inches

---

Try This

5. Use words or symbols to explain the rule for finding the perimeter of shapes made by placing hexagon pattern blocks side by side.

   _____

   _____

Name _____ Date _____ Time _____

3·2 | **Multiplication Facts**

1. Complete the Multiplication/Division Facts Table below.

*,/	1	2	3	4	5	6	7	8	9	10
1						6				
2										
3	3		9							
4		8								
5										
6										
7		14								
8										
9										
10										

2. List all the *factors* of 36. _____

3. List the *factor pairs* of 16. _____ and _____, _____ and _____, _____ and _____

4. Name the *product* of 8 and 7. _____

5. Name four *multiples* of 4. _____, _____, _____, _____

Practice

6. _____ = 91 − 38   **7.** _____ = 630 − 242   **8.** 1,462 − 697 = _____

Number Sense 3.0; Number Sense 4.0; Number Sense 4.1   **75**

LESSON 3·2 | Rectangular Arrays

Rectangular arrays can be used to model multiplication facts.
Follow these steps to build arrays with centimeter cubes.

1. Place a deck of number cards (1–10) facedown on the table.
Turn over 2 cards.

◆ Use one card for the number of rows in the array.

◆ Use the other card for the number of cubes in each row.

2. Use centimeter cubes to build the array.

Example: [4]   [2]

If ⌐4⌐ and ⌐2⌐ are turned
over, you can make either array:

2 rows,
4 cubes per row

4 rows,
2 cubes per row

3. Record some of the arrays you made in the table below.

How many rows?	How many cubes in each row?	How many cubes in all?	Number model
4	2	8	4 * 2 = 8

LESSON 3·2

Prime Numbers

A rectangular array shows two factors of a number.

SRB 7

1. On centimeter grid paper, draw as many arrays as you can for each of the following numbers:

2, 3, 4, 5, 6, 7, 11, 12, 15, 16

Example: Two different arrays can be made for 8.

    1, 2, 4, and 8 are factors of 8.

2. Write a number model for each array and its turn-around fact.

$1 * 8 = 8$ $8 * 1 = 8$

$4 * 2 = 8$
$2 * 4 = 8$

3. Record your results in the table.

Numbers with Only 1 Array	Numbers with More than 1 Array
	8

4. The numbers you listed in the left-hand column are called **prime numbers.** Use the data you collected to write a definition for prime numbers.

_____

_____

_____

_____

Try This

5. There are 20 other prime numbers that are less than 100. List them below.

_____

_____

STUDY LINK 3·3 Fact Triangles

Complete these Multiplication/Division Fact Triangles.

1.

*, /

3   8

2.

*, /

9   6

3.

*, /

4   7

4.

*, /

8   2

5.

*, /

5   9

6.

*, /

6   3

7.

*, /

4   10

8.

*, /

5   5

9.

*, /

6   8

Practice

10. Name 4 multiples of 7. _____, _____, _____, _____

11. List all the factors of 18. _____

12. Name the product of 9 and 6. _____

13. List all the factor pairs of 20.

_____ and _____, _____ and _____, _____ and _____

Number Sense 3.0; Number Sense 4.0

Name | Date | Time

Skip-Count Patterns

LESSON 3·3

SRB 16

1. Start at 0. Skip count by 2s.
Record the pattern.

									0
1	②	3	④	5	⑥	7	⑧	9	10
11	12	13	14	15	16	17	18	19	20
21	22	23	24	25	26	27	28	29	30
31	32	33	34	35	36	37	38	39	40
41	42	43	44	45	46	47	48	49	50
51	52	53	54	55	56	57	58	59	60
61	62	63	64	65	66	67	68	69	70
71	72	73	74	75	76	77	78	79	80
81	82	83	84	85	86	87	88	89	90
91	92	93	94	95	96	97	98	99	100

2. Start at 0. Skip count by 3s.
Record the pattern.

									0
1	2	3	4	5	6	7	8	9	10
11	12	13	14	15	16	17	18	19	20
21	22	23	24	25	26	27	28	29	30
31	32	33	34	35	36	37	38	39	40
41	42	43	44	45	46	47	48	49	50
51	52	53	54	55	56	57	58	59	60
61	62	63	64	65	66	67	68	69	70
71	72	73	74	75	76	77	78	79	80
81	82	83	84	85	86	87	88	89	90
91	92	93	94	95	96	97	98	99	100

3. Start at 0. Skip count by 4s.
Record the pattern.

									0
1	2	3	4	5	6	7	8	9	10
11	12	13	14	15	16	17	18	19	20
21	22	23	24	25	26	27	28	29	30
31	32	33	34	35	36	37	38	39	40
41	42	43	44	45	46	47	48	49	50
51	52	53	54	55	56	57	58	59	60
61	62	63	64	65	66	67	68	69	70
71	72	73	74	75	76	77	78	79	80
81	82	83	84	85	86	87	88	89	90
91	92	93	94	95	96	97	98	99	100

4. Start at 0. Skip count by 6s.
Record the pattern.

									0
1	2	3	4	5	6	7	8	9	10
11	12	13	14	15	16	17	18	19	20
21	22	23	24	25	26	27	28	29	30
31	32	33	34	35	36	37	38	39	40
41	42	43	44	45	46	47	48	49	50
51	52	53	54	55	56	57	58	59	60
61	62	63	64	65	66	67	68	69	70
71	72	73	74	75	76	77	78	79	80
81	82	83	84	85	86	87	88	89	90
91	92	93	94	95	96	97	98	99	100

5. On the back of this page, write about the skip-count patterns you see in each grid.

LESSON 3·3 | **Calculating Combinations**

Super Sweet sells ice-cream sundaes. Each sundae comes with one scoop of ice cream and one topping.

Ice-Cream Flavors	Toppings
chocolate	hot fudge
vanilla	whipped cream
strawberry	sprinkles
cookie dough	nuts
fudge swirl	

1. How many *different* sundaes that have one scoop of ice cream and one topping can Super Sweet sell?   _____ sundaes

Use an organized list, table, or picture to solve the problem. Show your work.

2. Super Sweet has decided to add butterscotch to the list of available toppings. How many *different* sundaes can Super Sweet sell now?   _____ sundaes

Explain how you found your answer.

_____

_____

3. Explain how you might use multiplication to solve a problem like this.

_____

_____

LESSON
3·4

Math Message

Name _____

Date _____

Ms. Chen's students took their first
50-facts test. These are their scores
for the first minute of the test.

26%, 8%, 36%, 18%, 18%, 20%, 40%,
10%, 22%

1. What is the median score? _____%

2. What is the mean score? _____%

Name _____

Date _____

Ms. Chen's students took their first
50-facts test. These are their scores
for the first minute of the test.

26%, 8%, 36%, 18%, 18%, 20%, 40%,
10%, 22%

1. What is the median score? _____%

2. What is the mean score? _____%

Name _____

Date _____

Ms. Chen's students took their first
50-facts test. These are their scores
for the first minute of the test.

26%, 8%, 36%, 18%, 18%, 20%, 40%,
10%, 22%

1. What is the median score? _____%

2. What is the mean score? _____%

Name _____

Date _____

Ms. Chen's students took their first
50-facts test. These are their scores
for the first minute of the test.

26%, 8%, 36%, 18%, 18%, 20%, 40%,
10%, 22%

1. What is the median score? _____%

2. What is the mean score? _____%

STUDY LINK 3·4 | Mystery Numbers

Find the mystery numbers.

1. I am thinking of a mystery number. If I multiply it by 4, the answer is 24. What is the number? _____

2. I am thinking of another number. If I multiply it by 3, the answer is 24. What is the number? _____

3. I multiplied a number by itself and got 36. What is the number? _____

4. If I multiply 7 by a number, I get 21. What is the number? _____

5. Write your own mystery number problem.

_____

_____

Fill in the missing numbers.

6. $4 * 5 =$ _____   _____ $* 4 = 20$

7. _____ $= 6 * 3$ $18 =$ _____ $* 3$

8. $7 * 7 =$ _____   _____ $* 7 = 49$

9. _____ $* 2 = 18$ $18 =$ _____ $* 9$

10. $35 =$ _____ $* 5$ _____ $* 7 = 35$

11. $28 =$ _____ $* 4$ _____ $* 7 = 28$

Practice

12. Name 4 multiples of 5. _____, _____, _____, _____

13. List all the factors of 24. _____

Mathematical Reasoning 2.0; Number Sense 3.0; Number Sense 4.0

LESSON 3·4   # Find the Mean

The table shows the number of books in several students' backpacks.

Student	John	Mito	Kate	Ezra	Lina	Luz	Nick
Number of Books	5	2	6	4	0	1	3

1. Place centimeter cubes on the bar graph below to show the number of books in each student's backpack.

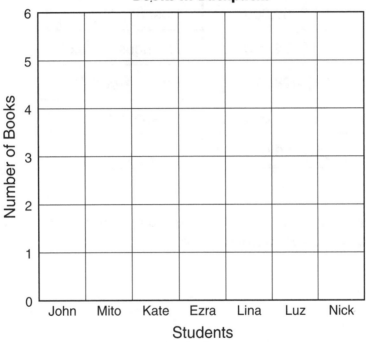

Books in Backpacks

2. Now move the cubes around so that all of the students have the same number of books.

How many books are in each student's backpack now? _____ books

When you "even out" the number of books so that each student's backpack has the same number of books, you are finding the **mean** or the **average** of the data set.

3. Complete the statement.

The mean, or average, number of books in the students' backpacks is _____.

LESSON 3·4 Compare the Mean and Median

Imagine that you are given a chance to play for a professional baseball team. Before you meet the owner, you will need to think about your salary demands.

Below is a list of some 2004 New York Yankees players' salaries.

Player	Salary	Player	Salary
Brown, Kevin	$15,714,286	Lofton, Kenny	$3,100,000
Cairo, Miguel	$900,000	Matsui, Hideki	$7,000,000
Clark, Tony	$750,000	Posada, Jorge	$9,000,000
Flaherty, John	$775,000	Rodriguez, Alex	$22,000,000
Giambi, Jason	$12,428,571	Sierra, Ruben	$1,000,000
Gordon, Tom	$3,500,000	Wilson, Enrique	$700,000
Jeter, Derek	$18,600,000		

Source: USA Today Salary Database

1. Would you want your salary to be based on the mean or the median of these players' salaries? Explain your answer.

_____

_____

2. When news organizations report the salaries of professional teams, they usually use the median. Why do you think they report the median instead of the mean?

_____

_____

3. If you were an owner of a team, would you rather report your players' mean or median salaries? Explain your answer.

_____

_____

_____

84

STUDY LINK 3·5 Missing Numbers

Complete each fact by filling in the missing numbers.
Use the Multiplication/Division Facts Table to help you.

1. 30 / 6 = _____

2. 21 / _____ = 3

3. 9 = _____ ÷ 8

4. 100 / _____ = 10

5. _____ / 4 = 8

6. 25 ÷ _____ = _____

7. _____ = 42 / _____

8. 8 / _____ = _____

9. 4 = _____ / _____

10. _____ ÷ _____ = 1

11. _____ / 2 = _____

12. 10 * _____ = _____

Try This

13. 5 * _____ * _____ = 30

14. 54 = _____ * _____ * _____

*,/	1	2	3	4	5	6	7	8	9	10
1	1	2	3	4	5	6	7	8	9	10
2	2	4	6	8	10	12	14	16	18	20
3	3	6	9	12	15	18	21	24	27	30
4	4	8	12	16	20	24	28	32	36	40
5	5	10	15	20	25	30	35	40	45	50
6	6	12	18	24	30	36	42	48	54	60
7	7	14	21	28	35	42	49	56	63	70
8	8	16	24	32	40	48	56	64	72	80
9	9	18	27	36	45	54	63	72	81	90
10	10	20	30	40	50	60	70	80	90	100

Practice

15. _____ = 989 + 657

16. 314 + 4,719 = _____

17. 887 − 598 = _____

18. _____ = 2,004 − 716

Algebra and Functions 1.0; Number Sense 3.0

Name _____ Date _____ Time _____

LESSON 3·5

Fractions and Division

Four friends want to share 3 pizzas evenly. Each person cannot have a whole pizza, so the pizzas need to be divided.

1. How many slices of pizza should each person get? _____ slices. Use a drawing to explain your answer.

2. Marisa says these expressions all mean the same thing:

$$\frac{1}{4} \text{ of } 3 \qquad \frac{3}{4} \qquad 3 \div 4 \qquad 4\overline{)3}$$

Do you agree or disagree? Explain your answer.

_____

_____

_____

✂ -

Name _____ Date _____ Time _____

LESSON 3·5

Fractions and Division

Four friends want to share 3 pizzas evenly. Each person cannot have a whole pizza, so the pizzas need to be divided.

1. How many slices of pizza should each person get? _____ slices. Use a drawing to explain your answer.

2. Marisa says these expressions all mean the same thing:

$$\frac{1}{4} \text{ of } 3 \qquad \frac{3}{4} \qquad 3 \div 4 \qquad 4\overline{)3}$$

Do you agree or disagree? Explain your answer.

_____

_____

_____

STUDY LINK 3·6 Number Stories about Egypt

1. The Nile in Africa is about 4,160 miles long. The Huang River in Asia is about 800 miles shorter than the Nile. How long is the Huang River?

   Number model: _____ About _____ miles

2. The Suez Canal links the Mediterranean and Red Seas. It is 103 miles long and was opened in 1869. For how many years has the Suez Canal been open?

   Number model: _____ _____ years

3. Egypt has about 3,079 miles of railroad. The United States has about 132,000 miles of railroad. How many fewer miles of railroad does Egypt have than the United States?

   Number model: _____ About _____ miles

4. The population of Cairo, the capital of Egypt, is about 10,834,000. The population of Washington, D.C., is about 563,000.

   a. True or false? About $10\frac{1}{2}$ million more people live in Cairo than in Washington, D.C.   _____

   b. Explain how you solved the problem.

   _____

   _____

Try This

5. The area of Egypt is about 386,700 square miles. The area of Wyoming is about 97,818 square miles.

   a. Egypt is about how many times as large as Wyoming? _____

   b. Explain how you solved the problem.

   _____

   _____

Practice

6. List all the factors of 12. _____

7. Name 4 multiples of 8. _____, _____, _____, _____

STUDY LINK 3·7 Map Scale

Here is a map of South Africa.
Use a ruler to measure the shortest
distance between cities. Measure
to the nearest $\frac{1}{4}$ inch. Use the map
scale to convert these measurements
to real distances.

SRB
145

Pretoria ✪
Johannesburg •

Upington •

Bloenfontein ✪

Durban •

LESOTHO

SOUTH AFRICA

Queenstown •

East London •

0   100   200 mi

Cape Town ✪
Cape of Good Hope

1 inch represents 200 miles

	Cities	Measurement on Map (inches)	Real Distance (miles)
1.	Cape Town and Durban		
2.	Durban and Pretoria		
3.	Cape Town and Johannesburg		
4.	Johannesburg and Queenstown		
5.	East London and Upington		
6.	_____ and _____		

Practice

7. _____ = 767 + 254

8. 193 + 6,978 = _____

9. 562 − 388 = _____

10. _____ = 4,273 − 678

Number Sense 3.1

LESSON 3·7 **Measure Line Segments**

Sometimes you do not need an exact measurement. Measuring to the nearest $\frac{1}{2}$ inch might be good enough.

Cut out the ruler at the bottom of the page. Use it to measure the line segments to the nearest $\frac{1}{2}$ inch. Record your measurements.

1. ─────────────────────────────────

Think: Is the measure of the line segment closer to 4 inches or $4\frac{1}{2}$ inches?

About _____ in.

2. ────────────────────

Think: Is the measure of the line segment closer to 2 inches or $2\frac{1}{2}$ inches?

About _____ in.

3. ───────────────────────────

Think: Is the measure of the line segment closer to $3\frac{1}{2}$ inches or 4 inches?

About _____ in.

4. Allison and Marta measured the line segment below to the nearest $\frac{1}{2}$ inch. Allison said, "The line segment measures about $5\frac{1}{2}$ inches." Marta said, "I think it measures about 6 inches." Who do you agree with? Explain your answer.

───────────────────────────────────

_____

_____

_____

5. On the back of this page, draw several line segments. Use your ruler to measure them to the nearest $\frac{1}{2}$ inch. Record your measurements.

0	$\frac{1}{2}$ 1	2	3	4	5	6

Inches (in.)

LESSON 3·7 **Compare Map Scales**

Different maps use different scales. On one map, 1 inch might represent 10 actual miles, but on another map, 1 inch might represent 100 miles.

1. Record the globe scale you used in Lesson 3-7. 1 inch → _____ miles

2. Locate the maps on pages *282–293* in your *Student Reference Book*. Record the map scale for each region.

   a. Region 1: Africa   1 in. → _____ miles

   b. Region 2: Europe   1 in. → _____ miles

   c. Region 3: South America 1 in. → _____ miles

   d. Region 4: Asia   1 in. → _____ miles

3. Do you think changing a map scale changes actual distances? Explain your answer.

   _____

   _____

4. Complete the table below to justify your answer to Problem 3. Measure to the nearest $\frac{1}{2}$ inch.

Distance Between	Measurement on Globe (inches)	Air Distance (miles)	Measurement on Region 3 Map (inches)	Air Distance (miles)
Bogotá, Colombia, and Brasilia, Brazil				
Quito, Ecuador, and Sucre, Bolivia				

Try This

5. A **cartographer** is a person who makes maps.

   a. Give an example of a map scale that would show very little detail.   _____ → _____

   b. Explain your answer.

   _____

   _____

STUDY LINK
3·8

Addition and Subtraction Number Stories

1. In 1896, the United Kingdom had the largest navy in the world with 659 ships. France had the second-largest navy with 457 ships. The United States was tenth with only 95 ships. How many more ships did the United Kingdom have than France?

_____ **Answer:** _____ more ships
(number model)

2. Rhode Island, the smallest state in the United States, has an area of 1,545 square miles. The area of the second-smallest state, Delaware, is 2,489 square miles. What is the combined area of these two states?

_____ **Answer:** _____ square miles
(number model)

3. A polar bear can weigh as much as 700 kilograms. An American black bear can weigh as much as 227 kilograms. How much more can a polar bear weigh than an American black bear?

_____ **Answer:** _____ kilograms more
(number model)

4. The Pacific leatherback turtle's maximum weight is about 1,552 pounds. The Atlantic leatherback turtle's maximum weight is about 1,018 pounds. What is the difference between the turtles' weights?

_____ **Answer:** _____ pounds
(number model)

5. According to the National Register of Historic Places, New York City has the most historic places in the United States with 624 sites. Philadelphia is second with 470 sites, and Washington, D.C., is third with 336 sites. How many historic sites are there in these three cities?

_____ **Answer:** _____ historic sites
(number model)

Practice

6. The numbers 81, 27, and 45 are multiples of _____.

7. List the first ten multiples of 6.

_____, _____, _____, _____, _____, _____, _____, _____, _____, _____

Number Sense 2.1, 3.0; Mathematical Reasoning 1.0, 2.3   **91**

Name _____ Date _____ Time _____

LESSON 3·8 | Situation Diagrams

Situation diagrams can help you organize the information in a number story and can help you decide what to do to solve the problem.

SRB
152 178

Decide which diagram to use for each problem. Complete the diagram.
Then solve the problem.

1. 283 students attended the football game. 371 students attended the soccer game. How many more students attended the soccer game? _____ students

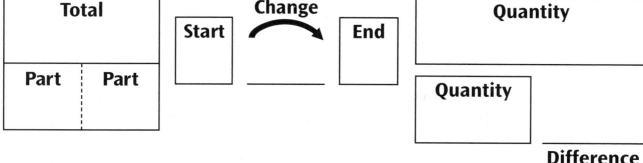

Total	
Part	Part

Change
| Start | | End |

Start ___

Quantity

Quantity

_____
Difference

2. Shawn had $145.00 in his bank account. He took out some money to buy a new bike. Now he has $85.00 in his account. How much did his bike cost? _____

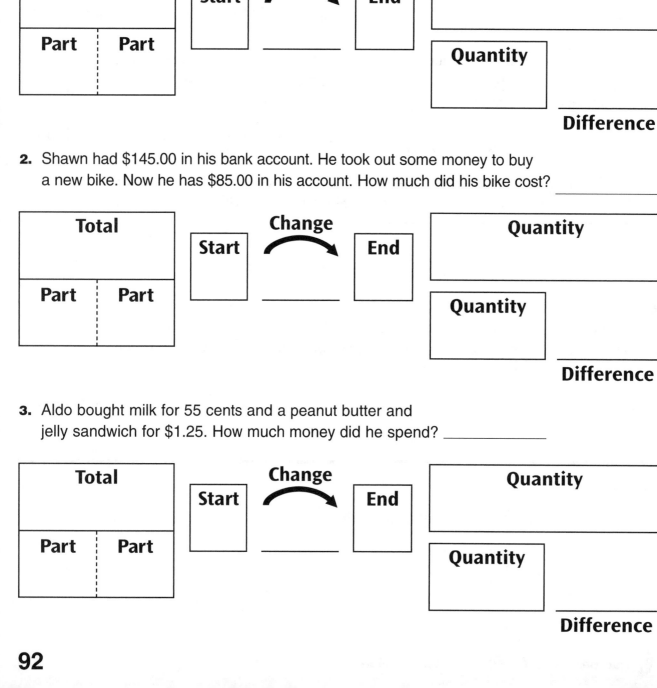

Total	
Part	Part

Change
| Start | | End |

Quantity

Quantity

_____
Difference

3. Aldo bought milk for 55 cents and a peanut butter and jelly sandwich for $1.25. How much money did he spend? _____

Total	
Part	Part

Change
| Start | | End |

Quantity

Quantity

_____
Difference

92

Copyright © Wright Group/McGraw-Hill

LESSON 3·8

The Great Pyramid and the Gateway Arch

Great Pyramid of Giza

Gateway Arch

The Great Pyramid of Giza is perhaps the greatest structure ever built by humans. It stands in the desert near Cairo, Egypt. Completed about 2580 B.C., it was the tomb of Pharaoh (king) Khufu. It is estimated that 100,000 workers labored more than 20 years to build the Great Pyramid. It contains more than 2 million stone blocks with an average weight of about $2\frac{1}{2}$ tons each.

Originally the Great Pyramid was about 147 meters tall. Over the years, stones were removed from its surface, reducing its height by about 9 meters. The Great Pyramid was the tallest structure in the world for 44 centuries, until the Eiffel Tower was built in Paris in 1889.

Today the tallest monument in the United States is the Gateway Arch, also known as the Jefferson National Expansion Memorial, in St. Louis, Missouri. The Gateway Arch was completed in 1965 and is about 192 meters tall.

1. How much taller is the Gateway Arch than the Great Pyramid?

About _____ meters

2. Underline the information in the essay that you used to solve Problem 1.

3. Use data from the essay above to write your own problem. Ask a partner to solve it.

_____

_____

_____

_____

93

STUDY LINK
3·9

Number Sentences

SRB
148

Next to each number sentence, write T if it is true, F if it is false, or ? if you can't tell.

1. $20 - 12 = 8 * 3$ _____

2. $7 = 14 * 2$ _____

3. $497 < 500$ _____

4. $16 / 4 = 4$ _____

5. $15 + 10 = 5$ _____

6. $24 > 11 + 11$ _____

7. $100 - 5 = 95$ _____

8. $33 - 4$ _____

9. Write two true number sentences. _____

_____

10. Write two false number sentences. _____

_____

11. a. Explain why $7 * 8$ is not a number sentence.

_____

_____

b. How could you change $7 * 8$ to make a true number sentence?

_____

_____

c. How could you change $7 * 8$ to make a false number sentence?

_____

_____

Practice

12. 24, _____, 48, _____, 72, _____   Rule: _____

13. _____, 108, 162, _____, 270, _____   Rule: _____

Algebra and Functions 1.0

LESSON 3·9 | **> and < Symbols**

Different symbols are used to show that numbers and amounts are not equal.

Example:

> means "is greater than"   < means "is less than"

Below are some ways to help you remember these symbols. Try each one.

The alligator eats the bigger number.

1. 3,568 ____ 3,896

2. 7 + 6 ____ 9 + 8

3. 600 + 900 ____ 700 + 300

4. 7 * 6 ____ 5 * 8

The less-than symbol looks like the fingers and thumb on your left hand. The words *left* and *less* start with the same letter. The less-than symbol points to the lesser number.

5. 13,009 ____ 13,053

6. 8 + 8 ____ 9 + 6

7. 500 + 800 ____ 700 + 700

8. 5 * 10 ____ 9 * 7

2 < 5   5 > 2

Mark two dots next to the greater number. Mark one dot next to the lesser number. Connect each of the two dots to the single dot, and the symbol will be correct.

9. 34,783 ____ 34,239

10. 11 − 6 ____ 12 − 8

11. 12,000 − 7,000 ____ 18,000 − 9,000

12. 36 / 9 ____ 25 / 5

13. What is your favorite way to remember the > and < symbols? Pick one from above, or tell about your own idea.

_____

_____

LESSON 3·9 **A Number-Sentence Puzzle**

1. Cut out the number tiles at the bottom of the page. Tape them in the number sentences below so that

   ◆ each number sentence is true,

   ◆ the same digit appears only one time in each row, and

   ◆ the same digit appears only one time in each column.

	*		=		*	
	*		>		*	
	*		<		*	

2. Explain the strategy you used to solve this problem.

_____

_____

_____

_____

_____

✂ -

2	2	2	3	3	3
4	4	4	6	6	6

STUDY LINK 3·10 Parentheses in Number Sentences

Write the missing number to make each number sentence true.

1. (45 / 5) * 3 = _____

2. 9 + (4 * 6) = _____

3. (20 ÷ 4) ÷ 5 = _____

4. _____ = (33 − 25) * 3

5. _____ = (25 / 5) + (8 * 4)

6. (33 + 7) / (3 + 2) = _____

Insert parentheses ( ) to make each number sentence true.

7. 3 * 6 + 4 = 30

8. 15 = 20 / 4 + 10

9. 7 + 7 * 3 = 4 * 7

10. 9 * 6 = 20 + 7 * 2

Try This

Insert two sets of parentheses to make each number sentence true.

11. 72 ÷ 9 = 2 * 3 + 18 ÷ 9

12. 35 ÷ 42 ÷ 6 = 10 − 6 + 1

Write T if it is true, F if it is false, or ? if you can't tell.

13. (6 * 5) / 3 _____

14. (3 * 7) / (15 − 12) _____

15. 30 = 1 + (4 * 6) _____

16. (4 * 6) + 13 = 47 − 10 _____

17. 15 > (7 * 6) * (10 − 9) _____

18. 20 < (64 ÷ 8) * (12 ÷ 4) _____

Practice

19. _____ = 494 + 3,769

20. 5,853 + 4,268 = _____

21. _____ = 8,210 − 654

22. 7,235 − 906 = _____

LESSON 3·10   Number Models with Parentheses

Joel and his parents were buying treats for his birthday party. He asked his mother and father, "How much is 6 plus 6 times 3?" His mother said "36," and his father said "24."

1. How did his mother get 36? _____

_____

2. How did his father get 24? _____

_____

Joel's parents both thought their answers were correct. Finally Joel said, "I want to buy 1 six-pack of vanilla cupcakes and 3 six-packs of chocolate cupcakes." Then Joel's parents knew whose answer made more sense.

3. Which answer, 36 or 24, makes more sense in this situation? Explain.

_____

--- ✂ --

Name   Date   Time

LESSON 3·10   Number Models with Parentheses

Joel and his parents were buying treats for his birthday party. He asked his mother and father, "How much is 6 plus 6 times 3?" His mother said "36," and his father said "24."

1. How did his mother get 36? _____

_____

2. How did his father get 24? _____

_____

Joel's parents both thought their answers were correct. Finally Joel said, "I want to buy 1 six-pack of vanilla cupcakes and 3 six-packs of chocolate cupcakes." Then Joel's parents knew whose answer made more sense.

3. Which answer, 36 or 24, makes more sense in this situation? Explain.

_____

Copyright © Wright Group/McGraw-Hill

98

STUDY LINK 3·11   Open Sentences

Write T if the number sentence is true and F if the number sentence is false.

1. $35 = 7 * 5$ _____

2. $43 > 34$ _____

3. $25 + 25 < 50$ _____

4. $49 - (7 \times 7) = 0$ _____

Make a true number sentence by filling in the missing number.

5. _____ $= 12 / (3 + 3)$

6. $(60 - 28) / 4 =$ _____

7. $(3 \times 8) \div 6 =$ _____

8. $30 - (4 + 6) =$ _____

Make a true number sentence by inserting parentheses.

9. $4 * 2 + 10 = 18$

10. $16 = 16 - 8 * 2$

11. $27 / 9 / 3 = 1$

12. $27 / 9 / 3 = 9$

Find the solution of each open sentence below. Write a number sentence with the solution in place of the variable. Check to see whether the number sentence is true.

Example: $6 + x = 14$ **Solution:** 8 **Number sentence:** $6 + 8 = 14$

Open sentence	Solution	Number sentence
13. $12 + x = 32$	_____	_____
14. $s = 200 - 3$	_____	_____
15. $5 * y = 40$	_____	_____
16. $7 = x / 4$	_____	_____

Practice

17. $366 + 7,565 =$ _____

18. $3,238 + 9,784 =$ _____

19. $9,325 - 756 =$ _____

20. $4,805 - 2,927 =$ _____

LESSON 3·11 | Solve Open Sentences

Rami picked up a Fact Triangle and asked,
"6 times 7 equals what number?"

Number sentence: $6 * 7 = ?$

Solution: $? = 42$

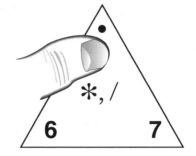

Cole picked up a different Fact Triangle and asked,
"3 times what number equals 15?"

Number sentence: $3 * ? = 15$

Solution: $? = 5$

Choose six Multiplication/Division Fact Triangles. Cover one corner with your thumb.
Write the number sentence and the solution.

1. Number sentence: _____ Solution: _____

2. Number sentence: _____ Solution: _____

3. Number sentence: _____ Solution: _____

4. Number sentence: _____ Solution: _____

5. Number sentence: _____ Solution: _____

6. Number sentence: _____ Solution: _____

Name _____ Date _____ Time _____

LESSON 3·11   Solve Open Sentences

Each letter in the animal names on this page has a value.

C	E	I	L	M	W	Y
8	17	2	12	9	10	4

A	D	K	N	O	P

Some of the values of the letters are known.   Some of the values of the letters are unknown.

Use the information below to find the unknown values.

COW is worth 23.   KOALA is worth 46.   DONKEY is worth 66.

MONKEY is worth 54.   LION is worth 35.   PANDA is worth 83.

--------------------------------✂--

Name _____ Date _____ Time _____

LESSON 3·11   Solve Open Sentences

Each letter in the animal names on this page has a value.

C	E	I	L	M	W	Y
8	17	2	12	9	10	4

A	D	K	N	O	P

Some of the values of the letters are known.   Some of the values of the letters are unknown.

Use the information below to find the unknown values.

COW is worth 23.   KOALA is worth 46.   DONKEY is worth 66.

MONKEY is worth 54.   LION is worth 35.   PANDA is worth 83.

101

Unit 4: Family Letter

Decimals and Their Uses

In previous grades, your child had many experiences with money written in decimal notation. In the next unit, the class will learn about other uses of decimals.

The class will focus on examples of decimals in everyday life. For example, some thermometers have marks that are spaced $\frac{2}{10}$ of a degree apart. These marks give a fairly precise measurement of body temperature, such as 98.6 °F.

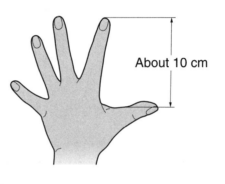

Normal body temperature is about 98.6 °F.

Students will explore how decimals are used in measuring distances, times, and gasoline mileage.

We will also begin a yearlong measurement routine. Students will find their own "personal references," which they will use to estimate lengths, heights, and distances in metric units. For example, your child might discover that the distance from the base of his or her thumb to the tip of his or her index finger is about 10 centimeters and then use this fact to estimate other distances.

About 10 cm

The World Tour will continue. In small groups, students will gather information about different countries in Africa and then share what they have learned with the class. Students can then compare and interpret data for a large number of countries from the same region.

Please keep this Family Letter for reference as your child works through Unit 4.

Vocabulary

Important terms in Unit 4:

centimeter (cm) In the metric system, a unit of length equivalent to $\frac{1}{100}$ of a meter; 10 millimeters; $\frac{1}{10}$ of a decimeter.

```
|||||||||||||||||||||||||||||||||||||||||||||||||||||||||||||||||||||||||||
0  CM  1     2     3     4     5     6     7
```

decimeter (dm) In the metric system, a unit of length equivalent to $\frac{1}{10}$ of a meter; 10 centimeters.

hundredths In base-10 *place-value* notation, the place in which a digit has a value equal to $\frac{1}{100}$ of itself; the second digit to the right of the decimal point.

meter (m) In the metric system, the unit of length from which other units of length are derived. One meter is the distance light will travel in a vacuum (empty space) in $\frac{1}{299,792,458}$ second; 100 centimeters; 10 decimeters.

millimeter (mm) A metric unit of length equivalent to $\frac{1}{1,000}$ of a meter; $\frac{1}{10}$ of a centimeter.

ONE Same as *whole.*

ones The place-value position in which a digit has a value equal to the digit itself.

personal measurement reference A convenient approximation for a standard unit of measurement. For example, many people have thumbs that are approximately one inch wide.

place value A number writing system that gives a digit a value according to its position, or place, in the number. In our standard, base-10 system, each place has a value ten times that of the place to its right and 1 tenth the value of the place to its left.

1,000s	100s	10s	1s		0.1s	0.01s	0.001s
Thousands	Hundreds	Tens	Ones	.	Tenths	Hundredths	Thousandths

tens The place-value position in which a digit has a value equal to 10 times itself.

tenths In base-10 *place-value* notation, the place in which a digit has a value equal to $\frac{1}{10}$ of itself; the first digit to the right of the decimal point.

thousandths In base-10 *place-value* notation, the place in which a digit has a value equal to $\frac{1}{1,000}$ of itself; the third digit to the right of the decimal point.

whole (or ONE, or unit) In *Everyday Mathematics,* an entire object, collection of objects, or quantity being considered; 100%. Same as the ONE or unit whole.

103

Do-Anytime Activities

To work with your child on the concepts taught in this unit, try the interesting activities listed below. For each activity, discuss the use of decimals and the meanings of place values.

1. Have your child track the sports statistics of a favorite athlete.

2. Have your child compare prices of items in the supermarket.

3. Help your child create and use new personal reference measures.

4. Together, find statistics about countries in the World Tour. Look in newspapers and almanacs.

Building Skills through Games

In Unit 4, your child will play the following games.

Baseball Multiplication See *Student Reference Book,* pages 231 and 232. The game provides practice with multiplication facts.

Fishing for Digits See *Student Reference Book,* page 242. The game provides practice in identifying digits, the values of the digits, adding, and subtracting.

Name That Number See *Student Reference Book,* page 254. The game provides practice with using operations to represent numbers in different ways.

Number Top-It (**Decimals**) See *Student Reference Book,* page 256. The game provides practice with comparing, ordering, reading, and identifying the value of digits in decimal numbers.

Polygon Pair-Up See *Student Reference Book,* page 258. The game provides practice in identifying properties of polygons.

Product Pile-Up See *Student Reference Book,* page 259. The game provides practice with multiplication facts.

As You Help Your Child with Homework

As your child brings assignments home, you may want to go over the instructions together, clarifying them as necessary. The answers listed below will guide you through some of the Study Links in this unit.

Study Link 4◆1

1.

1,000s	100s	10s	1s
6	8	5	4

3.

10s	1s		0.1s	0.01s	0.001s
7	3	.	0	0	4

Study Link 4◆3

Sample answers:

3. 5.05, 5.25, 5.95

4. 4.15, 4.55, 4.99

5. 21.4, 21.98, 21.57

6. 0.89, 0.85, 0.82

7. 2.155, 2.16, 2.159

8. 0.84, 0.88, 0.87

Study Link 4◆4

1. Seikan and Channel Tunnel

2. Between 90 and 130 miles

3. Sample answer: I rounded the tunnel lengths to "close-but-easier" numbers and added $35 + 30 + 20 + 15 + 15 = 115$ to find the total length.

4. 12 miles   **5.** 8 miles

Study Link 4◆5

1. 120.41   **2.** 1.46   **3.** 5.18   **4.** 0.03

5. >   **6.** <   **7.** >   **8.** >

9. Sample answer: 2.33 + 4.21

10. Sample answer: 6.83 − 5.31

Study Link 4◆6

1. a. $0.76   **b.** $2.43   **c.** $4.64   **d.** $2.95

2. $16.40   **3.** $2.57   **4.** $7.32   **5.** $18.10

6. $10.78

7. Loaf of bread; Sample answer: The price of a loaf of bread in 2000 was $0.88. The expected price of a loaf of bread in 2025 is $3.31. This was almost 4 times its cost in 2000.

Study Link 4◆7

1. $\frac{335}{1,000}$; 0.335   **2.** $\frac{301}{1,000}$; 0.301

3. $\frac{7}{100}$; 0.07   **4.** $1\frac{5}{100}$; 1.05

5. 0.346   **6.** 0.092   **7.** 0.003   **8.** 2.7

9. 0.536   **10.** 0.23   **11.** 7.008   **12.** 0.4

13. >   **14.** >   **15.** <   **16.** <

Study Link 4◆8

1. a. 7 cm **b.** 0.07 m   **2. a.** 12 cm **b.** 0.12 m

3. a. 4 cm **b.** 0.04 m   **4. a.** 6 cm   **b.** 0.06 m

5. a. 2 cm **b.** 0.02 m   **6. a.** 14 cm **b.** 0.14 m

Study Link 4◆9

2. 180 mm   **3.** 4 cm   **4.** 3,000 mm

5. 400 cm   **6.** 7 m   **7.** 460 cm

8. 794 cm   **9.** 4.5 m   **10.** 0.23 m

11. 60 cm   **12.** 8 cm   **13.** 7 cm

Study Link 4◆10

2. a. 65 mm   **b.** 2.6 cm   **c.** 610 cm

3. a. 50 mm   **b.** 3 cm   **c.** 300 cm

4. a. 800 mm   **b.** 11 cm   **c.** 5 m

5. a. 430 mm   **b.** 9.8 cm   **c.** 0.34 m

6. a. 6 mm   **b.** 0.4 cm   **c.** 5,200 mm

LESSON 4·1

Place-Value Number Lines

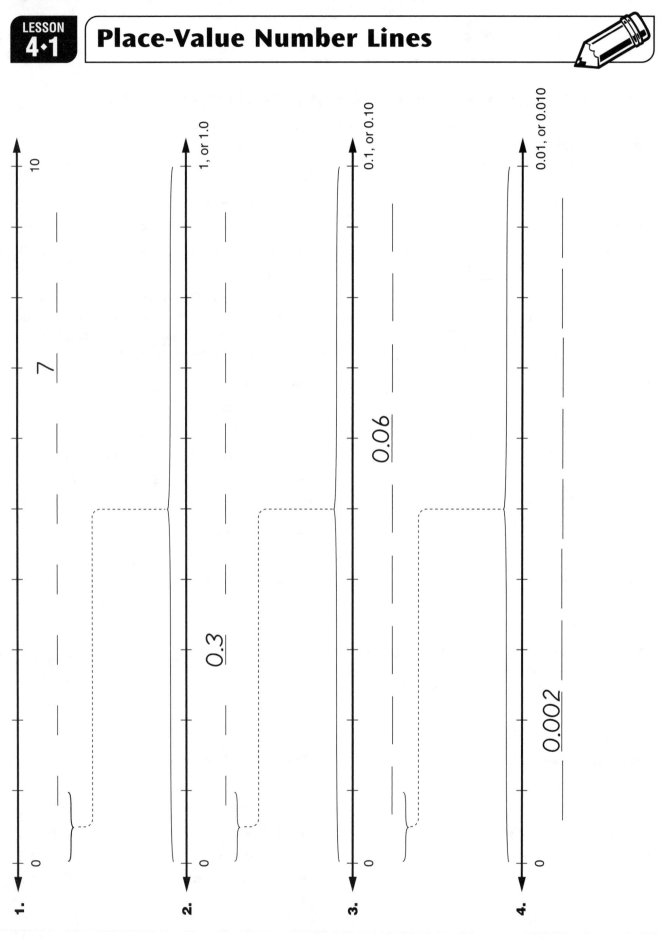

1. 0   7   10

2. 0   0.3   1, or 1.0

3. 0   0.06   0.1, or 0.10

4. 0   0.002   0.01, or 0.010

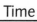

LESSON 4·1 Place-Value Chart

1,000s	100s	10s	1s						
Thousands	Hundreds	Tens	Ones ·						

STUDY LINK 4·1 | Place-Value Puzzles

Use the clues to write the digits in the boxes and find each number.

SRB
30 31

1. ◆ Write 5 in the tens place.

   ◆ Find $\frac{1}{2}$ of 24. Subtract 4. Write the result in the hundreds place.

   ◆ Add 7 to the digit in the tens place. Divide by 2. Write the result in the thousands place.

   ◆ In the ones place, write an even number greater than 2 that has not been used yet.

1,000s	100s	10s	1s

2. ◆ Divide 15 by 3. Write the result in the hundredths place.

   ◆ Multiply 2 by 10. Divide by 10. Write the result in the ones place.

   ◆ Write a digit in the tenths place that is 4 more than the digit in the hundredths place.

   ◆ Add 7 to the digit in the ones place. Write the result in the thousandths place.

100s	10s	1s	0.1s	0.01s	0.001s
		.			

3. ◆ Write the result of 6 ∗ 9 divided by 18 in the ones place.

   ◆ Double 8. Divide by 4. Write the result in the thousandths place.

   ◆ Add 3 to the digit in the thousandths place. Write the result in the tens place.

   ◆ Write the same digit in the tenths and hundredths place so that the sum of all the digits is 14.

10s	1s	0.1s	0.01s	0.001s
	.			

Practice

Write true or false.

4. $6 * 5 = 15 + 15$ _____   5. $15 + 7 < 13 - 8$ _____   6. $72 / 9 > 9$ _____

Number Sense 1.0

LESSON 4·1 | Money and Decimals

Use only $1 bills , dimes , and pennies .

1. Use as few bills and coins as possible to show each amount below. Record your work.

Amount	$1 bills	Dimes	Pennies
$1.26	1	2	6
$1.11			
$2.35			
$3.40			
$2.06			
$0.96			
$0.70			
$0.03			

2. Describe any patterns you see in the table.

_____

_____

_____

_____

3. You can use $1 bills, dimes, and pennies to make any amount of money.
   Why do you think we have nickels, quarters, and half-dollars?

_____

_____

_____

STUDY LINK 4·2 | **Decimals All Around**

Find examples of decimals in newspapers, in magazines, in books, or on food packages. Ask people in your family for examples.

Write your numbers below or, if an adult says you may, cut them out and tape them on this page. Be sure to write what the numbers mean. For example, "The body temperature of a hibernating dormouse may go down to 35.6°F."

_____

_____

_____

_____

_____

_____

_____

_____

_____

_____

_____

_____

_____

_____

Practice

Write true or false.

1. $286 + 286 = 462$ _____

2. $907 - 709 = 200$ _____

3. $641 + 359 = 359 + 641$ _____

4. $2,345 - 198 = 2,969 - 822$ _____

Number Sense 2.1

LESSON 4·2 | **The ONE**

Use base-10 blocks to help you solve the following problems.

1. If ▯ is ONE, then what is ▱? _____ What is ▦? _____

2. If ▦▦ is ONE, then what is ▯? _____ What is ▱? _____

3. If ▯▯▯▯▯ is ONE, then what is ▱? _____ What is ▦? _____

4. If ▱▱▱▱▱ is $\frac{1}{100}$, then what is the ONE? _____

5. If ▯▯▯ is $\frac{1}{10}$, then what is the ONE? _____

6. If ▯ ▱▱▱▱▱ is $\frac{1}{10}$, then what is the ONE? _____

What is $\frac{1}{100}$? _____

7. Explain how you solved Problem 6.

_____

_____

_____

_____

STUDY LINK 4·3 | **Ordering Decimals**

Mark the approximate locations of the decimals and fractions on the number lines below. Rename fractions as decimals as necessary.

1.

| 0.0 | 0.25 | 0.5 | 0.75 | 1 | 1.25 | 1.5 | 1.75 | 2 |

A 0.33   *B* 1.6   *C* 0.7   *D* 1.01

E 1.99   *F* 1.33   *G* 0.1   *H* 0.8

2.

| 0.0 | 0.1 | 0.2 | 0.3 | 0.4 | 0.5 | 0.6 | 0.7 | 0.8 | 0.9 | 1.0 | 1.1 | 1.2 |

I 0.67   *J* 0.05   *K* $\frac{75}{100}$ *L* 0.49   *M* 0.99

N 1.15   *O* $\frac{25}{100}$ *P* 0.101   *Q* 0.55   *R* 0.88

Use decimals. Write 3 numbers that are between the following:

3. $5 and $6 $_____ $_____ $_____

4. 4 centimeters and
5 centimeters   _____ cm   _____ cm   _____ cm

5. 21 seconds and
22 seconds   _____ sec   _____ sec   _____ sec

6. 8 dimes and 9 dimes $_____ $_____ $_____

7. 2.15 meters and
2.17 meters   _____ m   _____ m   _____ m

8. 0.8 meter and 0.9 meter   _____ m   _____ m   _____ m

Practice

9. $x + 17 = 23$ $x =$ _____   **10.** $5 * n = 35$ $n =$ _____   **11.** $32 / b = 4$ $b =$ _____

Number Sense **1.2**; Number Sense **1.9**

STUDY LINK 4·4 | **Railroad Tunnel Lengths**

The table below shows the five longest railroad tunnels in the world.

Tunnel	Location	Year Completed	Length in Miles
Seikan	Japan	1988	33.46
Channel	France/England	1994	31.35
Moscow Metro	Russia	1979	19.07
London Underground	United Kingdom	1939	17.30
Dai-Shimizu	Japan	1982	13.98

Use estimation to answer the following questions.

1. Which two tunnels have a combined length of about 60 miles?

_____ and _____

2. Which of the following is closest to the combined length of all five tunnels? Choose the best answer.

⊂⊃ Less than 90 miles   ⊂⊃ Between 90 and 130 miles

⊂⊃ Between 130 and 160 miles   ⊂⊃ More than 160 miles

3. Explain how you solved Problem 2.

_____

_____

4. About how many miles longer is the Channel Tunnel than the Moscow Metro Tunnel?

About _____ miles

Try This

5. The Cascade Tunnel in Washington State is the longest railroad tunnel in the United States. It is about $\frac{1}{4}$ the length of the Seikan. About how long is the Cascade Tunnel?

About _____ miles

Practice

6. $190 + b = 200$ $b =$ _____

7. $g - 500 = 225$ $g =$ _____

Items to Purchase

light bulbs
4-pack
$1.09

VCR tape
$3.25

tissues
$0.73

transparent tape
$0.84

batteries
4-pack
$3.59

toothpaste
$1.39

ballpoint pen
$0.39

tennis balls
can of 3
$2.59

paperback book
$2.99

MYSTERY TRAIN

LESSON 4·4 | **Estimate Purchase Cost**

SRB
34–37

Cost of Item 1	Cost of Item 2	Cost of Item 3	Number Model I Used to Estimate
$1.09	$1.39	$0.84	$1.00 + $1.40 + $1.00 = $3.40

- -

Name   Date   Time

LESSON 4·4 | **Estimate Purchase Cost**

SRB
34–37

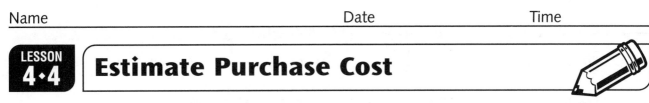

Cost of Item 1	Cost of Item 2	Cost of Item 3	Number Model I Used to Estimate
$1.09	$1.39	$0.84	$1.00 + $1.40 + $1.00 = $3.40

LESSON 4·4

Will I Run Out of Gas?

You are driving with your family from Denver, Colorado, to Des Moines, Iowa.
You know the following:

- Your car's gasoline tank holds about 12.1 gallons.

- Your car uses about 1 gallon of gasoline for every 30 miles on the highway.

- You start your trip with a full tank.

Here is a map of the route you follow.

Numbers indicate miles between cities.

Missouri River

Des Moines
Adair
Avoca
Omaha   40   60
Lincoln 50
North Platte 50
50
Ogallala 110
80 100 Kearney
130 Sterling
Iowa
Missouri
Colorado **Nebraska**
Denver **Kansas**

1. About how many gallons of gasoline would
   your car use traveling from Denver to Sterling?   About _____ gallons

2. When you get to Ogallala, you would expect your gas tank to be

   a. almost empty.   **b.** about $\frac{1}{4}$ full.   **c.** about $\frac{1}{2}$ full.   **d.** about $\frac{3}{4}$ full.

3. Is it OK to wait until you get to Kearney to buy more gas? Explain.

   _____

   _____

   _____

4. You stop at North Platte to buy more gasoline. If you buy
   7.6 gallons, about how many gallons are there in your tank now?   About _____ gallons

5. Could you get to Des Moines from North Platte without running
   out of gas if you filled your gasoline tank just one more time?   _____

   If so, where would you stop? _____

LESSON 4·4

Decimal Magic Square

Insert decimal points so that the sum of the numbers in each row, column, and diagonal is equal to 6.5.

3 0	1 6	9 0	2 2	1 5 0
2 0	8 0	2 1	1 4	2 0
7 0	2 5	1 3 0	1 0	1 9 0
2 4	1 2	5 0	1 8	6 0
1 1	4 0	1 7	1 0 0	2 3

✂ -

Name   Date   Time

LESSON 4·4

Decimal Magic Square

Insert decimal points so that the sum of the numbers in each row, column, and diagonal is equal to 6.5.

3 0	1 6	9 0	2 2	1 5 0
2 0	8 0	2 1	1 4	2 0
7 0	2 5	1 3 0	1 0	1 9 0
2 4	1 2	5 0	1 8	6 0
1 1	4 0	1 7	1 0 0	2 3

Copyright © Wright Group/McGraw-Hill

117

Name _____ Date _____ Time _____

LESSON 4·5

Math Message

What's wrong with this problem?
What is the correct answer?

```
  0.76
+ 0.2
------
  0.78
```

_____
_____
_____
_____
_____

✂ -

Name _____ Date _____ Time _____

LESSON 4·5

Math Message

What's wrong with this problem?
What is the correct answer?

```
  0.76
+ 0.2
------
  0.78
```

_____
_____
_____
_____
_____

✂ -

Name _____ Date _____ Time _____

LESSON 4·5

Math Message

What's wrong with this problem?
What is the correct answer?

```
  0.76
+ 0.2
------
  0.78
```

_____
_____
_____
_____
_____

✂ -

Name _____ Date _____ Time _____

LESSON 4·5

Math Message

What's wrong with this problem?
What is the correct answer?

```
  0.76
+ 0.2
------
  0.78
```

_____
_____
_____
_____

118

STUDY LINK 4•5 | **Addition and Subtraction of Decimals**

Add or subtract. Show your work.

1. $96.45 + 23.96 =$ _____

2. $1.06 + 0.4 =$ _____

3. $9.87 - 4.69 =$ _____

4. $0.4 - 0.37 =$ _____

Write $<$, $>$, or $=$ to make each statement true.

5. $2.78 + 9.1$ _____ $3.36 + 8.49$

6. $0.08 + 0.97$ _____ $1.04 + 0.03$

7. $13.62 - 4.9$ _____ $9.4 - 1.33$

8. $9.4 - 5.6$ _____ $8.3 - 4.7$

9. Name two 3-digit numbers whose sum is 6.54. _____ $+$ _____ $= 6.54$

10. Name two 3-digit numbers whose difference is 1.52. _____ $-$ _____ $= 1.52$

Practice

11. $13 = 7 + s$ $s =$ _____

12. $8 * g = 24$ $g =$ _____

13. $36 / p = 6$ $p =$ _____

14. $m / 9 = 8$ $m =$ _____

LESSON 4·5 A Hiking Trail

The Batona Trail is a hiking trail in southern New Jersey. The Batona Hiking Club measured the trail very carefully and found that it is about 47.60 kilometers long.

The trail crosses several roads, so it can be reached by car at a number of places.

Carpenter Spring is at the north end of the trail. Washington Road, near Batsto, is at the trail's south end.

Go to *Math Masters,* page 121.

Map of Batona Trail

Source: Batona Hiking Club of Philadelphia

120

LESSON 4·5   A Hiking Trail *continued*

The following table shows distances from several points of interest from the north to the south end of the trail. Fill in the missing distances.

Batona Trail		
Point of Interest	**Distance from Carpenter Spring (km)**	**Distance from Washington Road (km)**
Carpenter Spring	0	47.60
Deep Hollow Pond	1.91	45.69
Route 70	3.37	
Lebanon Headquarters	4.66	
Pakim Pond	9.91	
Route 72	12.10	
Route 563		33.56
Route 532	19.53	
Apple Pie Hill Fire Tower	21.31	
Carranza Memorial		19.80
Hay Road	33.05	
Quakerbridge	37.92	9.68
Washington Road	47.60	0

How can you check your answers?

_____

_____

_____

_____

LESSON 4·6

Keeping a Bank Balance

Date	Transaction		Current Balance
January 2	Deposit	$100.00	$ _100.00_
January 14	Deposit	$14.23	+ $ _14.23_ $ _114.23_
February 4	Withdrawal	$16.50	$ _____ $ _____
February 11	Deposit	$33.75	$ _____ $ _____
February 14	Withdrawal	$16.50	$ _____ $ _____
March 19	Deposit	$62.00	$ _____ $ _____
March 30	Withdrawal	$104.26	$ _____ $ _____
March 31	Interest	$0.78	$ _____ $ _____
April 1	Deposit	$70.60	$ _____ $ _____
April 3	Withdrawal	$45.52	$ _____ $ _____
April 28	Withdrawal	$27.91	$ _____ $ _____

STUDY LINK 4·6 | Rising Grocery Prices

The table below shows some USDA grocery prices for the year 2000 and estimates of grocery prices for the year 2025.

Grocery Item	Price in 2000	Estimated Price in 2025
dozen eggs	$1.02	$1.78
loaf of white bread	$0.88	$3.31
pound of butter	$2.72	$7.36
gallon of milk	$2.70	$5.65

1. How much more is each item predicted to cost in 2025?

   a. eggs _____   **b.** bread _____   **c.** butter _____   **d.** milk _____

2. The year is 2000. You buy bread and butter. You hand the cashier a $20 bill. How much change should you receive? _____

3. The year is 2025. You buy eggs and milk. You hand the cashier a $10 bill. How much change should you receive? _____

4. The year is 2000. You buy all 4 items. What is the total cost? _____

5. The year is 2025. You buy all 4 items. What is the total cost? _____

6. If the predictions are correct, how much more will you pay in 2025 for the 4 items than you paid in 2000? _____

7. Which item is expected to have the greatest price increase? _____

   Explain your answer. _____

   _____

   _____

Practice

8. List the first ten multiples of 3. ____, ____, ____, ____, ____, ____, ____, ____, ____, ____

9. List the first ten multiples of 7. ____, ____, ____, ____, ____, ____, ____, ____, ____, ____

LESSON 4·6   **"Goodie Bags"**

The table at the right shows different items that
the party store sells to make goodie bags. Use the
information in the table to answer the questions
below. Show or write what you did to solve each
problem.

Item	Price
erasers	$0.16 each
clay	2 cans for $1.22
key chains	$0.59 each
rubber balls	3 for $0.51
markers	4 packs for $5.60
stickers	$1.39 per pack
whistles	$0.18 each
marbles	$1.41 per bag
gum	3 packs for $1.86

1. Kareem put a pack of stickers, a rubber ball, and a pack of gum
in each of his goodie bags. What is the cost of each bag? _____

2. Ella created a bag that cost the same amount as Kareem's bag but was not
filled with the same things. What did Ella put in her bag?

_____

3. Create your own goodie bag. You must place 5 different items in your bag and
the total cost must be between $3.25 and $3.50. Tell what is in your bag and
how much you spent.

_____

_____

LESSON 4·7   Modeling Decimals

Base-10 Blocks					Fraction	Decimal
Total Cubes	Big Cubes	Flats	Longs	Cubes		
235	0	2	3	5	$\frac{235}{1,000}$	0.235
832						
408						
790						
64						
8						
200						
20						
2						
1,843						
27,051						

STUDY LINK 4·7 | **Tenths, Hundredths, Thousandths**

Complete the table. The big cube is the ONE.

Base-10 Blocks	Fraction Notation	Decimal Notation
1. ☐☐☐ |||		
2. ☐☐☐ .		
3. ||||| ||		
4. ☐☐ |||||		

Write each number in decimal notation.

5. $\frac{346}{1,000}$ _____

6. $\frac{92}{1,000}$ _____

7. $\frac{3}{1,000}$ _____

8. $2\frac{7}{10}$ _____

Write each of the following in decimal notation.

9. 536 thousandths _____

10. 23 hundredths _____

11. 7 and 8 thousandths _____

12. 4 tenths _____

Write < or >.

13. 0.407 _____ 0.074

14. 0.65 _____ 0.437

15. 0.672 _____ 0.7

16. 2.38 _____ 2.4

Practice

17. 6.05 + 1.24 = _____

18. _____ = 47.90 + 0.76

19. _____ = 8.71 − 2.78

20. 46.8 − 3.77 = _____

Number Sense 1.0; Number Sense **1.2**; Number Sense 1.6

LESSON 4·7 | **Batting Averages**

The women listed in this table were members of the 2004 U.S. Olympic Softball Team. These are their batting statistics after the 2004 Olympics in Athens, Greece.

Player	At Bats (AB)	Hits (H)	Batting Average $\left(\frac{H}{AB}\right)$
Berg, Laura	19	7	0.368
Bustos, Crystl	26	9	0.346
Fernandez, Lisa	22	12	0.545
Freed, Amanda	6	1	0.167
Jung, Lovieanne	20	6	0.300
Mendoza, Jessica	20	5	0.250
Nuveman, Stacey	16	5	0.313
O'Brien Amico, Leah	25	5	0.200
Topping, Jenny	6	4	0.667
Watley, Natasha	30	12	0.400

Source: U.S. Softball Official Web site

1. Which players have a better batting average than Crystl Bustos?

_____

2. If the coaches need a strong hitter to bat first, which player should they choose? Why?

_____

_____

3. Some players were up at bat more times than others. If a player is up at bat more times, does this mean she will have a higher batting average? Explain.

_____

_____

_____

4. a. Based on her batting average, if Mendoza went to bat 1,000 times, about how many hits should she get? _____ hits

    b. 100 times? _____ hits   **c.** 10 times? _____ hits

127

STUDY LINK
4·8

Measuring in Centimeters

Measure each line segment to the nearest centimeter. Record the measurement in centimeters and meters.

SRB
128 129

Example: _____

    a. About ____*5*____ centimeters   **b.** About ___*0.05*___ meter

1. _____

    a. About _____ centimeters   **b.** About _____ meter

2. _____

    a. About _____ centimeters   **b.** About _____ meter

3. _____

    a. About _____ centimeters   **b.** About _____ meter

4. _____

    a. About _____ centimeters   **b.** About _____ meter

5. _____

    a. About _____ centimeters   **b.** About _____ meter

6. _____

    a. About _____ centimeters   **b.** About _____ meter

Practice

7. _____ $= 10.06 + 10.04$ **8.** $38.93 + 92.4 =$ _____

9. $16.85 - 14.23 =$ _____   **10.** _____ $= 20.9 - 8.57$

     Number Sense 2.1

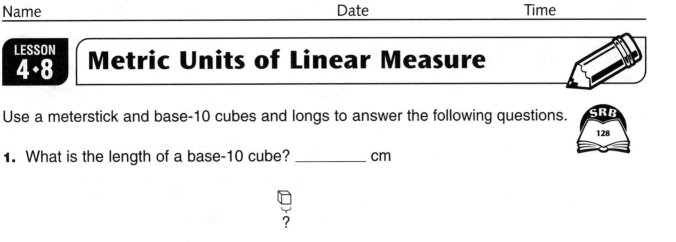

LESSON 4·8

Metric Units of Linear Measure

Use a meterstick and base-10 cubes and longs to answer the following questions.

SRB
128

1. What is the length of a base-10 cube? _____ cm

?

2. What is the length of a base-10 long? _____ cm

?

3. a. If you placed base-10 cubes side by side along a meterstick, how many cubes would you need to equal the length of 1 meter?

_____ cubes

METER STICK

b. How many centimeters are in 1 meter? _____ cm

4. a. If you placed base-10 longs side by side along a meterstick, how many longs would you need to equal the length of 1 meter?

_____ longs

METER STICK

b. A length of 10 centimeters is called a **decimeter.** How many decimeters are in 1 meter?

_____ decimeters

129

LESSON 4·8 Metric Prefixes

1. Research metric units of length and record your results in the table below.

Unit	Prefix	Number of Meters
terameter	tera–	1,000,000,000,000
meter		1
millimeter	milli–	$\frac{1}{1,000}$

2. Describe any patterns you see in the table.

_____

_____

_____

_____

STUDY LINK 4·9 | **Metric Measurements**

1. Use your personal references to estimate the lengths of 4 objects in metric units. Then measure each object. Record your estimates and measurements.

Object	Estimated Length	Actual Length

Complete.

2. 18 cm = _____ mm

3. _____ cm = 40 mm

4. 3 m = _____ mm

5. 4 m = _____ cm

6. _____ m = 700 cm

7. 4.6 m = _____ cm

8. 7.94 m = _____ cm

9. _____ m = 450 cm

10. _____ m = 23 cm

11. 0.6 m = _____ cm

Measure each line segment to the nearest $\frac{1}{2}$ cm.

12. _____

About _____ centimeters

13. _____

About _____ centimeters

Practice

Insert < or >.

14. 0.68 _____ 0.32

15. 9.13 _____ 9.03

16. 0.65 _____ 0.6

Number Sense 1.2

131

LESSON 4·9 — Matching Metric Units

Metric Units of Linear Measure	
millimeter (mm)	decimeter (dm)
centimeter (cm)	meter (m)

SRB
130

1. Write the abbreviation for the correct unit after each measurement below.

   a. A crayon is about 85 _____ long.

   b. A thumb is about 2 _____ across.

   c. An arm span is about 110 _____.

   d. A journal is about 280 _____ long.

   Everyday Mathematics

   e. The height of your table or desk is about 7 _____.

   f. A door opening is about 1 _____ wide.

2. Describe any patterns you see in the measurements and units above.

   _____

   _____

   _____

3. Make up 2 examples of your own. Measure the objects in a unit of your choice.

   _____

   _____

STUDY LINK 4·10 Decimals and Metric Units

Symbols for Metric Units of Length
meter (m)
centimeter (cm)
decimeter (dm)
millimeter (mm)

1 decimeter

0   1 dm

1 m = 10 dm   1 dm = 0.1 m

10 centimeters

0 1 2 3 4 5 6 7 8 9 10 cm

1 m = 100 cm   1 cm = 0.01 m
1 dm = 10 cm   1 cm = 0.1 dm

100 millimeters

0 10 20 30 40 50 60 70 80 90 100 mm

1 m = 1,000 mm   1 mm = 0.001 m
1 dm = 100 mm   1 mm = 0.01 dm
1 cm = 10 mm   1 mm = 0.1 cm

Use your tape measure or ruler to help you fill in the answers below.

1. a. 4.2 cm = __42__ mm   **b.** 64 mm = __6.4__ cm   **c.** 2.6 m = __260__ cm

2. a. 6.5 cm = _____ mm   **b.** 26 mm = _____ cm   **c.** 6.1 m = _____ cm

3. a. 5 cm = _____ mm   **b.** 30 mm = _____ cm   **c.** 3 m = _____ cm

4. a. 80 cm = _____ mm   **b.** 110 mm = _____ cm   **c.** _____ m = 500 cm

5. a. 43 cm = _____ mm   **b.** 98 mm = _____ cm   **c.** _____ m = 34 cm

6. a. 0.6 cm = _____ mm   **b.** 4 mm = _____ cm   **c.** 5.2 m = _____ mm

---

Practice

7. 21, 49, and 56 are multiples of _____.

8. 45, 63, and 18 are multiples of _____.

LESSON 4·10

Centimeters and Millimeters

Cut out the ruler below. Use it to measure the pencils to the nearest centimeter.

SRB 128

1. a.

Pencil A is about _____ cm long.

b.

Pencil B is about _____ cm long.

2. One pencil is longer than the other. Which pencil is longer? Circle your answer.

Pencil A   Pencil B

3. How did you figure out which pencil is longer?

_____

_____

_____

4. Marco wants to know the difference in length between the two pencils.
Can you tell him? Why or why not?

_____

_____

_____

| 0 | 1 | 2 | 3 | 4 | 5 | 6 | 7 | 8 | 9 | 10 | 11 | 12 | 13 | 14 | 15 |
Centimeters

134

STUDY LINK
4·11   # Unit 5: Family Letter

Big Numbers, Estimation, and Computation

In this unit, your child will begin to multiply 1- and 2-digit numbers using what we call the **partial-products method.** In preparation for this, students will learn to play the game *Multiplication Wrestling.* Ask your child to explain the rules to you and play an occasional game together. While students are expected to learn the partial-products method, they will also investigate the **lattice multiplication method,** which students have often enjoyed in the past.

If your child is having trouble with multiplication facts, give short (five-minute) reviews at home, concentrating on the facts he or she finds difficult.

Another important focus in this unit is on reading and writing big numbers. Students will use big numbers to solve problems and make reasonable estimates. Help your child locate big numbers in newspapers and other sources, and ask your child to read them to you. Or, you can read the numbers and have your child write them.

Sometimes it is helpful to write big numbers in an abbreviated form so that they are easier to work with. One way is to use **exponents,** which tell how many times a number, called the base, is used as a factor. For example, 100,000 is equal to $10 * 10 * 10 * 10 * 10$. So 100,000 can be written as 10^5. The small raised 5 is called an exponent, and 10^5 is read as "10 to the fifth power." This will be most students' first experience with exponents, which will be studied in depth during fifth and sixth grades.

The class is well into the World Tour. Students are beginning to see how numerical information about a country helps them get a better understanding of the country— its size, climate, location, and population distribution—and how these characteristics affect the way people live. The next stop on the World Tour will be Budapest, Hungary, the starting point for an exploration of European countries. Encourage your child to bring to school materials about Europe, such as articles in the travel section of your newspaper, magazine articles, and travel brochures.

Please keep this Family Letter for reference as your child works through Unit 5.

Vocabulary

Important terms in Unit 5:

billion 1,000,000,000, or 10^9; 1,000 million.

estimate A close, rather than exact, answer; an approximate answer to a computation; a number close to another number.

exponent See *exponential notation.*

exponential notation A way to show repeated multiplication by the same factor. For example, 2^3 is exponential notation for $2 * 2 * 2$. The small, raised 3 is the exponent. It tells how many times the number 2, called the base, is used as a factor.

extended multiplication fact A multiplication fact involving multiples of 10, 100, and so on. In an extended multiplication fact, each factor has only one digit that is not 0. For example, $400 * 6 = 2,400$ and $20 * 30 = 600$ are extended multiplication facts.

lattice multiplication A very old way to multiply multidigit numbers. The steps below show how to find the product $46 * 73$ using lattice multiplication.

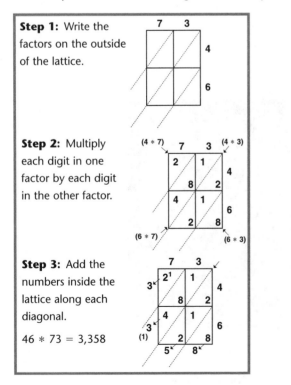

Step 1: Write the factors on the outside of the lattice.

Step 2: Multiply each digit in one factor by each digit in the other factor.

Step 3: Add the numbers inside the lattice along each diagonal.

$46 * 73 = 3,358$

magnitude estimate A rough estimate of whether a number is in the 1s, 10s, 100s, 1,000s, and so on.

million 1,000,000, or 10^6; 1,000 thousand.

partial-products multiplication A way to multiply in which the value of each digit in one factor is multiplied by the value of each digit in the other factor. The final product is the sum of the partial products. The example shows how to use the method to find $73 * 46$.

> **Partial–Products Multiplication**
> Multiply each part of one factor by each part of the other factor. Then add the partial products.
>
> ```
>                    73
>                 *  46
> 40 * 70 →     2,800
> 40 *  3 →       120
>  6 * 70 →       420
>  6 *  3 →  +     18
>              3,358
> ```

power of 10 A whole number that can be written as a product using only 10s as factors. For example, 100 is equal to $10 * 10$, or 10^2. 100 is 10 to the second power or the second power of 10 or 10 squared.

round a number To approximate a number to make it easier to work with or to make it better reflect the precision of data. Often, numbers are rounded to a nearest *power of 10*. For example, 12,964 rounded to the nearest thousand is 13,000.

136

Do-Anytime Activities

To work with your child on concepts taught in this unit, try these interesting and rewarding activities:

1. To help your child practice handling big numbers, have him or her look up the distances from Earth to some of the planets in the solar system, such as the distance from Earth to Mars, to Jupiter, to Saturn, and so on.

2. Have your child look up the box-office gross of one or more favorite movies.

3. Help your child look up the populations and land areas of the state and city in which you live and compare them with the populations and areas of other states and cities.

4. Have your child locate big numbers in newspapers and other sources and ask him or her to read them to you. Or, you can read the numbers and have your child write them.

Building Skills through Games

In Unit 5, your child will practice multiplication skills and build his or her understanding of multidigit numbers by playing the following games. For detailed instructions, see the *Student Reference Book.*

Beat the Calculator See *Student Reference Book* page 233.
This game develops automaticity with extended multiplication facts.

High-Number Toss See *Student Reference Book* page 252.
This game reinforces understanding of place value.

Multiplication Wrestling See *Student Reference Book* page 253.
This game reinforces understanding of the partial-products method for multiplication.

Number Top-It See *Student Reference Book* page 255.
This game strengthens understanding of place value.

Product Pile Up See *Student Reference Book* page 259.
This game develops automaticity with multiplication facts.

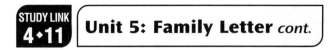

As You Help Your Child with Homework

As your child brings assignments home, you may want to go over the instructions together, clarifying them as necessary. The answers listed below will guide you through some of the Study Links in this unit.

Study Link 5·1

9. 1.48   **10.** 1.13   **11.** 8.17

Study Link 5·2

1. 42; 420; 420; 4,200; 4,200; 42,000

2. 27; 270; 270; 2,700; 2,700; 27,000

3. 32; 320; 320; 3,200; 3,200; 32,000

4. 3; 5; 50; 3; 3; 500

5. 6; 6; 60; 9; 900; 9,000

6. 5; 500; 50; 8; 80; 800

7. 15   **8.** 9.5   **9.** 4.26

Study Link 5·3

Sample answers:

1. $850 + 750 = 1,600$; 1,601

2. $400 + 1,000 + 500 = 1,900$; 1,824

3. $400 + 750 = 1,150$

4. $600 + 650 + 350 = 1,600$; 1,595

5. $300 + 300 + 500 = 1,100$

6. $800 + 700 = 1,500$; 1,547

7. $700 + 200 + 400 = 1,300$

8. $100 + 700 + 800 = 1,600$; 1,627

9. $750 + 400 + 200 = 1,350$

10. $600 + 800 = 1,400$

11. 4,800   **12.** 2,100   **13.** 45,000

Study Link 5·4

Sample answers:

1. $20 * 400 = 8,000$; 1,000s

2. $10 * 20 = 200$; 100s

3. $5 * 400 = 2,000$; 1,000s

4. $2 * 20 * 10,000 = 400,000$; 100,000s

5. Either 3 or 4 digits; $10 * 10 = 100$ and $90 * 90 = 8,100$

Study Link 5·5

1. 392   **2.** 2,200   **3.** 11,916

4. a. $7 * 200 = 1,400$; 1,000s   **b.** 1,267 hours

5. less   **6.** 7,884   **7.** 11,436

8. 1,258   **9.** 4,689

Study Link 5·6

1. 4,074   **2.** 1,680   **3.** 2,100   **4.** 486

5. 3,266   **6.** 17,000   **7.** 7,471   **8.** 37,632

9. 5,722   **10.** 10,751   **11.** 916   **12.** 2,769

Study Link 5·7

7. 6,552

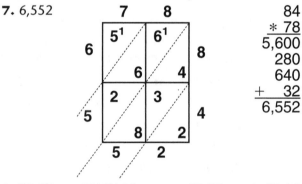

$$
\begin{array}{r}
84 \\
* \ 78 \\
\hline
5,600 \\
280 \\
640 \\
+ \quad 32 \\
\hline
6,552
\end{array}
$$

9. 39.57   **10.** 74.22   **11.** 33.77   **12.** 71.15

Study Link 5·8

92,106,954,873

12. 92 billion, 106 million, 954 thousand, 873

13. 370   **14.** 3,168   **15.** 1,656   **16.** 2,632

Study Link 5·9

7. 441   **8.** 2,970   **9.** 5,141

Study Link 5·10

2. Phoenix Mercury and San Antonio Stars; Sacramento Monarchs and Seattle Storm

4. 4,152   **5.** 798   **6.** 3,212

Study Link 5·11

1. China   **2.** France   **4.** Italy and the United States

STUDY LINK
5·1

Multiplication/Division Puzzles

Solve the multiplication/division puzzles mentally. Fill in the blank boxes.

SRB
17

Examples:

*, /	300	2,000
2	600	4,000
3	900	6,000

*, /	80	50
4	320	200
8	640	400

1.

*, /	70	400
8		
9		

2.

*, /	5	7
80		
600		

3.

*, /	9	4
50		
7,000		

4.

*, /		600
7	3,500	
		2,400

5.

*, /		80
30	2,700	
		56,000

6.

*, /	4,000	
	36,000	
20		10,000

Make up and solve some puzzles of your own.

7.

*, /		

8.

*, /		

Practice

9. _____ = 0.56 + 0.92

10. _____ = 2.86 − 1.73

11. 19.11 − 10.94 = _____

12. _____ = 0.52 + 0.25

STUDY LINK
5·2

Extended Multiplication Facts

Solve mentally.

1. $6 * 7 =$ _____

$6 * 70 =$ _____

$60 * 7 =$ _____

$60 * 70 =$ _____

$600 * 7 =$ _____

$60 * 700 =$ _____

2. $9 * 3 =$ _____

$9 * 30 =$ _____

$90 * 3 =$ _____

$90 * 30 =$ _____

$900 * 3 =$ _____

$90 * 300 =$ _____

3. $4 * 8 =$ _____

$4 * 80 =$ _____

$40 * 8 =$ _____

$40 * 80 =$ _____

$400 * 8 =$ _____

$40 * 800 =$ _____

4. $5 *$ _____ $= 15$

$30 *$ _____ $= 150$

$30 *$ _____ $= 1,500$

_____ $* 50 = 150$

_____ $* 500 = 1,500$

$30 *$ _____ $= 15,000$

5. _____ $* 9 = 54$

_____ $* 90 = 540$

_____ $* 90 = 5,400$

$60 *$ _____ $= 540$

$6 *$ _____ $= 5,400$

$6 *$ _____ $= 54,000$

6. $8 *$ _____ $= 40$

$8 *$ _____ $= 4,000$

$80 *$ _____ $= 4,000$

_____ $* 50 = 400$

_____ $* 5 = 400$

_____ $* 500 = 400,000$

Practice

7. _____ $= 6.3 + 8.7$

8. $7.36 + 2.14 =$ _____

9. _____ $= 9.74 - 5.48$

10. _____ $= 4.6 - 2.8$

140

Number Sense 3.0; Algebra and Functions 1.1; Mathematical Reasoning 1.1

LESSON 5·2 | Partial-Sums Addition

Example: $2,000 + 280 + 300 + 42 = ?$

$$
\begin{array}{r}
2,000 \\
280 \\
300 \\
+\quad 42 \\
\end{array}
$$

Add the thousands:	2,000	
Add the hundreds:	500	(200 + 300)
Add the tens:	120	(80 + 40)
Add the ones:	+ 2	
Find the total:	2,622	

Solve each problem.

1. $800 + 120 + 160 + 24 =$ _____

2. $700 + 420 + 50 + 30 =$ _____

3. _____ $= 600 + 180 + 40 + 12$

4. _____ $= 2,400 + 160 + 420 + 28$

5. _____ $= 1,500 + 90 + 240 + 24$

6. $5,600 + 420 + 400 + 30 =$ _____

LESSON 5·2

A *Multiplication Wrestling* Competition

1. Twelve players entered a *Multiplication Wrestling* competition. The numbers they chose are shown in the following table. The score of each player is the product of the two numbers. For example, Aidan's score is 741, because 13 * 57 = 741. Which of the 12 players do you think has the highest score? _____

Group A	Group B	Group C
Aidan: 13 * 57	Indira: 15 * 73	Miguel: 17 * 35
Colette: 13 * 75	Jelani: 15 * 37	Rex: 17 * 53
Emily: 31 * 75	Kuniko: 51 * 37	Sarah: 71 * 53
Gunnar: 31 * 57	Liza: 51 * 73	Tanisha: 71 * 35

Check your guess with the following procedure. *Do not do any arithmetic for Steps 2 and 3.*

2. In each pair below, cross out the player with the lower score. Find that player's name in the table above and cross it out as well.

Aidan; Colette	Indira; Jelani	Miguel; Rex
Emily; Gunnar	Kuniko; Liza	Sarah; Tanisha

3. Two players are left in Group A. Cross out the one with the lower score.
   Two players are left in Group B. Cross out the one with the lower score.
   Two players are left in Group C. Cross out the one with the lower score.

   Which 3 players are still left?

   _____

4. Of the 3 players who are left, which player has the lowest score? _____
   Cross out that player's name.

5. There are 2 players left. What are their scores? _____

   _____

6. Who won the competition? _____

LESSON 5·3 | Flight Coupons

The airline you are using on the World Tour will give you a $200 discount coupon for every 15,000 miles you fly. Suppose you have flown the distances shown in the table below.

Washington, D.C. → Cairo	5,980 mi
Cairo → Accra	2,420 mi
Accra → Cairo	2,420 mi
Cairo → Budapest	1,380 mi
Budapest → London	1,040 mi

1. Have you flown enough miles to get a discount coupon? _____

2. Describe the strategy you used to solve the problem.

_____

_____

_____

Name _____   Date _____   Time _____

LESSON 5·3 | Flight Coupons

The airline you are using on the World Tour will give you a $200 discount coupon for every 15,000 miles you fly. Suppose you have flown the distances shown in the table below.

Washington, D.C. → Cairo	5,980 mi
Cairo → Accra	2,420 mi
Accra → Cairo	2,420 mi
Cairo → Budapest	1,380 mi
Budapest → London	1,040 mi

1. Have you flown enough miles to get a discount coupon? _____

2. Describe the strategy you used to solve the problem.

_____

_____

STUDY LINK 5·3 | **Estimating Sums**

For all problems, write a number model to estimate the sum.

◆ If the estimate is greater than or equal to 1,500, find the exact sum.

◆ If the estimate is less than 1,500, **do not** solve the problem.

1. 867 + 734 = _____

Number model:

_____

2. 374 + 962 + 488 = _____

Number model:

_____

3. 382 + 744 = _____

Number model:

_____

4. 581 + 648 + 366 = _____

Number model:

_____

5. 318 + 295 + 493 = _____

Number model:

_____

6. 845 + 702 = _____

Number model:

_____

7. 694 + 210 + 386 = _____

Number model:

_____

8. 132 + 692 + 803 = _____

Number model:

_____

9. 756 + 381 + 201 = _____

Number model:

_____

10. 575 + 832 = _____

Number model:

_____

Practice

11. 60 * 80 = _____

12. 30 * 70 = _____

13. 50 * 900 = _____

14. 40 * 800 = _____

Mathematical Reasoning 2.2; Number Sense 1.4; Number Sense 2.1

LESSON 5·3 "Closer To" with Base-10 Blocks

You can use base-10 blocks to help you **round** numbers.

Example: Round 64 to the nearest ten.

◆ Build a model for 64 with base-10 blocks.

◆ *Think:* What **multiples of 10** are nearest to 64?
If I take the ones (cubes) away, I would have **60.**
If I add more ones to make the next ten, I would have **70.**

◆ Build models for 60 and 70.

60   64   70

Think: Is 64 closer to 60 or 70? 64 is closer to 60. So, 64 rounded to the nearest ten is 60.

Build models to help you choose the closer number.

1. Round 87 to the nearest ten.

List the three numbers you will build models for: _____, _____, _____

87 is closer to _____. So, 87 rounded to the nearest ten is _____.

2. Round 43 to the nearest ten.

List the three numbers you will build models for: _____, _____, _____

43 is closer to _____. So, 43 rounded to the nearest ten is _____.

3. Round 138 to the nearest ten.

List the three numbers you will build models for: _____, _____, _____

138 is closer to _____. So, 138 rounded to the nearest ten is _____.

4. Round 138 to the nearest *hundred.*

List the three numbers you will build models for: _____, _____, _____

138 is closer to _____. So, 138 rounded to the nearest hundred is _____.

145

LESSON 5·3 A Traveling Salesperson Problem

A salesperson plans to visit several cities. To save time and money, the trip should be as short as possible. If the salesperson were visiting only a few cities, it would be possible to figure the shortest route in a reasonable time. But what if the trip includes 10 cities? There would be 3,628,800 possible routes! Computer scientists are trying to find ways to solve this problem on the computer without having to do an impossible number of calculations.

Think like a computer. Imagine that you begin a trip in Seattle and have to visit Denver, Birmingham, and Bangor for business.

1. Estimate to find the shortest *route* that would include each city. Use the map on journal page 112.

2. Describe your route between each of the four cities.

_____

_____

_____

_____

_____

Try This

3. Describe a route that includes each city that would take the shortest amount of *time*.

_____

_____

_____

Name _____ Date _____ Time _____

LESSON 5·4 | **What Do Americans Eat?**

Answer the following questions:

1. How many eggs did you eat in the last 7 days? _____

2. How many cups of milk did you drink in the last 7 days? _____

3. How many cups of yogurt did you eat in the last 7 days? _____

✂ -

Name _____ Date _____ Time _____

LESSON 5·4 | **What Do Americans Eat?**

Answer the following questions:

1. How many eggs did you eat in the last 7 days? _____

2. How many cups of milk did you drink in the last 7 days? _____

3. How many cups of yogurt did you eat in the last 7 days? _____

✂ -

Name _____ Date _____ Time _____

LESSON 5·4 | **What Do Americans Eat?**

Answer the following questions:

1. How many eggs did you eat in the last 7 days? _____

2. How many cups of milk did you drink in the last 7 days? _____

3. How many cups of yogurt did you eat in the last 7 days? _____

STUDY LINK 5·4 | **Estimating Products**

Estimate whether the answer will be in the tens, hundreds, thousands, or more. Write a number model to show how you estimated. Then circle the box that shows your estimate.

1. A koala sleeps an average of 22 hours each day. About how many hours does a koala sleep in a year?

   Number model: _____

10s	100s	1,000s	10,000s	100,000s	1,000,000s

2. A prairie vole (a mouselike rodent) has an average of 9 babies per litter. If it has 17 litters in a season, about how many babies are produced?

   Number model: _____

10s	100s	1,000s	10,000s	100,000s	1,000,000s

3. Golfers lose, on average, about 5 golf balls per round of play. About how many golf balls will an average golfer lose playing one round every day for one year?

   Number model: _____

10s	100s	1,000s	10,000s	100,000s	1,000,000s

4. In the next hour, the people in France will save 12,000 trees by recycling paper. About how many trees will they save in two days?

   Number model: _____

10s	100s	1,000s	10,000s	100,000s	1,000,000s

Try This

5. How many digits can the product of two 2-digit numbers have? Give examples to support your answer.

   _____

Practice

6. 60 * 7 = _____   7. 4 * 80 = _____   8. _____ = 200 * 9

148

LESSON 5·4 A Curved Number Line

The number lines below are curved like hills. Use them to help you **round** numbers.

Example 1:

Round 64 to the nearest ten.

♦ Which **multiples of 10** are nearest to 64?

_____ and _____

♦ What number is halfway
between 60 and 70? _____

♦ Will 64 "slide" down
the hill to 60 or to 70? _____

♦ 64 rounded to the nearest ten is 60.

Example 2:

Round 175 to the nearest hundred.

♦ Which **multiples of 100** are nearest to 175?

_____ and _____

♦ What number is halfway
between 100 and 200? _____

♦ Will 175 "slide" down
the hill to 100 or 200? _____

♦ 175 rounded to the nearest hundred is 200.

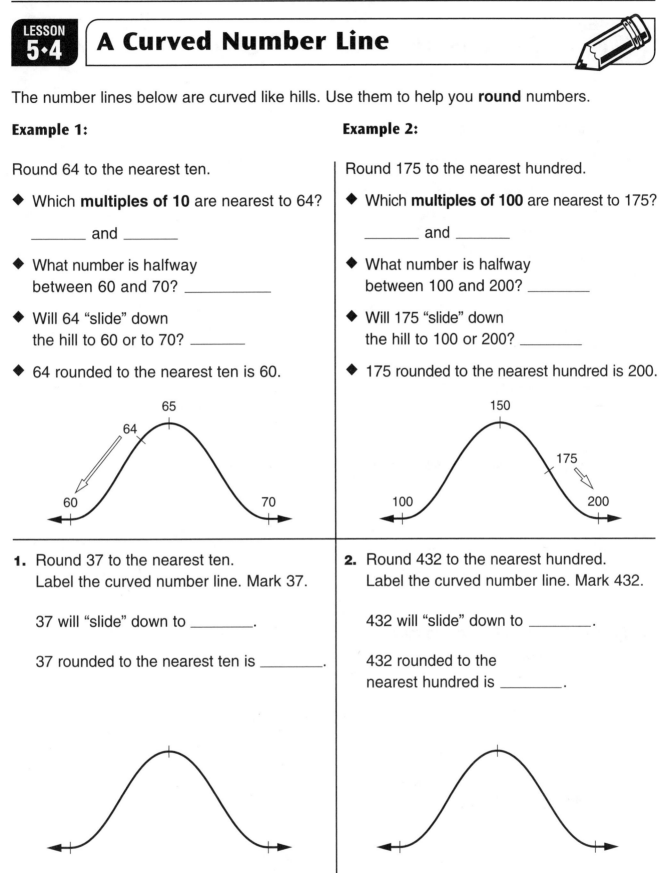

1. Round 37 to the nearest ten.
   Label the curved number line. Mark 37.

   37 will "slide" down to _____.

   37 rounded to the nearest ten is _____.

2. Round 432 to the nearest hundred.
   Label the curved number line. Mark 432.

   432 will "slide" down to _____.

   432 rounded to the
   nearest hundred is _____.

LESSON 5·4 **Missing Numbers and Digits**

1. Complete the number sentences.

◆ Fill in the circles using the numbers 3, 4, 6, or 7.

◆ Fill in the rectangles using the numbers 47, 62, 74, or 86.

◆ Some numbers will be used more than once.

a. $\bigcirc \times \boxed{} = 329$ **b.** $\bigcirc \times \boxed{} = 258$

c. $\bigcirc \times \boxed{} = 372$ **d.** $\bigcirc \times \boxed{} = 248$

e. $\bigcirc \times \boxed{} = 444$ **f.** $\bigcirc \times \boxed{} = 296$

2. For each problem, fill in the squares using the digits 4, 6, and 7.

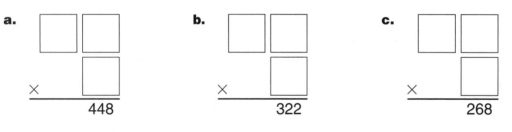

a. $\times$ 448   **b.** $\times$ 322   **c.** $\times$ 268

3. Use the digits 6, 7, 8, and 9 to make the largest product possible.

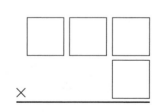

4. Use the digits 6, 7, 8, and 9 to make the smallest product possible.

STUDY LINK 5·5 **Multiplication**

Multiply using the partial-product method. Show your work in the grid below.

1. 56 * 7 = _____

2. 8 * 275 = _____

3. _____ = 1,324 * 9

4. Maya goes to school for 7 hours each day. If she does not miss any of the 181 school days, how many hours will Maya spend in school this year?

 a. Estimate whether the answer will be in the tens, hundreds, thousands, or more. Write a number model to show how you estimated. Circle the box that shows your estimate.

 Number model: _____

10s	100s	1,000s	10,000s	100,000s	1,000,000s

 b. Exact answer: _____ hours

5. The average eye blinks once every 5 seconds. Is that more than or less than a hundred thousand times per day? Explain your answer.

_____

_____

Practice

6. _____ = 495 + 7,389

7. 5,638 + 5,798 = _____

8. 3,007 − 1,749 = _____

9. _____ = 8,561 − 3,872

Number Sense 3.0, 3.2, 3.3

151

LESSON 5·5

Patterns in Extended Facts

1. Use base-10 blocks to help you solve the problems in the first 2 columns. Use the patterns to help you solve the problems in the third column. Use a calculator to check your work.

2 * 1 =	20 * 1 =	200 * 1 =
2 * 10 =	20 * 10 =	200 * 10 =
2 * 100 =	20 * 100 =	200 * 100 =

2. Use what you learned in Problem 1 to help you solve the problems in the table below. Use a calculator to check your work.

2 * 4 =	20 * 4 =	200 * 4 =
2 * 40 =	20 * 40 =	200 * 40 =
2 * 400 =	20 * 400 =	200 * 400 =

3. Explain how knowing 2 * 4 can help you find the answer to 20 * 40.

_____

_____

_____

_____

4. Make up and solve some problems of your own that use this pattern.

_____   _____

_____   _____

_____   _____

LESSON 5·5 | **An Old Puzzle**

An old puzzle begins like this: "A man has 6 houses. In each house, he keeps 6 cats. Each cat has 6 whiskers. On each whisker sit 6 fleas."

1. Answer the last line of the puzzle: "Houses, cats, whiskers, fleas—how many are there in all?"

_____

2. Use number models or illustrations to explain how you solved the puzzle.

✂ -

Name   Date   Time

LESSON 5·5 | **An Old Puzzle**

An old puzzle begins like this: "A man has 6 houses. In each house, he keeps 6 cats. Each cat has 6 whiskers. On each whisker sit 6 fleas."

1. Answer the last line of the puzzle: "Houses, cats, whiskers, fleas—how many are there in all?"

_____

2. Use number models or illustrations to explain how you solved the puzzle.

Name _____ Date _____ Time _____

STUDY LINK 5·6 More Multiplication

Multiply using the partial-products algorithm. Show your work.

1. 582 * 7 = _____

2. 56 * 30 = _____

3. 42 * 50 = _____

4. _____ = 27 * 18

5. _____ = 46 * 71

6. 340 * 50 = _____

Try This

7. _____ = 241 * 31

8. _____ = 768 * 49

Practice

9. _____ = 283 + 5,439

10. 6,473 + 4,278 = _____

11. 5,583 − 4,667 = _____

12. _____ = 9,141 − 6,372

154

Number Sense 3.2; Number Sense 3.3

Name _____ Date _____ Time _____

A Dart Game

Vanessa played a game of darts. She threw 9 darts.
Each dart hit the target. She scored 550 points.

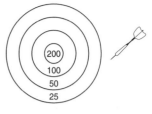

Where might each of her 9 darts have hit? Use the
table to show all possible solutions.

200	100	50	25

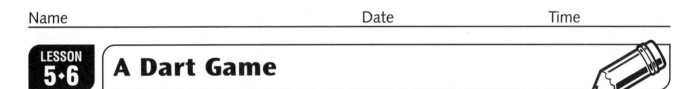

✂ -

Name _____ Date _____ Time _____

LESSON
5·6

A Dart Game

Vanessa played a game of darts. She threw 9 darts.
Each dart hit the target. She scored 550 points.

Where might each of her 9 darts have hit? Use the
table to show all possible solutions.

200	100	50	25

155

LESSON 5·6 | **Sorting Numbers**

Study the Venn diagrams in Problems 1 and 2. Label each circle and add at least one number to each section.

1.

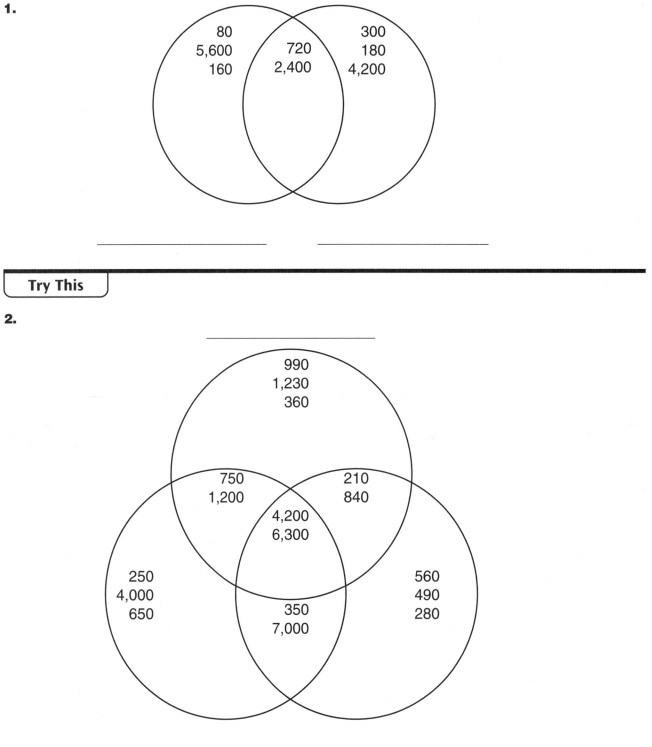

80		300
5,600	720	180
160	2,400	4,200

_____   _____

Try This

2.

_____

990
1,230
360

750   210
1,200   840

4,200
6,300

250   560
4,000   490
650   350   280
7,000

_____   _____

156

STUDY LINK 5·7 | Lattice Multiplication

Use the lattice method to find the following products.

1. 5 * 46 = _____

2. 8 * 67 = _____

3. 7 * 836 = _____

4. 4 * 329 = _____

5. 25 * 31 = _____

6. 49 * 52 = _____

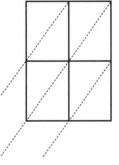

7. Use the lattice method and the partial-products method to find the product.

84 * 78 = _____

Practice

8. _____ = 33.67 + 5.9

9. 68.4 + 5.82 = _____

10. 71.44 − 37.67 = _____

11. _____ = 101.06 − 29.91

LESSON 5·7 | Napier's Rods

Scottish mathematician John Napier (1550–1617) devised a multiplication method using rods made of bone, wood, or heavy paper. These rods were used to solve multiplication and division problems.

Example 1:

4 * 67 = 268

Example 2:

8 * 5,239 = 41,912

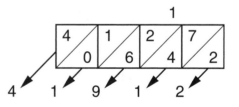

Cut out the rods on *Math Masters,* page 159. Use the rods and the board on *Math Masters,* page 160 to solve the following problems and some of your own. Use another method to check your answers.

1. 5 * 79 = _____

2. 7 * 92 = _____

3. _____ = 6 * 236

4. _____ = 9 * 5,841

| **Try This** |

5. Show a friend how you would use Napier's Rods to solve 3 * 407 or 9 * 5,038.

LESSON 5·7 **Napier's Rods** *continued*

Napier's Rods *continued*

1
2
3
4
5
6
7
8
9

LESSON 5·7 **Fact Lattice Patterns**

1. Look at a Multiplication/Division Facts Table. Find the shaded diagonal showing the doubles facts.

2. Find the doubles facts on the Fact Lattice on *Math Masters,* page 435. Shade the doubles facts lightly with a colored pencil.

3. Compare the two fact tables.

   a. List 3 things the tables have in common.

   _____

   _____

   _____

   _____

   b. List 3 things that are different on the Fact Lattice.

   _____

   _____

   _____

   _____

4. Describe 2 patterns that you see on the Fact Lattice.

   a. _____

   _____

   _____

   b. _____

   _____

   _____

5. Which of your Fact Lattice patterns is also in the Multiplication/Division Facts Table in your journal?

_____

LESSON 5·8

A 50-by-40 Array

STUDY LINK 5·8 Place-Value Puzzle

Use the clues below to fill in the place-value chart.

Billions				Millions				Thousands				Ones		
100B	10B	1B	,	100M	10M	1M	,	100Th	10Th	1Th	,	100	10	1

1. Find $\frac{1}{2}$ of 24. Subtract 4. Write the result in the hundreds place.

2. Find $\frac{1}{2}$ of 30. Divide the result by 3. Write the answer in the ten-thousands place.

3. Find $30 \div 10$. Double the result. Write it in the one-millions place.

4. Divide 12 by 4. Write the answer in the ones place.

5. Find $9 * 8$. Reverse the digits in the result. Divide by 3.
   Write the answer in the hundred-thousands place.

6. Double 8. Divide the result by 4. Write the answer in the one-thousands place.

7. In the one-billions place, write the even number greater than 0
   that has not been used yet.

8. Write the answer to $5 \div 5$ in the hundred-millions place.

9. In the tens place, write the odd number that has not been used yet.

10. Find the sum of all the digits in the chart so far.
    Divide the result by 5, and write it in the ten-billions place.

11. Write 0 in the empty column whose place value is less than billions.

12. Write the number in words. For example, 17,450,206 could be written as
    "17 million, 450 thousand, 206."

_____

Practice

13. $74 * 5 =$ _____

14. _____ $= 396 * 8$

15. _____ $= 92 * 18$

16. $56 * 47 =$ _____

LESSON 5·8 A Roomful of Dots

Suppose you filled your classroom from floor to ceiling with dot paper (2,000 dots per sheet).

SRB 180–184

1. About how many dots do you think there would be on all the paper needed to fill your classroom? Make a check mark next to your guess.

   _____ less than a million

   _____ between a million and a half billion

   _____ between half a billion and a billion

   _____ more than a billion

2. One ream of paper weighs about 5 pounds and has 500 sheets of paper. About how many pounds would the paper needed to fill your classroom weigh? Make a check mark next to your guess.

   _____ less than 100,000 pounds

   _____ between 100,000 pounds and 500,000 pounds

   _____ between 500,000 pounds and a million pounds

   _____ more than a million pounds

3. Now, work with your group to make more accurate estimates for Problems 1 and 2. Explain what you did.

   My group's estimates:

   Number of dots: _____

   Weight of the paper: _____

LESSON 5·8 | **How Much Is a Million?**

David M. Schwartz, the author of *How Much Is a Million?*, used 7 pages of his book to show approximately 100,000 tiny stars.

He wrote, "If this book had a million tiny stars, they would fill seventy pages.... If this book had a billion tiny stars, its pages spread side by side would stretch almost ten miles.... If you put a trillion of our stars onto a gigantic roll of paper, it would stretch all the way from New York to New Zealand."

1. About how many pages would be needed to show a trillion tiny stars? Explain.

_____

_____

2. Describe a strategy you could use, other than counting each star, to find the number of tiny stars on one page of *How Much Is a Million?*

_____

_____

✂ -

Name   Date   Time

LESSON 5·8 | **How Much Is a Million?**

David M. Schwartz, the author of *How Much Is a Million?*, used 7 pages of his book to show approximately 100,000 tiny stars.

He wrote, "If this book had a million tiny stars, they would fill seventy pages.... If this book had a billion tiny stars, its pages spread side by side would stretch almost ten miles.... If you put a trillion of our stars onto a gigantic roll of paper, it would stretch all the way from New York to New Zealand."

1. About how many pages would be needed to show a trillion tiny stars? Explain.

_____

_____

2. Describe a strategy you could use, other than counting each star, to find the number of tiny stars on one page of *How Much Is a Million?*

_____

LESSON 5·9 Place Value and Powers of 10

Millions	Hundred Thousands	Ten Thousands	Thousands	Hundreds	Tens	Ones
1,000,000			1,000	100		1
10 [100,000s]			10 [100s]	10 [10s]		10 [tenths]
		10 * 10 * 10 * 10		10 * 10		
	10^5		10^3	10^2		10^0

Fill in this place-value chart as follows:

1. Write standard numbers in Row 1.

2. In Row 2, write the value of each place to show that it is 10 times the value of the place to its right.

3. In Row 3, write the place values as products of 10s.

4. In Row 4, show the values as powers of 10. Use exponents. The exponent shows how many times 10 is used as a factor. It also shows how many zeros are in the standard number.

STUDY LINK 5·9 Many Names for Powers of 10

Below are different names for powers of 10. Write the names in the appropriate name-collection boxes. Circle the names that do not fit in any of the boxes.

1,000,000	10,000	1,000
100	10	10 [100,000s]
10 [10,000s]	10^6	10 [1,000s]
10^3	10 * 10 * 10 * 10	one thousand
10^5	10 * 10 * 10 * 10 * 10	10 [10s]
10 * 10	ten	10^1
10 [tenths]	10^0	1

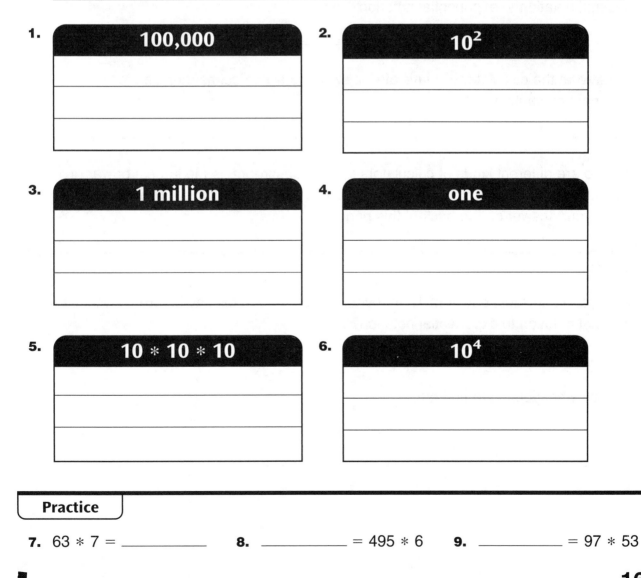

1. 100,000

2. 10^2

3. 1 million

4. one

5. 10 * 10 * 10

6. 10^4

Practice

7. 63 * 7 = _____

8. _____ = 495 * 6

9. _____ = 97 * 53

LESSON 5·9 | Powers of 10 on a Calculator

Experiment to see what happens when your calculator can no longer display all of the digits in a power of 10.

Clear your calculator's memory, then program it to multiply over and over by 10 as follows:

Calculator	Key Sequence
Calculator A	On/Off and Clear together
	Op1 ⊗ 10 Op1 10 Op1 Op1 Op1 ...
Calculator B	AC
	10 ⊗ ⊗ ⊟ ⊟ ⊟ ...

1. What is the largest power of 10 that your calculator can display before it switches from decimal notation to exponential notation?

_____

2. Write what the calculator displays after it switches from decimal notation to exponential notation.

_____

3. If there are different kinds of calculators in your classroom, is the largest power of 10 that they can display the same or different from your calculator? If it is different, tell how. Write your answer on the back of this page.

Try This

4. What is the smallest power of 10 that your calculator can display before it switches from decimal notation to exponential notation?

_____

Explain what you did to find out.

_____

_____

Name   Date   Time

STUDY LINK 5·10 Rounding

1. Round the seating capacities in the table below to the nearest thousand.

Women's National Basketball Association Seating Capacity of Home Courts		
Team	Seating Capacity	Rounded to the Nearest 1,000
Charlotte Sting	24,042	
Cleveland Rockers	20,562	
Detroit Shock	22,076	
New York Liberty	19,763	
Phoenix Mercury	19,023	
Sacramento Monarchs	17,317	
San Antonio Stars	18,500	
Seattle Storm	17,072	

2. Look at your rounded numbers. Which stadiums have about the same capacity?

_____

3. Round the population figures in the table below to the nearest million.

U.S. Population by Official Census from 1940 to 2000		
Year	Population	Rounded to the Nearest Million
1940	132,164,569	
1960	179,323,175	
1980	226,542,203	
2000	281,421,906	

Source for both tables: The World Almanac and Book of Facts 2004

Practice

4. _____ = 692 ∗ 6   5. _____ = 38 ∗ 21   6. 44 ∗ 73 = _____

Number Sense **1.1**; Number Sense **1.3**   **169**

LESSON 5·10 | **Number Lines**

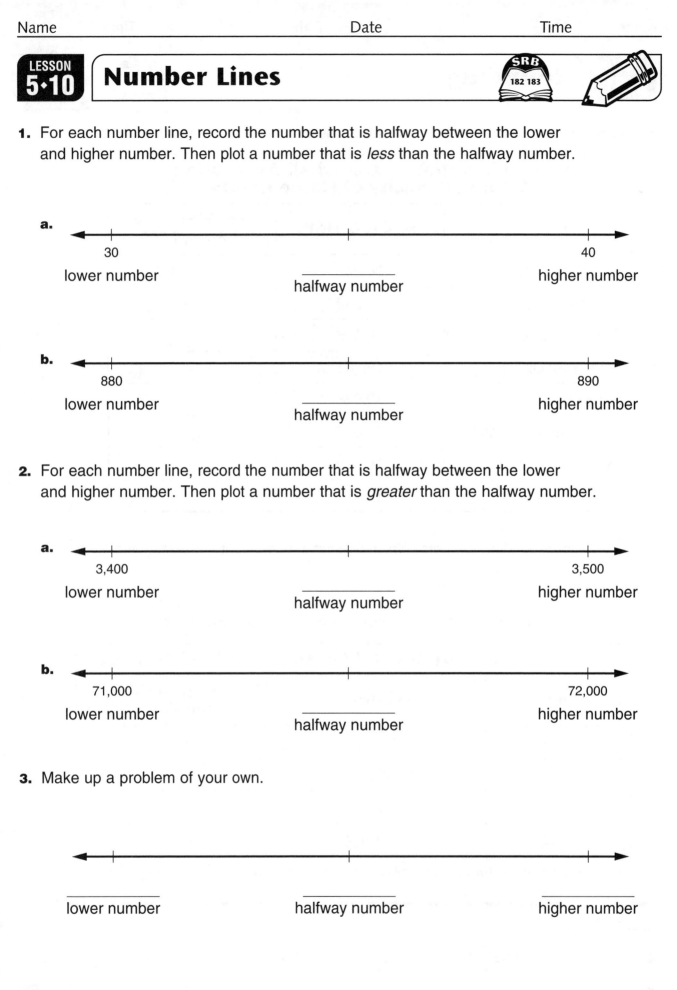

1. For each number line, record the number that is halfway between the lower and higher number. Then plot a number that is *less* than the halfway number.

a.

30
lower number

_____
halfway number

40
higher number

b.

880
lower number

_____
halfway number

890
higher number

2. For each number line, record the number that is halfway between the lower and higher number. Then plot a number that is *greater* than the halfway number.

a.

3,400
lower number

_____
halfway number

3,500
higher number

b.

71,000
lower number

_____
halfway number

72,000
higher number

3. Make up a problem of your own.

_____
lower number

_____
halfway number

_____
higher number

**LESSON
5·10**

Rounding Bar Graph Data

Each bar represents the 2003 population of a country.

SRB
76

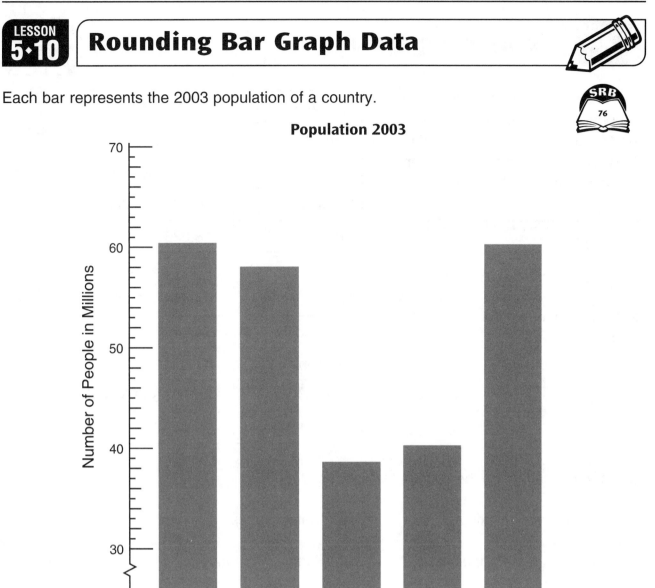

Population 2003

Source: The World Factbook

1. Estimate the population of each country to the nearest 10 million, to the nearest 5 million, and to the nearest 1 million.
   Organize your information in a table on the back of this sheet.

2. Describe the strategy you used to round to the nearest million.

_____

_____

_____

_____

_____

171

Name _____ Date _____ Time _____

Comparing Data

This table shows the number of pounds of fruit produced by the top 10 fruit-producing countries in 2001. Read each of these numbers to a friend or a family member.

Country	Pounds of Fruit
Brazil	77,268,294,000
China	167,046,420,000
France	26,823,740,000
India	118,036,194,000
Iran	28,599,912,000
Italy	44,410,538,000
Mexico	34,549,912,000
Philippines	27,028,556,000
Spain	36,260,392,000
United States	73,148,598,000

1. Which country produced the most fruit?

   _____

2. Which country produced the least fruit?

   _____

3. For each pair, circle the country that produced more fruit.

   a. India   Mexico   b. United States   Iran

   c. Brazil   Philippines   d. Spain   Italy

4. Which two countries together produced about as much fruit as India?

   _____

Practice

Estimate the sum. Write a number model.

5. 687 + 935 _____

6. 2,409 + 1,196 + 1,327 _____

7. 11,899 + 35,201 _____

Statistics, Data Analysis, and Probability 1.0; Number Sense **1.2**, 2.1

STUDY LINK 5·12

Unit 6: Family Letter

Division; Map Reference Frames; Measures of Angles

The first four lessons and the last lesson of Unit 6 focus on understanding the division operation, developing a method for dividing whole numbers, and solving division number stories.

Though most adults reach for a calculator to do a long-division problem, it is useful to know a paper-and-pencil procedure for computations such as $567 \div 6$ and $15\overline{)235}$. Fortunately, there is a method that is similar to the one most of us learned in school but is much easier to understand and use. This method is called the **partial-quotients method.**

Students have had considerable practice with extended division facts, such as $420 \div 7 = 60$, and questions, such as "About how many 12s are in 150?" Using the partial-quotients method, your child will apply these skills to build partial quotients until the exact quotient and remainder are determined.

This unit also focuses on numbers in map coordinate systems. For maps of relatively small areas, rectangular coordinate grids are used. For world maps and the world globe, the system of latitude and longitude is used to locate places.

Full-circle (360°) protractor

Because this global system is based on angle measures, the class will practice measuring and drawing angles with full-circle (360°) and half-circle (180°) protractors. If you have a protractor, ask your child to show you how to use this tool.

The class is well into the World Tour. Students have visited Africa and are now traveling in Europe. They are beginning to see how numerical information about a country helps them get a better understanding of the country—its size, climate, location,

Half-circle (180°) protractor

and population distribution—and how these characteristics affect the way people live. Your child may want to share with you information about some of the countries the class has visited. Encourage your child to take materials about Europe to school, such as magazine articles, travel brochures, and articles in the travel section of your newspaper.

Please keep this Family Letter for reference as your child works through Unit 6.

Vocabulary

Important terms in Unit 6:

acute angle An angle with a measure greater than 0° and less than 90°.

coordinate grid (also called a *rectangular coordinate grid*) A reference frame for locating points in a plane using *ordered number pairs,* or *coordinates.*

equal-groups notation A way to denote a number of equal-sized groups. The size of the groups is written inside square brackets and the number of groups is written in front of the brackets. For example, 3 [6s] means 3 groups with 6 in each group.

index of locations A list of places together with a reference frame for locating them on a map. For example, "Billings D3," indicates that Billings can be found within the rectangle where column 3 and row D of a grid meet on the map.

meridian bar A device on a globe that shows degrees of latitude north and south of the equator.

multiplication/division diagram A diagram used for problems in which a total is made up of several equal groups. The diagram has three parts: a number of groups, a number in each group, and a total number.

rows	chairs per row	chairs in all
6	4	24

obtuse angle An angle with a measure greater than 90° and less than 180°.

ordered number pair Two numbers that are used to locate a point on a *coordinate grid.* The first number gives the position along the horizontal axis, and the second number gives the position along the vertical axis. The numbers in an ordered pair are called *coordinates.* Ordered pairs are usually written inside parentheses: (2,3).

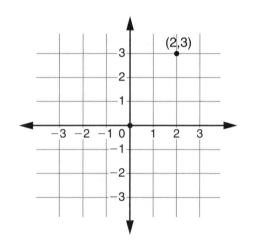

protractor A tool used for measuring or drawing angles. A half-circle protractor can be used to measure and draw angles up to 180°. A full-circle protractor can be used to measure and draw angles up to 360°. One of each type is on the Geometry Template.

quotient The result of dividing one number by another number. For example, in 35 ÷ 5 = 7, the quotient is 7.

reflex angle An angle with a measure greater than 180° and less than 360°.

straight angle An angle with a measure of 180°.

vertex The point at which the rays of an angle, the sides of a polygon, or the edges of a polyhedron meet. Plural is vertexes or vertices.

174

Copyright © Wright Group/McGraw-Hill

STUDY LINK 5·12 | **Unit 6: Family Letter** *cont.*

Do-Anytime Activities

To work with your child on concepts taught in this unit, try these interesting and rewarding activities:

1. Help your child practice division by solving problems for everyday situations.

2. Name places on the world globe and ask your child to give the latitude and longitude for each.

3. Encourage your child to identify and classify acute, right, obtuse, straight, and reflex angles in buildings, bridges, and other structures.

4. Work together with your child to construct a map, coordinate system, and index of locations for your neighborhood.

Building Skills through Games

In Unit 6, your child will practice using division and reference frames and measuring angles by playing the following games. For detailed instructions, see the *Student Reference Book.*

Angle Tangle See *Student Reference Book,* page 230.

This is a game for two players and will require a protractor. The game helps students practice drawing, estimating the measure of, and measuring angles.

Division Dash See *Student Reference Book,* page 241.

This is a game for one or two players. Each player will need a calculator. The game helps students practice division and mental calculation.

Grid Search See *Student Reference Book,* pages 250 and 251.

This is a game for two players, and each player will require *two* playing grids. The game helps students practice using a letter-number coordinate system and developing a search strategy.

Over and Up Squares See *Student Reference Book,* page 257.

This is a game for two players and will require a playing grid. The game helps students practice using ordered pairs of numbers to locate points on a rectangular grid.

Copyright © Wright Group/McGraw-Hill

175

As You Help Your Child with Homework

As your child brings assignments home, you may want to go over the instructions together, clarifying them as necessary. The answers listed below will guide you through some of the Study Links in this unit.

Study Link 6·1

1. 8 rows   **2.** 120,000 quills   **3.** 21 boxes

Study Link 6·2

1. 38   **2.** 23   **3.** 47

Study Link 6·3

1. 13 marbles; 5 left   **2.** 72 prizes, 0 left

3. 22 R3   **4.** 53 R3

Study Link 6·4

1. $15\frac{4}{8}$ or $15\frac{1}{2}$; Reported it as a fraction or decimal; Sample answer: You can cut the remaining strawberries into halves to divide them evenly among 8 students.

2. 21; Ignored it; Sample answer: There are not enough remaining pens to form another group of 16.

Study Link 6·5

1–7.

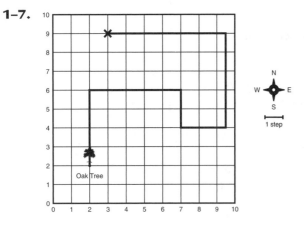

Study Link 6·6

1. >; 101°   **2.** <; 52°

3. >; 144°   **4.** <; 137°

6. 24   **7.** 8 R2   **8.** 157   **9.** 185 R3

Study Link 6·7

1. 60°   **2.** 150°   **3.** 84°   **4.** 105°

5. 32°   **6.** 300°

Study Link 6·8

1.

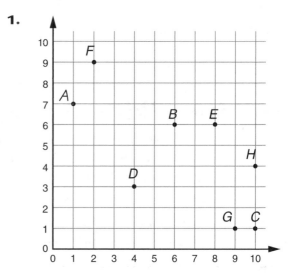

2. K (4,8);   L (7,7);   M (10,5);   N (1,8);   O (6,2);
P (8,4);   Q (10,2);   R (3,10)

Study Link 6·9

1.

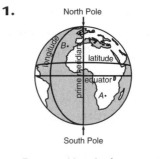

2. Eastern Hemisphere   **3.** water

4. 15 R2   **5.** 14   **6.** 43 R2   **7.** 134

Study Link 6·10

1. 8 pitchers; 0 oranges left

2. 22 bouquets; 8 flowers left

3. 45 R6   **4.** 69   **5.** 180

6. 2,233   **7.** 1,827   **8.** 16,287

STUDY LINK 6·1

Multiplication/Division Number Stories

Fill in each Multiplication/Division Diagram. Then write a number model. Be sure to include a unit with your answer.

SRB
22 23

1. Trung wants to rearrange his collection of 72 animals on a shelf in his room. How many equal rows of 9 animals can he make?

rows	animals per row	animals in all

Number model: _____

Answer: _____

2. An average porcupine has about 30,000 quills. About how many quills would 4 porcupines have?

porcupines	quills per porcupine	quills in all

Number model: _____

Answer: _____

3. There are 168 calculators for the students at Madison School. A box holds 8 calculators. How many boxes are needed to hold all of the calculators?

boxes	calculators per box	calculators in all

Number model: _____

Answer: _____

Practice

4. _____ = 6.17 + 8.77   **5.** _____ = 12.13 − 4.44

Number Sense **3.0**, **3.4**; Mathematical Reasoning 2.3   **177**

Equal-Grouping Division Problems

For Problems 1–3, fill in the multiples-of-10 list if it is helpful. If you prefer to solve the division problems in another way, show your work.

1. The community center bought 228 juice boxes for a picnic. How many 6-packs is that?

10 [6s] = _____   Number model: _____

20 [6s] = _____   Answer: _____ 6-packs

30 [6s] = _____

40 [6s] = _____

50 [6s] = _____

---

2. There are 8 girls on each basketball team. There are 184 girls in the league. How many teams are there?

10 [8s] = _____   Number model: _____

20 [8s] = _____   Answer: _____ teams

30 [8s] = _____

40 [8s] = _____

50 [8s] = _____

---

3. How many 3s are in 142?

10 [3s] = _____   Number model: _____

20 [3s] = _____   Answer: _____

30 [3s] = _____

40 [3s] = _____

50 [3s] = _____

Practice

4. _____ = 661 * 4   **5.** 13 * 96 = _____   **6.** _____ = 59 * 82

Number Sense 3.4; Mathematical Reasoning 1.2

Copyright © Wright Group/McGraw-Hill

LESSON 6·2   **Multiples of 10 and 100**

Fill in the missing numbers in the problems below.

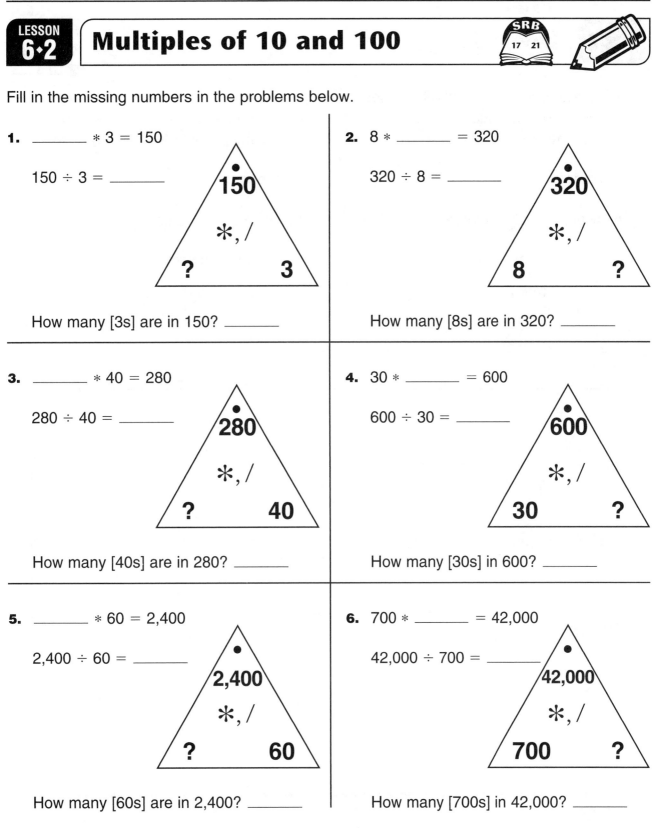

1. _____ * 3 = 150

150 ÷ 3 = _____

150

*, /

?   3

How many [3s] are in 150? _____

2. 8 * _____ = 320

320 ÷ 8 = _____

320

*, /

8   ?

How many [8s] are in 320? _____

3. _____ * 40 = 280

280 ÷ 40 = _____

280

*, /

?   40

How many [40s] are in 280? _____

4. 30 * _____ = 600

600 ÷ 30 = _____

600

*, /

30   ?

How many [30s] in 600? _____

5. _____ * 60 = 2,400

2,400 ÷ 60 = _____

2,400

*, /

?   60

How many [60s] are in 2,400? _____

6. 700 * _____ = 42,000

42,000 ÷ 700 = _____

42,000

*, /

700   ?

How many [700s] in 42,000? _____

7. Explain how solving one problem in each set helps you solve the other two problems.

_____

_____

179

STUDY LINK 6·3 | Division

SRB
22 23

1. Bernardo divided a bag of 83 marbles evenly among five friends and himself. How many marbles did each get?

   Number model: _____

   Answer: _____ marbles

   How many marbles are left over?

   _____ marbles

2. The carnival committee has 360 small prizes to share equally with 5 carnival booths. How many prizes will each booth get?

   Number model: _____

   Answer: _____ prizes

   How many prizes are left over?

   _____ prizes

3. 4)‾91‾   Answer: _____

4. 427 / 8   Answer: _____

Practice

5. _____ = 34.96 + 1.58

6. _____ = 300.2 + 2.378

7. 43.27 − 12.67 = _____

8. 74.6 − 31.055 = _____

Number Sense 3.2; Number Sense 3.4

LESSON 6·3

A Pen Riddle

Mrs. Swenson bought 2 pens for each of her 3 daughters.

◆ She gave the clerk a $10 bill.   ◆ Each pen cost the same amount.

◆ Her change was all in nickels.   ◆ No sales tax was charged.

◆ Her change was less than 50 cents.

1. What was the cost of each pen? _____

2. Show or explain how you got your answer.

✂ -

Name   Date   Time

LESSON 6·3

A Pen Riddle

Mrs. Swenson bought 2 pens for each of her 3 daughters.

◆ She gave the clerk a $10 bill.   ◆ Each pen cost the same amount.

◆ Her change was all in nickels.   ◆ No sales tax was charged.

◆ Her change was less than 50 cents.

1. What was the cost of each pen? _____

2. Show or explain how you got your answer.

Copyright © Wright Group/McGraw-Hill

STUDY LINK 6·4

Interpreting Remainders

1. Mrs. Patel brought a box of 124 strawberries to the party. She wants to divide the strawberries evenly among 8 people. How many strawberries will each person get?

   Picture:

   Number model: _____

   Answer: _____ strawberries

   What did you do about the remainder? Circle the answer.

   A. Ignored it

   B. Reported it as a fraction or decimal

   C. Rounded the answer up

   Why? _____
   _____
   _____

2. Mr. Chew has a box of 348 pens. He asks Maurice to divide the pens into groups of 16. How many groups can Maurice make?

   SRB 179

   Picture:

   Number model: _____

   Answer: _____ groups

   What did you do about the remainder? Circle the answer.

   A. Ignored it

   B. Reported it as a fraction or decimal

   C. Rounded the answer up

   Why? _____
   _____
   _____

Practice

3. $68 \div 7 =$ _____

4. _____ $= 74 \div 4$

5. $\dfrac{468}{9} =$ _____

6. $3\overline{)95} =$ _____

Number Sense 1.4, 3.4; Mathematical Reasoning 2.3

LESSON 6·4 | *A Remainder of One*

Use 25 centimeter cubes to represent the 25 ants in the story *A Remainder of One*.

1. Divide the cubes into 2 equal rows. Draw what you did.

How many cubes are in each row?

_____ cubes

How many cubes are left over?

_____ cube(s)

2. Divide the cubes into 3 equal rows. Draw what you did.

How many cubes are in each row?

_____ cubes

How many cubes are left over?

_____ cube(s)

3. Divide the cubes into 4 equal rows. Draw what you did.

How many cubes are in each row?

_____ cubes

How many cubes are left over?

_____ cube(s)

4. Divide the cubes into 5 equal rows. Draw what you did.

How many cubes are in each row?

_____ cubes

How many cubes are left over?

_____ cube(s)

LESSON 6·4 | Multiples Number Story

Paolo has fewer than 40 marbles in a bag. If he splits up the marbles among his 4 friends, he'll have 3 left over.

If he divides them among his 7 friends, he'll have 2 left over.

1. How many marbles are in the bag? _____ marbles

2. Show or explain how you got your answer.

Name _____ Date _____ Time _____

LESSON 6·4 | Multiples Number Story

Paolo has fewer than 40 marbles in a bag. If he splits up the marbles among his 4 friends, he'll have 3 left over.

If he divides them among his 7 friends, he'll have 2 left over.

1. How many marbles are in the bag? _____ marbles

2. Show or explain how you got your answer.

Copyright © Wright Group/McGraw-Hill

Treasure Hunt

Marge and her friends are playing Treasure Hunt. Help them find the treasure. Follow the directions. Draw the path from the oak tree to the treasure. Mark the spot where the treasure is buried.

SRB
107

1. Start at the dot under the oak tree; face north. Walk 4 steps.

2. Make a quarter turn, clockwise. Walk 5 steps.

3. Face south. Walk 2 steps.

4. Face east. Walk $2\frac{1}{2}$ steps.

5. Make a $\frac{3}{4}$ turn, clockwise. Walk 5 steps.

6. Make a $\frac{3}{4}$ turn, clockwise. Walk $6\frac{1}{2}$ steps.

7. Make an X to mark the spot where you end.

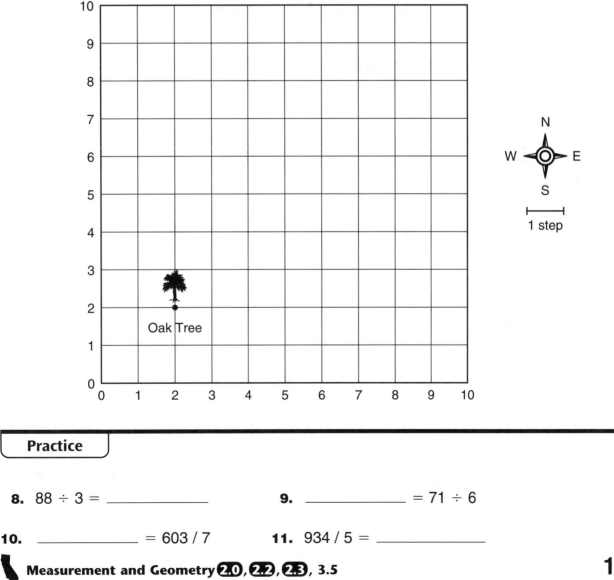

Practice

8. $88 \div 3 =$ _____

9. _____ $= 71 \div 6$

10. _____ $= 603 / 7$

11. $934 / 5 =$ _____

Measurement and Geometry 2.0, 2.2, 2.3, 3.5

185

LESSON 6·5 | Time (Analog)

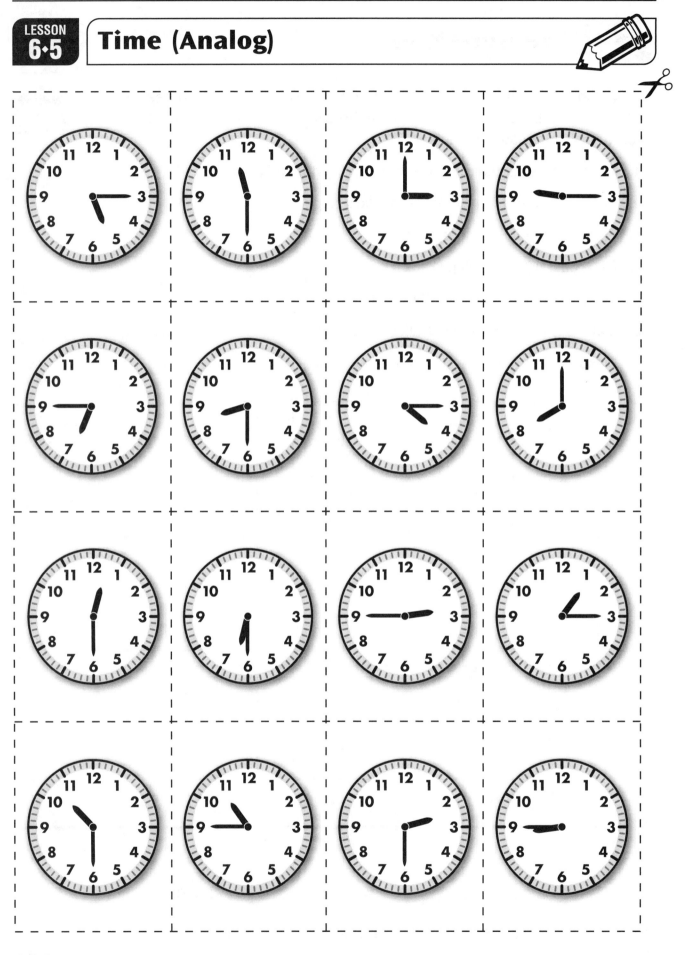

186

LESSON 6·5   **Time (Digital)**

LESSON 6·5 Time (Words)

8 o'clock	Half-past 2 o'clock	Quarter-to 7 o'clock	Quarter-past 5 o'clock
Half-past 8 o'clock	3 o'clock	Quarter-to 11 o'clock	Quarter-after 4 o'clock
Half-past 6 o'clock	Half-past 12 o'clock	Quarter-to 3 o'clock	Half-past 10 o'clock
Quarter-to 9 o'clock	Quarter-after 9 o'clock	Quarter-after 1 o'clock	Half-past 11 o'clock

LESSON 6·5 | **Clock Angle Challenge**

Use the full-circle protractor and the clock from journal pages 152 and 153 to help you solve the problems below.

SRB
141 142

1. How long does it take the *hour hand* to move 1°? _____

Explain. _____

_____

2. How long does it take the *minute hand* to move 1°? _____

Explain. _____

_____

_____

✂ --

Name _____ Date _____ Time _____

LESSON 6·5 | **Clock Angle Challenge**

Use the full-circle protractor and the clock from journal pages 152 and 153 to help you solve the problems below.

SRB
141 142

1. How long does it take the *hour hand* to move 1°? _____

Explain. _____

_____

2. How long does it take the *minute hand* to move 1°? _____

Explain. _____

_____

Copyright © Wright Group/McGraw-Hill

189

Measuring Angles

SRB
141 142

First estimate and then use your full-circle protractor to measure each angle.

1. This angle is _____ (>, <) 90°.

∠G: _____

2. This angle is _____ (>, <) 90°.

∠H: _____

3. This angle is _____ (>, <) 90°.

∠I: _____

4. This angle is _____ (>, <) 90°.

∠J: _____

Try This

5. On the back of this page, draw and label angles with the following degree measures:

∠ABC   78°   ∠DEF   145°   ∠GHI   213°   ∠JKL   331°

Practice

6. _____ = 96 ÷ 4

7. 66 ÷ 8 = _____

8. _____ = 314 ÷ 2

9. 928 ÷ 5 = _____

Measurement and Geometry 3.5; Number Sense 3.2

LESSON 6·6 | A Waxed-Paper Protractor

1. Follow the steps below to make a waxed-paper protractor.

Step 1: Take a sheet of waxed paper.

Step 2: Fold the paper in half. Be sure to crease it tightly.

fold

Step 3: Fold it in half again.

← fold

Step 4: Bring the folded edges together and fold it in half. Repeat this step again.

fold   fold

Step 5: Cut off the top.

Step 6: Unfold.

2. Use your waxed-paper protractor to measure the angles below.

a.

M

Angle *M* measures about _____ wedges.

b.

R

Angle *R* measures about _____ wedges.

3. Use a straightedge to draw more angles on the back of this sheet.
   Measure the angles and record the numbers of wedges.

191

STUDY LINK 6·7 | **Measuring Angles with a Protractor**

First estimate whether the angles measure more or less than 90°. Then use a half-circle protractor to measure them.

SRB 143

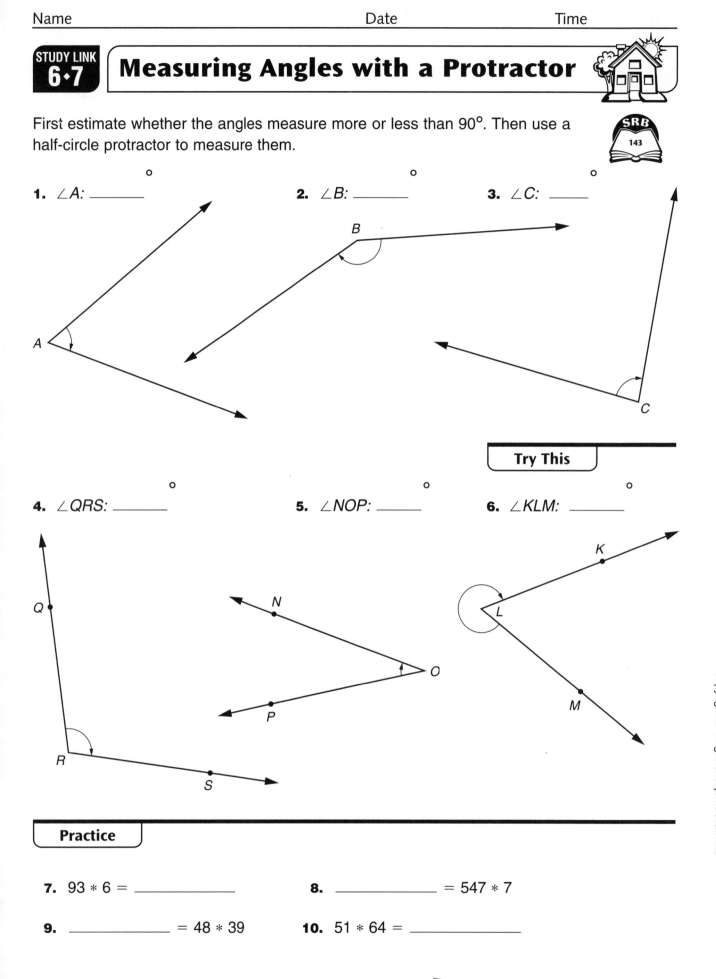

1. ∠A: _____

2. ∠B: _____

3. ∠C: _____

Try This

4. ∠QRS: _____

5. ∠NOP: _____

6. ∠KLM: _____

Practice

7. 93 * 6 = _____

8. _____ = 547 * 7

9. _____ = 48 * 39

10. 51 * 64 = _____

Measurement and Geometry **3.5**

LESSON 6·7 | # Exploring Triangle Measures

You need 2 sheets of paper, a straightedge, and a protractor.

SRB 143

1. Draw a large triangle on each sheet of paper. The 2 triangles should not look the same.

2. Label the vertices of one triangle *A, B,* and *C.* Label the vertices of the other triangle *D, E,* and *F.* Be sure to write the labels inside the triangles.

3. Using your protractor, measure each angle as accurately as you can. Record the degree measures in the tables below.

4. Find the sum of the degree measures in triangle *ABC* and in triangle *DEF.*

Angle	Degree Measure
$\angle A$	About _____ °
$\angle B$	About _____ °
$\angle C$	About _____ °
Sum	About _____ °

Angle	Degree Measure
$\angle D$	About _____ °
$\angle E$	About _____ °
$\angle F$	About _____ °
Sum	About _____ °

5. Write a true statement about the sum of the measures of the 3 angles of a triangle.

_____

_____

STUDY LINK 6·8 | **Coordinate Grids**

1. Plot and label each point on the coordinate grid.

SRB
144

A   (1,7)

B   (6,6)

C   (10,1)

D   (4,3)

E   (8,6)

F   (2,9)

G   (9,1)

H   (10,4)

2. Write the ordered number pair for each point plotted on the coordinate grid.

I   (_5_ , _3_)

J   (_7_ , _2_)

K   (____ , ____)

L   (____ , ____)

M   (____ , ____)

N   (____ , ____)

O   (____ , ____)

P   (____ , ____)

Q   (____ , ____)

R   (____ , ____)

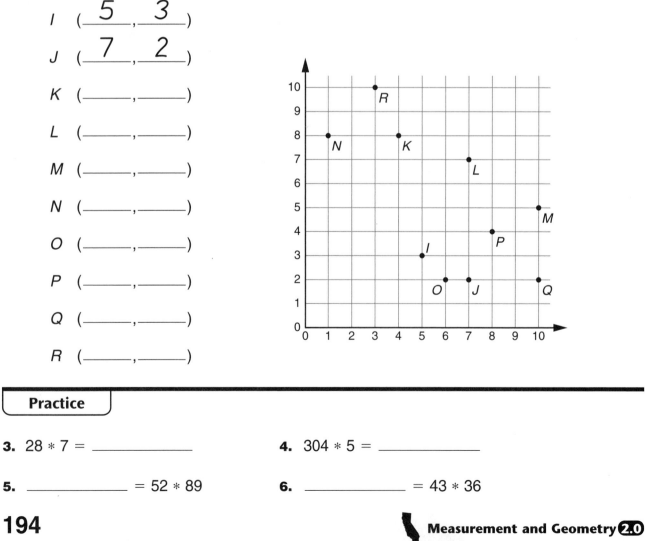

Practice

3. $28 * 7 =$ _____

4. $304 * 5 =$ _____

5. _____ $= 52 * 89$

6. _____ $= 43 * 36$

Measurement and Geometry 2.0

STUDY LINK 6·9 | **Latitude and Longitude**

Use your *Student Reference Book* to help you complete this Study Link.
Read the examples and study the figures on pages 272 and 273.

1. Do the following on the picture of the world globe.

   a. Label the North and South Poles.

   b. Draw and label the equator.

   c. Label the prime meridian.

   d. Draw and label a line of latitude that is north
   of the equator.

   e. Draw and label a line of longitude that is
   west of the prime meridian.

   f. Mark a point that is in the Southern
   Hemisphere and also in the Eastern
   Hemisphere. Label the point *A*.

   g. Mark a point that is in the Northern
   Hemisphere and also in the Western
   Hemisphere. Label the point *B*.

2. The entire continent of Africa is shown in the figure above. Is Africa
   mostly in the Western Hemisphere or in the Eastern Hemisphere?

   _____

3. Do the equator and prime meridian meet over water or over land? _____

Practice

4. _____ = 47 / 3

5. $7\overline{)98}$ _____

6. 217 ÷ 5 = _____

7. _____ = 804 / 6

LESSON 6·9 — Latitude and Longitude Cards

Latitude 0° Equator	Latitude 10° N or S	Latitude 20° N or S	Latitude 30° N or S	Latitude 40° N or S
Latitude 50° N or S	Latitude 60° N or S	Latitude 70° N or S	Latitude 80° N or S	Latitude 90° N or S
Longitude 0° Prime Meridian	Longitude 10° E or W	Longitude 20° E or W	Longitude 30° E or W	Longitude 40° E or W
Longitude 50° E or W	Longitude 60° E or W	Longitude 70° E or W	Longitude 80° E or W	Longitude 90° E or W
Longitude 100° E or W	Longitude 110° E or W	Longitude 120° E or W	Longitude 130° E or W	Longitude 140° E or W
Longitude 150° E or W	Longitude 160° E or W	Longitude 170° E or W	Longitude 180° International Date Line	Longitude PLAYER'S CHOICE

STUDY LINK 6·10 | **Division**

1. It takes 14 oranges to make a small pitcher of juice. Annette has 112 oranges. How many pitchers of juice can she make?

   Number model: _____

   Answer: _____ pitchers of juice

   How many oranges are left over? _____ oranges

2. Each bouquet needs 17 flowers. The florist has 382 flowers in his store. How many bouquets can the florist make?

   Number model: _____

   Answer: _____ bouquets

   How many flowers are left over? _____ flowers

3. $726 \div 16 =$ _____

4. $4\overline{)276}$ _____

Practice

5. $45 * 4 =$ _____

6. _____ $= 319 * 7$

7. _____ $= 29 * 63$

8. $89 * 183 =$ _____

LESSON 6·10 | **Division "Magic"**

1. Write a 3-digit number. _____ Enter it into your calculator twice to make a 6-digit number. For example, if you picked 259, then you would enter 259259 in your calculator.

2. Divide the 6-digit number by 7. Then divide the result by 11. Finally, divide that result by 13.

3. What is the final quotient? _____

4. Repeat Steps 1 and 2.   New number: _____   Final quotient: _____

5. Do you think this trick works with *any* three-digit number? Explain.

_____

_____

_____

Copyright © Wright Group/McGraw-Hill

✂ -

Name _____ Date _____ Time _____

LESSON 6·10 | **Division "Magic"**

1. Write a 3-digit number. _____ Enter it into your calculator twice to make a 6-digit number. For example, if you picked 259, then you would enter 259259 in your calculator.

2. Divide the 6-digit number by 7. Then divide the result by 11. Finally, divide that result by 13.

3. What is the final quotient? _____

4. Repeat Steps 1 and 2.   New number: _____   Final quotient: _____

5. Do you think this trick works with *any* three-digit number? Explain.

_____

_____

_____

Copyright © Wright Group/McGraw-Hill

STUDY LINK
6·11

Unit 7: Family Letter

Fractions and Their Uses; Chance and Probability

One of the most important ideas in mathematics is the concept that a number can be named in many different ways. For example, a store might advertise an item at $\frac{1}{2}$ off its original price or at a 50% discount—both mean the same thing. Much of the mathematics your child will learn involves finding equivalent names for numbers.

A few weeks ago, the class studied decimals as a way of naming numbers between whole numbers. Fractions serve the same purpose. After reviewing the meaning and uses of fractions, students will explore equivalent fractions—fractions that have the same value, such as $\frac{1}{2}, \frac{2}{4}, \frac{3}{6},$ and so on. As in past work with fractions, students will handle concrete objects and look at pictures, because they first need to "see" fractions in order to understand what fractions mean.

A measuring cup showing fractional increments

Fractions are also used to express the chance that an event will occur. For example, if we flip a coin, we say that it will land heads-up about $\frac{1}{2}$ of the time. The branch of mathematics that deals with chance events is called **probability.** Your child will begin to study probability by performing simple experiments.

Please keep this Family Letter for reference as your child works through Unit 7.

199

Vocabulary

Important terms in Unit 7:

denominator The number below the line in a fraction. In a fraction where the whole is divided into equal parts, the denominator represents the number of equal parts into which the whole (or ONE or unit whole) is divided. In the fraction $\frac{a}{b}$, b is the denominator.

$$\frac{5}{9} \qquad 5/9$$
denominator

equal chance outcomes or **equally likely outcomes** If each of the possible outcomes for a chance experiment or situation has the same chance of occurring, the outcomes are said to have an equal chance or to be equally likely. For example, there is an equal chance of getting heads or tails when flipping a coin, so heads and tails are equally likely outcomes.

equivalent fractions Fractions with different denominators that name the same number. For example, $\frac{1}{2}$ and $\frac{4}{8}$ are equivalent fractions.

fair (coin, die, or spinner) A device that is free from bias. Each side of a fair die or coin will come up about equally often. Each section of a fair spinner will come up in proportion to its area.

A die has six faces. If the die is fair, each face has the same chance of coming up.

fair game A game in which every player has the same chance of winning.

mixed number A number that is written using both a whole number and a fraction. For example, $2\frac{1}{4}$ is a mixed number equal to $2 + \frac{1}{4}$.

numerator The number above the line in a fraction. In a fraction where the whole (or ONE or unit whole) is divided into a number of equal parts, the numerator represents the number of equal parts being considered. In the fraction $\frac{a}{b}$, a is the numerator.

numerator
$$\frac{5}{9} \qquad 5/9$$

probability A number from 0 through 1 that tells the chance that an event will happen. The closer a probability is to 1, the more likely the event is to happen.

whole (or ONE or unit whole) The entire object, collection of objects, or quantity being considered; the ONE; the unit whole; 100%.

"whole" box In *Everyday Mathematics,* a box in which students write the name of the whole (or ONE or unit whole).

Whole
24 pennies

Do-Anytime Activities

To work with your child on concepts taught in this unit, try these interesting and rewarding activities:

1. Have your child look for everyday uses of fractions in grocery items, clothing sizes, cookbooks, measuring cups and spoons, and statistics in newspapers and on television.

2. Encourage your child to express numbers, quantities, and measures, such as a quarter of an hour, a quart of orange juice, a dozen eggs, and a pint of milk.

3. While grocery shopping, help your child compare prices by looking at shelf labels or calculating unit prices. Help your child make decisions about the "better buy." If a calculator is available, have your child take it to the store.

4. Have your child look for everyday uses of probabilities in games, sports, and weather reports. Ask your child to make a list of events that could never happen, might happen, and are sure to happen.

Building Skills through Games

In this unit, your child will work on his or her understanding of fractions and probability by playing the following games. For detailed instructions, see the *Student Reference Book.*

Chances Are See *Student Reference Book,* pages 236 and 237.
This game is for 2 players and requires one deck of *Chances Are* Event Cards and one deck of *Chances Are* Probability Cards. The game develops skill in using probability terms to describe the likelihood of events.

Fraction Match See *Student Reference Book,* page 243.
This game is for 2 to 4 players and requires one deck of *Fraction Match* cards. The game develops skill in naming equivalent fractions.

Fraction Of See *Student Reference Book,* pages 244 and 245.
This game is for 2 players and requires one deck of *Fraction Of* Fraction Cards and one deck of *Fraction Of* Set Cards. The game develops skill in finding the fraction of a number.

Fraction Top-It See *Student Reference Book,* page 247.
This is a game for 2 to 4 players and requires one set of 32 Fraction Cards. The game develops skill in comparing fractions.

Getting to One See *Student Reference Book,* page 248.
This is a game for 2 players and requires one calculator. The game develops skill in estimation.

Grab Bag See *Student Reference Book,* page 249.
This game is for 2 players or two teams of 2 and requires one deck of *Grab Bag* cards. The game develops skill in calculating the probability of an event.

STUDY LINK 6·11 | **Unit 7: Family Letter** *cont.*

As You Help Your Child with Homework

As your child brings assignments home, you may want to go over the instructions together, clarifying them as necessary. The answers listed below will guide you through some of the Study Links in this unit.

Study Link 7·2

1. **b.** 4   **c.** 12   **d.** 8   2. 6

3. 12   4. 7   5. 28

6. 10   7. 30   8. 10

9. 12   10. 12   11. $2\frac{1}{2}$

12. 23   13. $19\frac{2}{3}$ 14. 13

15. $41\frac{7}{9}$

Study Link 7·3

1. 50-50 chance   2. very unlikely

4. 5   5. 592   6. 3,948

7. 1,690   8. 16,170

Study Link 7·4

3. 8   4. 0.881   5. 9.845

6. 1.59   7. 0.028

Study Link 7·5

1. Less than $1.00; 0.75 + 0.10 = 0.85

2. $3\frac{3}{4}$ 3. $\frac{1}{6}$ 4. $2\frac{3}{8}$

5. Sample answers:

$\frac{1}{4} + \frac{1}{4} + \frac{1}{4} + \frac{1}{4} = 1$ $\frac{1}{4} + \frac{3}{12} + \frac{3}{6} = 1$

$\frac{2}{4} + \frac{3}{6} = 1$

6. 8   7. 45   8. 49   9. 22

Study Link 7·6

1. C, F, I   2. B, D   3. E, H   4. A, G

5. $\frac{2}{3}$ 7. $\frac{5}{6}$ 9. $\frac{1}{2}$ 10. $\frac{1}{6}$

Study Link 7·7

5. $23\frac{3}{4}$ 6. 19   7. 42

Study Link 7·8

Sample answers for 1–10:

1. $\frac{2}{10}$; $\frac{1}{5}$; $\frac{20}{100}$ 2. $\frac{6}{10}$; $\frac{3}{5}$; $\frac{60}{100}$

3. $\frac{5}{10}$; $\frac{1}{2}$; $\frac{50}{100}$ 4. $\frac{3}{4}$; $\frac{30}{40}$; $\frac{75}{100}$

5. 0.3   6. 0.63   7. 0.7   8. 0.4

9. 0.70; $\frac{70}{100}$ 10. 0.2; $\frac{2}{10}$ 11. 702   12. 3,227

13. 975

Study Link 7·9

1. >   2. <   3. =

4. =   5. <   6. >

7. Answers vary.   8. Answers vary.

9. $\frac{1}{4}$; $\frac{4}{10}$; $\frac{3}{7}$; $\frac{24}{50}$ 10. $\frac{1}{12}$; $\frac{3}{12}$; $\frac{7}{12}$; $\frac{8}{12}$; $\frac{11}{12}$

11. $\frac{1}{50}$; $\frac{1}{20}$; $\frac{1}{5}$; $\frac{1}{3}$; $\frac{1}{2}$ 12. $\frac{4}{100}$; $\frac{4}{12}$; $\frac{4}{8}$; $\frac{4}{5}$; $\frac{4}{4}$

13. 5   14. 100   15. 36

Study Link 7·10

3. 28   4. 27   5. 30   6. 36

Study Link 7·11

3. 29   4. $16\frac{1}{2}$ 5. 105   6. $141\frac{1}{5}$

Study Link 7·12

1. Answers vary.

2. Answers vary.

3. Answers vary.

4. **a.** $\frac{1}{4}$ **b.** $\frac{1}{4}$ **c.** $\frac{1}{2}$

5. Sample answer: I think it will be about the same fraction for 1000 times as it was for 20.

6. 336   7. 7,866   8. 3,870   9. 4,828

202

Name _____ Date _____ Time _____

Fractions

1. Divide the circle into 6 equal parts.
Color $\frac{5}{6}$ of the circle.

Whole
circle

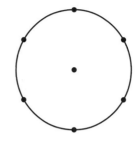

SRB
44 52

2. Divide the rectangle into 3 equal parts.
Shade $\frac{2}{3}$ of the rectangle.

Whole
rectangle

3. Divide each square into fourths.
Color $1\frac{3}{4}$ of the squares.

Whole
square

Fill in the missing fractions and mixed numbers on the number lines.

4.

0                  $\frac{7}{10}$ 1

5.

0    $\frac{1}{4}$ 1   2

Practice

6. 854 + 267 = _____

7. _____ = 3,398 + 2,635

8. _____ = 6,374 − 755

9. 5,947 − 3,972 = _____

Number Sense 1.5; Number Sense 1.7; Number Sense 1.9

203

Copyright © Wright Group/McGraw-Hill

LESSON 7·1 | Fraction Strips

Cut along the dashed lines.

1 Whole

0   1

Halves

Fourths

Eighths

Thirds

Sixths

LESSON 7·1   Fraction Number-Line Poster

1 Whole
Halves
Fourths
Eighths
Thirds
Sixths

LESSON 7·1   Constructing an Equilateral Triangle

An **equilateral triangle** is a triangle in which all 3 sides are the same length. Here is one way to construct an equilateral triangle using a compass and straightedge.

Step 1: Draw line segment *AB*.

Step 2: Place the anchor of the compass on *A* and the pencil on *B*. Without changing the compass opening, make an arc above the line segment.

Step 3: Place the anchor on *B*. Keeping the same compass opening, make a second arc that crosses the first arc. Label the point where the two arcs cross as *C*.

Step 4: Draw line segments *AC* and *BC*.

Use your compass and straightedge to construct a very large equilateral triangle on a separate sheet of paper. Cut out your triangle. Divide it into 6 equal parts. Color $\frac{1}{6}$ of it. Tape your triangle on the back of this sheet.

STUDY LINK 7·2 "Fraction-of" Problems

SRB
59

1. Theresa had 24 cookies. She gave $\frac{1}{6}$ to her sister and $\frac{3}{6}$ to her mother.

Whole

   a. Fill in the "whole" box.

   b. How many cookies did she give to her sister? _____ cookies

   c. How many did she give to her mother? _____ cookies

   d. How many did she have left? _____ cookies

Solve.

2. $\frac{1}{3}$ of 18 = _____

3. $\frac{2}{3}$ of 18 = _____

4. $\frac{1}{5}$ of 35 = _____

5. $\frac{4}{5}$ of 35 = _____

6. $\frac{1}{4}$ of 40 = _____

7. $\frac{3}{4}$ of 40 = _____

Try This

8. $\frac{5}{8}$ of 16 = _____

9. $\frac{4}{9}$ of 27 = _____

10. $\frac{3}{5}$ of 20 = _____

11. What is $\frac{1}{4}$ of 10? _____ Explain. _____

_____

_____

Practice

12. $92 \div 4 =$ _____

13. $59 / 3 =$ _____

14. _____ $= 104 / 8$

15. $9\overline{)376} =$ _____

Number Sense 1.5

207

LESSON 7·2 | **Hiking Trails**

Luis is staying in a large state park that has
8 hiking trails. In the table at the right, each trail
is labeled *easy, moderate,* or *rugged,* depending
on how difficult that trail is for hiking.

Luis figures that it would take him about
20 minutes to walk 1 mile on an easy trail,
about 30 minutes on a moderate trail, and
about 40 minutes on a rugged trail.

State Park Trails		
Trail	**Miles**	**Type**
Ice Age	$1\frac{1}{4}$	easy
Kettle	2	moderate
Pine	$\frac{3}{4}$	moderate
Bluff	$1\frac{3}{4}$	rugged
Cliff	$\frac{3}{4}$	rugged
Oak	$1\frac{1}{2}$	easy
Sky	$1\frac{1}{2}$	moderate
Badger	$3\frac{1}{2}$	moderate

1. About how long will it take Luis to walk
   the following trails?

   a. Kettle Trail: About _____ minutes

   b. Cliff Trail: About _____ minutes

   c. Oak Trail: About _____ minutes

   d. Bluff Trail: About _____ minutes

2. If Luis wants to hike for about $\frac{3}{4}$ of an
   hour, which trail should he choose?   _____

3. If he wants to hike for about 25 minutes,
   which trail should he choose?   _____

4. About how long would it take him
   to complete Pine Trail?   About _____ minutes

5. Do you think Luis could walk Badger Trail in less than 2 hours? _____

   Explain. _____

   _____

   _____

   _____

STUDY LINK 7·3 Color Tiles

SRB
45 80

There are 5 blue, 2 red, 1 yellow, and 2 green tiles in a bag.

1. Without looking, Maren picks a tile from the bag. Which of these best describes her chances of picking a blue tile?

Ⓐ likely

Ⓑ 50-50 chance

Ⓒ unlikely

Ⓓ very unlikely

2. Which of these best describes her chances of picking a yellow tile?

Ⓐ certain

Ⓑ likely

Ⓒ 50-50 chance

Ⓓ very unlikely

3. Find the probability of each event. Then make up an event and find the probability.

Event	Favorable Outcomes	Possible Outcomes	Probability
Pick a blue tile	5	10	$\frac{5}{10}$
Pick a red tile		10	$\frac{\square}{10}$
Pick a yellow tile		10	$\frac{\square}{10}$
Pick a green tile		10	$\frac{\square}{10}$
Pick a blue, red, or green tile		10	$\frac{\square}{10}$
		10	$\frac{\square}{10}$

4. Suppose you picked a color tile from the bag 10 times. After each pick, you put the tile back in the bag. How many times would you expect to pick a blue tile? _____ times

Try the experiment. Compare your prediction with the actual results.

Practice

5. $74 * 8 =$ _____

6. _____ $= 4 * 987$

7. _____ $= 65 * 26$

8. $35 * 462 =$ _____

Statistics, Data Analysis, and Probability 2.0, 2.2

209

Name _____ Date _____ Time _____

 LESSON 7·3   **A Deck of Regular Playing Cards**

1. How many cards, not including jokers,
   are in a deck of regular playing cards? _____ cards

2. Use the cards to help you fill in the chart.

Type of Card	Number of Cards in Deck	Type of Card	Number of Cards in Deck
Red		Spade ♠	
Black		Face card (jack, queen, king)	
Diamond ♦		Heart face card	
Heart ♥		9	
Club ♣		4	

✂ -

Name _____ Date _____ Time _____

LESSON 7·3   **A Deck of Regular Playing Cards**

1. How many cards, not including jokers,
   are in a deck of regular playing cards? _____ cards

2. Use the cards to help you fill in the chart.

Type of Card	Number of Cards in Deck	Type of Card	Number of Cards in Deck
Red		Spade ♠	
Black		Face card (jack, queen, king)	
Diamond ♦		Heart face card	
Heart ♥		9	
Club ♣		4	

LESSON 7·3 | **A Playing-Card Experiment**

1. Place 52 playing cards in a bag. Shake the bag.

2. Before you begin the experiment, predict the results for each event.

Event	Predicted Results for 52 Picks	Tallies	Actual Results for 52 Picks
Pick a black card	☐ 52		☐ 52
Pick a red card			
Pick a face card			
Pick a heart			
Pick an Ace			
Pick an Ace of spades			

3. Now do the experiment.

   Step 1: Pick a card from the bag.

   Step 2: Record a tally for each event that applies. For example, for the king of clubs put a tally mark next to *black card* and *face card.*

   Step 3: Mark an X in the grid to record the number of picks.

   Step 4: Return the card to the bag and shake it.

   Repeat Steps 1–4 until all 52 boxes in the grid have been filled in.

4. Describe how your actual results compare with your predicted results. Be sure to include anything that surprised you.

LESSON 7·4

Polygons

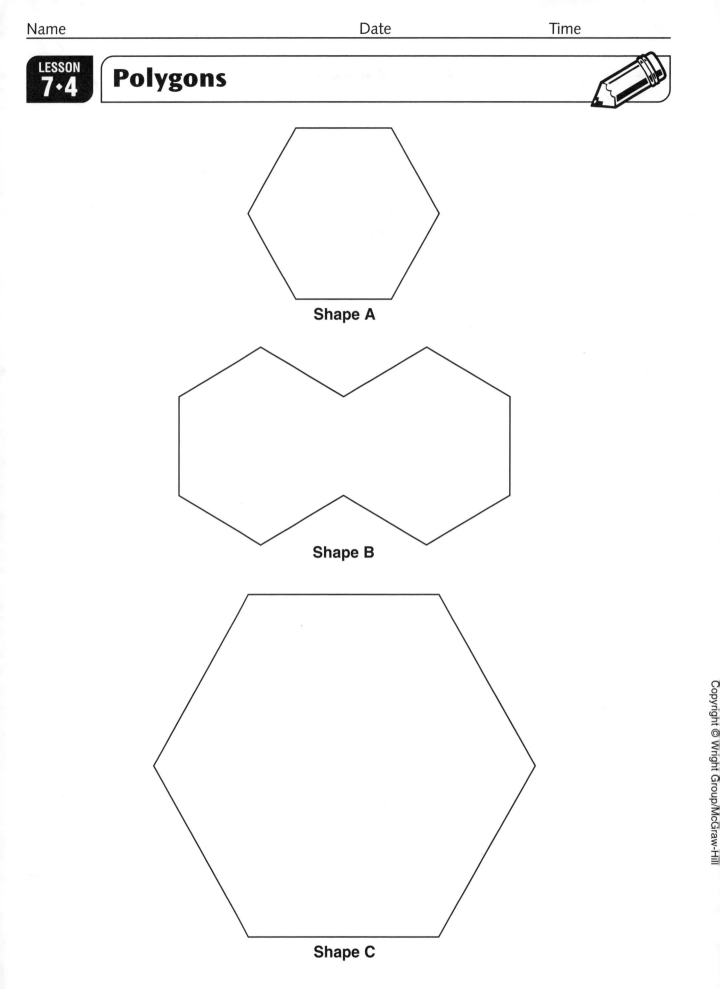

Shape A

Shape B

Shape C

STUDY LINK 7·4 | Dividing Squares

Use a straightedge and the dots below to help you divide each of the squares into equal parts.

Example: Squares A, B, C, and D are each divided in half in a different way.

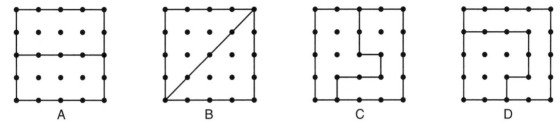

A   B   C   D

1. Square E is divided into fourths. Divide squares F, G, and H into fourths, each in a different way.

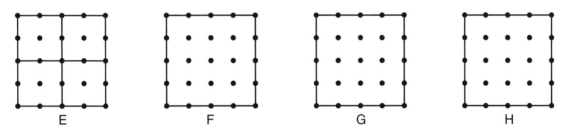

E   F   G   H

2. Square I is divided into eighths. Divide squares J, K, and L into eighths, each in a different way.

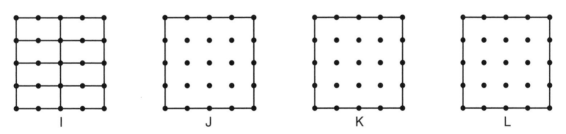

I   J   K   L

3. Rosa has 15 quarters and 10 nickels. She buys juice from a store for herself and her friends. The juice costs 35 cents per can. She gives the cashier $\frac{2}{3}$ of the quarters and $\frac{3}{5}$ of the nickels. The cashier does not give her any change.

How many cans of juice did she buy? _____ cans

Show your work on the back of this paper.

Practice

4. $0.636 + 0.245 =$ _____

5. _____ $= 9.085 + 0.76$

6. _____ $= 1.73 - 0.14$

7. $0.325 - 0.297 =$ _____

Number Sense 1.5; Number Sense 1.7

213

LESSON 7·4 | **Fractions of Rectangles**

Use red, blue, and green crayons to color the squares at the bottom of the page. Cut out the squares. If your teacher has colored tiles, use those instead.

SRB
49

Use your colored squares to build the following rectangles in at least two *different* ways. Record your work.

1. $\frac{1}{2}$ red and $\frac{1}{2}$ blue

2. $\frac{1}{3}$ red, $\frac{1}{3}$ blue, $\frac{1}{3}$ green

3. $\frac{1}{4}$ red, $\frac{1}{2}$ blue, $\frac{1}{4}$ green

4. Make up a problem of your own.

_____ red, _____ blue, _____ green

red	red	red	red	red	red	red	red	red	red
blue	blue	blue	blue	blue	blue	blue	blue	blue	blue
green	green	green	green	green	green	green	green	green	green

214

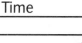

LESSON 7·4 | Exploring Tangrams

1. Cut out the tangram pieces at the top of *Math Masters,* page 441, and use all 7 pieces to create the large square at the bottom of the page.

2. If the large square is the whole, or the ONE, find the value of each of the tangram pieces.

Small Square	Large Triangle	Medium Triangle	Small Triangle	Parallelogram

3. Describe the strategy you used to find the value of the small triangle.

_____

_____

_____

_____

_____

4. Describe how you can prove that you found the correct value of the small triangle.

_____

_____

_____

_____

_____

Try This

5. Use several tangram pieces to create a polygon for which the small square is worth $\frac{2}{9}$. Trace the polygon on the back of this page. Give the value of each tangram piece in the polygon.

STUDY LINK 7·5 | Fractions

SRB 55 57

1. Jake has $\frac{3}{4}$ of a dollar. Maxwell has $\frac{1}{10}$ of a dollar. Do they have more or less than $1.00 in all? _____

   Number model: _____

2. Jillian draws a line segment $2\frac{1}{4}$ inches long. Then she makes the line segment $1\frac{1}{2}$ inches longer. How long is the line segment now? _____ inches

   $2\frac{1}{4}$ in. $1\frac{1}{2}$ in.

3. A pizza was cut into 6 slices. Benjamin ate $\frac{1}{3}$ of the pizza and Dana ate $\frac{1}{2}$. What fraction of the pizza was left?   _____

4. Rafael drew a line segment $2\frac{7}{8}$ inches long. Then he erased $\frac{1}{2}$ inch. How long is the line segment now?   _____ inches

   $2\frac{7}{8}$ in.

   ? $\frac{1}{2}$ in.

5. Two hexagons together are one whole. Draw line segments to divide each whole into trapezoids, rhombuses, and triangles. Write a number model to show how the parts add up to the whole.

   _____   _____   _____

Practice

6. $\frac{1}{4}$ of 32 = _____

7. _____ = $\frac{9}{10}$ of 50

8. $\frac{7}{8}$ of 56 = _____

9. _____ = $\frac{11}{12}$ of 24

LESSON 7·5 Divide *Gator Pie*

Use a straightedge to divide the pies below as Alvin and Alice did in *Gator Pie*. Make sure each gator gets an equal share. Write a number model to show what you did.

1. Two gators

   Number model:

   _____ + _____ = 1

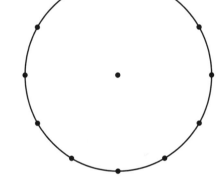

2. Three gators

   Number model:

   _____ + _____ + _____ = 1

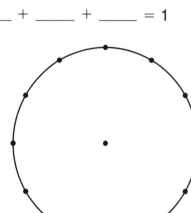

3. Four gators

   Number model:

   _____

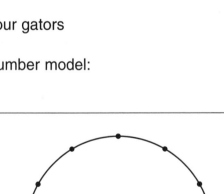

4. Eight gators

   Number model:

   _____

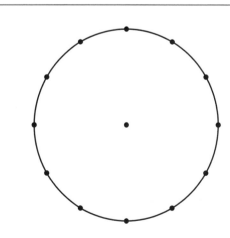

217

Name _____ Date _____ Time _____

Many Names for Fractions

Write the letters of the pictures that represent each fraction.

1. $\frac{1}{2}$ _C,_ _____

2. $\frac{3}{4}$ _____

3. $\frac{4}{5}$ _____

4. $\frac{2}{3}$ _____

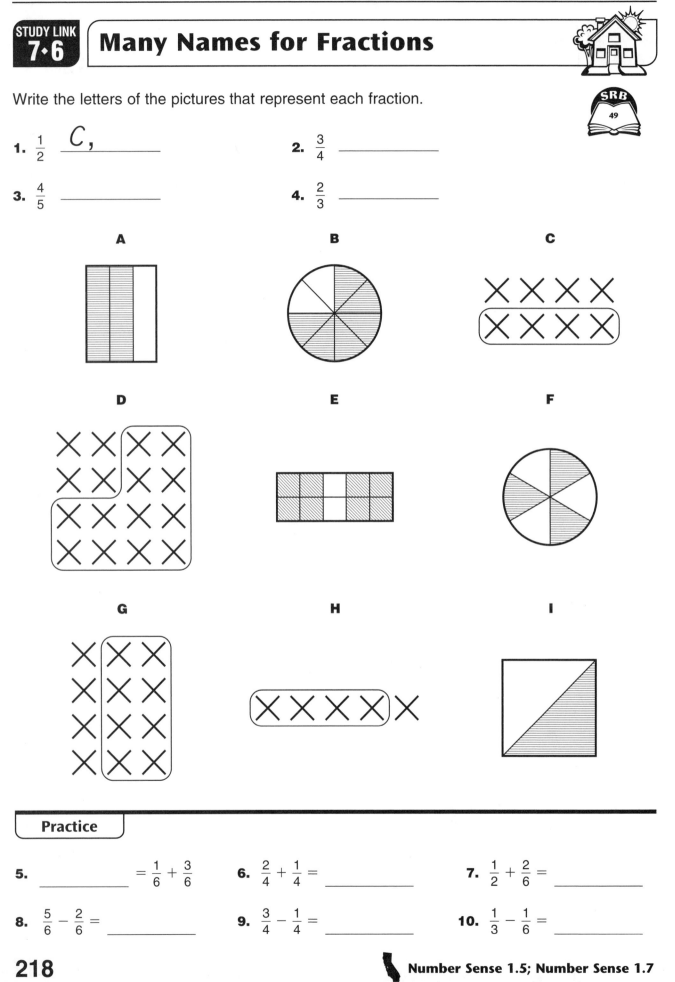

A

B

C

D

E

F

G

H

I

Practice

5. _____ $= \frac{1}{6} + \frac{3}{6}$

6. $\frac{2}{4} + \frac{1}{4} =$ _____

7. $\frac{1}{2} + \frac{2}{6} =$ _____

8. $\frac{5}{6} - \frac{2}{6} =$ _____

9. $\frac{3}{4} - \frac{1}{4} =$ _____

10. $\frac{1}{3} - \frac{1}{6} =$ _____

Number Sense 1.5; Number Sense 1.7

LESSON 7·6 **Fraction Circles**

Whole

219

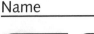 LESSON
7·6 | **Equivalent Fractions**

Follow these steps to find equivalent fractions:

◆ Cut out each circle on *Math Masters,* page 219.

◆ Label the parts of each circle with a fraction, and cut them apart along the dashed lines.

◆ Glue the cutout pieces onto the circles on this page and *Math Masters,* page 221 as directed.

◆ Fill in the missing numerators to complete the equivalent fractions.

1. Cover $\frac{1}{2}$ of the circle with fourths.   **2.** Cover $\frac{1}{4}$ of the circle with eighths.

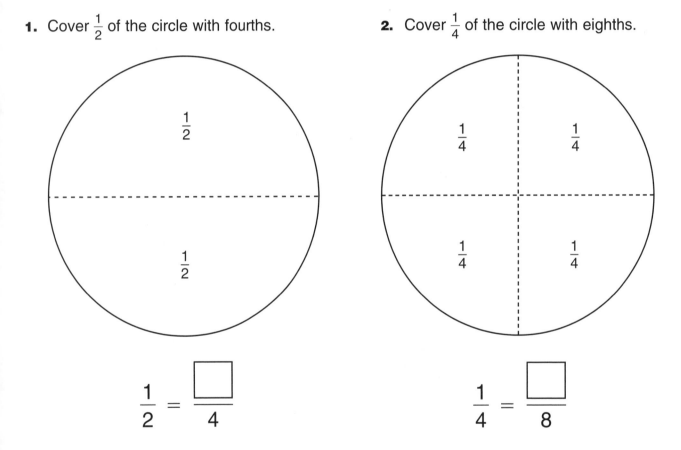

$$\frac{1}{2} = \frac{\square}{4}$$ $$\frac{1}{4} = \frac{\square}{8}$$

LESSON 7·6 | **Equivalent Fractions** *continued*

3. Cover $\frac{2}{4}$ of the circle with eighths.

4. Cover $\frac{1}{2}$ of the circle with sixths.

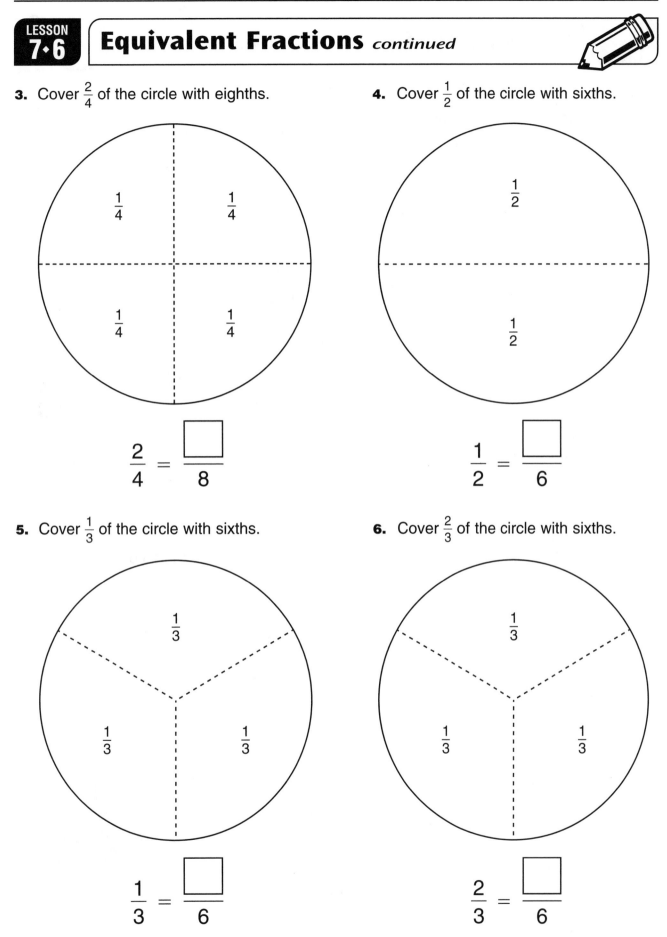

$\frac{1}{4}$ $\frac{1}{4}$

$\frac{1}{4}$ $\frac{1}{4}$

$$\frac{2}{4} = \frac{\Box}{8}$$

$\frac{1}{2}$

$\frac{1}{2}$

$$\frac{1}{2} = \frac{\Box}{6}$$

5. Cover $\frac{1}{3}$ of the circle with sixths.

6. Cover $\frac{2}{3}$ of the circle with sixths.

$\frac{1}{3}$

$\frac{1}{3}$ $\frac{1}{3}$

$$\frac{1}{3} = \frac{\Box}{6}$$

$\frac{1}{3}$

$\frac{1}{3}$ $\frac{1}{3}$

$$\frac{2}{3} = \frac{\Box}{6}$$

LESSON 7·6 | **Equivalent Clock Fractions**

1. Explain why a hexagon pattern block
   is useful for modeling equivalencies
   of fractions with denominators of
   2, 3, and 6.

   _____

   _____

   _____

   _____

2. Study the clock face. Which denominators can be
   modeled on the clock face?

   _____

   _____

   Explain your answer.

   _____

   _____

3. Using the denominators from Problem 2, name the fraction represented on each clock
   face in as many different ways as you can.

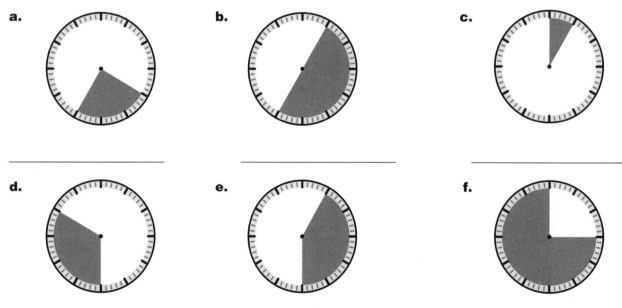

   a.   b.   c.

   d.   e.   f.

STUDY LINK 7·7   Fraction Name-Collection Boxes

In each name-collection box:

Write the missing number in each fraction so that the fraction belongs in the box. Write one more fraction that can go in the box.

1.
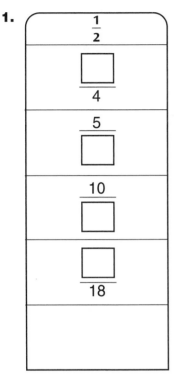

$$\frac{1}{2}$$

$$\frac{\square}{4}$$

$$\frac{5}{\square}$$

$$\frac{10}{\square}$$

$$\frac{\square}{18}$$

2.

$$\frac{2}{3}$$

$$\frac{\square}{9}$$

$$\frac{12}{\square}$$

$$\frac{20}{\square}$$

$$\frac{\square}{12}$$

3.
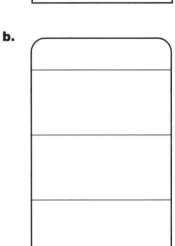

$$\frac{1}{4}$$

$$\frac{\square}{12}$$

$$\frac{5}{\square}$$

$$\frac{10}{\square}$$

$$\frac{\square}{100}$$

4. Make up your own name-collection box problems like the ones above. Ask a friend to solve your problems. Check your friend's work.

a.

b.

Practice

5. _____ = 95 / 4   **6.** 57 ÷ 3 = _____   **7.** _____ = 882 / 21

 Number Sense 1.5

LESSON 7·7   **Egyptian Fractions**

Ancient Egyptians only used fractions with 1 in the numerator. These are called **unit fractions.** They wrote non-unit fractions, such as $\frac{3}{4}$ and $\frac{4}{9}$, as sums of unit fractions. They did not use the same unit fraction more than once in a sum.

SRB
55 57

Examples:

$$\frac{3}{4} = \frac{1}{2} + \frac{1}{4}$$

$$\frac{4}{9} = \frac{1}{3} + \frac{1}{9}$$

Use drawings and what you know about equivalent fractions to help you find the Egyptian form of each fraction.

1. $\frac{3}{8}$ = _____

2. $\frac{5}{12}$ = _____

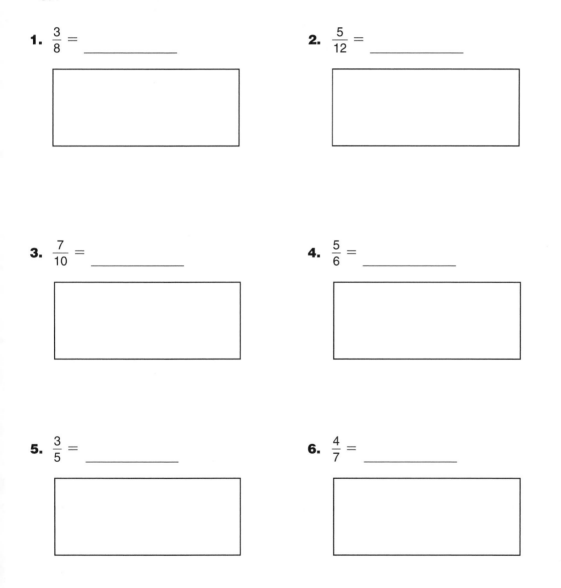

3. $\frac{7}{10}$ = _____

4. $\frac{5}{6}$ = _____

5. $\frac{3}{5}$ = _____

6. $\frac{4}{7}$ = _____

LESSON 7·7 | **An Equivalent Fractions Rule**

Margot says the value of a fraction does not change if you do the same thing to the numerator and denominator. Margot says that she added 2 to the numerator and the denominator in $\frac{1}{4}$ and got $\frac{3}{6}$.

$$\frac{1+2}{4+2} = \frac{3}{6}$$

Therefore, she says that $\frac{1}{4} = \frac{3}{6}$. How could you explain or show Margot that she is wrong?

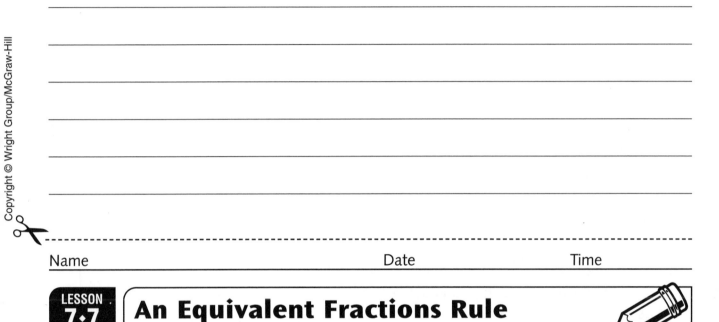

✂ -

Name   Date   Time

LESSON 7·7 | **An Equivalent Fractions Rule**

Margot says the value of a fraction does not change if you do the same thing to the numerator and denominator. Margot says that she added 2 to the numerator and the denominator in $\frac{1}{4}$ and got $\frac{3}{6}$.

$$\frac{1+2}{4+2} = \frac{3}{6}$$

Therefore, she says that $\frac{1}{4} = \frac{3}{6}$. How could you explain or show Margot that she is wrong?

STUDY LINK 7·8 **Fractions and Decimals**

Write 3 equivalent fractions for each decimal.

Example:

0.8 $\frac{8}{10}$ $\frac{4}{5}$ $\frac{80}{100}$

1. 0.20   _____   _____   _____

2. 0.6   _____   _____   _____

3. 0.50   _____   _____   _____

4. 0.75   _____   _____   _____

Write an equivalent decimal for each fraction.

5. $\frac{3}{10}$ _____   **6.** $\frac{63}{100}$ _____   **7.** $\frac{7}{10}$ _____   **8.** $\frac{2}{5}$ _____

9. Shade more than $\frac{53}{100}$ of the square and less than $\frac{8}{10}$ of the square. Write the value of the shaded part as a decimal and a fraction.

Decimal: _____

Fraction: _____

10. Shade more than $\frac{11}{100}$ of the square and less than $\frac{1}{4}$ of the square. Write the value of the shaded part as a decimal and a fraction.

Decimal: _____

Fraction: _____

Practice

11. _____ = 78 * 9   **12.** 461 * 7 = _____   **13.** _____ = 39 * 25

Number Sense 1.6; Number Sense 1.7

LESSON 7·8 **Fraction, Decimal, and Percent Grids**

Fill in the missing numbers. Shade the grids.

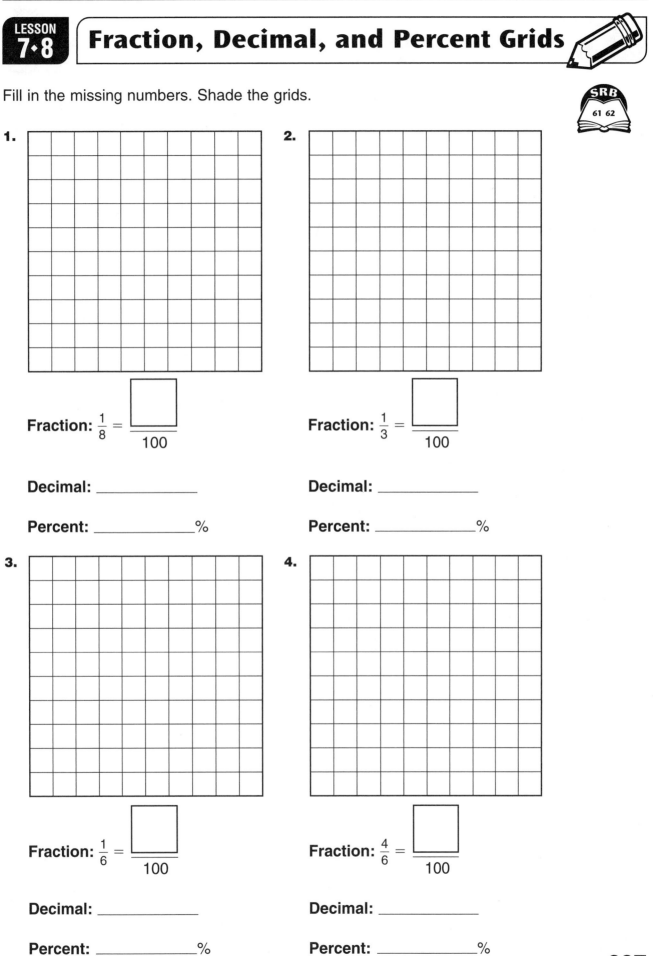

1.

Fraction: $\frac{1}{8}$ = $\dfrac{\boxed{}}{100}$

Decimal: _____

Percent: _____%

2.

Fraction: $\frac{1}{3}$ = $\dfrac{\boxed{}}{100}$

Decimal: _____

Percent: _____%

3.

Fraction: $\frac{1}{6}$ = $\dfrac{\boxed{}}{100}$

Decimal: _____

Percent: _____%

4.

Fraction: $\frac{4}{6}$ = $\dfrac{\boxed{}}{100}$

Decimal: _____

Percent: _____%

STUDY LINK 7·9

Compare and Order Fractions

SRB 53 54

Write $<$, $>$, or $=$ to make each number sentence true.

1. $\frac{5}{6}$ _____ $\frac{1}{6}$ **2.** $\frac{3}{10}$ _____ $\frac{3}{4}$ **3.** $\frac{2}{3}$ _____ $\frac{10}{15}$

4. $\frac{10}{40}$ _____ $\frac{4}{16}$ **5.** $\frac{4}{9}$ _____ $\frac{7}{9}$ **6.** $\frac{5}{6}$ _____ $\frac{5}{8}$

7. Explain how you solved Problem 1. _____

_____

8. Explain how you solved Problem 2. _____

_____

9. Circle each fraction that is less than $\frac{1}{2}$.

$\frac{7}{8}$ $\frac{1}{4}$ $\frac{4}{10}$ $\frac{7}{12}$ $\frac{5}{9}$ $\frac{3}{7}$ $\frac{24}{50}$ $\frac{67}{100}$

Write the fractions in order from smallest to largest.

10. $\frac{3}{12}$, $\frac{7}{12}$, $\frac{1}{12}$, $\frac{11}{12}$, $\frac{8}{12}$ _____ _____ _____ _____ _____

                                           smallest   **largest**

11. $\frac{1}{5}$, $\frac{1}{3}$, $\frac{1}{20}$, $\frac{1}{2}$, $\frac{1}{50}$ _____ _____ _____ _____ _____

                                           smallest   **largest**

12. $\frac{4}{5}$, $\frac{4}{100}$, $\frac{4}{4}$, $\frac{4}{8}$, $\frac{4}{12}$ _____ _____ _____ _____ _____

                                           smallest   **largest**

Practice

13. $\frac{1}{6}$ of 30 = _____   **14.** $\frac{3}{4}$ of _____ = 75   **15.** $\frac{4}{5}$ of 45 = _____

         Number Sense 1.9; Mathematical Reasoning 2.3

LESSON 7·9 | Sort Fractions

Cut out the cards. Sort the cards into groups according to the fractions shown on them, and tape them onto a separate sheet of paper. Next to each group, write why you chose to put the cards into the group.

44

229

LESSON 7·9   Two-Digit Fractions

Any fraction can be made from the digits 0–9. A fraction can have two digits like $\frac{3}{4}$ or $\frac{8}{7}$ or many digits like $\frac{347}{983}$. A fraction may not have a denominator of 0.

SRB
53

Use any two digits to make each of the following fractions.

1. The smallest possible fraction greater than 0 _____

2. The largest possible fraction _____

3. The largest fraction less than 1 _____

4. The smallest fraction greater than $\frac{1}{2}$ _____

5. Make up your own problem. _____

✂ -

Name   Date   Time

LESSON 7·9   Two-Digit Fractions

Any fraction can be made from the digits 0–9. A fraction can have two digits like $\frac{3}{4}$ or $\frac{8}{7}$ or many digits like $\frac{347}{983}$. A fraction may not have a denominator of 0.

SRB
53

Use any two digits to make each of the following fractions.

1. The smallest possible fraction greater than 0 _____

2. The largest possible fraction _____

3. The largest fraction less than 1 _____

4. The smallest fraction greater than $\frac{1}{2}$ _____

5. Make up your own problem. _____

STUDY LINK 7·10 **What Is the ONE?**

For Problems 1 and 2, use your Geometry Template or sketch the shapes.

1. Suppose ⬜ is $\frac{1}{4}$. Draw each of the following:

Example: $\frac{3}{4}$ **a.** 1   **b.** $1\frac{1}{2}$ **c.** 2

2. Suppose ◇ is $\frac{2}{3}$. Draw each of the following:

    a. $\frac{1}{3}$ **b.** 1   **c.** $\frac{4}{3}$ **d.** 2

Use counters to solve the following problems.

3. If 14 counters are $\frac{1}{2}$, then what is the ONE?

_____ counters

4. If 9 counters are $\frac{1}{3}$, then what is the ONE?

_____ counters

5. If 12 counters are $\frac{2}{5}$, then what is the ONE? _____ counters

6. If 16 counters are $\frac{4}{9}$, then what is the ONE? _____ counters

---

Practice

7. _____ $= \frac{1}{4} + \frac{1}{2}$ **8.** $\frac{1}{3} + \frac{1}{6} =$ _____

9. $\frac{3}{4} - \frac{1}{4} =$ _____   **10.** _____ $= \frac{5}{6} - \frac{1}{3}$

Number Sense 1.5; Number Sense 1.7   **231**

Name _____ Date _____ Time _____

LESSON 7·10 | **A Whole Candy Bar**

Two friends cut a large candy bar into equal pieces. Harriet ate $\frac{1}{4}$ of the pieces. Nisha ate $\frac{1}{2}$ of the remaining pieces. Six pieces were left over.

1. How many pieces was the candy bar originally divided into? _____ pieces

2. Explain how you got your answer. Include a drawing and number models as part of your explanation.

_____

_____

_____

_____

- -

Name _____ Date _____ Time _____

LESSON 7·10 | **A Whole Candy Bar**

Two friends cut a large candy bar into equal pieces. Harriet ate $\frac{1}{4}$ of the pieces. Nisha ate $\frac{1}{2}$ of the remaining pieces. Six pieces were left over.

1. How many pieces was the candy bar originally divided into? _____ pieces

2. Explain how you got your answer. Include a drawing and number models as part of your explanation.

_____

_____

_____

232

LESSON 7·11 | **Spinner Experiments**

1. Use a paper clip and pencil to make a spinner.

   a. Spin the paper clip 4 times. Record the number of times it lands on the shaded part and on the white part.

shaded	white

   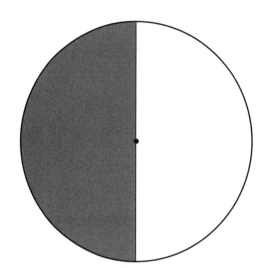

   b. Record the number of times the paper clip lands on the shaded part and on the white part **for the whole class.**

shaded	white

2. Make another spinner. Color the circle blue and red so that the paper clip is **twice as likely** to land on blue as on red.

   a. Spin the paper clip 4 times. Record the number of times it lands on blue and on red.

blue	red

   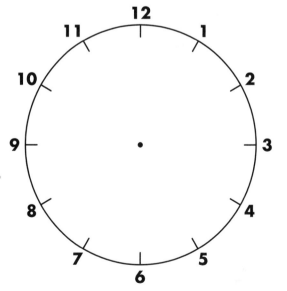

   b. Record the number of times the paper clip lands on blue and on red **for the whole class.**

blue	red

   c. What would you expect after spinning the paper clip 300 times?

blue	red

233

Spinners and Fractions

1. Design your own spinner with as many colors as you wish. Use a pencil until you are satisfied with your work, then color your spinner.

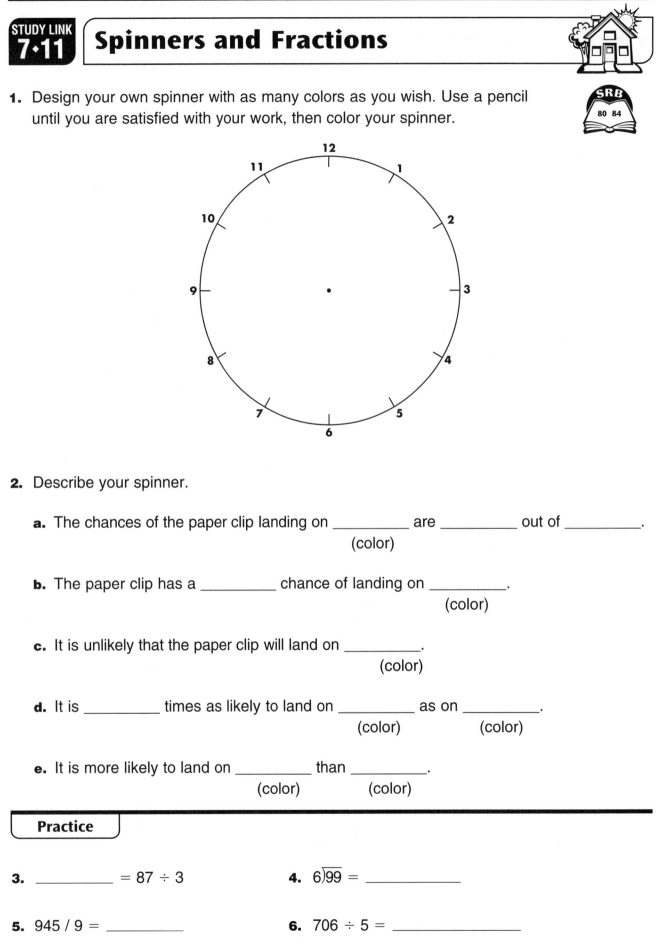

2. Describe your spinner.

a. The chances of the paper clip landing on _____ are _____ out of _____.
   (color)

b. The paper clip has a _____ chance of landing on _____.
   (color)

c. It is unlikely that the paper clip will land on _____.
   (color)

d. It is _____ times as likely to land on _____ as on _____.
   (color)   (color)

e. It is more likely to land on _____ than _____.
   (color)   (color)

Practice

3. _____ = 87 ÷ 3

4. 6)99̄ = _____

5. 945 / 9 = _____

6. 706 ÷ 5 = _____

Statistics, Data Analysis, and Probability 2.2; Number Sense **3.2**

STUDY LINK 7·11   Layout of a Kitchen

Pages 235 and 236 will be needed to do Lesson 8-1 in the next unit. Please complete the pages and return them to class.

Every kitchen needs a stove, a sink, and a refrigerator. Notice how the stove, sink, and refrigerator are arranged in the kitchen below. The triangle shows the work path in the kitchen. Walking from the stove to the sink and to the refrigerator forms an invisible "triangle" on the floor.

Front View of Kitchen

Bird's-Eye View of Kitchen
(looking down at appliances
and countertops)

The side of a grid square represents 1 foot.

1. Put one coin or other marker on the floor in front of your sink, one in front of your stove, and one in front of your refrigerator.

2. Measure the distance between each pair of markers. Use feet and inches, and record your measurements below.

Distance between

  a. stove and refrigerator   About _____ feet _____ inches

  b. refrigerator and sink   About _____ feet _____ inches

  c. sink and stove   About _____ feet _____ inches

Statistics, Data Analysis, and Probability 1.1

STUDY LINK
7·11

Layout of a Kitchen *continued*

SRB
131 133

3. On the grid below, make a sketch that shows how the stove, sink, and refrigerator are arranged in your kitchen.

Your sketch should show a bird's-eye view of these 3 appliances (including all countertops).

If your oven is separate from your stove, sketch the stove top only.

Use the following symbols in your sketch:

stove   refrigerator   sink   double sink

Statistics, Data Analysis, and Probability 1.1

LESSON 7·11

Fractions of Circles

Divide each circle into equal parts and color as directed.

1. Divide into 2 equal parts.
Color $\frac{1}{2}$ yellow.

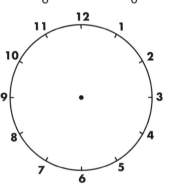

2. Divide into 3 equal parts.
Color $\frac{1}{3}$ red and $\frac{1}{3}$ blue.

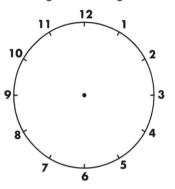

3. Divide into 6 equal parts.
Color $\frac{1}{6}$ green and $\frac{2}{6}$ orange.

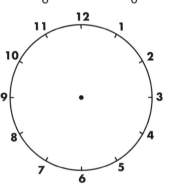

4. Divide into 6 equal parts.
Color $\frac{1}{6}$ green and $\frac{1}{3}$ orange.

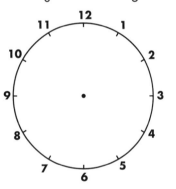

5. Divide into 12 equal parts.
Color $\frac{1}{3}$ red.

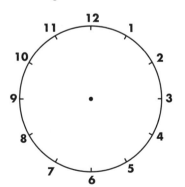

6. Divide into 12 equal parts.
Color $\frac{1}{3}$ red in a different way.

LESSON 7·12

A Cube-Drop Experiment

Color the squares in the grid above.

The table at the right shows the number of squares you must use for each color.

How to Color the Grid	
Color	**Number of Squares**
yellow	1
red	4
green	10
blue	35
white	50
Total	**100**

STUDY LINK 7·12 | **What Are the Chances?**

SRB
81

1. You are going to toss 2 pennies 20 times. How many times do you expect the 2 pennies will come up as

   a. 2 heads? _____ times

   b. 2 tails? _____ times

   c. 1 head and 1 tail? _____ times

2. Now toss 2 pennies together 20 times. Record the results in the table.

A Penny Toss	
Results	**Number of Times**
2 heads	
2 tails	
1 head and 1 tail	

3. What fraction of the tosses came up as

   a. 2 heads? _____

   b. 2 tails? _____

   c. 1 head and 1 tail? _____

4. Suppose you were to flip the coins 1,000 times. What fraction do you expect would come up as

   a. 2 heads? _____

   b. 2 tails? _____

   c. 1 head and 1 tail? _____

5. Explain how you got your answers for Problem 4.

   _____

   _____

   _____

Practice

6. $7 * 48 =$ _____

7. $874 * 9 =$ _____

8. _____ $= 45 * 86$

9. _____ $= 34 * 142$

LESSON 7·12 | **Fractions and Percents on Grids**

Fractions and percents can be modeled with base-10 blocks.

$\frac{47}{100}$ = 47 out of 100 = 47%

SRB 62

Build each fraction with base-10 blocks. Shade the grid, and fill in the missing numbers.

1.

$\frac{30}{100}$ = _____ out of 100 = _____%

2.

$\frac{76}{100}$ = _____ out of 100 = _____%

3.

$\frac{4}{100}$ = _____ out of 100 = _____%

4. Create your own.

$\frac{\boxed{}}{100}$ = _____ out of 100 = _____%

These grids are the whole. Find the percent of each grid that is shaded.

5.

$\frac{\boxed{}}{50}$ = $\frac{\boxed{}}{100}$ = _____ out of 100 = _____%

6.

$\frac{\boxed{}}{50}$ = $\frac{\boxed{}}{100}$ = _____ out of 100 = _____%

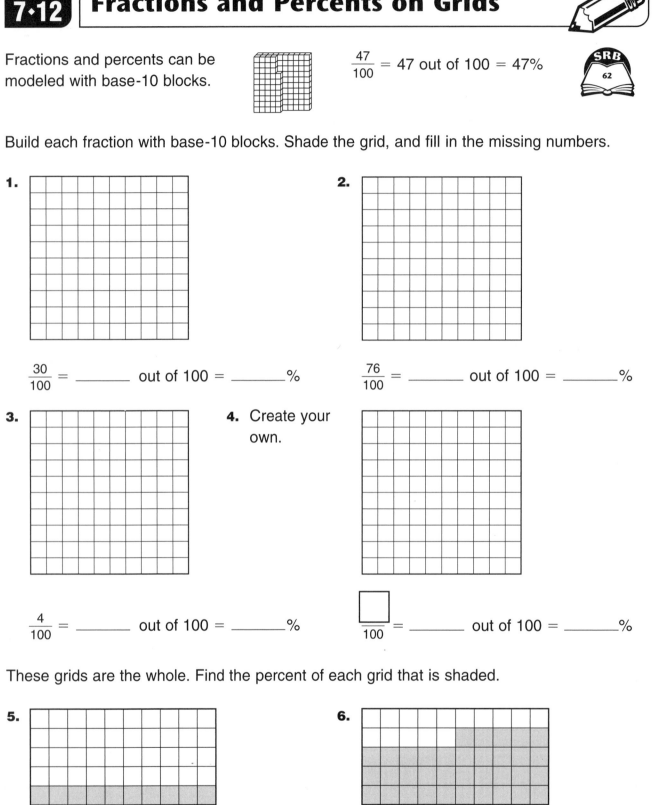

LESSON 7·12 **Results for 50 Cube Drops**

Results for 50 Cube Drops

Color	Number of Drops
yellow	
red	
green	
blue	
white	
Total	**50**

Results for 50 Cube Drops

Color	Number of Drops
yellow	
red	
green	
blue	
white	
Total	**50**

Results for 50 Cube Drops

Color	Number of Drops
yellow	
red	
green	
blue	
white	
Total	**50**

Results for 50 Cube Drops

Color	Number of Drops
yellow	
red	
green	
blue	
white	
Total	**50**

Results for 50 Cube Drops

Color	Number of Drops
yellow	
red	
green	
blue	
white	
Total	**50**

Results for 50 Cube Drops

Color	Number of Drops
yellow	
red	
green	
blue	
white	
Total	**50**

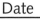

LESSON 7·12 — Class Results for 1,000 Cube Drops

Students

Color	S1	S2	S3	S4	S5	S6	S7	S8	S9	S10	S11	S12	S13	S14	S15	S16	S17	S18	S19	S20	Number of drops	Percent
yellow																						
red																						
green																						
blue																						
white																						
Total	50	50	50	50	50	50	50	50	50	50	50	50	50	50	50	50	50	50	50	50	1,000	100%

Most of the percents you calculate will not be whole-number percents. You can record them as percents in tenths or round them to the nearest whole percent. For example, 96 out of 1,000 is equivalent to 9.6 out of 100. This could be recorded either as 9.6% or 10%. If the answers are rounded, the total might not add up to 100%.

Unit 8: Family Letter

STUDY LINK
7·13

Perimeter and Area

In previous grades, your child studied the *perimeter* (distance around) and the *area* (amount of surface) of various geometric figures. This next unit will extend your child's understanding of geometry by developing and applying formulas for the areas of figures such as rectangles, parallelograms, and triangles.

Area of a Rectangle

Area = base * height (or length * width)

$A = b * h$ (or $l * w$)

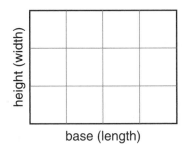

Area of a Parallelogram

Area = base * height

$A = b * h$

Area of a Triangle

Area = $\frac{1}{2}$ of (base * height)

$A = \frac{1}{2} * b * h$

Students will learn how to make scale drawings and apply their knowledge of perimeter, area, and scale drawing by analyzing the arrangement of the appliances in their kitchens and the furniture in their bedrooms.

Students will also calculate the area of the skin that covers their entire body. A rule of thumb is that the area of a person's skin is about 100 times the area of one side of that person's hand. Ask your child to show you how to calculate the area of your own skin.

The World Tour will continue. Students will examine how geographical areas are measured and the difficulties in making accurate measurements. They will compare areas for South American countries by using division to calculate the ratio of areas.

Please keep this Family Letter for reference as your child works through Unit 8.

Vocabulary

Important terms in Unit 8:

area The amount of surface inside a closed 2-dimensional (flat) boundary. Area is measured in *square units,* such as square inches or square centimeters.

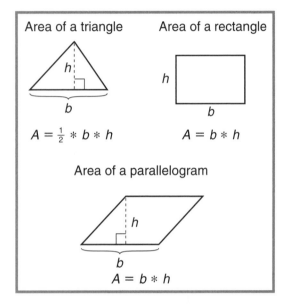

Area of a triangle

$A = \frac{1}{2} * b * h$

Area of a rectangle

$A = b * h$

Area of a parallelogram

$A = b * h$

formula A general rule for finding the value of something. A formula is often written using letter *variables,* which stand for the quantities involved.

length The distance between two points on a 1-dimensional figure. Length is measured in units such as inches, meters, and miles.

perimeter The distance around a 2-dimensional shape along the boundary of the shape. The perimeter of a circle is called its circumference. The perimeter of a polygon is the sum of the lengths of its sides.

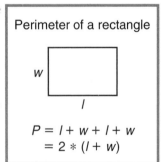

Perimeter of a rectangle

$P = l + w + l + w$
$= 2 * (l + w)$

perpendicular Crossing or meeting at right angles. Lines, rays, line segments, and planes that cross or meet at right angles are perpendicular. The symbol ⊥ means "is perpendicular to," as in "line *CD* ⊥ line *AB*." The symbol ⌐ indicates a right angle.

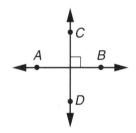

Perpendicular lines

scale The ratio of the distance on a map, globe, drawing, or model to an actual distance.

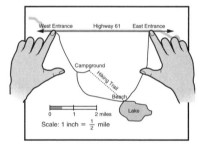

scale drawing A drawing of an object or a region in which all parts are drawn to the same scale as the object. Architects and builders often use scale drawings.

square unit A unit used to measure area. For example, a square that measures one inch on each side has an area of one square inch.

variable A letter or other symbol that represents a number. A variable can represent one specific number, or it can stand for many different numbers.

width The length of one side of a rectangle or rectangular object, typically the shorter side.

Do-Anytime Activities

To work with your child on concepts taught in this unit, try these interesting and engaging activities:

1. Have your child pretend that he or she is a carpenter whose job is to redesign a room—for example, a bedroom, the kitchen, or the living room. Have him or her make a rough estimate of the area of the room. Then help your child check the estimate by finding the actual area using a tape measure or, if possible, blueprints.

2. Have your child pretend that he or she is an architect. Give him or her some dimensions and space requirements to work with. Then have your child design a "dream house," "dream bedroom," or sports stadium, and make a scale drawing for that design.

3. Work with your child to make a scale drawing of your neighborhood. Or have your child make a scale drawing of the floor plan of your house or apartment.

4. Have your child compare the areas of continents, countries, states, or major cities.

Building Skills through Games

In this unit, your child will calculate perimeter and area, compare fractions, identify equivalent fractions, find fractions of collections, and calculate expected probabilities by playing the following games. For detailed instructions, see the *Student Reference Book.*

Fraction Match See *Student Reference Book,* page 243.
This is a game for 2 to 4 players and requires a deck of *Fraction Match* Cards. The game provides practice recognizing equivalent fractions.

Fraction Of See *Student Reference Book,* pages 244 and 245.
This is a game for 2 players and requires 1 deck of *Fraction Of* Fraction Cards, 1 deck of *Fraction Of* Set Cards, and 1 *Fraction Of* Gameboard and Record Sheet. The game provides practice finding fractions of collections.

Fraction Top-It See *Student Reference Book,* page 247.
This is a game for 2 to 4 players and requires a set of Fraction Cards 1 and 2. The game provides practice comparing fractions.

Grab Bag See *Student Reference Book,* page 249.
This is a game for 2 players or two teams of 2 players. It requires 1 deck of *Grab Bag* Cards, 2 *Grab Bag* Record Sheets, and 3 six-sided dice. The game provides practice with variable substitution and calculating probabilities of events.

Rugs and Fences See *Student Reference Book,* pages 260 and 261.
This is a game for 2 players and requires a *Rugs and Fences* Polygon Deck and an Area and Perimeter Deck. The game provides practice finding and comparing the area and perimeter of polygons.

STUDY LINK 7·13 Unit 8: Family Letter *cont.*

As You Help Your Child with Homework

As your child brings assignments home, you may want to go over the instructions together, clarifying them as necessary. The answers listed below will guide you through some of the Study Links in this unit.

Study Link 8·1

1. 17 feet **2.** 54 inches

3. Sample answer:

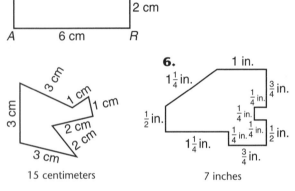

B ─── E
3 cm
L ── 5 cm ── U

4. Sample answer:

F ─── M
2 cm
A ── 6 cm ── R

5.

3 cm, 3 cm, 1 cm, 1 cm, 2 cm, 2 cm, 3 cm
15 centimeters

6.

1 in.
$1\frac{1}{4}$ in.
$\frac{1}{2}$ in.
$1\frac{1}{4}$ in.
$\frac{1}{4}$ in. $\frac{3}{4}$ in.
$\frac{1}{4}$ in. $\frac{1}{4}$ in. $\frac{1}{2}$ in.
$\frac{3}{4}$ in.
7 inches

Study Link 8·2

1. a. 52 miles **b.** 117 miles

c. $32\frac{1}{2}$ miles **d.** $175\frac{1}{2}$ miles

3.

Rectangle	Height in Drawing	Actual Height
A	$\frac{1}{2}$ in.	12 ft
B	$1\frac{1}{4}$ in.	30 ft
C	2 in.	48 ft
D	$1\frac{3}{4}$ in.	42 ft
E	1 in.	24 ft

Study Link 8·3

1. 24 square centimeters

2. 24 square centimeters

2., continued Sample answer:

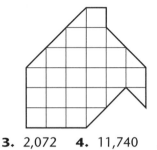

3. 2,072 **4.** 11,740 **5.** 3,593 **6.** 2,848

Study Link 8·4

1. 87,500; 35 grid squares

2. 17,500; 7 grid squares

3. 88.71 **4.** 58.08 **5.** 386.174 **6.** 18.098

Study Link 8·5

1. 48 square feet **2.** 21 square inches

3. 864 square centimeters

4. 300 square meters

5. 9 inches **6.** 10 centimeters

7. 9, 15, 18, 21 **8.** 28, 35, 49, 56

9. 36, 54, 60, 66 **10.** 24, 48, 72, 84

Study Link 8·6

1. 9 * 4 = 36 **2.** 3 * 8 = 24

3. 4 * 6 = 24 **4.** 65 * 72 = 4,680

5. 13 inches **6.** 85 meters

Study Link 8·7

1. $\frac{1}{2} * (8 * 4) = 16$ **2.** $\frac{1}{2} * (12 * 5) = 30$

3. $\frac{1}{2} * (10 * 2) = 10$

4. $\frac{1}{2} * (34 * 75) = 1,275$

5. 3 inches **6.** 6 meters

7. 27, 36, 54, 72 **8.** 8, 24, 40, 48

246

STUDY LINK 8·1 **Perimeter**

SRB
131

---

1. Perimeter = _____ feet

5'
3'   3'
2' 1' 1' 2'

2. Perimeter = _____ inches

20" 12" 13"
21"

---

3. Draw a rectangle *BLUE* whose perimeter is 16 centimeters. Label the length of the sides.

4. Draw a different rectangle *FARM* whose perimeter is also 16 centimeters. Label the length of its sides.

---

5. Measure the sides of the figure to the nearest centimeter. Label the length of its sides. Find its perimeter.

Perimeter = _____ centimeters

6. Measure the sides of the figure to the nearest $\frac{1}{4}$ inch. Label the length of its sides. Find its perimeter.

Perimeter = _____ inches

Practice

7. $\frac{1}{4}$ of 24 = _____

8. _____ = $\frac{2}{3}$ of 24

9. _____ = $\frac{5}{8}$ of 40

Measurement and Geometry 1.0, 1.3, 1.4

247

LESSON 8·1   Geoboard Perimeters

On a geoboard, make rectangles or squares with the perimeters given below.
Record the lengths of the long side and short side of each shape.

1 unit

1 unit

Perimeter (units)	Long side (units)	Short side (units)
12		
12		
12		
14		
14		
14		
16		
16		
16		
16		

✂ --

Name   Date   Time

LESSON 8·1   Geoboard Perimeters

On a geoboard, make rectangles or squares with the perimeters given below.
Record the lengths of the long side and short side of each shape.

1 unit

1 unit

Perimeter (units)	Long side (units)	Short side (units)
12		
12		
12		
14		
14		
14		
16		
16		
16		
16		

LESSON 8·1 | Pattern-Block Perimeters

1. Use the following pattern blocks to create shapes with as many *different* perimeters as you can: 1 hexagon, 3 trapezoids, 3 blue rhombi, and 3 triangles.

   ◆ Every shape must include all 10 pattern blocks.

   ◆ Each side of a pattern block measures 1 unit. The long side of a trapezoid pattern block measures 2 units.

   ◆ At least one side of every pattern block must *line up exactly* with a side of another pattern block. See figures.

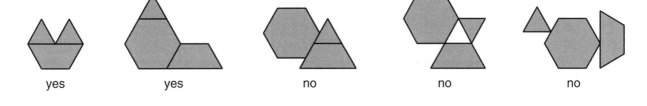

     yes   yes   no   no   no

2. Use your Geometry Template to record your shapes on a separate sheet of paper. The polygons should all have different perimeters. Write the perimeter next to each shape.

3. What was the smallest perimeter you were able to make? _____ units Describe the strategy you used to find this perimeter.

   _____

   _____

   _____

4. What was the largest perimeter you were able to make? _____ units Describe the strategy you used to find this perimeter.

   _____

   _____

   _____

STUDY LINK 8·2 | **Scale**

SRB 145

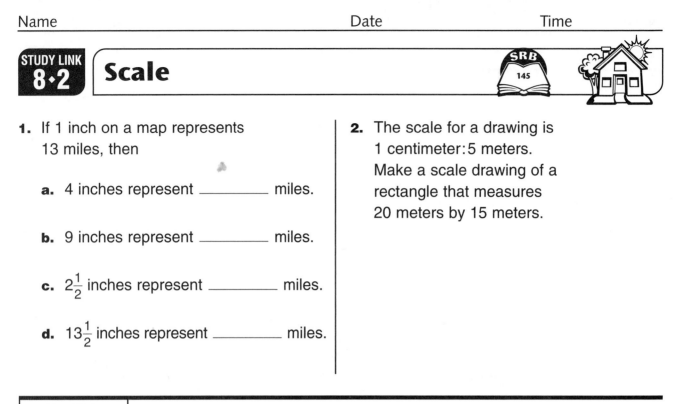

1. If 1 inch on a map represents 13 miles, then

   a. 4 inches represent _____ miles.

   b. 9 inches represent _____ miles.

   c. $2\frac{1}{2}$ inches represent _____ miles.

   d. $13\frac{1}{2}$ inches represent _____ miles.

2. The scale for a drawing is 1 centimeter : 5 meters. Make a scale drawing of a rectangle that measures 20 meters by 15 meters.

Try This

3. Scale: $\frac{1}{4}$ inch represents 6 feet. Measure the height of each rectangle to the nearest $\frac{1}{4}$ inch. Complete the table.

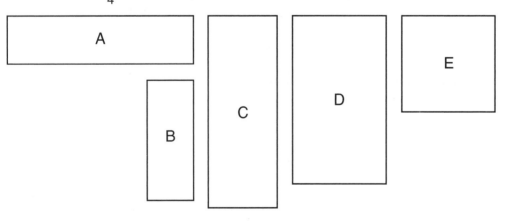

Rectangle	Height in Drawing	Actual Height
A		
B		
C		
D		
E		

Measurement and Geometry 1. 0

LESSON 8·2 Foot-Long Foot

1 foot

6 inches or $\frac{1}{2}$ foot

0 feet

251

LESSON 8·2

My Bedroom Floor Plan

Make a scale drawing of your bedroom floor. Round your measurements to the nearest $\frac{1}{4}$ foot (3 inches).

Scale: $\frac{1}{2}$ inch represents 1 foot.

Name   Date   Time

LESSON 8·2   My Bedroom Floor Plan *continued*

Make a scale drawing of each piece of furniture in your bedroom. Round your measurements to the nearest $\frac{1}{4}$ foot (3 inches). Cut out the scale drawings and tape them in place on your scale drawing of your bedroom floor.

Scale: $\frac{1}{2}$ inch represents 1 foot.

STUDY LINK
8·3 | **Exploring Area**

1. Rectangle A at the right is drawn on a 1-centimeter grid. Find its area.

   Area = _____ cm²

SRB
133 134

A

2. Rectangle B has the same area as Rectangle A. Cut out Rectangle B. Then cut it into 5 pieces any way you want.

   Rearrange the pieces into a new shape that is not a rectangle. Then tape the pieces together in the space below. What is the area of the new shape?

   Area of new shape = _____ cm²

B

Practice

3. 1,778 + 294 = _____

4. _____ = 6,096 + 5,644

5. 4,007 − 414 = _____

6. _____ = 8,030 − 5,182

Measurement and Geometry 1. 0, 1.1, 1.4

Name _____ Date _____ Time _____

Areas of Irregular Figures

1. Below is a map of São Paulo State in Brazil. Each grid square represents 2,500 square miles. Estimate the area of São Paulo State.

   I counted about _____ grid squares.

   The area is about _____ square miles.

2. To the right is a map of Rio de Janeiro State in Brazil. Each grid square represents 2,500 square miles. Estimate the area of Rio de Janeiro State.

   I counted about _____ grid squares.

   The area is about _____ square miles.

Practice

3. _____ = 73.04 + 15.67

4. 86.05 − 27.97 = _____

5. _____ = 312.11 + 74.064

6. 57.1 − 39.002 = _____

Measurement and Geometry 1.0

255

STUDY LINK 8·5

Areas of Rectangles

SRB
134

Find the area of each rectangle.

1.

8'

6'

Number model: _____

Area = _____ square feet

2.

3"

7"

Number model: _____

Area = _____ square inches

3.

36 cm

24 cm

Number model: _____

Area = _____ square centimeters

4.

12 m

25 m

Number model: _____

Area = _____ square meters

Try This

The area of each rectangle is given. Find the missing length.

5.

3 in.

?

Area = 27 in^2

height = _____ in.

6.

?

12 cm

Area = 120 cm^2

base = _____ cm

Practice

7. 3, 6, _____, 12, _____, _____, _____

8. 14, 21, _____, _____, 42, _____, _____

9. 30, _____, 42, 48, _____, _____, _____

10. 12, _____, 36, _____, 60, _____, _____

Algebra and Functions 1.1, 1.4; Measurement and Geometry 1.1, 1.4

LESSON 8·5 | **Area of a Rectangle**

1. Take turns rolling a die. The first roll represents the length of the base of a rectangle. The second roll represents the height of the rectangle.

2. Use square pattern blocks to build the rectangle. Count squares to find the area.

Example:

First roll 4, second roll 3

height | base

Area: 12 square units

3. Record your results in the table.

First Roll (length of base)	Second Roll (height)	Area (square units)
4	3	12

4. Describe a pattern in your table.

_____

_____

5. Without building the rectangle, can you use this pattern to find the area of a rectangle with a base of 8 units and a height of 7 units? Explain your answer.

_____

_____

257

LESSON 8·5 # The Tennis Court

Area of rectangle = length * width

Tennis can be played either by 2 people or by 4 people. When 2 people play, it is called a game of singles. When 4 people play, it is called a game of doubles.

Here is a diagram of a tennis court. The net divides the court in half.

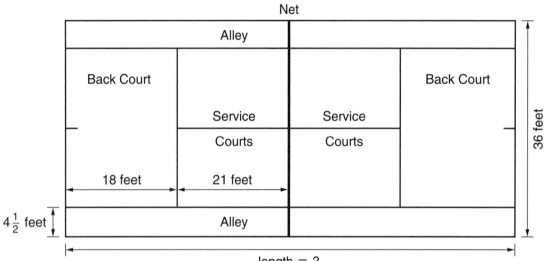

The two *alleys* are used only in doubles. They are never used in singles.

1. What is the total length of a tennis court? _____

2. The court used in a game of doubles is 36 feet wide. Each alley is $4\frac{1}{2}$ feet wide. What is the width of the court used in a game of singles? _____

3. What is the **area** of a singles court? _____

4. What is the **area** of a doubles court? _____

5. Do you think a player needs to cover more court in a game of singles or in a game of doubles? Explain.

_____

_____

_____

_____

258

LESSON 8·5 | Perimeter and Area

1. Tape together two copies of 1-inch grid paper (*Math Masters,* page 444).

SRB
131 134

2. Use a 24-inch string loop to find as many different rectangles as possible that have a perimeter of 24 inches.

3. Record your results in the table.

Length of Base (in.)	Height (in.)	Perimeter (in.)	Area (in²)
$/\ /$	$/$	24	
		24	
		24	
		24	
		24	
		24	
$10\frac{1}{2}$		24	
	$4\frac{1}{2}$	24	

4. Use your results to describe a relationship between the lengths of sides and areas of rectangles that have the same perimeter.

_____

_____

_____

5. What is another name for the rectangle with the largest area? _____

259

LESSON 8·6 | Areas of Parallelograms

Cut out Parallelogram A. (Use the second Parallelogram A if you make a mistake.) Cut it into 2 pieces so that it can be made into a rectangle. Tape the rectangle onto page 236 in your journal.

Do the same with Parallelograms B, C, and D.

STUDY LINK 8·6 Areas of Parallelograms

Find the area of each parallelogram.

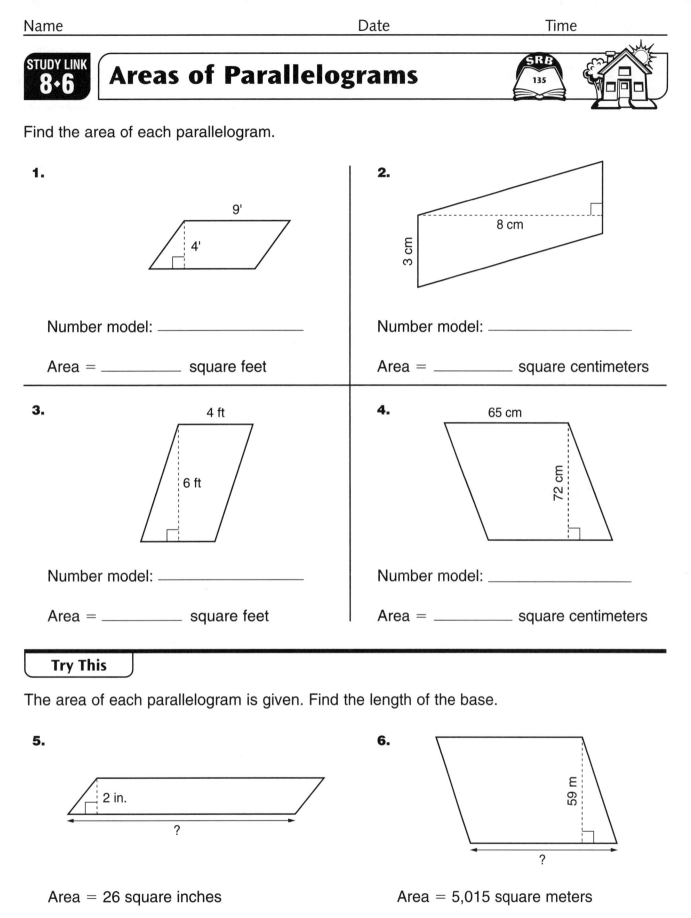

1.

9'

4'

Number model: _____

Area = _____ square feet

2.

8 cm

3 cm

Number model: _____

Area = _____ square centimeters

3.

4 ft

6 ft

Number model: _____

Area = _____ square feet

4.

65 cm

72 cm

Number model: _____

Area = _____ square centimeters

Try This

The area of each parallelogram is given. Find the length of the base.

5.

2 in.

?

Area = 26 square inches

base = _____ inches

6.

59 m

?

Area = 5,015 square meters

base = _____ meters

Algebra and Functions 1.1, 1.4; Measurement and Geometry 1.0, 1.4   **261**

Percents in My World

STUDY LINK 8·6

Percent means "per hundred" or "out of a hundred." *1 percent* means $\frac{1}{100}$ or 0.01.

"48 percent of the students in our school are boys" means that out of every 100 students in the school, 48 are boys.

Percents are written in two ways: with the word *percent,* as in the sentence above, and with the symbol %.

Collect examples of percents. Look in newspapers, magazines, books, almanacs, and encyclopedias. Ask people at home to help. Write the examples below. Also tell where you found them. If an adult says you may, cut out examples and bring them to school.

Encyclopedia: 91% of the area of New Jersey is land, and 9% is covered by water.

Newspaper: 76 percent of the seniors in Southport High School say they plan to attend college next year.

LESSON 8·6 | Perimeter and Area

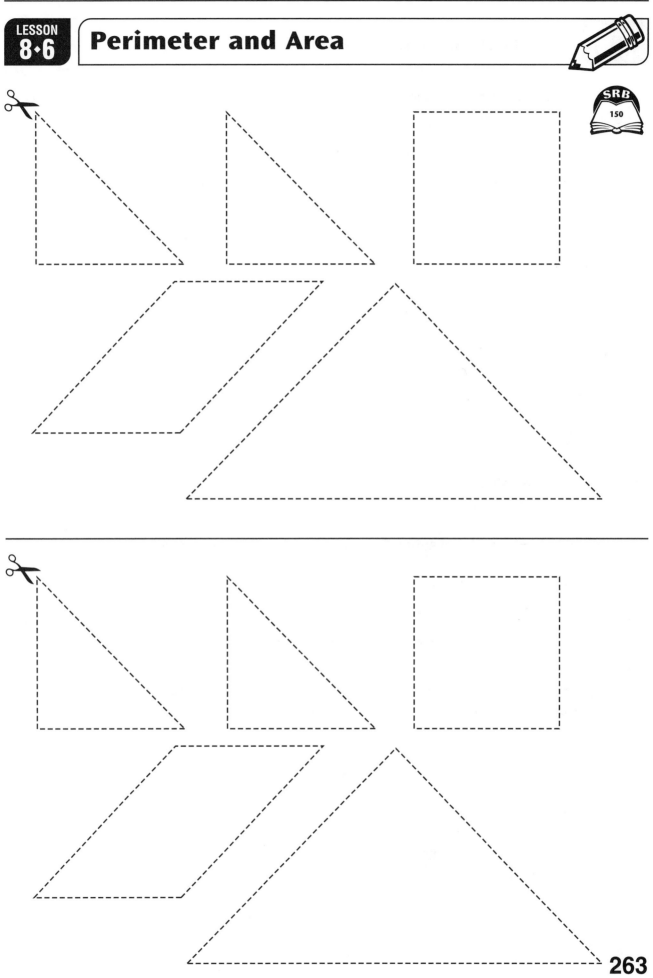

LESSON 8·6 | **Perimeter and Area** *continued*

Cut out and use only the shapes in the *top half* of *Math Masters,*
page 263 to complete Problems 1–5.

1. Make a square out of 4 of the shapes. Draw the square on the centimeter dot
   grid on *Math Masters,* page 437. Your picture should show how you put the
   square together.

2. Make a triangle out of 3 of the shapes. One of the shapes should be the
   shape you did not use to make the square in Problem 1. Draw the triangle
   on *Math Masters,* page 437.

3. Find the area of the following:

   a. the small triangle   _____ cm²

   b. the square   _____ cm²

   c. the parallelogram   _____ cm²

4. **a.** What is the perimeter of the large square
   you made in Problem 1?   _____ cm

   b. What is the area of that square?   _____ cm²

5. What is the area of the large triangle you
   made in Problem 2?   _____ cm²

Try This

6. Cut out the 5 shapes in the bottom half of *Math Masters,* page 263 and add
   them to the other shapes. Use at least 6 pieces each to make the following
   shapes.

   a. a square   **b.** a rectangle

   c. a trapezoid   **d.** any shape you choose

   Tape your favorite shape onto the back of this sheet. Next to the shape, write
   its perimeter and area.

LESSON 8·7

Areas of Triangles

Cut out Triangles A and B. Tape them together at the shaded corners to form a parallelogram. Tape the parallelogram in the space next to Triangle A on page 240 in your journal.

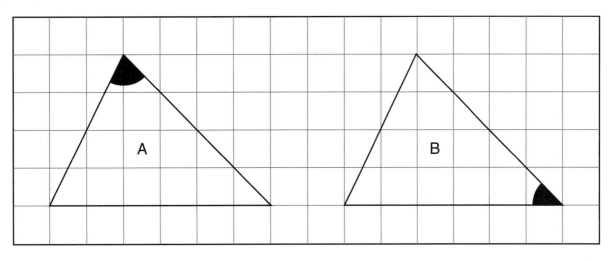

Do the same with the other 3 pairs of triangles.

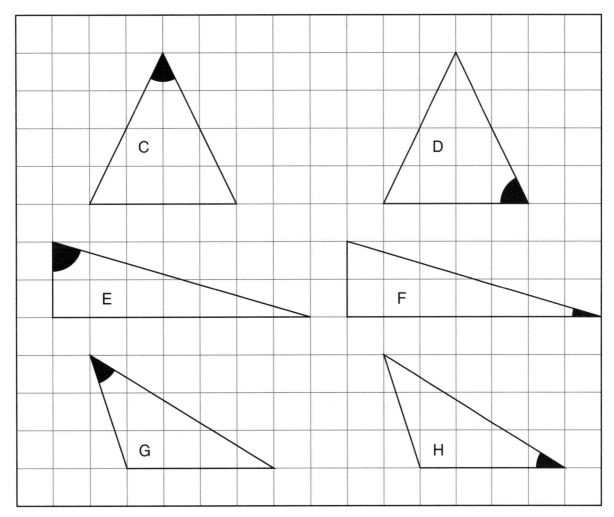

265

STUDY LINK 8·7 | Areas of Triangles

SRB
136

Find the area of each triangle.

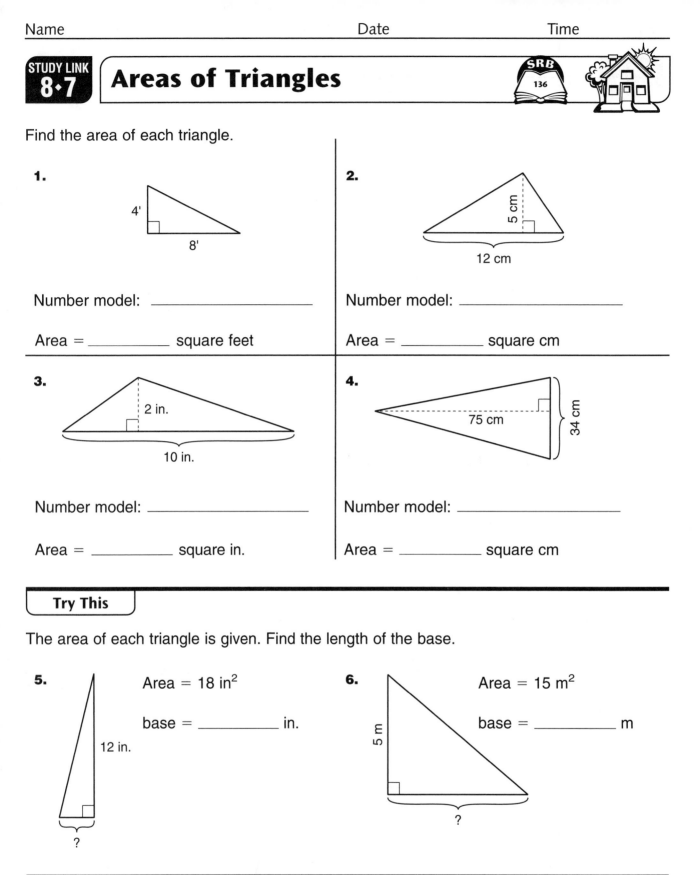

1.

4'

8'

Number model: _____

Area = _____ square feet

2.

5 cm

12 cm

Number model: _____

Area = _____ square cm

3.

2 in.

10 in.

Number model: _____

Area = _____ square in.

4.

75 cm

34 cm

Number model: _____

Area = _____ square cm

Try This

The area of each triangle is given. Find the length of the base.

5.

12 in.

?

Area = 18 in²

base = _____ in.

6.

5 m

?

Area = 15 m²

base = _____ m

Practice

7. 18, _____, _____, 45, _____, 63, _____

8. _____, 16, _____, 32, _____, _____, 56

Algebra and Functions 1.1, 1.2, 1.4; Measurement and Geometry 1.0, 1.4

LESSON 8·7 | **Comparing Areas**

1. Cut out the hexagon below. Then cut out the large equilateral triangle.
You should end up with one large triangle and three smaller triangles.

2. Use the large triangle and the three smaller triangles to form a rhombus.

   a. Sketch the rhombus in the
      space to the right.

   b. Is the area of the rhombus the
      same as the area of the hexagon? _____

   c. Is it possible for two different
      shapes to have the same area? _____

3. Put all the pieces back together to form a hexagon with an equilateral
triangle inside.

How can you show that the area of the hexagon is twice the area of the
large triangle?

_____

_____

_____

There are 4 triangles in the hexagon.

◆ The large triangle is called an **equilateral
triangle.** All 3 sides are the same length.

◆ The smaller triangles are called **isosceles
triangles.** Each of these triangles has
2 sides that are the same length.

LESSON
8·7

Area and Perimeter

1. Find the area of the hexagon below *without* counting squares.
   Hint: Divide the hexagon into figures for which you can calculate
   the areas: rectangles, parallelograms, and triangles. Use a formula
   to find the area of each of the figures. Record your work.

   Total area of hexagon = _____ cm²

2. Find the perimeter of the hexagon. Use a centimeter ruler.

   Perimeter = _____ cm

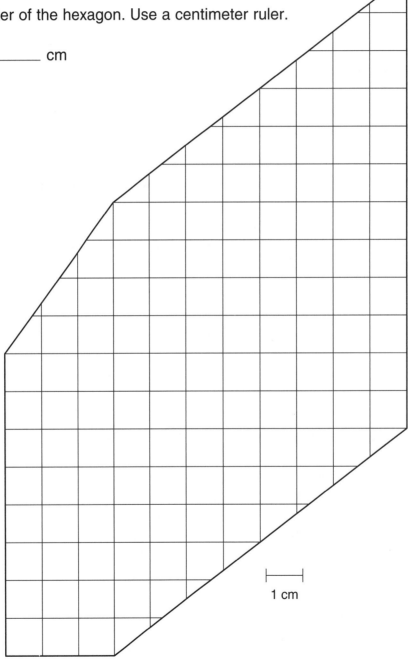

1 cm

268

Name _____ Date _____ Time _____

Turtle Weights

Turtle	Weight (pounds)
Pacific leatherback	1,552
Atlantic leatherback	1,018
Green sea	783
Loggerhead	568
Alligator snapping	220
Flatback sea	171
Hawksbill sea	138
Kemps Ridley	133
Olive Ridley	110
Common snapping	85

Source: The Top 10 of Everything 2004

1. The Atlantic leatherback is about 10 times heavier than the _____ turtle.

2. The loggerhead is about _____ times the weight of the common snapping turtle.

3. Which turtle weighs about
   3 times as much as the loggerhead? _____

4. The flatback sea turtle and the alligator snapping
   turtle together weigh about half as much as the _____ turtle.

5. About how many common snapping turtles would
   equal the weight of two alligator snapping turtles? _____

6. The Atlantic leatherback is about $\dfrac{\square}{\square}$ the weight of the Pacific leatherback.

Practice

Name the factors.

7. 50 _____   8. 63 _____

9. 90 _____

Statistics, Data Analysis, and Probability 1.0

LESSON 8·8 | Compare Area

1. Cut out the shapes below and combine them with the shapes cut out by the other members of your group.

2. On a separate sheet of paper, use "times as many" and "fraction-of" language to compare the areas of different pairs of shapes.

Examples:

◆ The area of Shape B is about 4 times the area of Shape A.

◆ The area of Shape D is about $\frac{2}{3}$ the area of Shape C.

Name   Date   Time

Weight on Different Planets

Mercury has about $\frac{1}{3}$ the gravitational pull on your body mass as does Earth—about 0.37 to be more precise. You would weigh about $\frac{1}{3}$ as much on Mercury as you do on Earth.

The table below shows how much Rich, his brother Jean-Claude, and his sister Gayle would weigh on each planet.

1. Use your calculator to find each planet's gravitational pull relative to Earth's.

Planet	Gravitational Pull Relative to Earth's	Weight in Pounds			
		Rich	Jean-Claude	Gayle	Me
Earth	1	86	75	50	
Mercury	0.37	31.82	27.75	18.5	
Venus		77.4	67.5	45	
Mars		31.82	27.75	18.5	
Jupiter		202.1	176.25	117.5	
Saturn		78.26	68.25	45.5	
Uranus		75.68	66	44	
Neptune		96.32	84	56	

Source: NASA Kids

2. Explain the strategy you used to determine the gravitational pulls.

_____

_____

Try This

3. Use the information in the table to calculate your own weight on each planet and record it in the "Me" column in the table above.

271

Similar Figures

Imagine that you used a copying machine to enlarge the original figures below and on
Math Masters, page 273 to get **similar** figures. Find the perimeter of each original shape
and of its enlargement.

1 cm

1.   **Original**   **Enlargement**

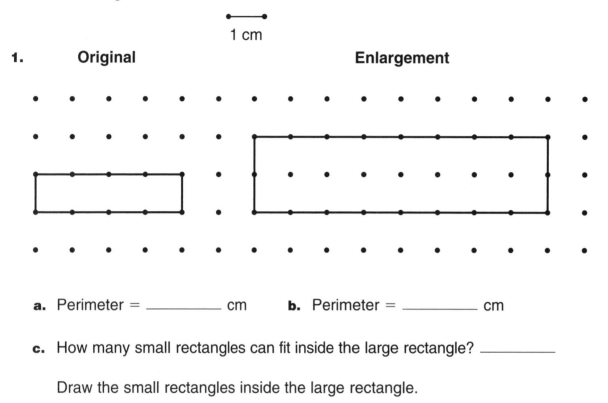

a. Perimeter = _____ cm   **b.** Perimeter = _____ cm

c. How many small rectangles can fit inside the large rectangle? _____

Draw the small rectangles inside the large rectangle.

2.   **Original**   **Enlargement**

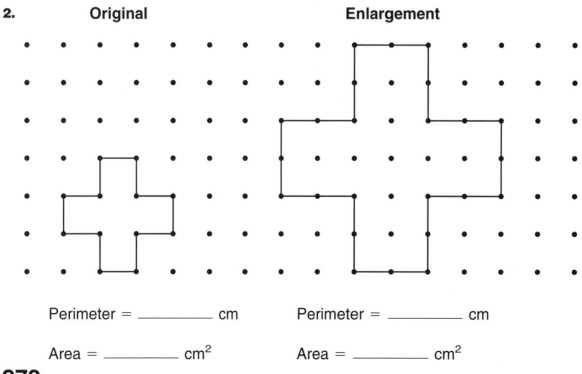

Perimeter = _____ cm   Perimeter = _____ cm

Area = _____ cm^2 Area = _____ cm^2

272

LESSON 8·8   **Similar Figures** *continued*

1 cm

3.   **Original**   **Enlargement**

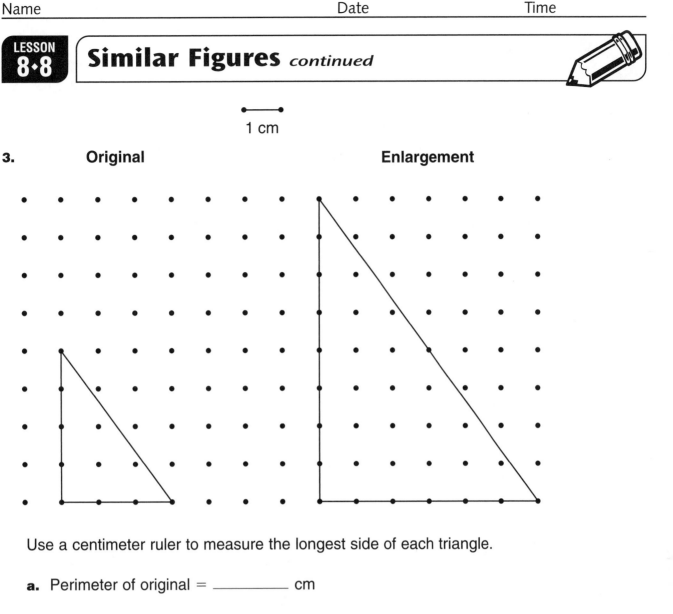

Use a centimeter ruler to measure the longest side of each triangle.

a. Perimeter of original = _____ cm

b. Perimeter of enlargement = _____ cm

c. How many small triangles can fit inside the large triangle? _____

d. Draw the small triangles inside the large triangle.

4. Complete the statements.

a. When you enlarge the sides of a shape to twice their original size, the perimeter of the enlargement is _____ times as large as the perimeter of the original shape.

b. When you enlarge the sides of a shape to twice their original size, the area of the enlargement is _____ times as large as the area of the original shape.

273

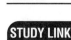

STUDY LINK
8·9

Unit 9: Family Letter

Fractions, Decimals, and Percents

In Unit 9, we will be studying percents and their uses in everyday situations. Your child should begin finding examples of percents in newspapers and magazines, on food packages, on clothing labels, and so on, and bring them to class. They will be used to illustrate a variety of percent applications.

As we study percents, your child will learn equivalent values for percents, fractions, and decimals. For example, 50% is equivalent to the fraction $\frac{1}{2}$ and to the decimal 0.5. The class will develop the understanding that **percent** always refers to a **part out of 100.**

Converting "easy" fractions, such as $\frac{1}{2}$, $\frac{1}{5}$, $\frac{1}{10}$, and $\frac{3}{4}$, to decimal and percent equivalents should become automatic for your child. Such fractions are common in percent situations and are helpful with more difficult fractions, decimals, and percents. To help memorize the "easy" fraction/percent equivalencies, your child will play *Fraction/Percent Concentration.*

"Easy" Fractions	Decimals	Percents
$\frac{1}{2}$	0.50	50%
$\frac{1}{4}$	0.25	25%
$\frac{3}{4}$	0.75	75%
$\frac{2}{5}$	0.40	40%
$\frac{7}{10}$	0.70	70%
$\frac{2}{2}$	1.00	100%

Throughout the unit, your child will use a calculator to convert fractions to percents and will learn how to use the percent key (%) to calculate discounts, sale prices, and percents of discount.

As part of the World Tour, your child will explore population data, such as literacy rates and percents of people who live in rural and urban areas.

Finally, the class will begin to apply the multiplication and division algorithms to problems that contain decimals. The approach used in *Everyday Mathematics* is straightforward: Students solve the problems as if the numbers were whole numbers. Then they estimate the answers to help them locate the decimal point in the exact answer. In this unit, we begin with fairly simple problems. Your child will solve more difficult problems in *Fifth* and *Sixth Grade Everyday Mathematics.*

Please keep this Family Letter for reference as your child works through Unit 9.

274

Vocabulary

Important terms in Unit 9:

discount The amount by which the regular price of an item is reduced in a sale, usually given as a fraction or percent of the original price, or as a "percent off."

illiterate An illiterate person cannot read or write.

life expectancy The average number of years a person may be expected to live.

literate A literate person can read and write.

100% box The entire object, the entire collection of objects, or the entire quantity being considered.

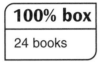

100% box

24 books

percent (%) Per hundred or out of a hundred. For example, "48% of the students in the school are boys" means that, on average, 48 out of 100 students in the school are boys; $48\% = \frac{48}{100} = 0.48$

percent of literacy The percent of the total population that is literate; the number of people out of 100 who are able to read and write. For example, 92% of the population in Mexico is literate—this means that, on average, 92 out of 100 people can read and write.

percent or fraction discount The percent or fraction of the regular price that you save in a "percent off" sale. See example under *regular price*.

rank To put in order by size; to sort from smallest to largest or vice versa.

	Countries Ranked from Smallest to Largest Percent of Population, Rural	
1	Australia	8%
2	Japan	21%
3	Russia	27%
4	Iran	33%
5	Turkey	34%
6	China	61%
7	Thailand	68%
8	India	72%
9	Vietnam	74%
10	Bangladesh	76%

regular price or list price The price of an item without a discount.

Regular Price	Sale!	Sale Price	You Saved
$19.95	25% OFF	$14.96	$4.99

rural In the country

sale price The amount you pay after subtracting the discount from the regular price. See example under *regular price*.

urban In the city

275

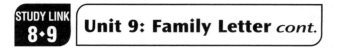

Do-Anytime Activities

To work with your child on the concepts taught in this unit, try these interesting and rewarding activities:

1. Help your child compile a percent portfolio that includes examples of the many ways percents are used in everyday life.

2. Encourage your child to incorporate such terms as "whole," "halves," "thirds," and "fourths" into his or her everyday vocabulary.

3. Practice renaming fractions as percents, and vice versa, in everyday situations. For example, when preparing a meal, quiz your child on what percent $\frac{3}{4}$ of a cup would be.

4. Look through advertisements of sales and discounts. If the original price of an item and the percent of discount are given, have your child calculate the amount of discount and the sale price. If the original price and sale price are given, have your child calculate the amount and percent of discount.

Building Skills through Games

In this unit, your child will play the following games:

Fraction Match See *Student Reference Book,* page 243.
This game is for 2 to 4 players and requires one deck of *Fraction Match* cards. The game develops skill in naming equivalent fractions.

Fraction/Percent Concentration See *Student Reference Book,* page 246.
Two or three players need 1 set of Fraction/Percent Tiles and a calculator to play this game. Playing *Fraction/Percent Concentration* helps students recognize fractions and percents that are equivalent.

Over and Up Squares See *Student Reference Book,* page 257.
This is a game for 2 players and will require a playing grid. The game helps students practice using ordered pairs of numbers to locate points on a rectangular grid.

Polygon Pair-Up See *Student Reference Book,* page 258.
This game provides practice in identifying properties of polygons. It requires a *Polygon Pair-Up* Property Deck and Polygon Deck.

Rugs and Fences See *Student Reference Book,* pages 260 and 261.
This is a game for 2 players and requires a *Rugs and Fences* Polygon Deck, Area and Perimeter Deck, and Record Sheet. The game helps students practice computing the area and perimeter of polygons.

As You Help Your Child with Homework

As your child brings assignments home, you may want to go over the instructions together, clarifying them as necessary. The answers listed below will guide you through this unit's Study Links.

Study Link 9·1

1. $\frac{90}{100}$; 90%   **2.** $\frac{53}{100}$; 53%   **3.** $\frac{4}{100}$; 4%

4. $\frac{60}{100}$; 0.60   **5.** $\frac{25}{100}$; 0.25   **6.** $\frac{7}{100}$; 0.07

7. 0.50; 50%   **8.** 0.75; 75%   **9.** 0.06; 6%

Study Link 9·2

1. 100; $\frac{1}{100}$; 0.01; 1%   **2.** 20; $\frac{1}{20}$; 0.05; 5%

3. 10; $\frac{1}{10}$; 0.10; 10%   **4.** 4; $\frac{1}{4}$; 0.25; 25%

5. 2; $\frac{1}{2}$; 0.50; 50%   **6.** 0.75; 75%

7. 0.20; 20%

Study Link 9·3

1.

$\frac{1}{2}$	0	.	5					
$\frac{1}{3}$	0	.	3	3	3	3	3	3
$\frac{1}{4}$	0	.	2	5				
$\frac{1}{5}$	0	.	2					
$\frac{1}{6}$	0	.	1	6	6	6	6	6
$\frac{1}{7}$	0	.	1	4	2	8	5	7
$\frac{1}{8}$	0	.	1	2	5			
$\frac{1}{9}$	0	.	1	1	1	1	1	1
$\frac{1}{10}$	0	.	1					
$\frac{1}{11}$	0	.	0	9	0	9	0	9
$\frac{1}{12}$	0	.	0	8	3	3	3	3
$\frac{1}{13}$	0	.	0	7	6	9	2	3
$\frac{1}{14}$	0	.	0	7	1	4	2	8
$\frac{1}{15}$	0	.	0	6	6	6	6	6
$\frac{1}{16}$	0	.	0	6	2	5		
$\frac{1}{17}$	0	.	0	5	8	8	2	3
$\frac{1}{18}$	0	.	0	5	5	5	5	5
$\frac{1}{19}$	0	.	0	5	2	6	3	1
$\frac{1}{20}$	0	.	0	5				
$\frac{1}{21}$	0	.	0	4	7	6	1	9
$\frac{1}{22}$	0	.	0	4	5	4	5	4
$\frac{1}{23}$	0	.	0	4	3	4	7	8
$\frac{1}{24}$	0	.	0	4	1	6	6	6
$\frac{1}{25}$	0	.	0	4				

Study Link 9·4

1. 34%   **2.** 67%   **3.** 84%   **4.** 52%

5. 85%   **6.** 20%   **7.** 25%   **8.** 30%

9. 62.5%   **10.** 70%   **11.** 15%   **12.** 37.5%

13. Sample answer: I divided the numerator by the denominator and then multiplied by 100.

14. 86%   **15.** 3%   **16.** 14%   **17.** 83.5%

Study Link 9·5

1. 7%; 7%; 7%; 8%; 10%; 11%; 10%; 10%; 9%; 8%; 7%

3. Sample answer: I divided the number of marriages for each month by the total number of marriages, then multiplied by 100 and rounded to the nearest whole number.

Study Link 9·6

1. The varsity team. They won $\frac{8}{10}$ or 80% of their games. The junior varsity team only won $\frac{6}{8}$ or 75% of their games.

2. 2: 11; $\frac{5}{11}$; 45%   3: 3; $\frac{3}{3}$; 100%

4: 11; $\frac{9}{11}$; 82%   5: 7; $\frac{4}{7}$; 57%

6: 16; $\frac{11}{16}$; 69%   7: 10; $\frac{6}{10}$; 60%

8: 2; $\frac{1}{2}$; 50%

Study Link 9·7

1. 50%   **2.** Tuvalu   **3.** 5%

4. Dominica; Antigua and Barbuda; and Palau

5. 300%

Study Link 9·8

1. 25.8   **2.** 489.6   **3.** 45.12   **4.** 112.64

7. Sample answer: I estimated that the answer should be about $5 * 20 = 100$.

8. 212.4   **9.** 38.64   **10.** 382.13

Study Link 9·9

1. 14.8   **2.** 0.2700   **3.** 24.96   **4.** 0.860

5. 23.4   **6.** 58.32

7. Sample answer: I estimated that the answer should be about $\frac{100}{4} = 25$.

8. 4.2   **9.** 38.7   **10.** 0.65

LESSON 9·1   **Playing *Fraction Match***

1. Katrina is playing *Fraction Match.* The target card is $\frac{3}{4}$. She has the following cards in her hand. Circle the card she may play.

2. Suppose she had a WILD card in her hand. Write a different fraction, equivalent to $\frac{3}{4}$, that she could name. _____

   WILD   WILD
   WILD
   Name an equivalent fraction with a denominator of 2, 3, 4, 5, 6, 8, 9, 10, or 12.

3. Imagine that a WILD card allowed Katrina to name *any* fraction equivalent to $\frac{3}{4}$. Write two fractions that she could name.

   _____   _____

✂ -

Name   Date   Time

LESSON 9·1   **Playing *Fraction Match***

1. Katrina is playing *Fraction Match.* The target card is $\frac{3}{4}$. She has the following cards in her hand. Circle the card she may play.

   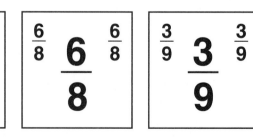

2. Suppose she had a WILD card in her hand. Write a different fraction, equivalent to $\frac{3}{4}$, that she could name. _____

   WILD   WILD
   WILD
   Name an equivalent fraction with a denominator of 2, 3, 4, 5, 6, 8, 9, 10, or 12.

3. Imagine that a WILD card allowed Katrina to name *any* fraction equivalent to $\frac{3}{4}$. Write two fractions that she could name.

   _____   _____

Fractions, Decimals, and Percents

SRB
61 62

Rename each decimal as a fraction and a percent.

1. $0.90 = \dfrac{\square}{100} =$ _____%

2. $0.53 = \dfrac{\square}{100} =$ _____%

3. $0.04 = \dfrac{\square}{100} =$ _____%

Rename each percent as a fraction and a decimal.

4. $60\% = \dfrac{\square}{100} =$ ___._____

5. $25\% = \dfrac{\square}{100} =$ ___._____

6. $7\% = \dfrac{\square}{100} =$ ___._____

Rename each fraction as a decimal and a percent.

7. $\dfrac{50}{100} =$ ___._____ $=$ _____%

8. $\dfrac{75}{100} =$ ___._____ $=$ _____%

9. $\dfrac{6}{100} =$ ___._____ $=$ ___%

10. Shade more than $\dfrac{10}{100}$ and less than $\dfrac{30}{100}$ of the grid.
Write the value of the shaded part as a decimal and a percent.

Decimal: _____

Percent: _____

11. Shade more than 25% and less than 60% of the grid.
Write the value of the shaded part as a decimal and a percent.

Decimal: _____

Percent: _____

12. Shade more than 0.65 and less than 0.85 of the grid.
Write the value of the shaded part as a decimal and a percent.

Decimal: _____

Percent: _____

Practice

Order the fractions from smallest to largest.

13. $\dfrac{3}{6}, \dfrac{3}{3}, \dfrac{3}{5}, \dfrac{3}{7}$ _____

14. $\dfrac{2}{3}, \dfrac{6}{7}, \dfrac{1}{2}, \dfrac{19}{20}$ _____

Number Sense 1.6

STUDY LINK 9·1 | **Trivia Survey**

Conduct the survey below. The results will be used in Lesson 9-6.

Find at least five people to answer the following survey questions. You can ask family members, relatives, neighbors, and friends.

BE CAREFUL! You will not ask every person every question. Pay attention to the instructions that go with each question.

Record each answer with a tally mark in the Yes or No column.

Question	Yes	No
1. Is Monday your favorite day? (Ask everyone younger than 20.)		
2. Have you gone to the movies in the last month? (Ask everyone older than 8.)		
3. Did you eat breakfast today? (Ask everyone over 25.)		
4. Do you keep a map in your car? (Ask everyone who owns a car.)		
5. Did you eat at a fast-food restaurant yesterday? (Ask everyone.)		
6. Did you read a book during the last month? (Ask everyone over 20.)		
7. Are you more than 1 meter tall? (Ask everyone over 20.)		
8. Do you like liver? (Ask everyone.)		

 Statistics, Data Analysis, and Probability 1.0, 1.1

LESSON 9·1 | **50% of a Square**

Benito and Silvia each shaded 50% of a grid.

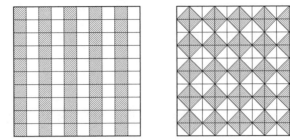

1. Do you think they shaded the grids correctly? Explain your reasoning.

_____

_____

2. Shade 50% of the grids below in different ways. Explain how you know
   you have shaded 50%.

   a.

   b.

   _____   _____

   _____   _____

   _____   _____

   _____   _____

Try This

3. Shade 50% of the grid. Explain how you know you have shaded 50%.

   _____

   _____

281

Coins as Percents of $1

SRB
38 39

1. How many pennies in $1? _____ What fraction of $1 is 1 penny? _____

   Write the decimal that shows what part of $1 is 1 penny. _____

   What percent of $1 is 1 penny? _____%

2. How many nickels in $1? _____ What fraction of $1 is 1 nickel? _____

   Write the decimal that shows what part of $1 is 1 nickel. _____

   What percent of $1 is 1 nickel? _____%

3. How many dimes in $1? _____ What fraction of $1 is 1 dime? _____

   Write the decimal that shows what part of $1 is 1 dime. _____

   What percent of $1 is 1 dime? _____%

4. How many quarters in $1? _____ What fraction of $1 is 1 quarter? _____

   Write the decimal that shows what part of $1 is 1 quarter. _____

   What percent of $1 is 1 quarter? _____%

5. How many half-dollars in $1? _____ What fraction of $1 is 1 half-dollar? _____

   Write the decimal that shows what part of $1 is 1 half-dollar. _____

   What percent of $1 is 1 half-dollar? _____%

6. Three quarters (75¢) is $\frac{3}{4}$ of $1.

   Write the decimal. _____

   What percent of $1 is

   3 quarters? _____%

7. Two dimes (20¢) is $\frac{2}{10}$ of $1.

   Write the decimal. _____

   What percent of $1 is

   2 dimes? _____%

Practice

8. _____ = 748 * 6   9. 51 * 90 = _____   10. _____ = 28 * 903

Number Sense 1.6

LESSON 9·2 | **Percent Patterns**

Complete each set of statements. Use grids or base-10 blocks,
or draw pictures to help you. Look for patterns in your answers.

Example:

50% is the same as 50 per 100.

If there are 50 per 100, then there are

____5____ per 10. __500__ per 1,000.

___10___ per 20. __100__ per 200.

1. 20% is the same as 20 per 100.

If there are 20 per 100, then there are

_____ per 10.   _____ per 1,000.

_____ per 20.   _____ per 200.

2. 30% is the same as 30 per 100.

If there are 30 per 100, then there are

_____ per 10.   _____ per 1,000.

_____ per 20.   _____ per 200.

3. 80% is the same as 80 per 100.

If there are 80 per 100, then there are

_____ per 10.   _____ per 1,000.

_____ per 20.   _____ per 200.

4. 60% is the same as 60 per 100.

If there are 60 per 100, then there are

_____ per 10.   _____ per 1,000.

_____ per 20.   _____ per 200.

Try This

5. 75% is the same as 75 per 100.

If there are 75 per 100, then there are

_____ per 10.   _____ per 1,000.

_____ per 20.   _____ per 200.

6. 120% is the same as 120 per 100.

If there are 120 per 100, then there are

_____ per 10.   _____ per 1,000.

_____ per 20.   _____ per 200.

STUDY LINK 9·3 | **Calculator Decimals**

1. Use your calculator to rename each fraction below as a decimal.

$\frac{1}{2}$	0	.	5					
$\frac{1}{3}$	0	.	3	3	3	3	3	3
$\frac{1}{4}$								
$\frac{1}{5}$								
$\frac{1}{6}$								
$\frac{1}{7}$								
$\frac{1}{8}$								
$\frac{1}{9}$								
$\frac{1}{10}$								
$\frac{1}{11}$								
$\frac{1}{12}$								
$\frac{1}{13}$								

$\frac{1}{14}$								
$\frac{1}{15}$								
$\frac{1}{16}$								
$\frac{1}{17}$								
$\frac{1}{18}$								
$\frac{1}{19}$								
$\frac{1}{20}$								
$\frac{1}{21}$								
$\frac{1}{22}$								
$\frac{1}{23}$								
$\frac{1}{24}$								
$\frac{1}{25}$								

2. Make up some of your own.

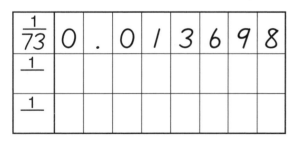

$\frac{1}{73}$	0	.	0	1	3	6	9	8
$\frac{1}{}$								
$\frac{1}{}$								

$\frac{1}{}$							
$\frac{1}{}$							
$\frac{1}{}$							

Practice

3. $6\overline{)96}$ = _____

4. 91 / 5 = _____

5. _____ = 864 ÷ 8

6. 575 ÷ 7 = _____

Number Sense 1.6

STUDY LINK 9·4 Fractions and Decimals to Percents

Do NOT use a calculator to convert these fractions to percents.
On the back of this page, show your work for Problems 3–6.

1. $\dfrac{34}{100} =$ _____%

2. $\dfrac{67}{100} =$ _____%

3. $\dfrac{42}{50} =$ _____%

4. $\dfrac{13}{25} =$ _____%

5. $\dfrac{17}{20} =$ _____%

6. $\dfrac{25}{125} =$ _____%

Use a calculator to convert these fractions to percents.

7. $\dfrac{23}{92} =$ _____%

8. $\dfrac{12}{40} =$ _____%

9. $\dfrac{20}{32} =$ _____%

10. $\dfrac{49}{70} =$ _____%

11. $\dfrac{60}{400} =$ _____%

12. $\dfrac{21}{56} =$ _____%

13. Describe how you used your calculator to convert the fractions
in Problems 7–12 to percents.

_____

_____

_____

Do NOT use a calculator to convert these decimals to percents.

14. $0.86 =$ _____%

15. $0.03 =$ _____%

16. $0.140 =$ _____%

17. $0.835 =$ _____%

Practice

Order the fractions from smallest to largest.

18. $\dfrac{7}{16}, \dfrac{7}{8}, \dfrac{7}{12}, \dfrac{7}{9}$ _____

19. $\dfrac{7}{15}, \dfrac{3}{15}, \dfrac{8}{15}, \dfrac{4}{15}$ _____

20. $\dfrac{5}{9}, \dfrac{15}{16}, \dfrac{1}{4}, \dfrac{9}{10}$ _____

Number Sense 1.6

285

LESSON 9·4 | **"Percent-of" Problems**

Use counters to solve the problems on this page.

1. If ○ ○ ○ ○ ○ is 100%, draw 50%.

    50% of 10 = _____

2. If ○ ○ ○ ○ is 100%, draw 25%.

    25% of 16 = _____

3. If ○ ○ ○ ○ ○ is 100%, draw 10%.

    10% of 20 = _____

4. If ○ ○ ○ is 50%, draw 100%.

    50% of _____ = 6

5. If ○ ○ ○ is 75%, draw 100%.

    75% of _____ = 9

6. If ○ ○ ○ ○ is 40%, draw 100%.

    40% of _____ = 8

7. Pick one of the problems from above and explain how you got your answer.

    Problem _____

_____

_____

_____

LESSON 9·4 | **Discount Number Stories**

1. A store is having a sale on gym shoes.

   ◆ The regular price of the High Flyers is $50. Now they are on sale for $38.

   ◆ The Zingers are $15 off the regular price. When not on sale, the Zingers cost $75 a pair.

   Which pair has the greater "percent-of" discount? Explain your answer.

   _____

   _____

   _____

   _____

2. The same store is also having a sale on tennis rackets.

   ◆ The regular price of the Smasher is $54.00. It is on sale for 25% off the regular price.

   ◆ The regular price of the Fast Flight is $75.00. It is on sale for 20% off the regular price.

   For which tennis racket are you getting more money taken off the regular price? Explain your answer.

   _____

   _____

   _____

   _____

Name _____   Date _____   Time _____

STUDY LINK 9·5 | Renaming Fractions as Percents

In 2001, there were about 2,317,000 marriages in the United States.
The table below shows the approximate number of marriages each month.

1. Use a calculator to find the percent of the total number of marriages that
   occurred each month. Round the answers to the nearest whole-number percent.

Month	Approximate Number of Marriages	Approximate Percent of Total Marriages
January	147,000	6%
February	159,000	
March	166,000	
April	166,000	
May	189,000	
June	237,000	
July	244,000	
August	225,000	
September	224,000	
October	217,000	
November	191,000	
December	152,000	

Source: U.S. Department of Health and Human Services

2. According to the table, what is the most popular month for a wedding? _____

   What is the least popular month for a wedding? _____

3. Describe how you used your calculator to find the percent for each month.

   _____

   _____

Practice

Name all the factors of each number.

4. 63 _____   5. 28 _____

288   **Number Sense 1.6**

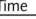

LESSON 9·5 | **Rounding Percents**

The number lines below are curved like hills. You can use them to help you **round** percents to the nearest whole-number percent.

Example:

Round 89.7% to the nearest whole-number percent.

◆ Think: Which whole-number percents are nearest to 89.7%?

◆ If I look at the number line, **89%** is the whole-number percent to the left of 89.7%.

◆ If I look at the number line, **90%** is the whole-number percent to the right of 89.7%.

◆ What number would be exactly halfway between 89% and 90%?

Mark 89.7% on the curved number line.

Would 89.7% slide down to 89% or 90%?

89.7% rounded to the nearest whole-number percent is 90%.

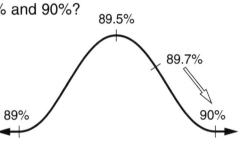

1. Round 23.6% to the nearest whole-number percent.

   Label the curved number line. Mark 23.6%.

   23.6% would slide down to _____.

   23.6% rounded to the
   nearest whole-number percent is _____.

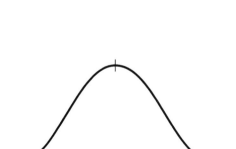

2. Round 92.1% to the nearest whole-number percent.

   Label the curved number line. Mark 92.1%.

   92.1% would slide down to _____.

   92.1% rounded to the
   nearest whole-number percent is _____.

LESSON 9·6 | # Trivia Survey Data Chart

Class Results for the Trivia Survey

Question	Yes	No	Total	$\dfrac{\text{Yes}}{\text{Total}}$	% Yes
1. Monday					
2. movies					
3. breakfast					
4. map					
5. fast food					
6. read					
7. meter					
8. liver					

STUDY LINK 9·6 | Use Percents to Compare Fractions

SRB
62 207

1. The girls' varsity basketball team won 8 of the 10 games it played. The junior varsity team won 6 of 8 games. Which team has the better record? Explain your reasoning.

_____

_____

2. Complete the table of shots taken (not including free throws) during a game. Calculate the percent of shots made to the nearest whole percent.

Player	Shots Made	Shots Missed	Total Shots	Shots Made / Total Shots	% of Shots Made
1	5	12	17	$\frac{5}{17}$	29%
2	5	6			
3	3	0			
4	9	2			
5	4	3			
6	11	5			
7	6	4			
8	1	1			

3. The basketball game is tied. Your team has the ball. There is only enough time for one more shot. Based only on the information in the table, which player would you choose to take the shot? Why?

_____

_____

_____

_____

Practice

4. $\frac{1}{3} + \frac{1}{6} =$ _____

5. _____ $= \frac{3}{4} - \frac{1}{2}$

6. _____ $= \frac{7}{10} + \frac{1}{5}$

7. $\frac{5}{8} - \frac{1}{4} =$ _____

Number Sense 3.0; Mathematical Reasoning 2.3; Mathematical Reasoning 3.1

291

LESSON 9·6   "Fraction-of" a Collection

Part One

1. Estimate the total number of pattern blocks in the jar given to you by your teacher. _____ pattern blocks

2. Estimate the total number of red trapezoids in the jar.

   _____ red trapezoids

3. Write your estimates as a fraction.

   $$\frac{\text{total number of red trapezoids}}{\text{total number of pattern blocks}} = \frac{\boxed{}}{\boxed{}}$$

4. Record the estimates made by the members of your group.

   _____   _____   _____   _____

Part Two

5. Count the number of pattern blocks in the jar. _____ pattern blocks

6. Count the number of red trapezoids in the jar. _____ red trapezoids

7. Record the counts as a fraction.

   $$\frac{\text{total number of red trapezoids}}{\text{total number of pattern blocks}} = \frac{\boxed{}}{\boxed{}}$$

Part Three

8. Which of your group members' estimates do you think was closest to the actual fraction of trapezoids in the jar? _____

   Explain why you think so.

   _____

   _____

   _____

292

LESSON 9·7 | **Map of Region 4**

SRB
301

Title: _____

Name _____ Date _____ Time _____

STUDY LINK 9·7 | Least-Populated Countries

The table below shows the approximate population for the 10 least-populated countries in the world. Use the data to estimate answers to the problems.

Country	Population
Vatican City	900
Tuvalu	11,000
Nauru	13,000
Palau	20,000
San Marino	28,000
Monaco	32,000
Liechtenstein	33,000
St. Kitts and Nevis	39,000
Antigua and Barbuda	68,000
Dominica	69,000

Source: Top Ten of Everything 2004

1. The population of Liechtenstein is about _____% of the population of Dominica.

2. What country's population is about 33% of Liechtenstein's population? _____

3. The population of Vatican City is about _____% of the population of Palau.

4. The population of the 10 countries listed is 314,900. What 3 country populations together equal about 50% of that total?

_____

5. The population of St. Kitts and Nevis is about _____% of Nauru's population.

Practice

6. 27 * 4 = _____

7. _____ = 508 * 8

8. _____ = 63 * 86

9. 849 * 52 = _____

294   Statistics, Data Analysis, and Probability 1.0; Number Sense 3.2

LESSON 9·7 | Color-Coded Map for Percent of Literacy

A **literate** person is a person who can read and write. People who cannot read and write are said to be **illiterate.**

Percent of literacy is the fraction of the total population that is literate—the number of people out of 100 who are literate. Young children are not counted until they reach an age at which they are expected to read and write.

1. Make a prediction: Do you think there is a relationship among population statistics on literacy, age, and rural or urban living? _____

2. In the table below, list the countries in Region 4 from *greatest* to *least* according to the percent of the population that is literate. (See *Student Reference Book,* page 299.)

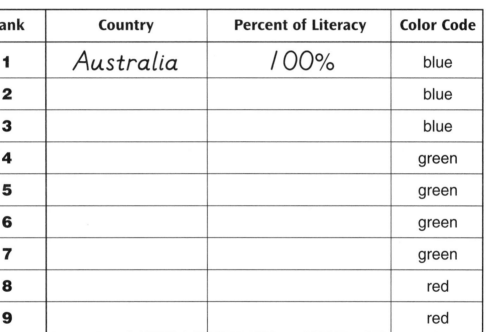

Rank	Country	Percent of Literacy	Color Code
1	*Australia*	*100%*	blue
2			blue
3			blue
4			green
5			green
6			green
7			green
8			red
9			red
10			red

3. Color these countries on the map on *Math Masters,* page 293 according to the color code in the table.

4. Compare this map with the population ages 0–14 and percent rural maps. Do the data support the prediction you made in Problem 1? _____

   Explain your answer on the back of this page. Include reasons why you think a country might be colored red or blue on all three maps.

STUDY LINK 9·8 — Multiplying Decimals

For each problem below, the multiplication has been done correctly, but the decimal point is missing in the answer. Correctly place the decimal point in the answer.

1. 6 * 4.3 = 2 5 8

2. 72 * 6.8 = 4 8 9 6

3. 0.96 * 47 = 4 5 1 2

4. 5.12 * 22 = 1 1 2 6 4

5. 8,457 * 9.8 = 8 2 8 7 8 6

6. 0.04 * 140 = 5 6

7. Explain how you decided where to place the decimal point in Problem 4.

_____

_____

_____

Try This

Multiply. Show your work.

8. 5.9 * 36 = _____

9. 0.46 * 84 = _____

10. _____ = 7.21 * 53

Practice

11. _____ = 96 ÷ 6

12. 4)67 = _____

13. _____ = 411 / 3

14. 9)903 = _____

Number Sense 3.3; Mathematical Reasoning 2.1

LESSON 9·8

Multiplying Whole Numbers

Write a number model to estimate each product. Then multiply with a paper-and-pencil algorithm. Show your work.

SRB 18 19

1. $7 * 68 =$ _____

Number model:

_____

2. $534 * 6 =$ _____

Number model:

_____

3. _____ $= 58 * 67$

Number model:

_____

4. $33 * 275 =$ _____

Number model:

_____

Try This

5. Margo's favorite socks are on sale for $2.89 per pair. She has $25. Can she buy 6 pairs? _____

Explain how to solve this problem without using a paper-and-pencil algorithm.

_____

_____

_____

STUDY LINK 9·9 | **Dividing Decimals**

For each problem below, the division has been done correctly, but the decimal point is missing in the answer. Correctly place the decimal point in the answer.

1. 88.8 / 6 = 1 4 8

2. 1.35 / 5 = 2 7 0 0

3. 99.84 / 4 = 2 4 9 6

4. 2.58 / 3 = 8 6 0

5. 163.8 / 7 = 2 3 4

6. 233.28 / 4 = 5 8 3 2

7. Explain how you decided where to place the decimal point in Problem 3.

_____

_____

_____

Try This

Divide. Show your work.

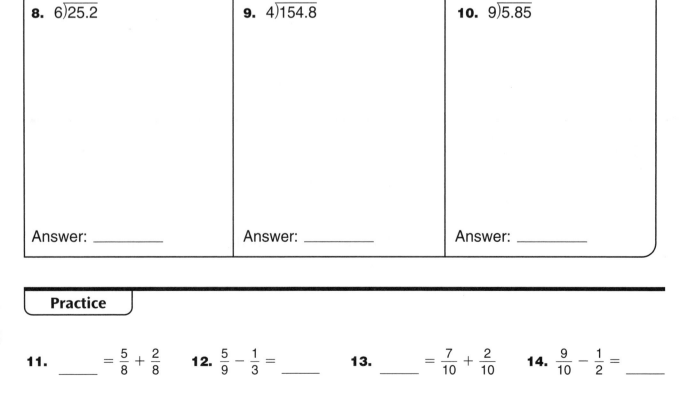

8. 6)25.2

Answer: _____

9. 4)154.8

Answer: _____

10. 9)5.85

Answer: _____

Practice

11. _____ = $\frac{5}{8} + \frac{2}{8}$ **12.** $\frac{5}{9} - \frac{1}{3}$ = _____ **13.** _____ = $\frac{7}{10} + \frac{2}{10}$ **14.** $\frac{9}{10} - \frac{1}{2}$ = _____

Number Sense **3.2**, 3.4; Mathematical Reasoning 2.3

Dividing Whole Numbers

Write a number model to estimate each quotient. Then divide with a
paper-and-pencil algorithm. Show your work.

SRB
22 23

1. 79 / 6 = _____
Number model:

_____

2. 92 / 3 = _____
Number model:

_____

3. _____ = 573 / 4
Number model:

_____

4. 945 / 18 = _____
Number model:

_____

Try This

5. The school has $357 to spend on new science books.
If the books cost $9 each, how many books can they buy? _____ books

Explain how to solve this problem without using a paper-and-pencil algorithm.

_____

_____

_____

STUDY LINK 9·10

Unit 10: Family Letter

Reflections and Symmetry

In this unit, your child will take another look at geometry, with an emphasis on symmetry. Many objects in nature are symmetrical: flowers, insects, and the human body, to name just a few. Symmetry is all around—in buildings, furniture, clothing, and paintings.

The class will focus on **reflectional symmetry,** also called **line symmetry** or **mirror symmetry,** in which half of a figure is the mirror image of the other half. Encourage your child to look for symmetrical objects, and if possible, to collect pictures of symmetrical objects from magazines and newspapers. For example, the right half of the printed letter T is the mirror image of the left half. If you have a small hand mirror, have your child check letters, numbers, and other objects to see whether they have line symmetry. The class will use a device called a **transparent mirror,** which is pictured below. Students will use it to see and trace the mirror image of an object.

Geometry is not only the study of figures (such as lines, rectangles, and circles), but also the study of transformations or "motions" of figures. These motions include **reflections** (flips), **rotations** (turns), and **translations** (slides). Your child will use these motions to create pictures like the ones below, called **frieze patterns.**

Students will also work with positive and negative numbers, looking at them as reflections of each other across zero on a number line. They will develop skills of adding positive and negative numbers by thinking in terms of credits and debits for a new company, and they will practice these skills in the *Credits/Debits Game.*

Please keep this Family Letter for reference as your child works through Unit 10.

Vocabulary

Important terms in Unit 10:

frieze pattern A geometric design in a long strip in which an element is repeated over and over. The element may be rotated, translated, and reflected. Frieze patterns are often found on the walls of buildings, on the borders of rugs and tiled floors, and on clothing.

image The reflection of an object that you see when you look in the mirror. Also a figure that is produced by a transformation (reflection, translation, or rotation) of another figure. See *preimage*.

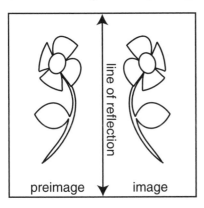

preimage   image

line of reflection A line halfway between a figure (preimage) and its reflected image. In a reflection, a figure is "flipped over" the line of reflection.

line of symmetry A line drawn through a figure that divides the figure into two parts that are mirror images of each other. The two parts look alike, but face in opposite directions.

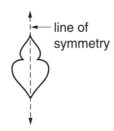

line of symmetry

negative number A number that is less than zero; a number to the left of zero on a horizontal number line or below zero on a vertical number line. The symbol "−" may be used to write a negative number. For example, "negative 5" is usually written as −5.

preimage A geometric figure that is somehow changed (by a *reflection*, a *rotation*, or a *translation*, for example) to produce another figure. See *image*.

reflection (flip) The "flipping" of a figure over a line (the *line of reflection*) so that its image is the mirror image of the original (preimage).

reflection

rotation (turn) A movement of a figure around a fixed point, or axis; a "turn."

symmetric Having the same size and shape on either side of a line, or looking the same when turned by some amount less than 360°.

transformation Something done to a geometric figure that produces a new figure. The most common transformations are translations (slides), reflections (flips), and rotations (turns).

translation A movement of a figure along a straight line; a "slide." In a translation, each point of the figure slides the same distance in the same direction.

translation

301

Do-Anytime Activities

To work with your child on concepts taught in this unit, try these interesting and rewarding activities:

1. Have your child look for frieze patterns on buildings, rugs, floors, and clothing. If possible, have your child bring pictures to school or make sketches of friezes that he or she sees.

2. Encourage your child to study the mathematical qualities of the patterns of musical notes and rhythms. Composers of even the simplest of tunes use reflections and translations of notes and chords (groups of notes).

3. Encourage your child to incorporate transformation vocabulary—**symmetric, reflected, rotated,** and **translated**—into his or her everyday vocabulary.

Building Skills through Games

In this unit, your child will play the following games to develop his or her understanding of addition and subtraction of positive and negative numbers, practice estimating and measuring angles, practice plotting ordered pairs in the first quadrant of a coordinate grid, and identify properties of polygons. For detailed instructions, see the *Student Reference Book.*

Angle Tangle See *Student Reference Book,* page 230. Two players need a protactor, straightedge, and several sheets of blank paper to play this game. This game provides practice estimating and measuring angle sizes.

Credits/Debits Game See *Student Reference Book,* page 238. Playing the *Credits/Debits Game* offers students practice adding and subtracting positive and negative numbers.

Over and Up Squares See *Student Reference Book,* page 257. Two players need a gameboard and record sheet, 2 different-colored pencils, and 2 six-sided dice to play this game. Playing this game provides practice plotting ordered pairs and developing a winning game strategy.

Polygon Pair-Up See *Student Reference Book,* page 258. To play this game, two players need a deck of polygon cards, a deck of property cards, and paper and pencils for sketching. Playing this game provides students with practice identifying properties of polygons.

STUDY LINK 9·10 | **Unit 10: Family Letter** *cont.*

As You Help Your Child with Homework

As your child brings assignments home, you may want to go over the instructions together, clarifying them as necessary. The answers listed below will guide you through some of the Study Links in this unit.

Study Link 10·2

1.

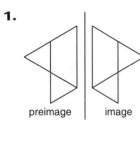

preimage | image

3. preimage

image

5.

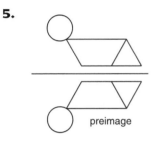

preimage

Study Link 10·3

1. preimage   image

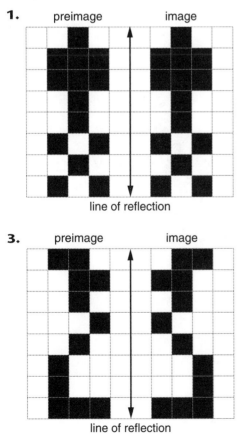

line of reflection

3. preimage   image

line of reflection

Study Link 10·4

2.

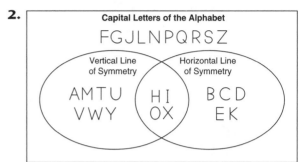

3. Sample answers:

horizontal	vertical
BOX	TAX
KID	YOU
BOOK	MAT
KICK	HIM

Study Link 10·5

1. a. reflection   **b.** translation   **c.** rotation

Study Link 10·6

1. <   **2.** <   **3.** <   **4.** >

5. $-8, -3.4, -\frac{1}{4}, \frac{1}{2}, 1.7, 5$

6. $-43, -3, 0, \frac{14}{7}, 5, 22$

7. Sample answers: $\frac{1}{4}, \frac{1}{2}, \frac{3}{4}, 1$

8. Sample answers: $-2, -1, -\frac{1}{2}, -\frac{1}{4}$

9. a. 13   **b.** -5 **c.** -13

10. a. 8   **b.** -2 **c.** -8

11. a. 15   **b.** 11   **c.** -15

Copyright © Wright Group/McGraw-Hill

303

LESSON 10·1 | Buzz....

Beetrice, the bee, wants to gather pollen from each flower and then return to her hive. Use your transparent mirror to help Beetrice fly around.

LESSON 10·1   **Build a Clown**

Use a transparent mirror to put a hat on the clown's head. When the hat is where you want it, draw the hat. Do the same thing with the other missing parts to complete the clown picture. Then color the picture and cut it out.

STUDY LINK 10·1   A Reflected Image

There is a simple design in the box in the middle of this page. It is the **preimage.**

Hold this page in front of a mirror, with the printed side facing the mirror. On a blank piece of paper, sketch what the design looks like in the mirror—the **image.**

Compare your sketch (image) with the design on the Study Link page (preimage). Bring both the preimage and image to school tomorrow.

Sketch the design as
it looks in the mirror.

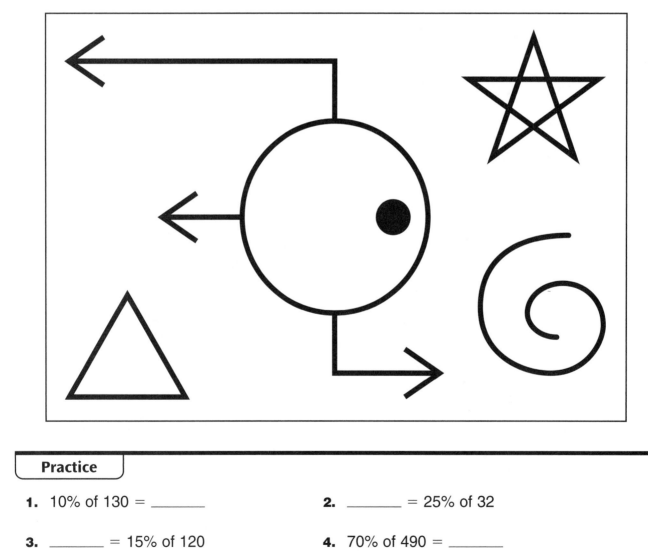

Practice

1. 10% of 130 = _____

2. _____ = 25% of 32

3. _____ = 15% of 120

4. 70% of 490 = _____

Measurement and Geometry 3.4

STUDY LINK 10·2 — Lines of Reflection

For each preimage and image, draw the line of reflection.

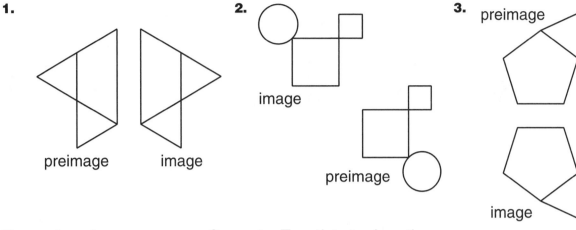

1.

preimage   image

2.

image

preimage

3. preimage

image

For each preimage, use your Geometry Template to draw the image on the other side of the line of reflection.

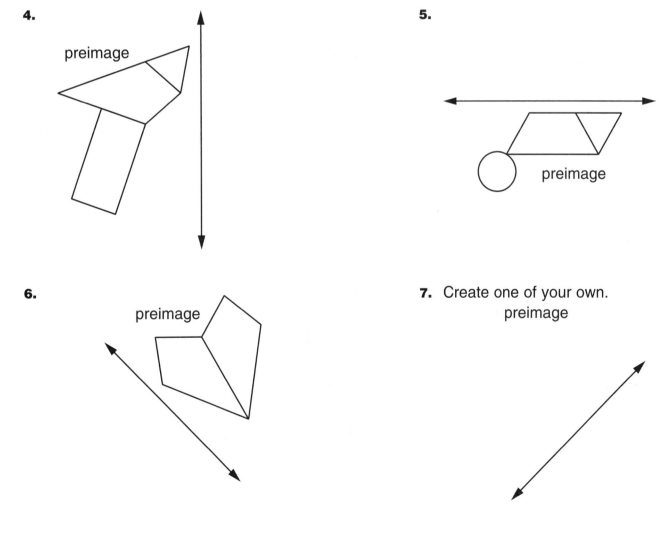

4.

preimage

5.

preimage

6.

preimage

7. Create one of your own.

preimage

LESSON 10·2

Paper-Folding Puzzles

For each design, circle the pieces that could be unfolded to match it.
For some problems, there is more than one correct answer.

The dashed lines represent folds. The pieces in Problems 3 and 4
have been folded two times.

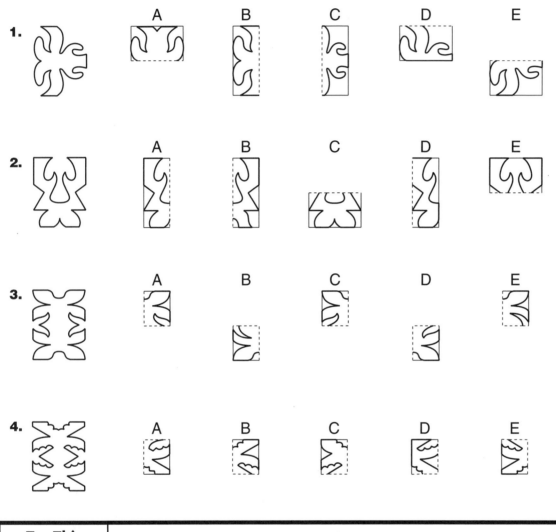

Try This

Match the folded piece to the correct unfolded design. Circle it.

308

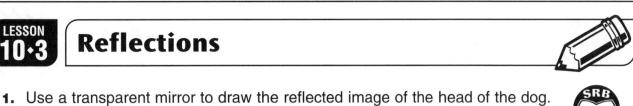

LESSON
10·3 **Reflections**

1. Use a transparent mirror to draw the reflected image of the head of the dog.

SRB
106

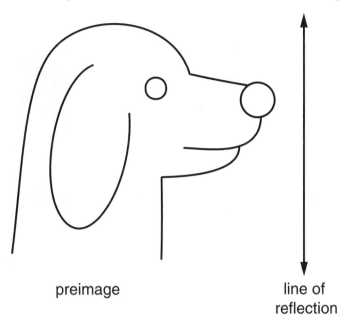

preimage   line of   image
                                reflection

2. On the back of this page, describe how the two drawings in Problem 1
   are alike and how they are different.

3. Draw a picture on the left side of the line. Ask your partner to use
   a transparent mirror to draw the reflected image of your picture.

preimage   line of   image
                                reflection   **309**

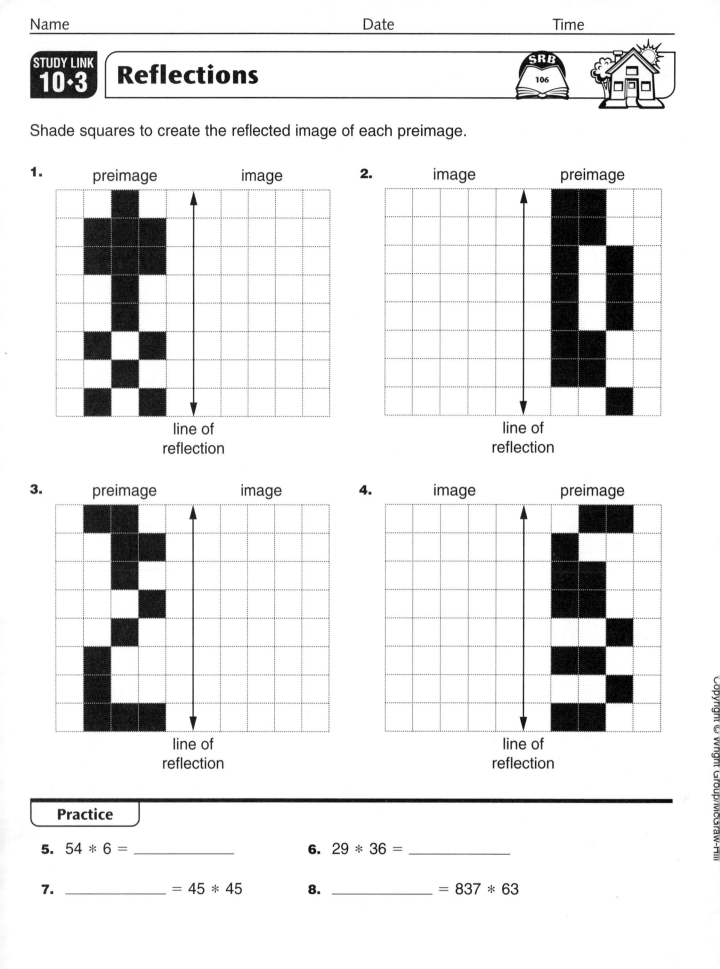

STUDY LINK 10·3 | **Reflections**

Shade squares to create the reflected image of each preimage.

1. preimage — image

line of reflection

2. image — preimage

line of reflection

3. preimage — image

line of reflection

4. image — preimage

line of reflection

Practice

5. $54 * 6 =$ _____

6. $29 * 36 =$ _____

7. _____ $= 45 * 45$

8. _____ $= 837 * 63$

Measurement and Geometry 3.4; Number Sense 3.2

LESSON 10·4 Half-Pictures

311

LESSON 10·4   Symmetric Pictures

SRB 109

LESSON 10·4   **Polygons A–E**

SRB
109

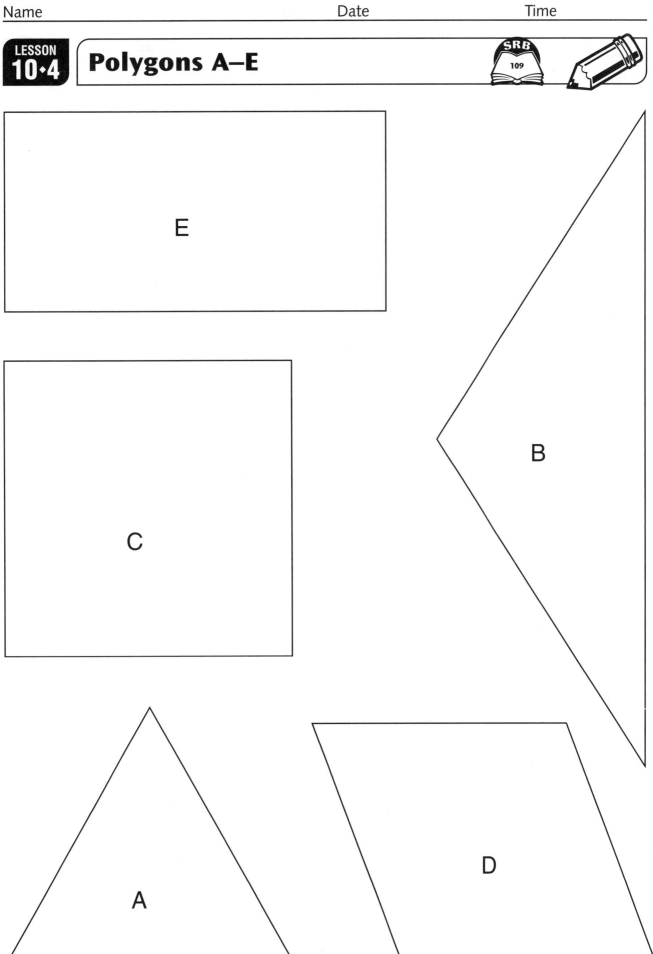

313

LESSON 10·4 **Polygons F–J**

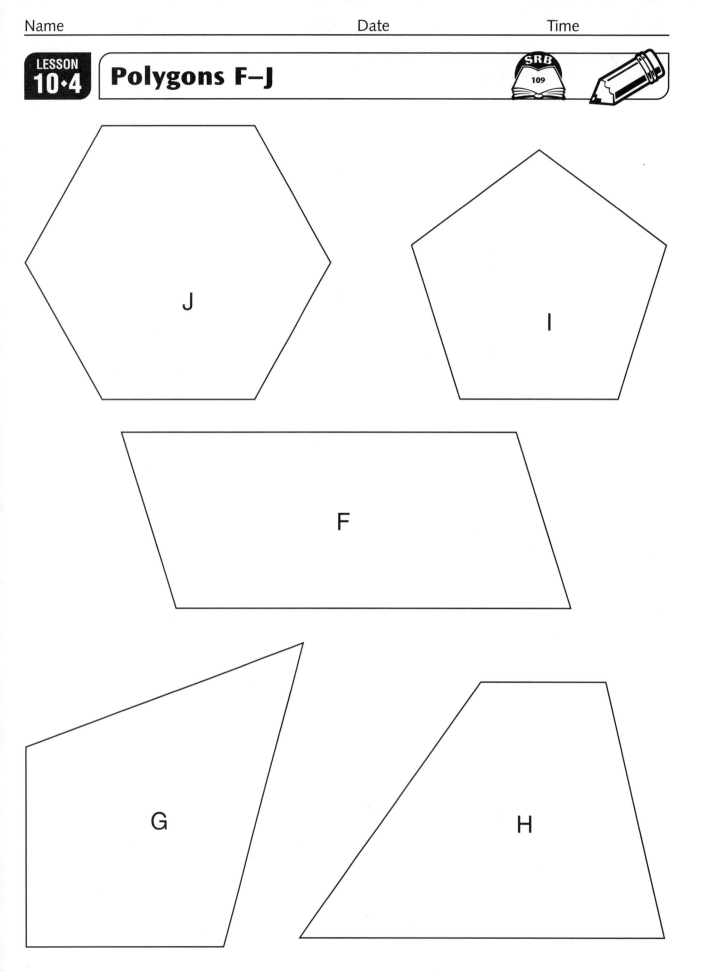

STUDY LINK 10·4 | **Line Symmetry in the Alphabet**

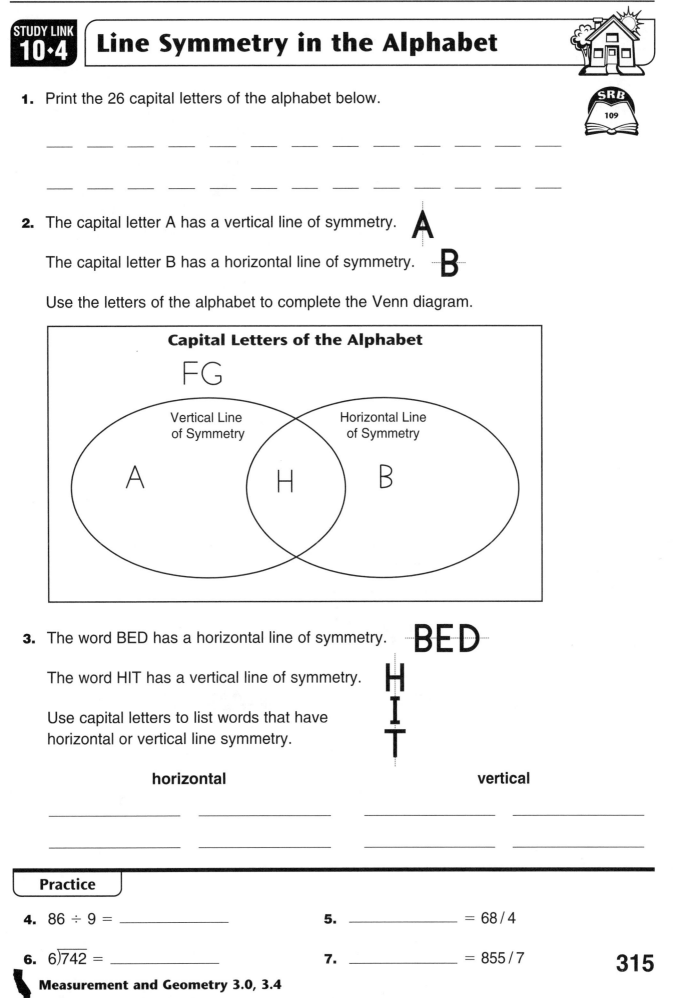

1. Print the 26 capital letters of the alphabet below.

— — — — — — — — — — — — —

— — — — — — — — — — — — —

2. The capital letter A has a vertical line of symmetry. A

The capital letter B has a horizontal line of symmetry. B

Use the letters of the alphabet to complete the Venn diagram.

Capital Letters of the Alphabet

FG

Vertical Line of Symmetry   Horizontal Line of Symmetry

A   H   B

3. The word BED has a horizontal line of symmetry. BED

The word HIT has a vertical line of symmetry. HIT

Use capital letters to list words that have horizontal or vertical line symmetry.

horizontal   **vertical**

_____ _____   _____ _____

_____ _____   _____ _____

Practice

4. $86 \div 9 =$ _____

5. _____ $= 68 / 4$

6. $6\overline{)742} =$ _____

7. _____ $= 855 / 7$

315

Measurement and Geometry 3.0, 3.4

LESSON 10·4   **Interpreting a Cartoon**

1. What answer does Ruthie's brother expect? _____

2. Explain and draw pictures to show why both of Ruthie's answers are correct.

Name   Date   Time

LESSON 10·4   **Interpreting a Cartoon**

1. What answer does Ruthie's brother expect? _____

2. Explain and draw pictures to show why both of Ruthie's answers are correct.

LESSON 10·4 | **Line Symmetry**

SRB
109

Use pattern blocks to create shapes with the given number of lines of symmetry.
Use your Geometry Template to record the shapes and draw the lines of symmetry.

1. 1 yellow hexagon, 2 orange squares
   2 lines of symmetry

2. 1 orange square, 4 green triangles
   0 lines of symmetry

3. 2 red trapezoids
   6 lines of symmetry

4. 5 orange squares
   1 line of symmetry

Try This

5. 5 red trapezoids
   1 line of symmetry
   Show two different ways.

6. On the back of this page, make up a problem of your own. Give it to a partner to solve.

STUDY LINK 10·5 | Geometric Patterns

1. Continue each pattern. Then tell if you continued the pattern by using a reflection, rotation, or translation of the original design.

SRB 106–108

a. _____

b. _____

c. _____

2. Make up your own pattern.

Practice

3. 50% of $25.00 = _____

4. 25% of $10.00 = _____

5. _____ = 40% of $150.00

6. _____ = 20% of $250.00

Measurement and Geometry 3.4

LESSON 10·5   Making Frieze Patterns

1. Use an index card as a template for making frieze patterns.

SRB
108

   a. Trim your index card to make a 3-inch by 3-inch square.

   b. Draw a simple design in the middle of the square.

   c. Cut out your design. If you need to cut through the edge of the index card, then use tape to repair the cut.

2. Make a frieze pattern with your template.

   a. Draw a long line on a large sheet of paper.

   b. Put your template at the left end of the line.

   c. Trace the shape of the design you cut out. Make a mark on the line at the right edge of the template.

   d. Move your template to the right along the line. Line up the left side of the template with the mark you made on the line.

   e. Repeat Steps c and d. To make more complicated patterns, give your template a turn or a flip every time you move it.

319

Name _____ Date _____ Time _____

LESSON 10·6 **Positive and Negative Numbers**

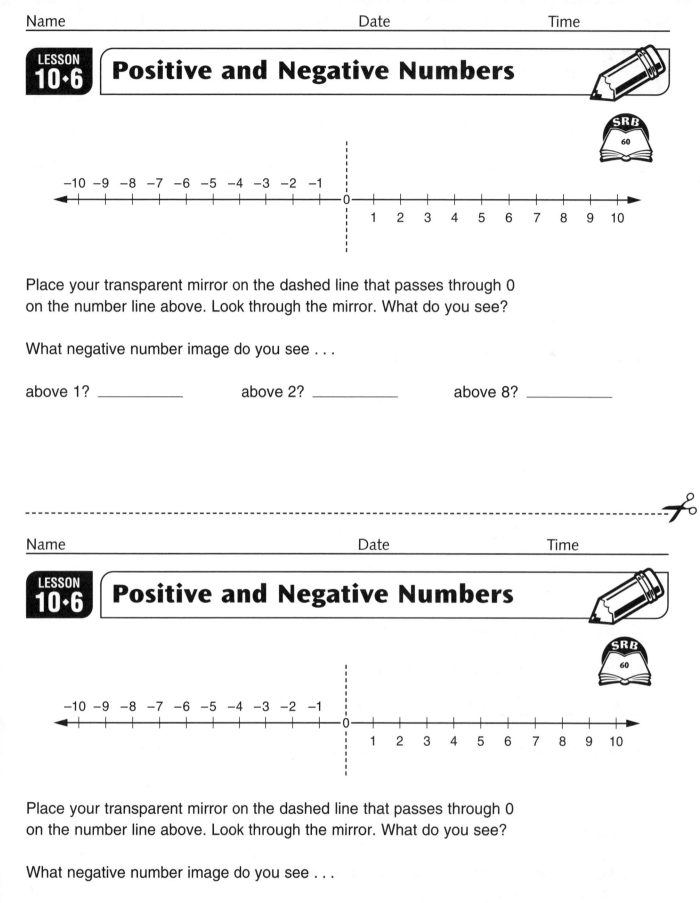

Place your transparent mirror on the dashed line that passes through 0
on the number line above. Look through the mirror. What do you see?

What negative number image do you see . . .

above 1? _____   above 2? _____   above 8? _____

Name _____ Date _____ Time _____

LESSON 10·6 **Positive and Negative Numbers**

Place your transparent mirror on the dashed line that passes through 0
on the number line above. Look through the mirror. What do you see?

What negative number image do you see . . .

above 1? _____   above 2? _____   above 8? _____

320

LESSON 10·6 | Ledger

Transaction	Start	Change	End/Start of Next Transaction

```
  -10 -9  -8  -7  -6  -5  -4  -3  -2  -1    0    1   2   3   4   5   6   7   8   9  10
◄──┼───┼───┼───┼───┼───┼───┼───┼───┼───┼────┼────┼───┼───┼───┼───┼───┼───┼───┼───┼──►
```

STUDY LINK 10·6 | **Positive and Negative Numbers**

SRB 60

Write < or > to make a true number sentence.

1. 3 _____ 14   **2.** −7 _____ 7   **3.** 19 _____ 20   **4.** −8 _____ −10

List the numbers in order from least to greatest.

5. 5, −8, $\frac{1}{2}$, −$\frac{1}{4}$, 1.7, −3.4

_____ _____ _____ _____ _____ _____

least   **greatest**

6. −43, 22, $\frac{14}{7}$, 5, −3, 0

_____ _____ _____ _____ _____ _____

least   **greatest**

7. Name four positive numbers
less than 2.   _____ _____ _____ _____

8. Name four negative numbers
greater than −3.   _____ _____ _____ _____

Use the number line to help you solve Problems 9–11.

-15 -14 -13 -12 -11 -10 -9 -8 -7 -6 -5 -4 -3 -2 -1 0 1 2 3 4 5 6 7 8 9 10 11 12 13 14 15

9. a. 4 + 9 = _____   **b.** 4 + (−9) = _____   **c.** (−4) + (−9) = _____

10. a. 5 + 3 = _____   **b.** (−5) + 3 = _____   **c.** (−5) + (−3) = _____

11. a. _____ = 2 + 13   **b.** _____ = (−2) + 13   **c.** _____ = (−2) + (−13)

Practice

12. 1.02 + 12.88 = _____   **13.** 7.26 − 1.94 = _____

14. _____ + 5.84 = 8.75   **15.** 3.38 − _____ = 2.62

Number Sense 1.8

STUDY LINK
10·7

Unit 11: Family Letter

3-D Shapes, Weight, Volume, and Capacity

Our next unit introduces several new topics, as well as reviewing some of the work with geometric solids from previous grades and some of the main ideas your child has been studying this past year.

We begin with a lesson on weight, focusing on grams and ounces. Students handle and weigh a variety of objects, trying to develop "weight sense" so that they can estimate weights effectively. The class participates in creating a Gram & Ounce Museum by displaying everyday objects labeled with their weights.

As part of a review of the properties of 3-dimensional shapes (prisms, pyramids, cylinders, and cones), your child will construct models of geometric solids using straws and paper patterns. They will use these models as they discuss vocabulary such as *face, edge,* and *vertex* and compare features of geometric solids.

By experimenting with cubes, the class will develop and apply a formula for finding the volumes of rectangular prisms (solids that look like boxes).

We will consider familiar units of capacity (cups, pints, quarts, gallons) and the relationships among them.

Your child will also explore subtraction of positive and negative numbers by playing a variation of the *Credits/Debits Game* introduced in Unit 10.

1 kg   1,000 g

In Lesson 11-1, a pan balance is used to measure weight in grams.

Please keep this Family Letter for reference as your child works through Unit 11.

323

Vocabulary

Important terms in Unit 11:

capacity (1) The amount of space occupied by a 3-dimensional shape. Same as *volume*. (2) Less formally, the amount a container can hold. Capacity is often measured in units such as quarts, gallons, cups, or liters. (3) The maximum *weight* a scale can measure.

cone A 3-dimensional shape that has a circular base, a *curved surface,* and one vertex, which is called the apex. The points on the curved surface of a cone are on straight lines connecting the apex and the circumference of the base.

cubic unit A unit used in measuring *volume,* such as a cubic centimeter or a cubic foot.

curved surface A 2-dimensional surface that is rounded rather than flat. Spheres, *cylinders,* and *cones* each have one curved surface.

cylinder A 3-dimensional shape that has two circular or elliptical bases that are parallel and congruent and are connected by a *curved surface.* A can is shaped like a cylinder.

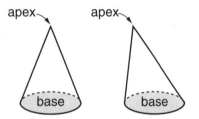

dimension A measure along one direction of an object, typically length, width, or height. For example, the dimensions of a box might be 24 cm by 20 cm by 10 cm.

formula A general rule for finding the value of something. A formula is often written using letters, called variables, that stand for the quantities involved.

geometric solid The surface or surfaces that make up a 3-dimensional shape, such as a *prism, cylinder, cone,* or sphere. Despite its name, a geometric solid is hollow; it does not contain the points in its interior.

prism A 3-dimensional shape with two parallel and congruent polygonal regions for bases and lateral faces formed by all the line segments with endpoints on corresponding edges of the bases. The lateral faces are all parallelograms.

triangular prism   rectangular prism   hexagonal prism

pyramid A 3-dimensional shape with a polygonal region for a base, a point (apex) not in the plane of the base, and all of the line segments with one endpoint at the apex and the other on an edge of the base. All faces except the base are triangular.

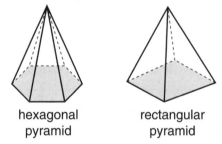

hexagonal pyramid   rectangular pyramid

3-dimensional (3-D) shape A shape whose points are not all in a single plane. Examples include *prisms, pyramids,* and spheres, all of which have length, width, and height.

volume The amount of space occupied by a 3-dimensional shape. Same as *capacity.* The amount a container can hold. Volume is often measured in cubic units, such as cm³, cubic inches, or cubic feet.

weight A measure of the force of gravity on an object. Weight is measured in metric units such as grams, kilograms, and milligrams and in U.S. customary units such as pounds and ounces.

Do-Anytime Activities

To work with your child on the concepts taught in this unit, try these interesting and rewarding activities:

1. Have your child compile a list of the world's heaviest objects or things. For example, which animal has the heaviest baby? What is the world's heaviest human-made structure? What is the greatest amount of weight ever hoisted by a person?

2. Have your child compile a portfolio of 3-dimensional shapes. Images can be taken from newspapers, magazines, photographs, and so on.

3. Encourage your child to create his or her own mnemonics and/or sayings for converting between units of capacity and weight. One such example is the old English saying "A pint's a pound the world around." (1 pint = 16 oz = 1 lb)

Building Skills through Games

In Unit 11, your child will play the following games. For detailed instructions, see the *Student Reference Book.*

Chances Are See *Student Reference Book,* page 236.
This game is for 2 players and requires one deck of *Chances Are* Event Cards and one deck of *Chances Are* Probability Cards. The game develops skill in using probability terms to describe the likelihood of events.

Credits/Debits Game See *Student Reference Book,* page 238.
This is a game for 2 players. Game materials include 1 complete deck of number cards and a recording sheet. The *Credits/Debits Game* helps students practice addition of positive and negative integers.

Credits/Debits Game (**Advanced Version**) See *Student Reference Book,* page 239.
This game is similar to the *Credits/Debits Game* and helps students practice addition and subtraction of positive and negative integers.

As You Help Your Child with Homework

As your child brings assignments home, you may want to go over the instructions together, clarifying them as necessary. The answers listed below will guide you through this unit's Study Links.

Study Link 11·1

1. 59   2. 96,640

3. Bagel and pumpkin; or taco and gingerbread man

4. Pasta, Chocolate bar, Hamburger, Ice cream sundae

6. −$50   7. −$75   8. $0

9. $30

Study Link 11·2

1. a. square pyramid   b. cone

   c. sphere   d. cylinder

   e. rectangular prism f. triangular prism

2.

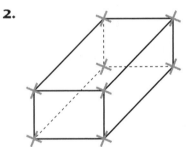

3. 6   4. 7,000; 63,560; and 91

5. 24; 120; 600

Study Link 11·3

1. cone   2. square pyramid

3. hexagonal prism   4. octahedron

6. $10   7. −$70

8. −$15   9. −$100

10. −$55   11. −$400

Study Link 11·4

4. 24   5. 17 R1, or $17\frac{1}{5}$

6. 29   7. 89 R2, or $89\frac{2}{4}$

Study Link 11·5

1. a. 39   b. 30

2. a. (3 * 3) * 6 = 54; 54

   b. (2 * 5) * 9.7 = 97; 97

3. a. 150   b. 150

4. −49   5. −40   6. 29   7. 73

Study Link 11·6

1. −110   2. −8   3. −8

4. 15   5. 14   6. −19

7. −70   8. 18

11. <   12. <   13. >

14. >   15. >   16. >

17. −14, −2.5, −0.7, $\frac{30}{6}$, 5.6, 8

18. −7, −$\frac{24}{6}$, −$\frac{3}{5}$, 0.02, 0.46, 4

19. 2,652   20. 44,114   21. 158

22. 106 R4, or $106\frac{4}{7}$

Study Link 11·7

Answers vary for Problems 1–4.

5. 4   6. 48   7. 2

8. 3   9. 3   10. 10

11. 4   12. −4   13. −40

14. −120

326

STUDY LINK 11·1 The World's Largest Foods

Food	Weight	Date	Location
Apple	3 pounds 11 ounces	October 1997	Linton, England
Bagel	714 pounds	July 1998	Mattoon, Illinois
Bowl of pasta	7,355 pounds	February 2004	Hartford, New York
Chocolate bar	5,026 pounds	March 2000	Turin, Italy
Garlic	2 pounds 10 ounces	1985	Eureka, California
Gingerbread man	372.13 pounds	November 2003	Vancouver, Canada
Hamburger	6,040 pounds	September 1999	Sac, Montana
Ice cream sundae	22.59 tons	July 1988	Alberta, Canada
Pumpkin	1,337 pounds	October 2002	Topsfield, Massachusetts
Taco	1,654 pounds	March 2003	Mexicali, Mexico

Source: www.guinnessworldrecords.com

Use the information in the table to solve the following problems.

1. The largest apple weighed _____ ounces.

2. A typical hamburger weighs about 4 ounces. The largest hamburger weighed

   _____ ounces.

3. Which 2 foods together weigh about a ton? _____ and

   _____

4. A kilogram is a little more than 2 pounds. Which 4 foods each weigh more than 1,000 kilograms?

   _____

5. On the back of this page, use data from the table to write and solve your own problem.

Practice

6. −$75 + $25 = _____

7. _____ = −$45 + (−$30)

8. _____ = −$60 + $60

9. $55 + (−$25) = _____

327

Statistics, Data Analysis, and Probability 1.0

STUDY LINK
11·2

Solids

1. The pictures below show objects that are shaped approximately like geometric solids. Identify each object as one of the following: **cylinder, cone, sphere, triangular prism, square pyramid,** or **rectangular prism.**

SRB
101 102

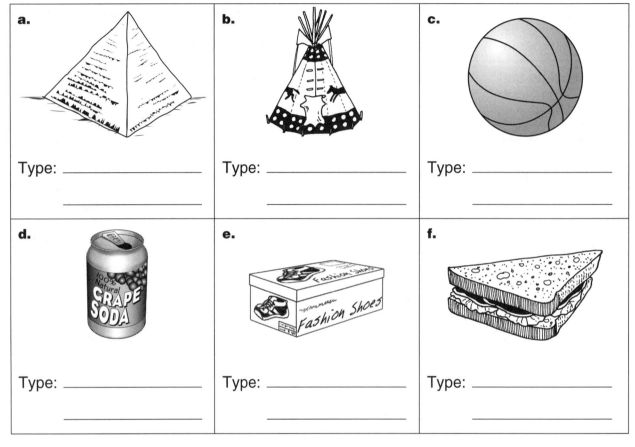

a.	b.	c.
Type: _____	Type: _____	Type: _____
_____	_____	_____

d.	e.	f.
Type: _____	Type: _____	Type: _____
_____	_____	_____

2. Mark *X*s on the vertices of the rectangular prism.

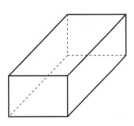

3. How many edges does the tetrahedron have? _____ edges

___

Practice

4. Circle the numbers that are multiples of 7.   132   7,000   63   560   834   91

5. Circle the numbers that are multiples of 12.   24   120   38   600   100   75

Measurement and Geometry 3.0; Measurement and Geometry 3.6

Geometry Riddles

Answer the following riddles.

SRB
101–103

1. I am a geometric solid.
I have two surfaces.
One of my surfaces is formed by a circle.
The other surface is curved.

What am I? _____

2. I am a geometric solid.
I have one square base.
I have four triangular faces.
Some Egyptian pharaohs were buried
in tombs shaped like me.

What am I? _____

3. I am a polyhedron.
I am a prism.
My two bases are hexagons.
My other faces are rectangles.

What am I? _____

4. I am a polyhedron.
All of my faces are the same.
All of my faces are equilateral triangles.
I have eight faces.

What am I? _____

Try This

5. Write your own geometry riddle.

_____

_____

_____

_____

_____

_____

_____

Practice

6. −$20 + $30 = _____

7. _____ = −$35 + (−$35)

8. _____ = $10 + (−$25)

9. $0 + (−$100) = _____

10. −$15 + (−$40) = _____

11. _____ = −$300 + (−$100)

Volume

Cut out the pattern below and tape it together to form an open box.

SRB
137 138

1. Find and record two items in your home that have volumes equal to about $\frac{1}{2}$ of the volume of the open box.

   _____   _____

2. Find and record two items in your home that have about the same volume as the open box.

   _____   _____

3. Find and record two items in your home that have volumes equal to about 2 times the volume of the open box.

   _____   _____

Practice

4. $96 \div 4 =$ _____

5. $86 / 5 =$ _____

6. $\frac{232}{8} =$ _____

7. $4\overline{)358} =$ _____

TAB   TAB

TAB   TAB

Measurement and Geometry 3.6; Number Sense 3.2

Name _____ Date _____ Time _____

STUDY LINK 11·5 · Volume

1. Find the volume of each stack of centimeter cubes.

a.

Volume = _____ cm³

b.

Volume = _____ cm³

2. Calculate the volume of each rectangular prism.

a.

6 cm
3 cm
3 cm

Number model: _____

Volume = _____ cm³

b.

2 cm
5 cm
9.7 cm

Number model: _____

Volume = _____ cm³

3. What is the total number of cubes needed to completely fill each box?

a.

_____ cubes

b.

_____ cubes

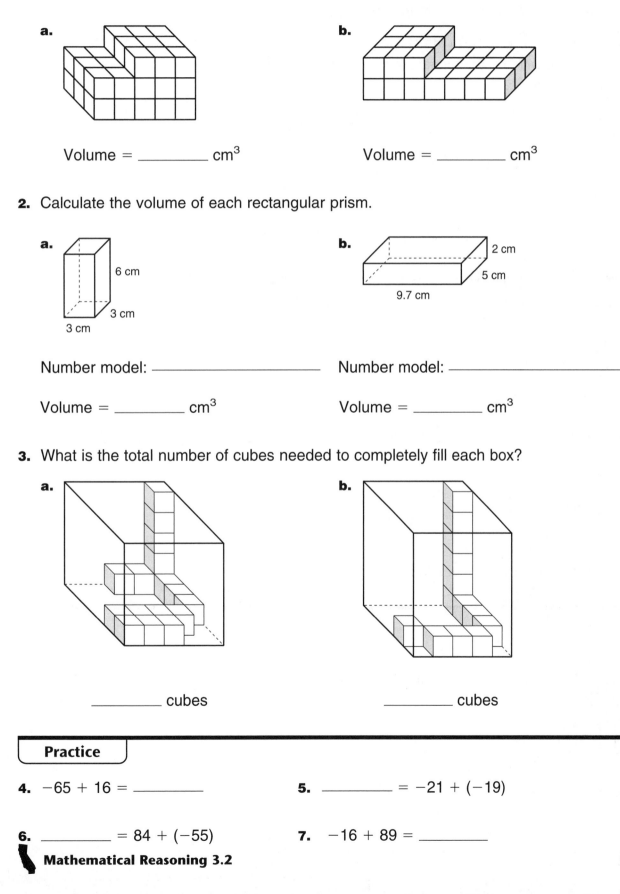

Practice

4. −65 + 16 = _____

5. _____ = −21 + (−19)

6. _____ = 84 + (−55)

7. −16 + 89 = _____

Mathematical Reasoning 3.2   **331**

LESSON 11·5 | Hidden Cubes

1. The stacks of cubes shown below are called *soma cubes* and were first designed in 1936 by Piet Hein, a Danish poet and scientist.

Use interlocking cubes to build the stacks shown below. Use a small stick-on note to label each stack with the appropriate letter. Then record the number of cubes needed to build each stack.

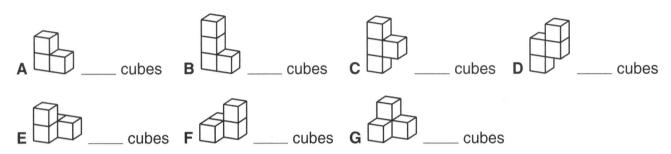

A _____ cubes B _____ cubes C _____ cubes D _____ cubes

E _____ cubes F _____ cubes G _____ cubes

Use the cube stacks that you made above to build each of the figures below. The figures do not have any hidden holes. Record the number of cubes needed to build each figure and the cube stacks that you used.

2. _____ cubes

I used the following cube stacks to build the figure: _____

3. _____ cubes

I used the following cube stacks to build the figure: _____

Try This

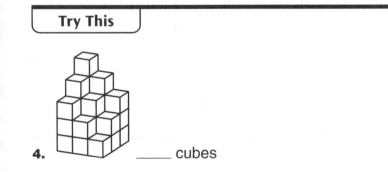

4. _____ cubes

I used the following cube stacks to build the figure: _____

STUDY LINK 11·6

Positive and Negative Numbers

SRB
6 60

Add or subtract.

1. $-40 + (-70) = $ _____

2. $12 - 20 = $ _____

3. _____ $= -14 - (-6)$

4. _____ $= 10 - (-5)$

5. $15 + (-1) = $ _____

6. $-12 - 7 = $ _____

7. _____ $= 60 + (-130)$

8. _____ $= -2 - (-20)$

9. Write two subtraction problems with an answer of -8.

_____ $-$ _____ $= -8$ _____ $-$ _____ $= -8$

10. Write two addition problems with an answer of -30.

_____ $+$ _____ $= -30$ _____ $+$ _____ $= -30$

Write $<$ or $>$ to make a true number sentence.

11. $0 - 7$ _____ -6

12. -11 _____ $-13 - (-5)$

13. $7 + (-2)$ _____ -8

14. $18 + (-8)$ _____ -18

15. $26 - (-14)$ _____ $27 + (-16)$

16. $9 - (-11)$ _____ $0 + (-20)$

List the numbers in order from least to greatest.

17. $\frac{30}{6}$, 8, -14, -0.7, 5.6, -2.5

_____ _____ _____ _____ _____ _____

least   greatest

18. 0.02, $-\frac{3}{5}$, -7, 4, 0.46, $-\frac{24}{6}$

_____ _____ _____ _____ _____ _____

least   greatest

Practice

19. _____ $= 34 * 78$

20. _____ $= 46 * 959$

21. $632 \div 4 = $ _____

22. $746 / 7 = $ _____

Number Sense 1.8; Number Sense 3.2

333

STUDY LINK
11·7 | **Capacity**

Find at least one container that holds each of the amounts listed below.
Describe each container and record all the capacity measurements on the label.

SRB
137

1. Less than 1 Pint

Container	Capacity Measurements on Label
bottle of hot chili sesame oil	5 fl oz, 148 mL

2. 1 Pint

Container	Capacity Measurements on Label
bottle of cooking oil	16 fl oz, 473 mL

3. 1 Quart

Container	Capacity Measurements on Label

4. More than 1 Quart

Container	Capacity Measurements on Label

Complete.

5. 2 quarts = _____ pints

6. 3 gallons = _____ cups

7. _____ pints = 4 cups

8. _____ quarts = 12 cups

9. 6 pints = _____ quarts

10. _____ quarts = $2\frac{1}{2}$ gallons

Practice

11. $-3 + 7 =$ _____

12. _____ $= 3 + (-7)$

13. _____ $= 40 + (-80)$

14. $-60 + (-60) =$ _____

334

STUDY LINK 11·8

Unit 12: Family Letter

Rates

For the next two or three weeks, your child will be studying rates. Rates are among the most common applications of mathematics in daily life.

A rate is a comparison involving two different units. Familiar examples come from working (dollars per hour), driving (miles per hour), eating (calories per serving), reading (pages per day), and so on.

Our exploration of rates will begin with students collecting data on the rate at which their classmates blink their eyes. The class will try to answer the question "Does a person's eye-blinking rate depend on what the person is doing?"

During this unit, students will collect many examples of rates and might display them in a Rates All Around Museum. Then they will use these examples to make up rate problems, such as the following:

1. If cereal costs $2.98 per box, how much will 4 boxes cost?

2. If a car's gas mileage is about 20 miles per gallon, how far can the car travel on a full tank of gas (16 gallons)?

3. If I make $6.25 per hour, how long must I work to earn enough to buy shoes that cost $35?

Then the class will work together to develop strategies for solving rate problems.

The unit emphasizes the importance of mathematics to educated consumers. Your child will learn about unit-pricing labels on supermarket shelves and how to use these labels to decide which of two items is the better buy. Your child will see that comparing prices is only *part* of being an educated consumer. Other factors to consider include quality, the need for the product, and, perhaps, the product's effect on the environment.

This unit provides a great opportunity for your child to help with the family shopping. Have your child help you decide whether the largest size is really the best buy. Is an item that is on sale necessarily a better buy than a similar product that is not on sale?

Nutrition Facts
Serving Size 1 link (45 g)
Servings per Container 10
Amount per Serving
Calories 150   Calories from Fat 120
% Daily Value
Total Fat 13 g   20%
Total Carbohydrate 1 g   <1%
Protein 7 g

Finally, students will look back on their experiences in the yearlong World Tour project and 50-facts test routine and share them with one another.

Please keep this Family Letter for reference as your child works through Unit 12.

Vocabulary

Important terms in Unit 12:

comparison shopping Comparing prices and collecting other information needed to make good decisions about which of several competing products or services to buy.

consumer A person who acquires products or uses services.

per *For each,* as in ten chairs per row or six tickets per family.

rate A comparison by division of two quantities with different units. For example, a speed such as 55 miles per hour is a rate that compares distance with time.

rate table A way of displaying *rate* information as in the miles per gallon table below.

Miles	35	70	105	140	175	210
Gallons	1	2	3	4	5	6

unit price The price *per* item or unit of measure. For example, if a 5-ounce package of something costs $2.50, then $0.50 per ounce is the unit price.

unit rate A *rate* with 1 in the denominator. For example, 600 calories per 3 servings or $\frac{600 \text{ calories}}{3 \text{ servings}}$ is not a unit rate, but 200 calories per serving $\left(\frac{200 \text{ calories}}{1 \text{ serving}}\right)$ is a unit rate.

Do-Anytime Activities

To work with your child on concepts taught in this unit, try these interesting and rewarding activities:

1. Have your child examine the Nutrition Facts labels on various cans and packages of food. The labels list the number of servings in the container and the number of calories per serving. Have your child use this information to calculate the total number of calories in the full container or package. *For example:*

   A can of soup has 2.5 servings.
   There are 80 calories per serving.
   So the full can has 2.5 ∗ 80 = 200 calories.

2. Have your child point out rates in everyday situations. *For example:*

   store price rates: cost per dozen, cost per 6-pack, cost per ounce
   rent payments: dollars per month or dollars per year
   fuel efficiency: miles per gallon
   wages: dollars per hour
   sleep: hours per night
   telephone rates: cents per minute
   copy machine rates: copies per minute

3. Use supermarket visits to compare prices for different brands of an item and for different sizes of the same item. Have your child calculate unit prices and discuss best buys.

Building Skills through Games

In this unit, your child will play the following games. For more detailed instructions, see the *Student Reference Book.*

Credits/Debits Game **(Advanced Version)** See *Student Reference Book,* page 239.
This game for 2 players simulates bookkeeping for a small business. A deck of number cards represents "credits" and "debits." Transactions are entered by the players on recording sheets. The game offers practice in addition and subtraction of positive and negative integers.

Fraction Top-It See *Student Reference Book,* page 247.
This game is for 2 to 4 players and requires one set of 32 Fraction Cards.
The game develops skills in comparing fractions.

Name That Number See *Student Reference Book,* page 254.
This game is for 2 or 3 players and requires 1 complete deck of number cards.
The game develops skills in representing numbers in different ways.

As You Help Your Child with Homework

As your child brings assignments home, you may want to go over the instructions together, clarifying them as necessary. The answers listed below will guide you through this unit's Study Links.

Study Link 12·1

2. $\frac{3}{5}$ **3.** $\frac{1}{8}$

4. 1 **5.** $\frac{5}{6}$

Study Link 12·2

1. $315

2. $12

3. 14 hours

4. a. 364 minutes per week

 b. 156 minutes

5. 9,096 **6.** 54,810

7. 81 R4 **8.** 13

Study Link 12·3

1. 2,100 feet

2. a. 3,500 pounds

 b. 420 gallons

3. 25 feet per second

4. a. 375 gallons

 b. 1,500 quarts

5. a. 480 feet

 b. 754 minutes, or $12\frac{1}{2}$ hours

6. 1,593 **7.** 55,080

8. 180 R4 **9.** 67

Study Link 12·4

1. 8 cents

2. $0.69

3. $0.35

4. Answers vary.

5. 1, 12; 2, 6; 3, 4

6. 1, 50; 2, 25; 5, 10

Study Link 12·5

1. $0.63

2. $0.37

3. $0.15

4. $0.35

5. $1.02

6. Sample answer: The 8-ounce cup is the better buy. The 8-ounce cup costs 9 cents per ounce, and the 6-ounce cup costs 10 cents per ounce.

7. Answers vary.

8. 1, 2, 3, 6, 7, 14, 21, 42

9. 1, 23

Study Link 12·6

1. 1,245 miles

2. About 9 times

3. a. About 69%

 b. About 49%

4. $\frac{8}{54}$, or $\frac{4}{27}$

5. a. China

 b. 6

 c. 9

 d. $9\frac{1}{2}$

STUDY LINK 12·1 | **Examples of Rates**

1. Look for examples of rates in newspapers, in magazines, and on labels.

    Study the two examples below, and then list some of the examples you find.
    If possible, bring your samples to class.

Example: *Label on a can of corn says "Servings Per Container $3\frac{1}{2}$"*

Nutrition Facts
Serving Size 110 g
Servings Per Container 3 1/2
Amount Per Serving

Example: *Lightbulbs come in packages of 4 bulbs. The package doesn't say so, but there are always 4 bulbs in each package.*

Example: _____

_____

_____

_____

Example: _____

_____

_____

_____

Example: _____

_____

_____

_____

Practice

2. $\frac{4}{5} - \frac{1}{5} =$ _____

3. _____ $= \frac{7}{8} - \frac{3}{4}$

4. _____ $= \frac{1}{9} + \frac{8}{9}$

5. $\frac{1}{3} + \frac{3}{6} =$ _____

LESSON 12·1 | **Median and Mean**

Anthony's first 4 test scores for his weekly 20-word spelling tests were 80%, 90%, 100%, and 75%.

1. What is Anthony's *median* score? _____%

2. What score must Anthony get on his next test to maintain his median score? _____% Explain your answer.

_____

_____

3. Anthony would like to raise his *mean* score to 90% or higher. If he takes one more spelling test, can he do it? _____ Explain your answer.

_____

_____

✂ -

Name _____ Date _____ Time _____

LESSON 12·1 | **Median and Mean**

Anthony's first 4 test scores for his weekly 20-word spelling tests were 80%, 90%, 100%, and 75%.

1. What is Anthony's *median* score? _____%

2. What score must Anthony get on his next test to maintain his median score? _____% Explain your answer.

_____

_____

3. Anthony would like to raise his *mean* score to 90% or higher. If he takes one more spelling test, can he do it? _____ Explain your answer.

_____

STUDY LINK
12·2 Rates

SRB
175 176

Solve the problems.

1. Hotels R Us charges $45 per night for a single room.
   At that rate, how much does a single room cost *per week*? $_____

2. The Morales family spends about $84 each week for
   food. On average, how much do they spend *per day*? $_____

3. Sharon practices playing the piano the same amount
   of time each day. She practiced a total of 4 hours
   on Monday and Tuesday combined. At that rate,
   how many hours would she practice *in a week*?   _____ hours

Hours							
Days	1	2	3	4	5	6	7

Try This

4. People in the United States spend an average of 6 hours and 4 minutes
   each week reading newspapers.

   a. That's how many minutes *per week*?   _____ minutes per week

   b. At that rate, how much time does an average
      person spend reading newspapers in a *3-day period*?   _____ minutes

Minutes							
Days	1	2	3	4	5	6	7

Practice

5. _____ = 24 * 379   6. 870 * 63 = _____

7. 652 ÷ 8 = _____   8. 546 ÷ 42 = _____

STUDY LINK 12·3

Mammal Rates

SRB
47

1. A mole can dig a tunnel 300 feet long in one night.
   How far could a mole dig in one week?   About _____ feet

2. An elephant may eat 500 pounds of hay and drink
   60 gallons of water in one day.

   a. About how many pounds of hay could an
      elephant eat per week?   About _____ pounds

   b. About how many gallons of water could an
      elephant drink per week?   About _____ gallons

3. The bottle-nosed whale can dive to a depth
   of 3,000 feet in 2 minutes. About how many
   feet is that per second?   About _____ feet per second

4. A good milking cow will give up to 1,500 gallons of milk in a year.

   a. About how many gallons is that in 3 months?   About _____ gallons

   b. About how many *quarts* is that in 3 months?   About _____ quarts

---

Try This

5. Sloths spend up to 80 percent of their lives sleeping. Not only is a sloth extremely
   sleepy, but it is also very slow. A sloth travels on the ground at a speed of about
   7 feet per minute. In the trees, its speed is about 15 feet per minute.

   a. After one hour, how much farther would a sloth have
      traveled in the trees than on the ground (if it didn't
      stop to sleep)?   About _____ feet

   b. About how long would it take a sloth to travel 1 mile
      on the ground? (*Hint:* There are 5,280 feet in a mile.)   About _____ minutes,

                                                        or _____ hours

---

Practice

6. $59 * 27 =$ _____   7. _____ $= 648 * 85$

8. $904 \div 5 =$ _____   9. _____ $= 536 / 8$

Mathematical Reasoning 1.1; Number Sense 3.3; Number Sense 3.4

LESSON 12·3 | **Mammal 100-Yard Dash**

It could not happen, of course, but suppose that you, an elephant, and a cheetah were to race a distance of 100 yards, or 300 feet. Which of you would win? Which would come in second? Third?

1. My Prediction: First _____ Second _____ Third _____

2. On the diagram below, show the winner crossing the finish line. Estimate where you think the second-place and third-place mammals would be when the fastest mammal wins. Write "C" for the cheetah, "E" for the elephant, and "Me" for yourself.

| 0 | 30 | 60 | 90 | 120 | 150 | 180 | 210 | 240 | 270 | 300 feet |

Start   Finish

3. What information would help you predict the winner?

_____

_____

4. Complete the table below by using the "last race results" to find each mammal's top sprint speed in feet per second.

Mammal	Last Race Results	Top Sprint Speed (approximate)
Fourth Grader	84 yards in 12 seconds	_____ ft/sec
Cheetah	2,448 inches in 2 seconds	_____ ft/sec
Elephant	36 yards in 3 seconds	_____ ft/sec

343

LESSON 12·3 | **Mammal 100-Yard Dash** *continued*

5. According to the ft/sec rates, how would the 300-foot race among an elephant, a cheetah, and a fourth grader turn out?

First _____ Second _____ Third _____

6. About how long would it take for the winner of the race to run 300 feet?   About _____ seconds

7. By the time the winner crosses the finish line, how far would the other mammals have run?

Second-place mammal   About _____ feet

Third-place mammal   About _____ feet

8. Would it be a close race?   _____

9. On the diagram below, show which mammal will win the race and where the other two mammals will be when the winner crosses the finish line.

| | | | | | | | | | | |
0   30   60   90   120   150   180   210   240   270   300
                                                                    feet
Start   Finish

10. About how many times faster is the first-place mammal than

a. the second-place mammal?   _____

b. the third-place mammal?   _____

11. The top sprint speed for a squirrel is 18 feet per second. Does this mean that you could catch a squirrel by running after it? Explain.

_____

_____

_____

344

STUDY LINK 12·4 | Unit Prices

Solve the unit price problems below. Complete the tables if it is helpful to do so.

SRB
47

1. A 12-oz bag of pretzels costs 96 cents. The unit price is _____ per ounce.

Dollars				0.96
Ounces	1	3	9	12

2. A package of 3 rolls of paper towels costs $2.07. The unit price is _____ per roll.

Dollars			2.07
Rolls	1	2	3

3. A 4-liter bottle of water costs $1.40. The unit price is _____ per liter.

Dollars				1.40
Liters	1	2	3	4

4. Choose 4 items from newspaper ads. In the table below, record the name, price, and quantity of each item. Leave the Unit Price column blank.

Item	Quantity	Price	Unit Price
Golden Sun Raisins	24 ounces	$2.99	

Practice

Name the factor pairs for each number.

5. 12 _____   **6.** 50 _____

Number Sense 3.3; Number Sense 3.4; Mathematical Reasoning 1.1

345

LESSON 12·4 Stock-Up Sale

Party Town is having a summer stock-up sale. The ad below shows the original price of each item and the sale price if you buy a certain number of items. Use bills and coins to help you find the stock-up price per item.

1.
Party Music CDs

$8.00 each

Stock-Up Price: Buy 5 for $25.00.

You pay _$5.00_ per CD.

2.
String in a Can

$3.00 each

Stock-Up Price: Buy 8 for $16.00.

You pay _____ per can.

3.
Mylar Balloon

$1.99 each

Stock-Up Price: Buy 12 for $14.40.

You pay _____ per balloon.

4.
Piñata

$14.99 each

Stock-Up Price: Buy 3 for $29.97.

You pay _____ per piñata.

5.
Glow bracelets

$2.50 each

Stock-Up Price: Buy 6 for $10.50.

You pay _____ per bracelet.

6.
Party Hats

$9.99 for a package of 45

Stock-Up Price: Buy 4 packages for $19.96.

You pay _____ per package.

STUDY LINK 12·5 **Unit Pricing**

1. A package of 3 muffins costs $1.89.
   What is the price *per muffin?* _____

2. A 5-pound bag of rice costs $1.85.
   What is the price *per pound?* _____

3. Chewy worms are sold at $2.40 per pound.
   What is the price *per ounce?* _____

4. A 6-pack of bagels costs $2.11.
   What is the price *per bagel?* _____

5. A 2-pound bag of frozen corn costs $2.03.
   What is the price *per pound?* _____

6. A store sells yogurt in two sizes: The 8-ounce cup costs 72 cents, and the 6-ounce cup costs 60 cents. Which is the better buy? Explain your answer.

   _____

   _____

   _____

   _____

7. Make up your own "better buy" problem. Then solve it.

   _____

   _____

   _____

   _____

   _____

Practice

Name all the factors.

8. 42 _____

9. 23 _____

Mathematical Reasoning 1.1; Mathematical Reasoning 2.3   **347**

LESSON 12·5 | **Which is the Better Buy?**

For each problem, draw pictures and use bills and coins to decide
which product is the better buy.

1. A 12-oz bottle of sports drink costs $0.75.
   A six-pack of 12-oz sports drink costs $3.60.

   Which is the better buy? _____
   Explain how you know.

2. One pencil costs $0.10. A box of 12 pencils costs $1.80.

   Which is the better buy? _____
   Explain how you know.

3. A cup of yogurt costs $0.90. A four-pack of yogurt costs $3.00.

   Which is the better buy? _____
   Explain how you know.

4. Write and solve your own "better buy" problem.

   _____

   _____

   _____

LESSON 12·5 Measuring Air Pressure with a Barometer

Some people think that air does not weigh anything. But it does—you can prove this by doing a simple experiment. Weigh a deflated soccer ball or basketball. Next, pump it full of air. Weigh it again. The ball will weigh more after you have pumped air into it. This shows that the air you pumped in does have weight.

In 1643, Evangelista Torricelli, a student of Galileo, invented an instrument for measuring air pressure—how much the weight of air pushes on a surface. He made a glass tube about $3\frac{1}{2}$ feet long, closed it at one end, and filled it with mercury. Then he turned the tube upside down and put it into an open container that held more mercury. When he did that, the mercury in the tube fell a few inches and then stopped.

You may wonder why some of the mercury remained in the tube. Why didn't *all* the mercury flow out of the tube and mix with the mercury in the container? The reason is that the air above the open container pushes down on the mercury. This, in turn, supports the mercury in the tube. The greater the air pressure, the higher the level of the mercury in the tube.

An early model mercury barometer

The instrument Torricelli invented is called a mercury barometer. The height of the mercury in the tube depends on the barometric pressure. When a weather forecaster reports that the barometric pressure is 30.25, this means that the mercury in the tube has reached a level of 30.25 inches.

Barometers are used to predict the weather. In fact, Torricelli's barometer came to be known as the "weather glass." When the weather pattern is changing, the barometric pressure also changes. When the barometer readings fall steadily or suddenly, a storm is probably on its way. The faster the barometer readings fall and the lower the reading, the more severe the storm is likely to be. When the barometer readings rise, you can expect fair weather.

349

LESSON 12·5

Measuring Air Pressure with a Barometer *cont.*

Aneroid barometer

Mercury barometers are awkward to carry from one place to another. A more convenient type of barometer is the aneroid barometer. This is the sort of barometer you may have in your school or at home. *Aneroid* means "without liquid." The units on an aneroid barometer have the same meaning as the units on a mercury barometer. If your aneroid barometer reads 29.85, a mercury barometer would show 29.85 inches of mercury in the tube.

Aneroid barometers have two needles. One needle moves when the barometric pressure changes. (It is the needle pointing to 30 in the picture.) The other needle stays in place unless someone moves it. If you move the smaller needle to today's reading, later you will be able to measure how much the barometric pressure has changed.

Barometric pressure is affected by elevation—how high the land is above sea level. The average barometric pressure at sea level is about 30 inches. At higher elevations, the average barometric pressure will be less.

The Elevation Rule

◆ For every 100 feet you climb, the barometer reading will drop about 0.1 inch.

◆ For every 1,000 feet you climb, the reading will drop about 1 inch.

Denver, Colorado, is about 5,000 feet above sea level; the average barometric pressure in Denver is about 25 inches.

Here is a map of the island of Hawaii. The numbers on the map give barometer readings for the cities shown—all taken under similar weather conditions. All readings were also taken at the same time. They vary because the cities are at different heights, or elevations, above sea level.

HAWAII

Pacific Ocean

Wainea
■ 27.0

Waikii
26.5 ■

Mauna
+ Kea

Hualalai
○ Crater

Pohauloa
23.4 ■

Hilo
30.0 ■

Mauna
Loa +

Kilauea
Crater
○

Keaau
29.6 ■

Kau
Desert

Papa
■ 28.4

Numbers below cities
are barometer readings.

LESSON 12·5 | **The Barometer and Elevation**

Refer to the map of Hawaii and the Elevation Rule on *Math Masters,*
page 350 to answer the following questions.

1. Hilo is the largest city on the island of Hawaii.
It is at sea level. This means that its elevation
is 0 feet above sea level. What is the barometer
reading in Hilo?

About _____ inches

2. Compare Keaau to Wainea.

    a. What is the barometer reading in Keaau?

About _____ inches

    b. What is the barometer reading in Wainea?

About _____ inches

    c. Which is higher above sea level:
    Keaau or Wainea?

_____

3. Compare Waikii to Hilo.

    a. What is the barometer reading in Waikii?

About _____ inches

    b. How much less is the barometer reading
    in Waikii than in Hilo?

_____ inches less

    c. What is the elevation of Waikii?

About _____ feet
above sea level

4. The barometer reading at the top of Kilauea Crater
is 1.7 inches less than at the top of Hualalai Crater.

    a. Which crater has a higher elevation?

_____

    b. About how much higher is it?

About _____ feet

5. The Kau Desert is about 2,500 feet above sea level.
What should the barometer reading be there?

About _____ inches

6. The highest mountains on Hawaii are Mauna Loa
and Mauna Kea. Their heights are nearly the same. If
the barometer reads 16.4 inches at the top of these
mountains, what is their elevation?

About _____ feet
above sea level

351

STUDY LINK
12·6

Country Statistics

SRB
175 176

1. China has the longest border in the world—13,759 miles.
   Russia has the second longest border in the world—12,514 miles.
   How much shorter is Russia's border than China's border?   _____ miles

2. The area of Russia is about 1,818,629 square miles. The area of
   Spain, including offshore islands, is about 194,897 square miles.
   About how many times larger is Russia than Spain?   _____ times larger

3. Students in China attend school about 251 days per year.
   Students in the United States attend school about 180 days
   per year.

   a. About what percent of the year do Chinese students
      spend in school?   _____%

   b. About what percent of the year do American students
      spend in school?   _____%

4. English is officially spoken in 54 countries. Portuguese is
   officially spoken in 8 countries. Portuguese is spoken in about
   what fraction of the number of English-speaking countries?   _____

5. The table to the right shows
   the countries in the world with
   the most neighboring countries.

Country	Number of Neighbors
Brazil	10
China	15
Dem. Rep. of Congo	9
Germany	9
Russia	14
Sudan	9

   Use the data in the table to answer the following questions.

   a. Which country has the maximum number of neighbors? _____

   b. What is the range? _____

   c. What is the mode? _____

   d. What is the median? _____

Number Sense 3.0; Statistics, Data Analysis, and Probability 1.2

LESSON 12·6 | Interpreting the Remainder

Draw a picture to illustrate the problem. Then solve the problem.

1. The roller coaster holds 24 people per ride. There are 65 people waiting in line. How many times does the roller coaster need to run before everyone in line gets a turn to ride?

   Number model: _____   Picture:

   Answer: _____ times

   What did you do about the remainder? Circle the answer.

   Ignored it.

   Reported it as a fraction or decimal.

   Rounded the answer up.

   Why?

   _____

   _____

2. Cedric's teacher is ordering pizza for an end-of-year party. He has $35.00 to spend. A large cheese pizza costs $8.00. How many pizzas can he order?

   Number model: _____   Picture:

   Answer: _____ pizzas

   What did you do about the remainder? Circle the answer.

   Ignored it.

   Reported it as a fraction or decimal.

   Rounded the answer up.

   Why?

   _____

   _____

STUDY LINK 12·7 Family Letter

Congratulations!

By completing *Fourth Grade Everyday Mathematics,* your child has accomplished a great deal. Thank you for all of your support.

This Family Letter is a resource to use throughout your child's vacation. It includes an extended list of Do-Anytime Activities, directions for games that can be played at home, a list of mathematics-related books to check out over vacation, and a sneak preview of what your child will be learning in *Fifth Grade Everyday Mathematics.* Enjoy the vacation!

Do-Anytime Activities

Mathematics means more when it is rooted in real-life situations. To help your child review many of the concepts he or she has learned in fourth grade, we suggest the following activities for you and your child to do together over vacation. These activities will help your child build on the skills he or she has learned this year and help prepare him or her for *Fifth Grade Everyday Mathematics.*

1. Have your child practice any multiplication and division facts that he or she has not yet mastered. Include some quick drills.

2. Provide items for your child to measure. Have your child use personal references, as well as U.S. customary and metric measuring tools.

3. Use newspapers and magazines as sources of numbers, graphs, and tables that your child may read and discuss.

4. Have your child practice multidigit multiplication and division using the algorithms that he or she is most comfortable with.

5. Ask your child to look at advertisements and find the sale prices of items using the original prices and rates of discount or find rates of discount using original prices and sale prices. Have your child use a calculator and calculate unit prices to determine best or better buys.

6. Continue the World Tour by reading about other countries.

Family Letter *cont.*

Building Skills through Games

The following section lists rules for games that can be played at home. You will need a deck of number cards, which can be made from index cards or by modifying a regular deck of cards as follows:

A regular deck of playing cards includes 54 cards (52 regular cards plus 2 jokers). Use a permanent marker to mark some of the cards:

◆ Mark each of the four aces with the number 1.

◆ Mark each of the four queens with the number 0.

◆ Mark the four jacks and four kings with the numbers 11 through 18.

◆ Mark the two jokers with the numbers 19 and 20.

Beat the Calculator

Materials   number cards 1–10 (4 of each); calculator

Players   3

Directions

1. One player is the "Caller," one is the "Calculator," and one is the "Brain."

2. Shuffle the deck of cards and place it facedown.

3. The Caller draws two cards from the number deck and asks for their product.

4. The Calculator solves the problem with a calculator. The Brain solves it without a calculator. The Caller decides who got the answer first.

5. The Caller continues to draw two cards at a time from the number deck and asks for their product.

6. Players trade roles every 10 turns or so.

Example: The Caller draws a 10 and 7 and calls out "10 times 7." The Brain and the Calculator solve the problem.

The Caller decides who got the answer first.

Variation 1: To practice extended multiplication facts, have the Caller draw two cards from the number deck and attach a 0 to either one of the factors or to both factors before asking for the product.

Example: If the Caller turns over a 4 and a 6, he or she may make up any one of the following problems:

4 ∗ 60   40 ∗ 6   40 ∗ 60

Variation 2: Use a full set of number cards: 4 each of the numbers 1–10, and 1 each of the numbers 11–20.

Building Skills through Games

Name That Number

Materials   1 complete deck of number cards

Players   2 or 3

Object of the game To collect the most cards

Directions

1. Shuffle the cards and deal five cards to each player. Place the remaining cards number-side down. Turn over the top card and place it beside the deck. This is the **target number** for the round.

2. Players try to match the target number by adding, subtracting, multiplying, or dividing the numbers on as many of their cards as possible. A card may be used only once.

3. Players write their solutions on a sheet of paper or a slate. When players have written their best solutions:

   ◆ They set aside the cards they used to name the target number.

   ◆ Replace them by drawing new cards from the top of the deck.

   ◆ Put the old target number on the bottom of the deck.

   ◆ Turn over a new target number, and play another hand.

4. Play continues until there are not enough cards left to replace all of the players' cards. The player who sets aside more cards wins the game.

   Example: Target number: 16   A player's cards: 7   5   8   2   10

   Some possible solutions:

   $10 + 8 - 2 = 16$ (*three cards used*)

   $7 * 2 + 10 - 8 = 16$ (*four cards used*)

   $8 / 2 + 10 + 7 - 5 = 16$ (*all five cards used*)

   The player sets aside the cards used to make a solution and draws the same number of cards from the top of the deck.

STUDY LINK 12·7 Family Letter *cont.*

Vacation Reading with a Mathematical Twist

Books can contribute to children's learning by presenting mathematics in a combination of real-world and imaginary contexts. The titles listed below were recommended by teachers who use *Everyday Mathematics* in their classrooms. They are organized by mathematical topic. Visit your local library and check out these mathematics-related books with your child.

Geometry

A Cloak for the Dreamer by Aileen Friedman

The Greedy Triangle by Marilyn Burns

Measurement

The Magic School Bus Inside the Earth by Joanna Cole

The Hundred Penny Box by Sharon Bell Mathis

Numeration

Alexander, Who Used to be Rich Last Sunday by Judith Viorst

If You Made a Million by David M. Schwartz

Fraction Action by Loreen Leedy

How Much Is a Million? by David M. Schwartz

Operations

Anno's Mysterious Multiplying Jar by Masaichiro Anno

The King's Chessboard by David Birch

One Hundred Hungry Ants by Elinor J. Pinczes

A Remainder of One by Elinor J. Pinczes

Patterns, Functions, and Sequences

Eight Hands Round by Ann Whitford Paul

Visual Magic by David Thomas

Reference Frames

The Magic School Bus: Inside the Human Body by Joanna Cole

Pigs on a Blanket by Amy Axelrod

Looking Ahead: Fifth Grade Everyday Mathematics

Next year your child will . . .

◆ Develop skills with decimals and percents

◆ Continue to practice multiplication and division skills, including operations with decimals

◆ Investigate methods for solving problems using mathematics in everyday situations

◆ Work with number lines, times, dates, and rates

◆ Collect, organize, describe, and interpret numerical data

◆ Further explore the properties, relationships, and measurement of 2- and 3-dimensional objects

◆ Read, write, and use whole numbers, fractions, decimals, percents, negative numbers, and exponential notation

◆ Explore scientific notation

Again, thank you for all of your support this year. Have fun continuing your child's mathematical experiences throughout the vacation!

Project Masters

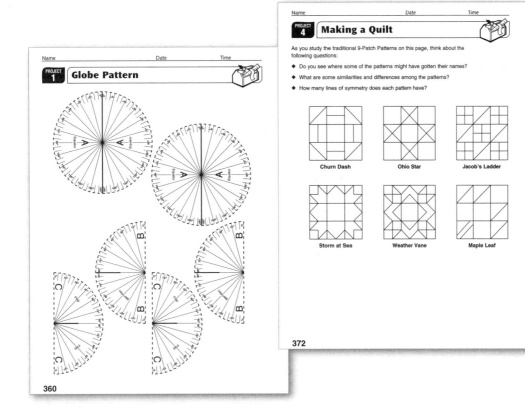

PROJECT 1

Globe Pattern

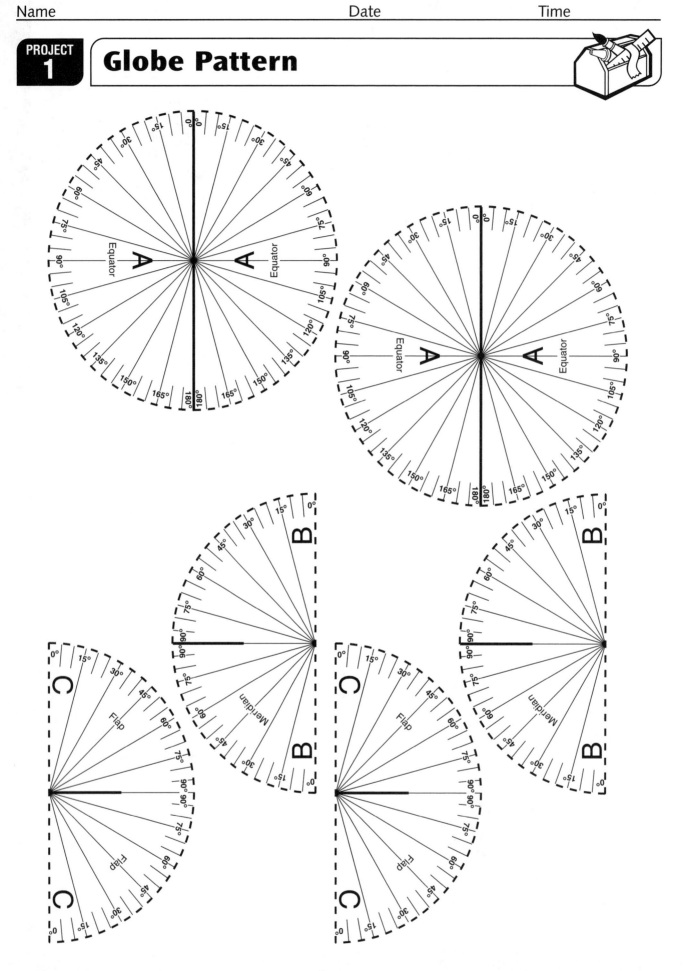

PROJECT 1

How to Make a Cutaway Globe

Figure 1

Figure 2

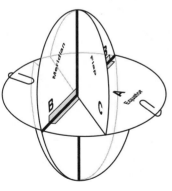

Figure 3

Directions:

Step 1: Carefully cut out one of the circles A along the dashed lines.

Step 2: Cut out one of the semicircles B; cut the thin slit on the semicircle.

Step 3: Lay semicircle B on circle A so that the base of the semicircle aligns with the 0° to 180° diameter shown on circle A. Tape the pieces together on both sides of the semicircle. Adjust the semicircle so that it stands straight up. See Figure 1.

Step 4: Cut out one of the semicircles C and cut along the slit. Fold the semicircle in half at the 90° line. Fold it back and forth several times at the same place until you have made a good crease.

Step 5: Slide the slit of semicircle C through the slit of semicircle B. See Figure 2.

Step 6: Repeat Steps 1–5 to make a second hemisphere.

Step 7: Put the two hemispheres together with paper clips to make a full globe. Put the 0° labels on circles A together. See Figure 3.

361

PROJECT 2

A Paper Compass

PROJECT 2

Making a Compass

In ancient times, sailors had only the sun, moon, and stars to aid them in navigation. The most important navigational instrument was the **compass.** The compass was invented more than 1,000 years ago. The first compass was a small bar of magnetized iron that floated on a reed in a bowl of water. The magnet in the iron would make the reed point to the magnetically charged North Pole. Using a compass, sailors could tell in which direction they were traveling.

You, too, can make a floating compass.

1. Magnetize a steel sewing needle by stroking it with one pole of a strong bar magnet. Slowly stroke the needle from end to end **in one direction only.** Be sure to lift your hand up in the air before coming down for another stroke.

2. Slice a round ($\frac{1}{2}$-inch-thick) piece from a cork stopper. Cut a groove across the center of the top of the cork. Put the needle in the groove.

3. Place the cork into a glass, china, or aluminum dish filled with water. Add a teaspoon of detergent to the water. The detergent will lower the surface tension of the water and prevent the cork from moving to one side of the dish and staying there.

The needle will behave like a compass needle. It will assume a North-South position because of Earth's magnetic field.

Source: Science for the Elementary School. New York: Macmillan, 1993.

PROJECT 3 | A Carnival Game

The class "quilt" of colored grids is placed on the floor and used as a target mat. The player stands about five feet from the mat and tosses a centimeter cube onto the mat. If the cube does not land on the mat, the player gets another turn. If the cube lands on more than one color, the color that is covered by most of the cube is used. The player may win a money prize, depending upon the color on which the cube lands. For each play, the player must buy a ticket for 10 cents.

1. Suppose that you bought 50 tickets.

   a. How much would you pay for 50 tickets?   _____

   Suppose that your 50 tosses landed on the colors you recorded in the table at the bottom of page 215 of *Math Journal 2.*

   b. How much prize money would you have won?   _____

   c. Would you win or lose money on the game?   _____

                                   How much?   _____

2. Suppose that the class decided to use the game to raise money to buy computer software. Pretend that students sold 1,000 tickets and that the cubes landed on the colors as shown on the board or on *Math Masters,* page 238.

   a. How much would the class collect on the sale of tickets? _____

   b. How much prize money would the class pay?   _____

   c. How much money would the class raise?   _____

PROJECT 3

A Carnival Game *continued*

3. Work with your group to make up your own version of the carnival game.

a. Record how much you would charge for a ticket and what the prizes would be for each color.

Ticket Price

_____ per toss

Prizes

yellow _____

red _____

green _____

blue _____

white _____

---

b. Use the results for 1,000 cube drops shown on the board or on *Math Masters,* page 242 to answer the following questions:

Would the class have won or lost money? _____

How much? _____

4. Suppose that the class ran your game on Parents' Night.

a. How many tickets do you estimate the class would sell? _____

b. How much money would the class get from ticket sales? _____

c. About how much money should you expect to pay in prizes? _____

d. About how much money should the class expect to earn? _____

365

PROJECT 4 — Patchwork Quilts

Throughout American history, women have worked together to make **patchwork quilts.** Because cloth was expensive and scarce, quilts were often made out of pieces of worn-out clothing or leftovers from another project. The quilters began by sewing together pieces of different colors, shapes, and textures to create a square pattern. Then they made more "patchwork" squares with the same pattern. When they had enough squares, they sewed them together to form the top of the quilt. Next they added a layer of wool fleece or cotton, called *batting,* and a cloth backing. They made a "sandwich" of the three layers—the backing on the bottom, the batting in the middle, and the patchwork on the top. They stretched the "sandwich" on a wooden frame and sewed the three layers together with tiny stitches.

The quilt was put together at a party, called a **quilting bee.** While cutting and sewing, the women would tell stories and share what went on in their lives. When the quilt was finished, the men joined the women for supper and dancing.

Buggy Wheel

Many patchwork patterns have become traditions. Their names and designs have come from the everyday lives of the people who created them. For example, the "Buggy Wheel" pattern was probably inspired by a trip in a buggy. Along with walking and riding horses, buggies were a popular form of transportation in early America.

Does and Darts

Although early quilters may not have studied geometry in school, we can see geometry in many of their designs. Patchwork quilting involves the cutting of fabric into various geometric shapes and sewing them together into patterns. The pattern may be repeated over and over to form a quilt, or it may be rotated or reflected as the patches are assembled. Many patchwork patterns, such as the "Buggy Wheel" and "Does and Darts," are symmetric. Others, such as the "Crazy Quilt," seem to have been created at random.

The beauty of a quilt lies in its uniqueness. No two patches need ever be the same because there are many possible arrangements of fabrics and colors.

Crazy Quilt

PROJECT 4

Symmetric Patterns

Each pattern to the right of the "Pinwheel" pattern below has been colored in a different way. Notice how each color arrangement changes the number of lines of symmetry.

Pinwheel Pattern

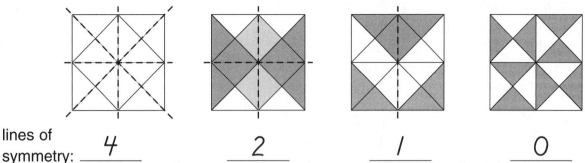

lines of symmetry: _4_   _2_   _1_   _0_

For each pattern below, draw all the lines of symmetry and record the number of lines of symmetry.

1. Bow-Tie Pattern

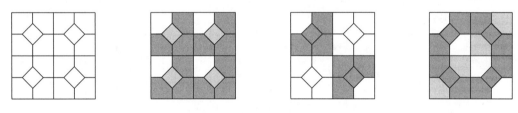

lines of symmetry: _____   _____   _____   _____

2. Ohio Star Pattern

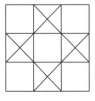

lines of symmetry: _____   _____   _____   _____

3. Pineapple Log Cabin Pattern

   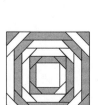

lines of symmetry: _____   _____   _____   _____

367

PROJECT 4 | Traditional 9-Patch Patterns

Some patterns, called **9-Patch Patterns,** look like they are made up of 9 squares. You can make your own 9-Patch Pattern on a 3-by-3 grid.

Take out *Math Masters,* pages 369 and 370. Color 6 squares on *Math Masters,* page 369 in one color and the other 6 in a different color. Cut out the 12 squares. Then make triangles by cutting 6 of the squares in half along a diagonal. Make rectangles by cutting the other 6 squares in half along a line through the middle.

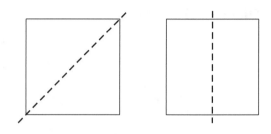

Now arrange some of the pieces on the grid on *Math Masters,* page 370 to make a pattern. Follow the directions below. When you have completed a pattern, draw and color it on one of the 3-by-3 grids below.

1. Make one or two patterns having 4 lines of symmetry.

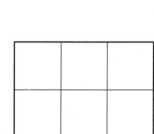

2. Make one or two patterns having 2 lines of symmetry.

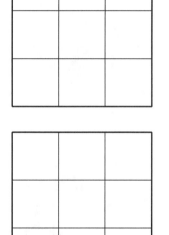

3. Make one or two patterns having no lines of symmetry.

PROJECT 4

9-Patch Pattern Pieces

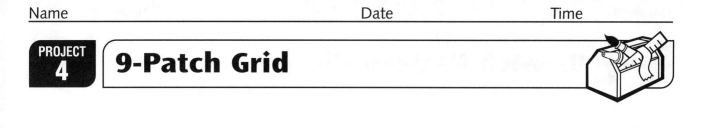

PROJECT 4

9-Patch Grid

PROJECT 4 — Rotating Patterns

Many traditional American quilts are made by rotating the square patterns as they are assembled into a quilt.

The first patchwork pattern below is a variation of the traditional "Grandmother's Fan" pattern. The patterns to the right of it show the pattern after it has been rotated clockwise a $\frac{1}{4}$, $\frac{1}{2}$, and $\frac{3}{4}$ turn.

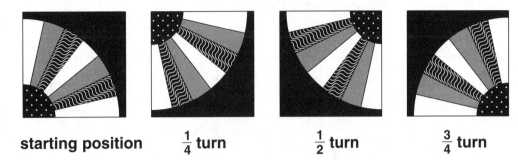

| **starting position** | $\frac{1}{4}$ **turn** | $\frac{1}{2}$ **turn** | $\frac{3}{4}$ **turn** |

This is what part of the quilt might look like if some of the patterns are rotated:

The "Wrench" pattern at the right, also known as the "Monkey Wrench," is a classic pattern that can be found in Amish and Mennonite quilts. Describe what it would look like if it were rotated a $\frac{1}{4}$, $\frac{1}{2}$, and $\frac{3}{4}$ turn.

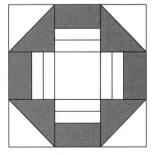

_____

_____

How many lines of symmetry does it have? _____

371

PROJECT 4

Making a Quilt

As you study the traditional 9-Patch Patterns on this page, think about the following questions:

◆ Do you see where some of the patterns might have gotten their names?

◆ What are some similarities and differences among the patterns?

◆ How many lines of symmetry does each pattern have?

Churn Dash

Ohio Star

Jacob's Ladder

Storm at Sea

Weather Vane

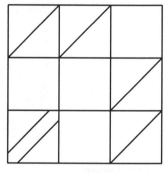

Maple Leaf

PROJECT 4

Making a Quilt *continued*

Work with two partners to make a quilt.

1. Each of you needs three copies of *Math Masters,* page 375. Cut out the 3-by-3 grid on each sheet. **Make sure you include the border with the dots.**

2. Cut out the quilting pattern shapes on *Math Masters,* page 374.

3. With your partners, choose one of the patterns on *Math Masters,* page 372. Decide on a way to color it. The colored pattern your group chooses **should not have more than two lines of symmetry.** Each group member should then copy this design onto three 3-by-3 grids. Use the pieces you cut out of *Math Masters,* page 374 to trace the pattern onto the 3-by-3 grids. Then color the pattern. Or you can trace the pieces onto colored paper, cut out the tracings, and paste them onto the 3-by-3 grids. Your group should end up with nine square "patches" that **look exactly alike.**

4. Punch holes through the dots along the border of the patches.

5. Lay all 9 square patches on the floor and arrange them so that some of the square patterns are rotated. When your group has agreed on an arrangement, line up the holes on the edges of the squares. Then fasten the pieces together by weaving yarn in and out of the holes. If you wish, make a ruffle for your quilt out of a strip of crepe paper. Pleat and glue the ruffle around the outer edges of the quilt.

Here is an example of a quilt with the "Maple Leaf" pattern:

373

PROJECT 4

Quilting Pattern Shapes

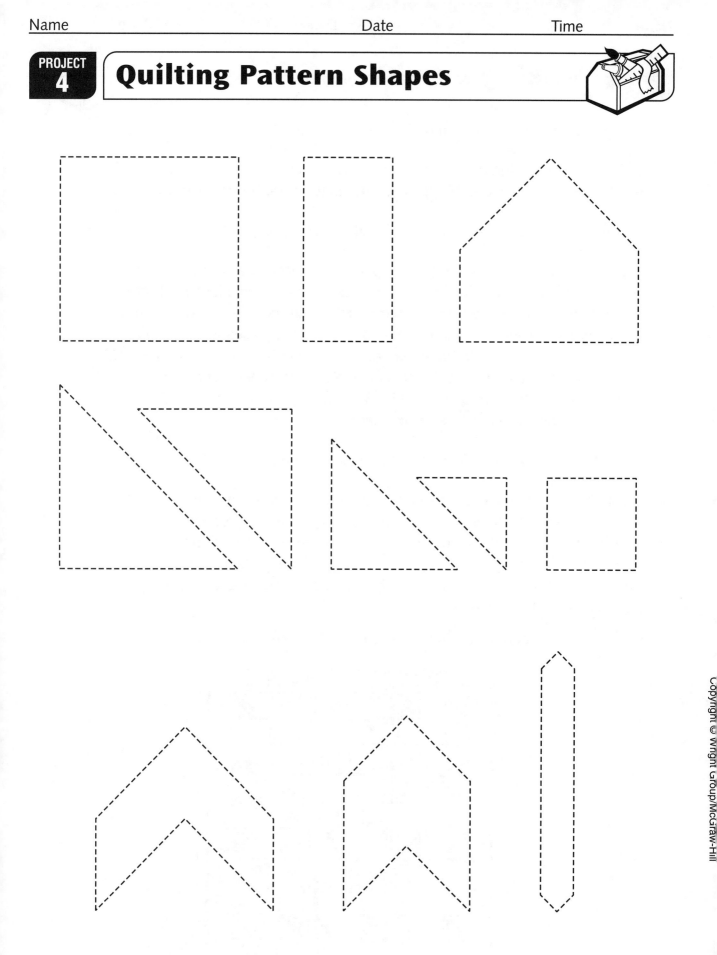

9-Patch Grid with Border

PROJECT 5

Which Soft Drink Would You Buy?

For each set of soft-drink cups, record the following information:

◆ The name of the place from which the cups come

◆ The size of the cup (small, medium, or large)

◆ The price

◆ The capacity in fluid ounces

Then calculate each unit price in cents per fluid ounce, rounded to the nearest tenth of a cent.

Soft-Drink Cups from			
Size	**Price**	**Capacity (fl oz)**	**Unit Price (¢/fl oz)**

Soft-Drink Cups from			
Size	**Price**	**Capacity (fl oz)**	**Unit Price (¢/fl oz)**

Soft-Drink Cups from			
Size	**Price**	**Capacity (fl oz)**	**Unit Price (¢/fl oz)**

PROJECT 5

Consumer Report: Best Soft-Drink Prices

Imagine that you have been assigned by *Kids' Consumer Reports* to investigate and report on the prices of soft drinks. Use the information your group recorded on *Math Masters,* page 376 to prepare a group report for the magazine. Your report might contain graphs, tables, and pictures. Try to answer some of the following questions in your report:

◆ Do small (or medium or large) cups at different places contain the same amount?

◆ Are prices similar for similar sizes? (For example, are the small-size drinks about the same price at different places?)

◆ Which places have the least expensive soft drinks? The most expensive soft drinks?

◆ Is the largest size always the best value?

◆ Which types of businesses offer better values? (For example, do restaurants generally offer better values than movie theaters?)

◆ What would you recommend to consumers? Do some places offer free refills? If so, how would this affect your recommendation?

_____

_____

_____

_____

_____

_____

_____

_____

_____

_____

_____

PROJECT 6 Blueprints

Sample Blueprint

back

1	2	2	2
0	0	0	1
0	1	1	1
0	2	2	1

left side | right side

front

Blueprint Mat

back

left side | right side

front

front view

left-side view

back view

right-side view

Group _____

Cut the sheet apart along the dashed line. Build your own structure on the Blueprint Mat (upper right). Then record the front view and the left-side view in the grid squares below. Leave your structure so that other students can find it, using these views.

front view   left-side view

If you make a mistake, use the grids below to draw the corrected views.

front view   left-side view

PROJECT 6

Building Structures

1. Use the blueprint at the right to build a structure on the Blueprint Mat (*Math Masters*, page 378). Use centimeter cubes.

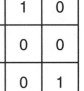

2	1	1	0
0	0	0	0
1	2	0	1
0	1	1	0

   a. Compare your structure to the structure built by your partner. They *should* look the same.

   b. Draw all 4 views of your structure by shading squares.

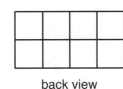

   front view   left-side view   back view   right-side view

   c. Compare your views to those drawn by your partner. They *should* be the same.

2. Build any structure you wish on your Blueprint Mat. *Reminder:* Use no more than 2 centimeter cubes on a square.

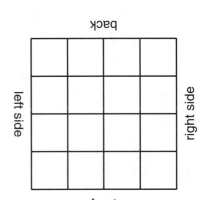

   a. Record your structure on the blueprint at the right.

   b. Draw all 4 views of your structure by shading the squares below. Ask your partner to check your work.

   front view   left-side view   back view   right-side view

   c. Compare the views of opposite sides of your structure.

3. Here is the front view of a structure. Draw its back view.

   front view   back view

379

PROJECT 6

More Structures

1. Here are 2 views of a structure. Draw its other 2 views.

front view   left-side view   back view   right-side view

2. Here is the front view, as well as the left-side view, of a structure.

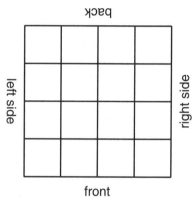

front view   left-side view

      back

      left side   right side

      front

   a. Build a structure that has these views. Record it on the blueprint at the right.

   b. Compare your structure and blueprint with your partner's. Are they the same?

3. Work with your partner. Use the following front view and left-side view to build 3 different structures. Record each structure on one of the blueprints.

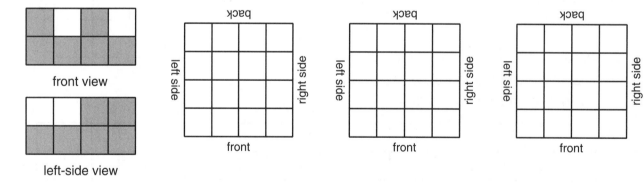

front view

left-side view

  back   back   back

left side   right side   left side   right side   left side   right side

front   front   front

4. a. Is it possible to build 2 different structures from the same front

     and left-side views? _____

   b. Is it possible to build 2 different structures from the same front,

     left-side, back, and right-side views? _____

PROJECT 7

Numbers, Mayan Style

The ancient Maya used a writing system made of pictures. The Maya had words and numerals for numbers, just as we do. Below are the Mayan picture words and numerals for 0–10, and the pronunciation of those words.

Mayan picture words	Mayan numerals/ pronunciation	
	mi	0 zero
	hun	1 one
	ca	2 two
	ox	3 three
	can	4 four
	ho	5 five
	uac	6 six
	uuc	7 seven
	uaxac	8 eight
	bolon	9 nine
	lahun	10 ten

The Maya are the native people who have lived for thousands of years in a 120,000-square-mile area of Central America stretching from the Valley of Mexico through Guatemala. Today there are about 6 million Maya in Central America.

The ancient Mayan civilization reached its height in A.D. 250 and flourished for more than 600 years. The Mayan people built large cities and tall limestone pyramids where they performed religious ceremonies. They traded cloth, cacao beans for making chocolate, and other items throughout Central America. Children, parents, grandparents, and even great-grandparents all lived together, and everyone helped with the housework and farming. The ancient Maya had no schools. Children learned everything by watching and helping adults.

The ancient Maya invented a number system using place value with dots and dashes to represent numbers, and a special symbol for zero. Their numbers read from top to bottom.

In our place-value system, we group numbers by tens and powers of ten. When we write a number like 2,457, we really mean $(2 * 1{,}000) + (4 * 100) + (5 * 10) + (7 * 1)$. The Mayan place-value system works similarly with 20s and powers of 20. But while we use 10 different symbols to write all of our numbers (the digits 0–9), the ancient Maya used only three symbols.

Mayan Number Symbols

(shell)	0
•	1
—	5

Our Place-Value System	Mayan Place-Value System
10,000s (10 * 10 * 10 * 10)	160,000s (20 * 20 * 20 * 20)
1,000s (10 * 10 * 10)	8,000s (20 * 20 * 20)
100s (10 * 10)	400s (20 * 20)
10s	20s
1s	1s

To write the number 837 using the Mayan system, put a 2 in the 400s place, a 1 in the 20s place, and 17 in the 1s place:

••	$2 * 400 =$	800
•	$1 * 20 =$	20
•• (over three bars)	$17 * 1 =$	+ 17
		837

381

Teaching Aid Masters

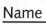

+, − Fact Triangles 1

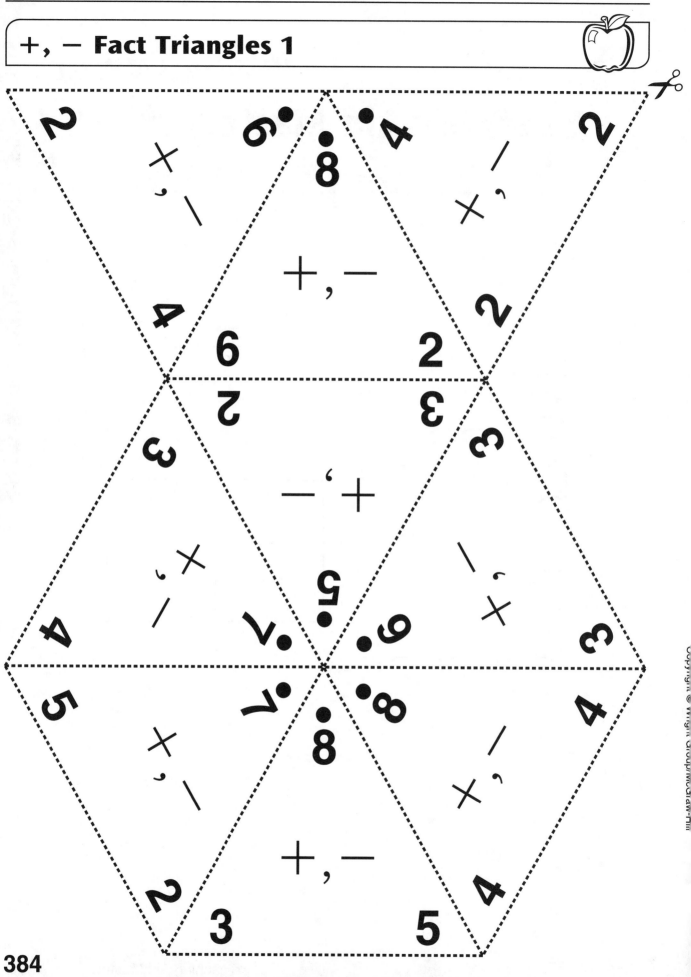

+, − Fact Triangles 2

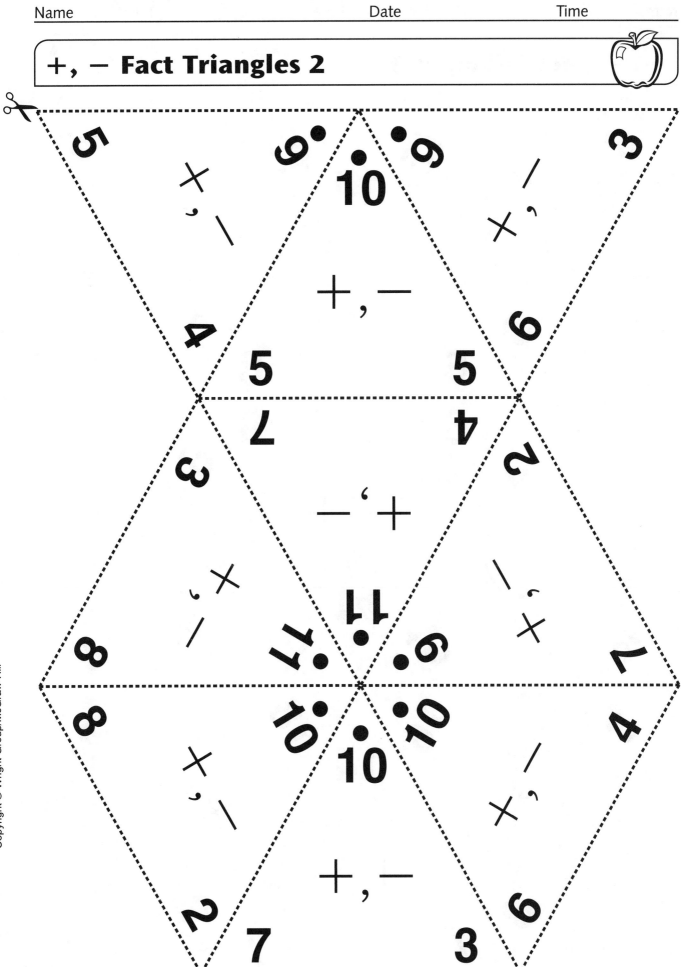

+, − Fact Triangles 3

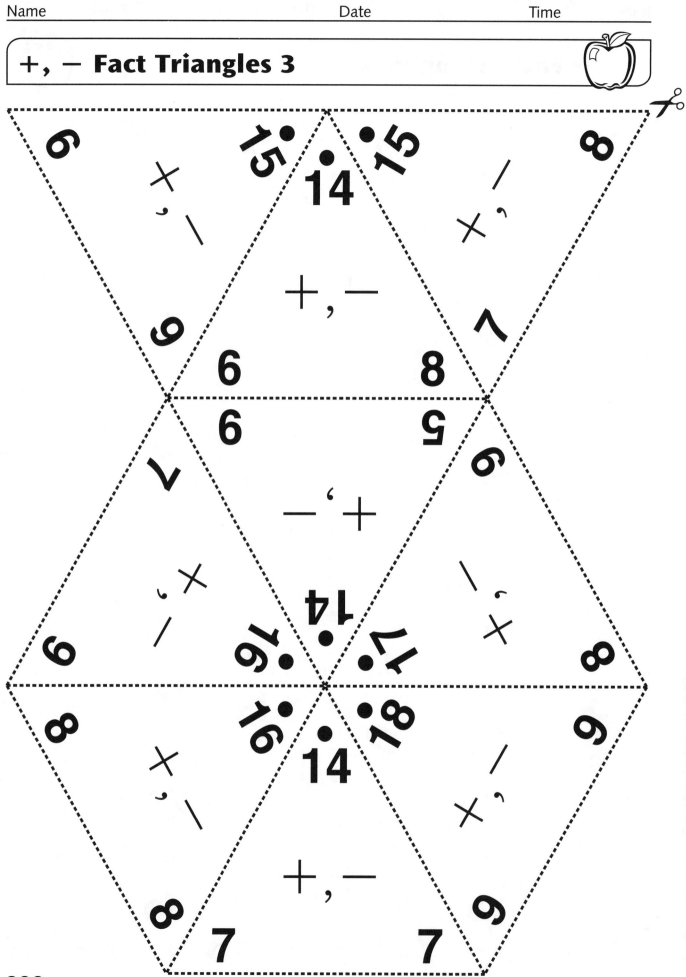

+, − Fact Triangles 4

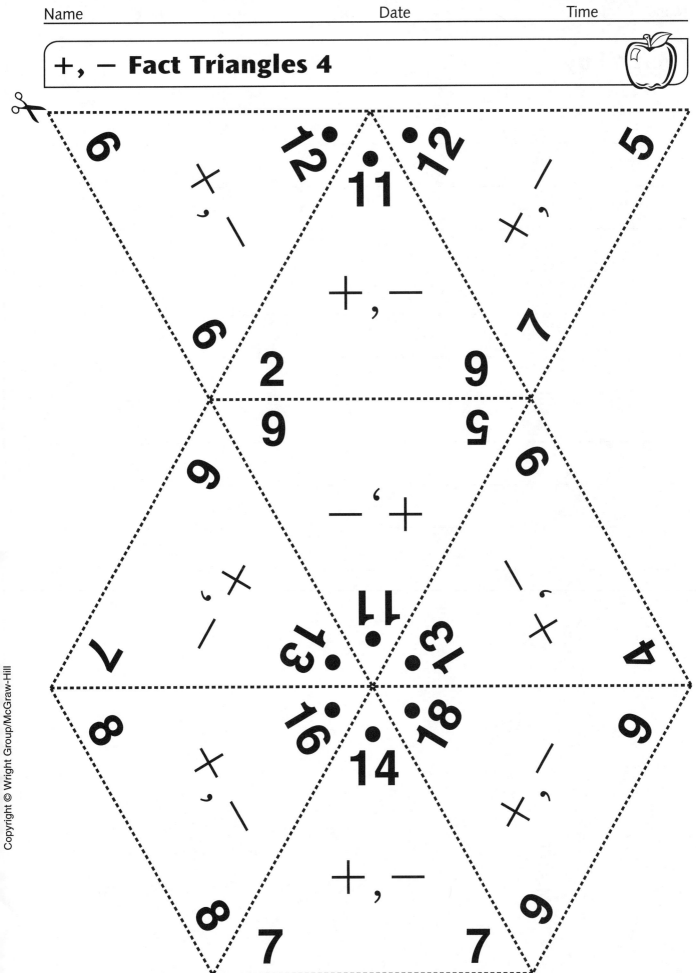

Math Log

Exit Slip

Exit Slip

Venn Diagram

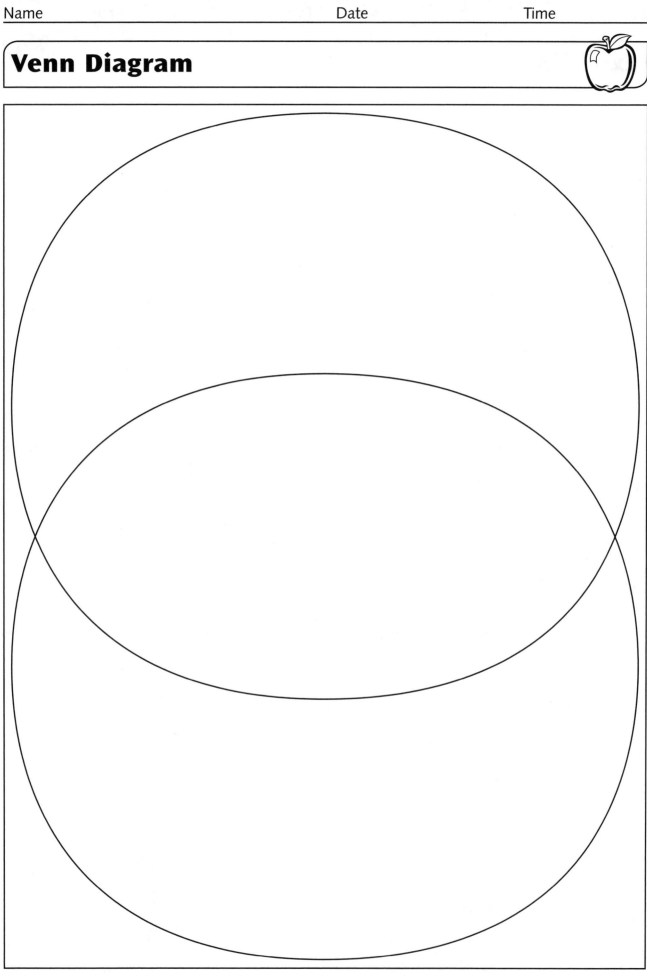

Timed Test 1: Addition & Subtraction Facts

$4 + 1 =$ _____	$9 + 9 =$ _____	$6 - 4 =$ _____	$12 - 4 =$ _____
$6 + 3 =$ _____	$8 + 7 =$ _____	$5 - 2 =$ _____	$16 - 8 =$ _____
$3 + 0 =$ _____	$6 + 9 =$ _____	$6 - 3 =$ _____	$13 - 9 =$ _____
$4 + 4 =$ _____	$5 + 8 =$ _____	$7 - 1 =$ _____	$12 - 7 =$ _____
$6 + 2 =$ _____	$9 + 3 =$ _____	$11 - 2 =$ _____	$14 - 6 =$ _____
$3 + 4 =$ _____	$7 + 7 =$ _____	$12 - 6 =$ _____	$11 - 4 =$ _____
$8 + 2 =$ _____	$5 + 6 =$ _____	$8 - 0 =$ _____	$15 - 6 =$ _____
$3 + 5 =$ _____	$7 + 9 =$ _____	$11 - 3 =$ _____	$17 - 9 =$ _____
$2 + 2 =$ _____	$6 + 7 =$ _____	$10 - 6 =$ _____	$15 - 8 =$ _____
$1 + 9 =$ _____	$9 + 5 =$ _____	$9 - 3 =$ _____	$13 - 7 =$ _____
$5 + 4 =$ _____	$8 + 6 =$ _____	$7 - 5 =$ _____	$14 - 9 =$ _____
$2 + 5 =$ _____	$4 + 7 =$ _____	$8 - 7 =$ _____	$18 - 9 =$ _____
$2 + 7 =$ _____	$9 + 8 =$ _____	$10 - 3 =$ _____	$13 - 5 =$ _____

Timed Test 2: Addition & Subtraction Facts

$4 + 5 =$ ___	$8 + 8 =$ ___	$7 - 2 =$ ___	$13 - 6 =$ ___
$0 + 8 =$ ___	$7 + 6 =$ ___	$6 - 5 =$ ___	$12 - 5 =$ ___
$7 + 2 =$ ___	$5 + 9 =$ ___	$10 - 7 =$ ___	$14 - 8 =$ ___
$1 + 4 =$ ___	$6 + 8 =$ ___	$6 - 2 =$ ___	$11 - 7 =$ ___
$5 + 2 =$ ___	$7 + 8 =$ ___	$5 - 3 =$ ___	$15 - 9 =$ ___
$5 + 3 =$ ___	$9 + 6 =$ ___	$6 - 3 =$ ___	$14 - 5 =$ ___
$2 + 2 =$ ___	$9 + 7 =$ ___	$11 - 8 =$ ___	$18 - 9 =$ ___
$7 + 1 =$ ___	$7 + 4 =$ ___	$10 - 4 =$ ___	$13 - 8 =$ ___
$3 + 6 =$ ___	$8 + 9 =$ ___	$9 - 6 =$ ___	$17 - 8 =$ ___
$4 + 3 =$ ___	$8 + 5 =$ ___	$4 - 1 =$ ___	$15 - 7 =$ ___
$2 + 8 =$ ___	$3 + 9 =$ ___	$11 - 9 =$ ___	$12 - 8 =$ ___
$4 + 4 =$ ___	$7 + 7 =$ ___	$12 - 6 =$ ___	$16 - 8 =$ ___
$2 + 6 =$ ___	$6 + 5 =$ ___	$9 - 0 =$ ___	$13 - 4 =$ ___

Name   Date   Time

Frames and Arrows

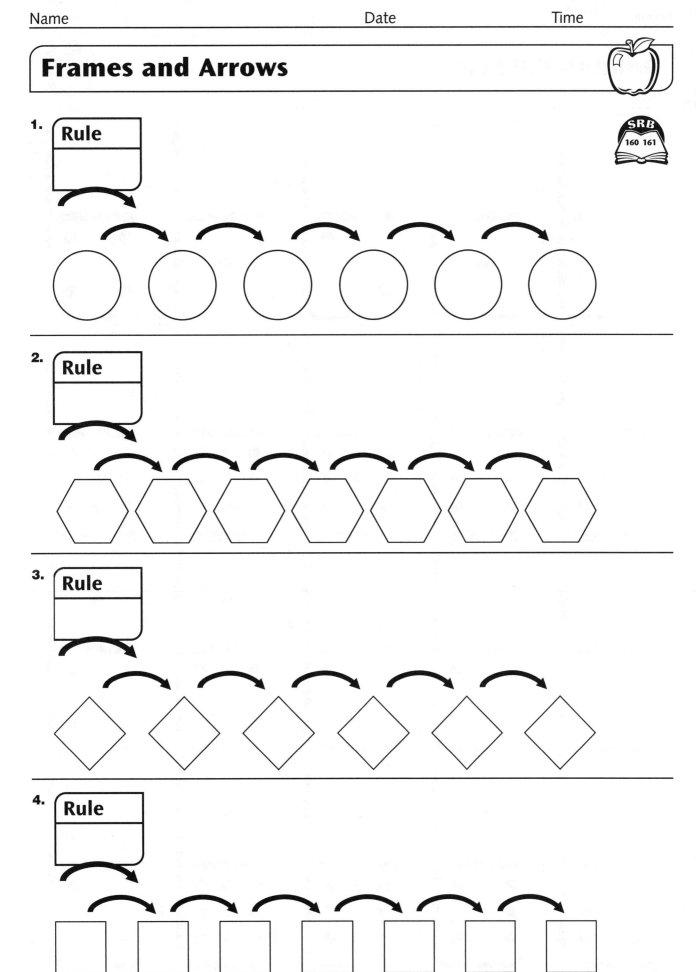

1. Rule

2. Rule

3. Rule

4. Rule

393

Domino Cutouts

Domino Cutouts *continued*

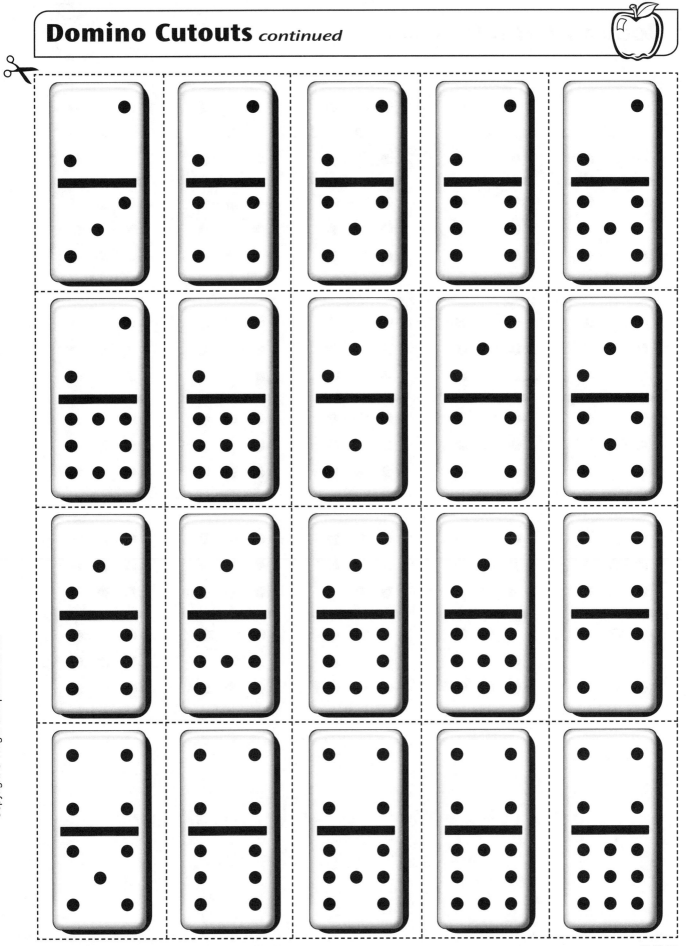

Name _____ Date _____ Time _____

Domino Cutouts *continued*

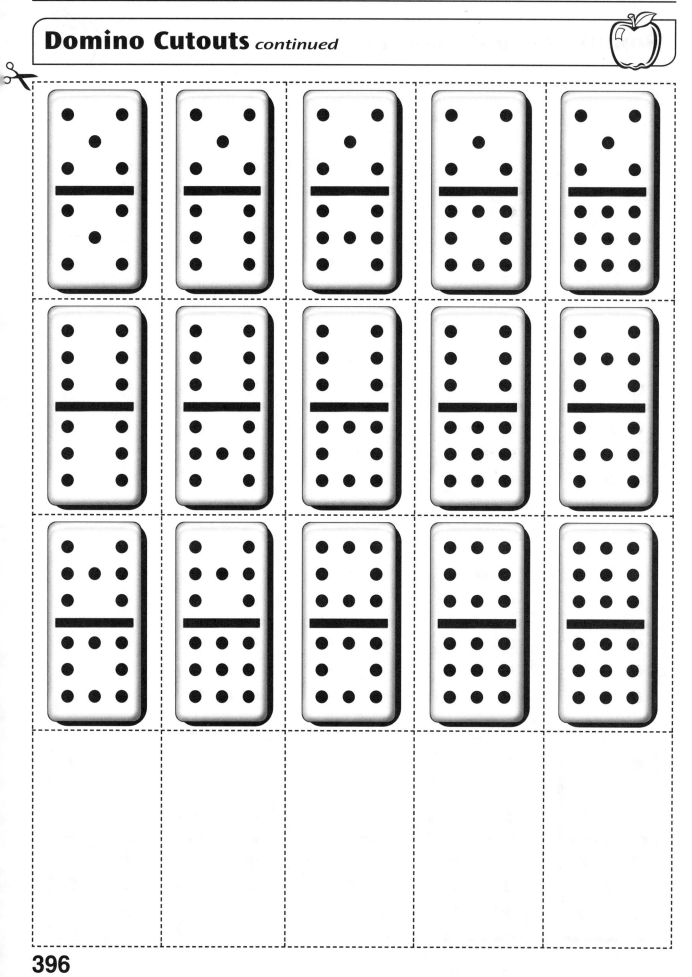

Name-Collection Boxes

Name _____

Date _____

Name _____

Date _____

Name _____

Date _____

Name _____

Date _____

Place-Value Chart

Number	Hundred Millions 100M	Ten Millions 10M	Millions M	Hundred Thousands 100K	Ten Thousands 10K	Thousands K	Hundreds H	Tens T	Ones O

Compact Place-Value Flip Book

1. Cut each page along the dashed lines. Do NOT cut any of the solid lines.

2. Cut along the vertical dashed lines to separate the digits.

3. Assemble the pages in order.

4. Staple the assembled book. (Ask your teacher for help if you need it.)

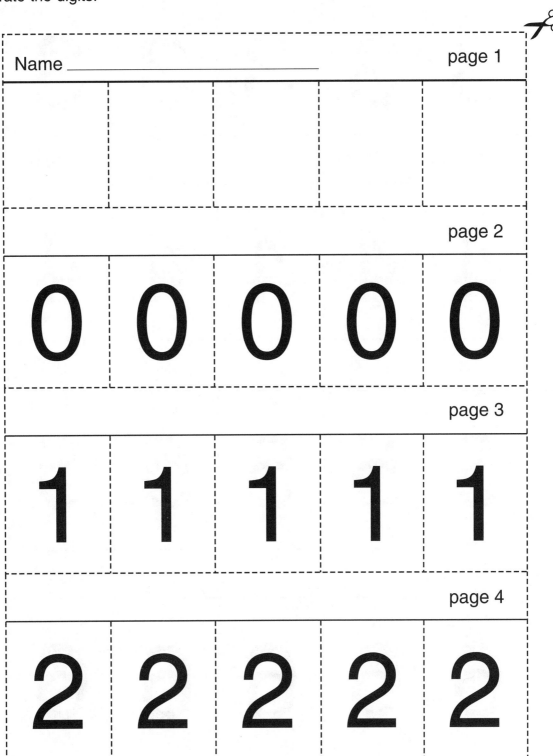

Name _____ page 1

page 2

0 0 0 0 0

page 3

1 1 1 1 1

page 4

2 2 2 2 2

399

Compact Place-Value Flip Book *continued*

page 5

3 3 3 3 3

page 6

4 4 4 4 4

page 7

5 5 5 5 5

page 8

6 6 6 6 6

Compact Place-Value Flip Book *continued*

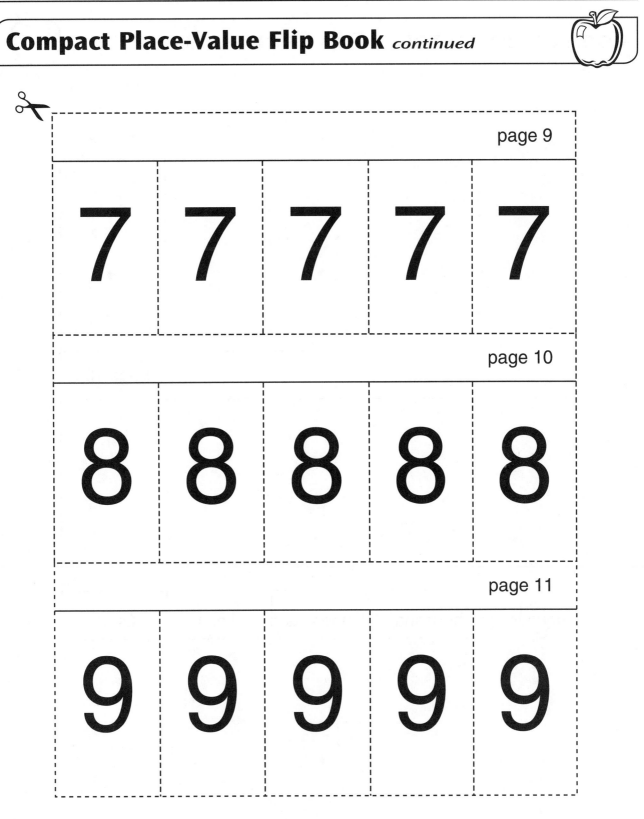

page 9

| 7 | 7 | 7 | 7 | 7 |

page 10

| 8 | 8 | 8 | 8 | 8 |

page 11

| 9 | 9 | 9 | 9 | 9 |

Compact Place-Value Flip Book *continued*

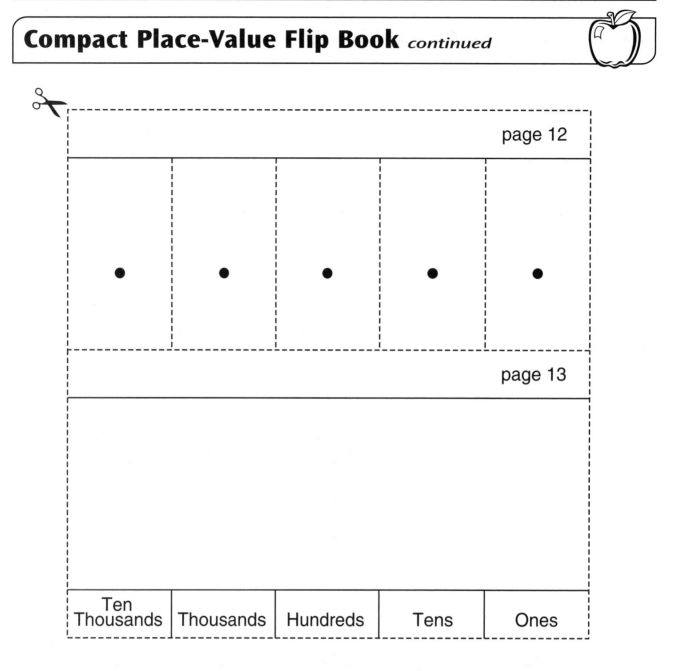

page 12

page 13

Ten Thousands	Thousands	Hundreds	Tens	Ones

Grid Paper (1 cm)

Computation Grids

404

Parts-and-Total Diagram

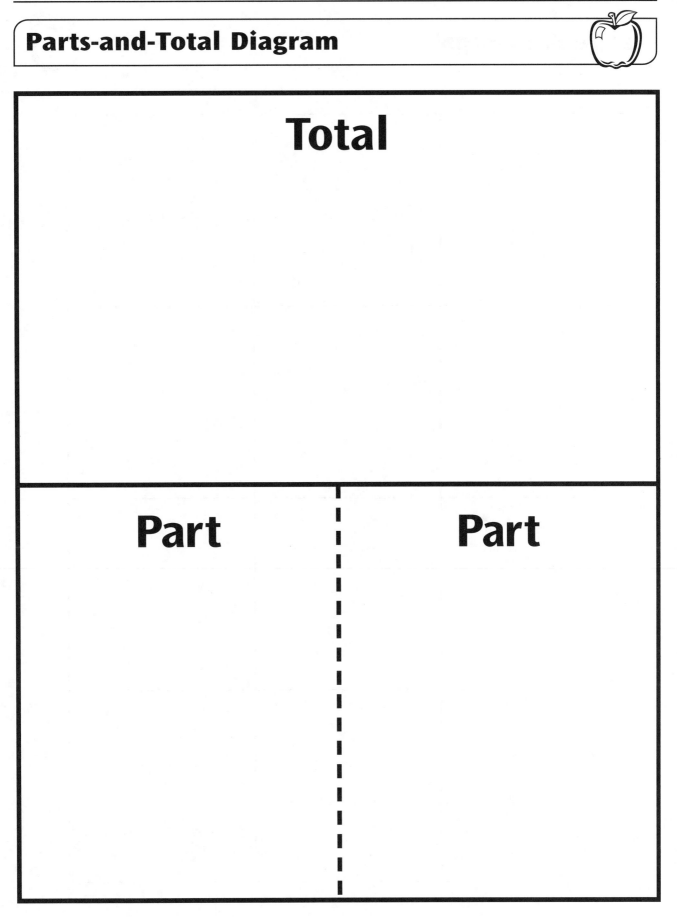

Large Bar Graph

"What's My Rule?"

SRB 162–166

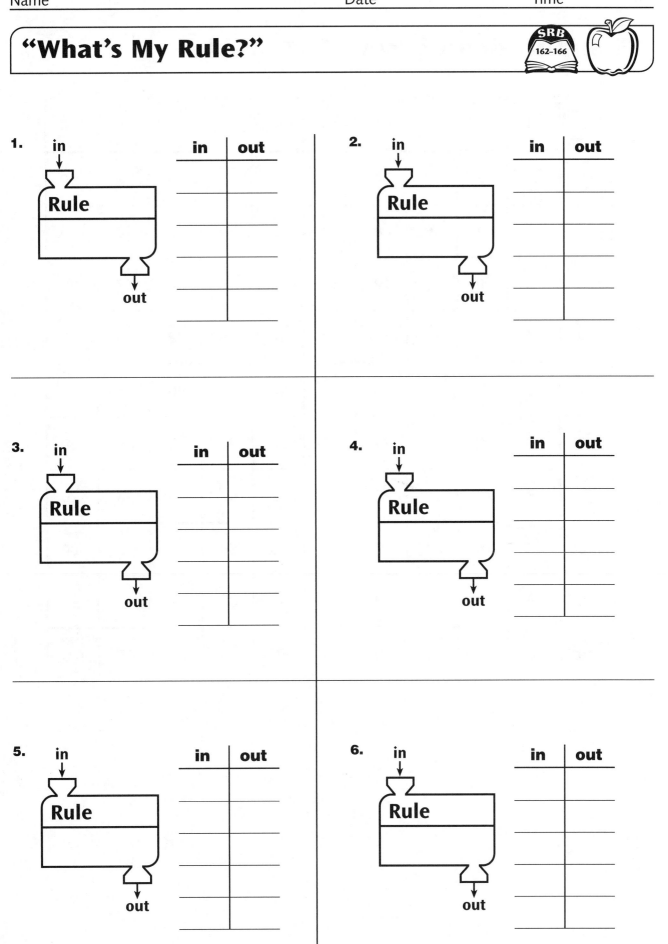

1.   in

Rule

out

in	out

2.   in

Rule

out

in	out

3.   in

Rule

out

in	out

4.   in

Rule

out

in	out

5.   in

Rule

out

in	out

6.   in

Rule

out

in	out

Multiplication/Division Facts Table

*, /	1	2	3	4	5	6	7	8	9	10
1	1	2	3	4	5	6	7	8	9	10
2	2	4	6	8	10	12	14	16	18	20
3	3	6	9	12	15	18	21	24	27	30
4	4	8	12	16	20	24	28	32	36	40
5	5	10	15	20	25	30	35	40	45	50
6	6	12	18	24	30	36	42	48	54	60
7	7	14	21	28	35	42	49	56	63	70
8	8	16	24	32	40	48	56	64	72	80
9	9	18	27	36	45	54	63	72	81	90
10	10	20	30	40	50	60	70	80	90	100

*, / Fact Triangle

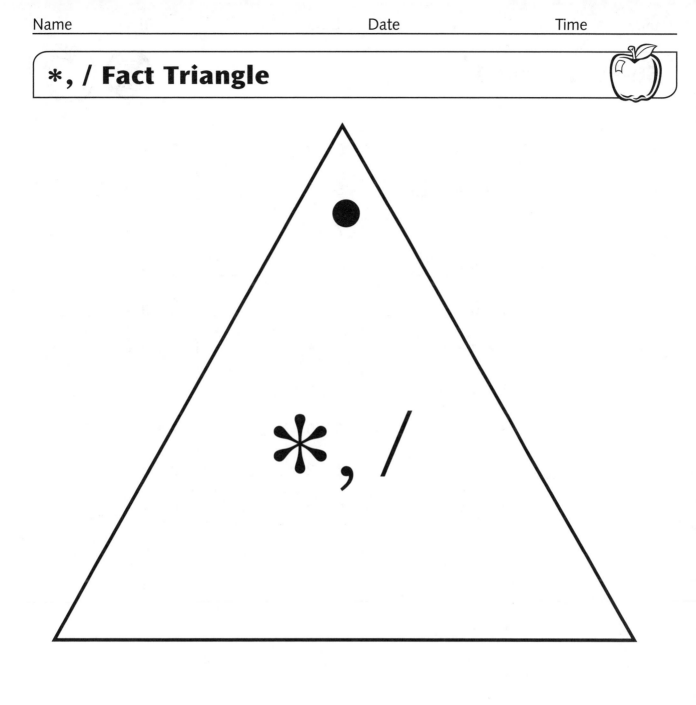

50-Facts Test 1

7 * 7 = _____	9 * 8 = _____	5 * 8 = _____	5 * 7 = _____
5 * 6 = _____	4 * 7 = _____	5 * 3 = _____	5 * 2 = _____
3 * 8 = _____	2 * 0 = _____	7 * 8 = _____	9 * 4 = _____
7 * 9 = _____	4 * 9 = _____	6 * 4 = _____	6 * 9 = _____
0 * 4 = _____	1 * 0 = _____	3 * 9 = _____	8 * 9 = _____
6 * 6 = _____	2 * 7 = _____	7 * 6 = _____	7 * 3 = _____
4 * 5 = _____	8 * 4 = _____	5 * 5 = _____	5 * 4 = _____
3 * 5 = _____	8 * 2 = _____	9 * 9 = _____	9 * 7 = _____
9 * 5 = _____	2 * 6 = _____	7 * 2 = _____	9 * 6 = _____
4 * 1 = _____	4 * 8 = _____	2 * 9 = _____	8 * 7 = _____
2 * 4 = _____	8 * 6 = _____	4 * 4 = _____	7 * 5 = _____
5 * 9 = _____	6 * 5 = _____	8 * 8 = _____	3 * 3 = _____
4 * 3 = _____	6 * 3 = _____		

1-Minute Score: _____ = _____ = _____%
                 50   100

3-Minute Score: _____ = _____ = _____%
                 50   100

50-Facts Test 2

6 * 6 = _____	4 * 7 = _____	8 * 3 = _____	7 * 7 = _____
5 * 0 = _____	4 * 2 = _____	6 * 5 = _____	6 * 9 = _____
4 * 4 = _____	5 * 8 = _____	5 * 5 = _____	4 * 6 = _____
6 * 3 = _____	5 * 9 = _____	9 * 8 = _____	3 * 6 = _____
8 * 7 = _____	2 * 5 = _____	8 * 2 = _____	9 * 5 = _____
2 * 7 = _____	8 * 8 = _____	7 * 8 = _____	9 * 9 = _____
4 * 9 = _____	4 * 8 = _____	8 * 6 = _____	8 * 5 = _____
5 * 3 = _____	6 * 8 = _____	9 * 7 = _____	7 * 6 = _____
8 * 1 = _____	7 * 3 = _____	3 * 3 = _____	5 * 4 = _____
3 * 8 = _____	9 * 6 = _____	7 * 5 = _____	3 * 7 = _____
7 * 9 = _____	7 * 4 = _____	9 * 4 = _____	9 * 2 = _____
6 * 7 = _____	4 * 3 = _____	4 * 5 = _____	8 * 9 = _____
3 * 5 = _____	9 * 3 = _____		

1-Minute Score: _____ = _____ = _____%
                   50   100

3-Minute Score: _____ = _____ = _____%
                   50   100

50-Facts Test 3

2 * 0 = _____	6 * 9 = _____	4 * 6 = _____	9 * 2 = _____
3 * 3 = _____	7 * 6 = _____	9 * 3 = _____	7 * 9 = _____
5 * 7 = _____	6 * 5 = _____	5 * 6 = _____	5 * 9 = _____
5 * 5 = _____	8 * 6 = _____	3 * 7 = _____	9 * 4 = _____
4 * 8 = _____	7 * 2 = _____	9 * 5 = _____	4 * 5 = _____
4 * 4 = _____	2 * 6 = _____	9 * 9 = _____	6 * 8 = _____
3 * 9 = _____	9 * 7 = _____	8 * 5 = _____	6 * 3 = _____
2 * 4 = _____	6 * 7 = _____	2 * 3 = _____	3 * 8 = _____
9 * 6 = _____	1 * 1 = _____	7 * 7 = _____	4 * 7 = _____
8 * 7 = _____	8 * 4 = _____	7 * 5 = _____	5 * 4 = _____
9 * 8 = _____	8 * 8 = _____	6 * 4 = _____	6 * 6 = _____
3 * 5 = _____	8 * 9 = _____	7 * 8 = _____	3 * 6 = _____
3 * 4 = _____	8 * 3 = _____		

1-Minute Score: _____ = _____ = _____%
                 50   100

3-Minute Score: _____ = _____ = _____%
                 50   100

50-Facts Test 4

$4 * 8 =$	$7 * 5 =$	$9 * 9 =$	$7 * 6 =$
$3 * 7 =$	$4 * 9 =$	$5 * 7 =$	$3 * 4 =$
$6 * 6 =$	$5 * 8 =$	$8 * 5 =$	$4 * 5 =$
$8 * 3 =$	$1 * 3 =$	$6 * 8 =$	$8 * 8 =$
$6 * 9 =$	$7 * 9 =$	$4 * 4 =$	$9 * 4 =$
$2 * 4 =$	$9 * 8 =$	$7 * 4 =$	$9 * 6 =$
$4 * 6 =$	$2 * 8 =$	$8 * 9 =$	$7 * 3 =$
$7 * 0 =$	$5 * 5 =$	$9 * 7 =$	$2 * 9 =$
$9 * 3 =$	$3 * 1 =$	$1 * 1 =$	$6 * 4 =$
$6 * 7 =$	$8 * 6 =$	$5 * 9 =$	$3 * 6 =$
$2 * 5 =$	$1 * 0 =$	$5 * 6 =$	$6 * 2 =$
$4 * 3 =$	$3 * 5 =$	$7 * 7 =$	$8 * 7 =$
$4 * 7 =$	$7 * 2 =$		

1-Minute Score: _____ = _____ = _____%
                   50   100

3-Minute Score: _____ = _____ = _____%
                   50   100

My 50-Facts Test Scores

Write the date on the bottom line. Using a pencil, make a dot above each date to record your 1-minute score. Using a pen, make a dot above each date to record your 3-minute score. Connect the pencil dots. Then connect the pen dots.

My 50-Facts Test Scores *continued*

Tape this page to *Math Masters,* page 414 if that page is filled up.

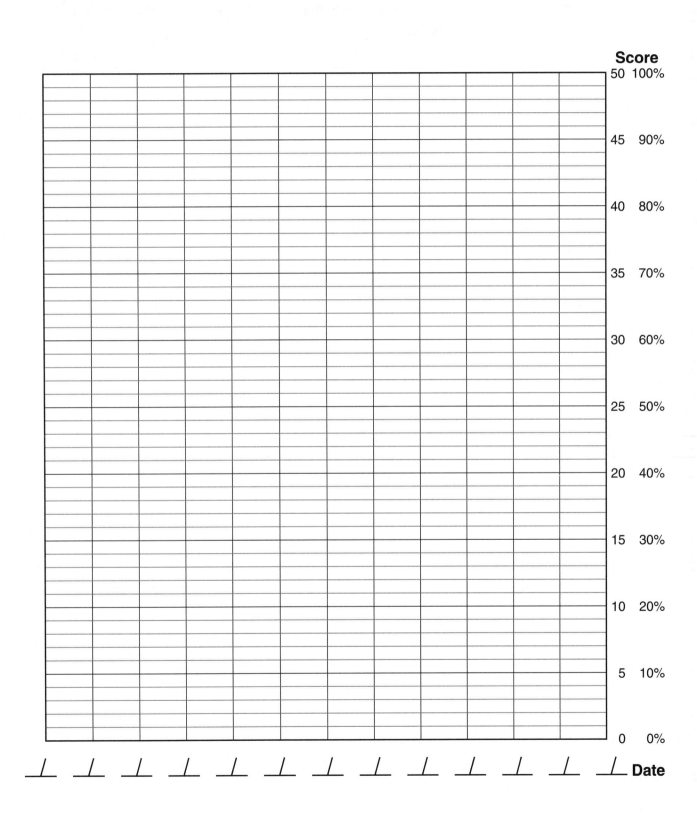

Class 50-Facts Test Scores

Write the date on the bottom line. Make a dot above each date to record each student's 1-minute score. On the gridline above each date, mark "M" for the class median score and "A" for the class mean, or average, score.

Class 50-Facts Test Scores *continued*

Tape this page to *Math Masters,* page 416 if that page is filled up.

Score

Fact Families

Complete each Fact Triangle. Write the fact family for each Fact Triangle.

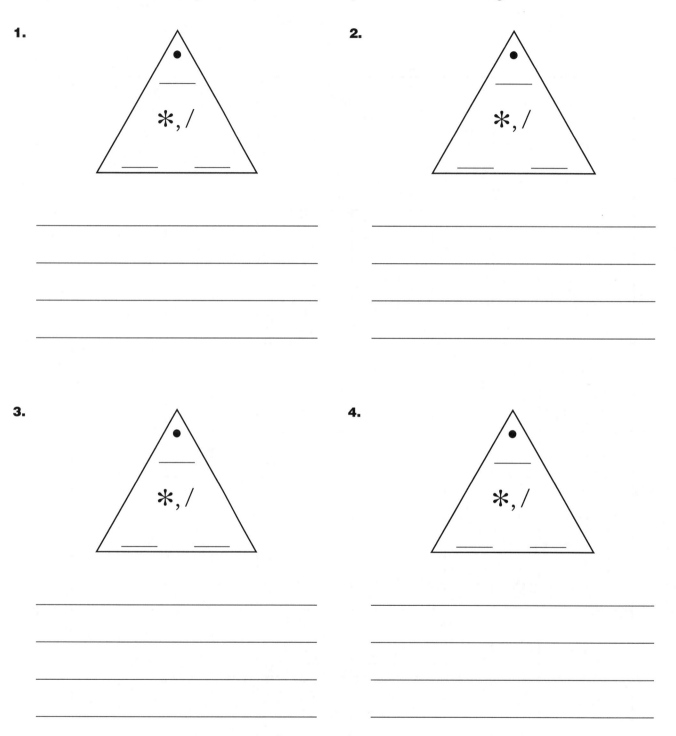

1.

*, /

_____

_____

_____

_____

2.

*, /

_____

_____

_____

_____

3.

*, /

_____

_____

_____

_____

4.

*, /

_____

_____

_____

_____

My Country Notes

A. Facts about the country

_____ is located in _____.
name of country   name of continent

1. It is bordered by _____
                          countries, bodies of water

_____.

2. Population: _____ Area: _____ square miles

3. Languages spoken: _____

_____

4. Monetary unit: _____

5. Exchange rate (optional): 1 _____ = _____

B. Facts about the capital of the country

_____ Population: _____
name of capital

1. When it is noon in my hometown, it is _____ in _____.
                                              time (A.M. or P.M.?)   name of capital

2. In _____ / _____, the average high temperature in _____
        month   month   name of capital

is about _____ °F. The average low temperature is about _____ °F.

3. What kinds of clothes should I pack for my visit to this capital? Why?

_____

_____

_____

_____

My Country Notes *continued*

4. Turn to the Route Map found on journal pages 172 and 173.
   Draw a line from the last city you visited to the capital of this country.

5. If your class is using the Route Log, record the information on journal page 171 or *Math Masters,* page 421.

6. Can you find any facts on pages 302–305 in your *Student Reference Book* that apply to this country? For example, is one of the 10 tallest mountains in the world located in this country? List all the facts you can find.

_____

_____

_____

_____

_____

C. My impressions about the country

Do you know anyone who has visited or lived in this country? If so, ask that person for an interview. Read about the country's customs and about interesting places to visit there. Use encyclopedias, travel books, the travel section of a newspaper, or library books. Try to get brochures from a travel agent. Then describe below some interesting things you have learned about this country.

_____

_____

_____

_____

_____

_____

_____

My Route Log

Date	Country		Capital	Air distance from last capital	Total distance traveled so far
	1	U.S.A.	Washington, D.C.	████	
	2	Egypt	Cairo		
	3				
	4				
	5				
	6				
	7				
	8				
	9				
	10				
	11				
	12				
	13				
	14				
	15				
	16				
	17				
	18				
	19				
	20				

A Guide for Solving Number Stories

1. **Understand the problem.**
   - ◆ Read the problem. Can you retell it in your own words?
   - ◆ What do you want to find out?
   - ◆ What do you know?
   - ◆ Do you have all the information needed to solve the problem?

2. **Plan what to do.**
   - ◆ Is the problem like one that you have solved before?
   - ◆ Is there a pattern you can use?
   - ◆ Can you draw a picture or a diagram?
   - ◆ Can you write a number model or make a table?
   - ◆ Can you use counters, base-10 blocks, or some other tool?
   - ◆ Can you estimate the answer and check if you're right?

3. **Carry out the plan.**
   - ◆ After you decide what to do, do it. Be careful.
   - ◆ Make a written record of what you do.
   - ◆ Answer the question.

4. **Look back.**
   - ◆ Does your answer make sense?
   - ◆ Does your answer agree with your estimate?
   - ◆ Can you write a number model for the problem?
   - ◆ Can you solve the problem in another way?

Situation Diagrams

423

Broken Calculator Record Sheet

Broken Key:

To Solve:

Broken Key:

To Solve:

Broken Key:

To Solve:

Broken Key:

To Solve:

Broken Key:

To Solve:

Broken Key:

To Solve:

Broken Calculator

Broken Key:

To Solve:

Base-10 Grids

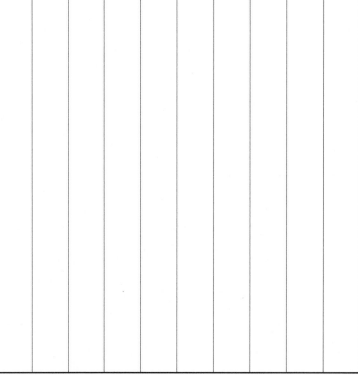

Number Grid (Decimal Version)

									0
0.01	0.02	0.03	0.04	0.05	0.06	0.07	0.08	0.09	0.10
0.11	0.12	0.13	0.14	0.15	0.16	0.17	0.18	0.19	0.20
0.21	0.22	0.23	0.24	0.25	0.26	0.27	0.28	0.29	0.30
0.31	0.32	0.33	0.34	0.35	0.36	0.37	0.38	0.39	0.40
0.41	0.42	0.43	0.44	0.45	0.46	0.47	0.48	0.49	0.50
0.51	0.52	0.53	0.54	0.55	0.56	0.57	0.58	0.59	0.60
0.61	0.62	0.63	0.64	0.65	0.66	0.67	0.68	0.69	0.70
0.71	0.72	0.73	0.74	0.75	0.76	0.77	0.78	0.79	0.80
0.81	0.82	0.83	0.84	0.85	0.86	0.87	0.88	0.89	0.90
0.91	0.92	0.93	0.94	0.95	0.96	0.97	0.98	0.99	1.00

$1 and $10 Bills

A cm/mm Ruler

Multiplication/Division Puzzles

Solve the multiplication/division puzzles mentally. Fill in the blank boxes.

Examples:

*,/	400	6,000
5	2,000	30,000
8	3,200	48,000

*,/	90	20
3	270	60
7	630	140

1.

*,/		

2.

*,/		

3.

*,/		

4.

*,/		

5.

*,/		

6.

*,/		

Make up and solve some puzzles of your own.

7.

*,/		

8.

*,/		

Computation Grids

Array Grid

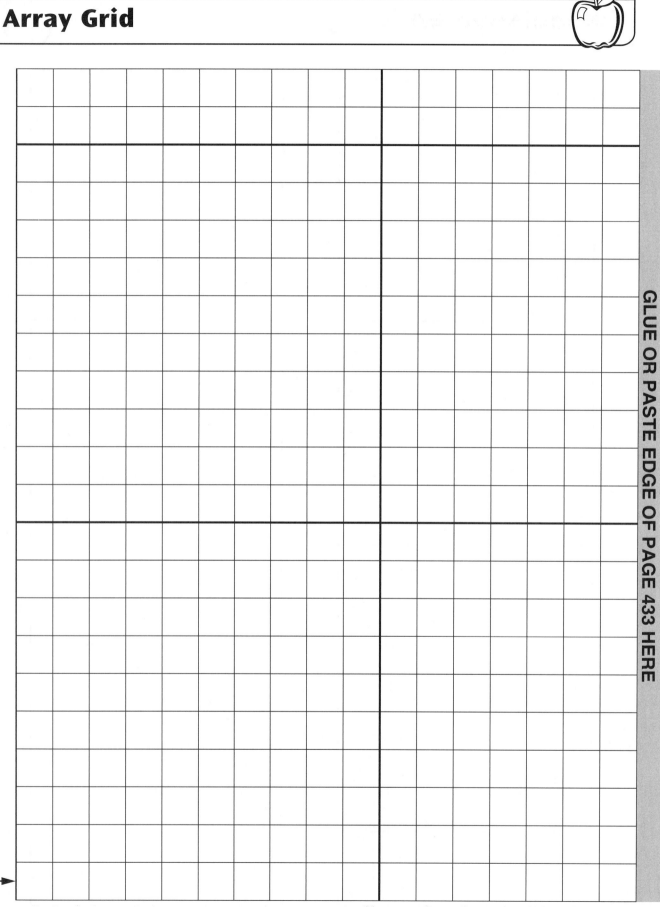

GLUE OR PASTE EDGE OF PAGE 433 HERE

Copyright © Wright Group/McGraw-Hill

Start here.

Array Grid *continued*

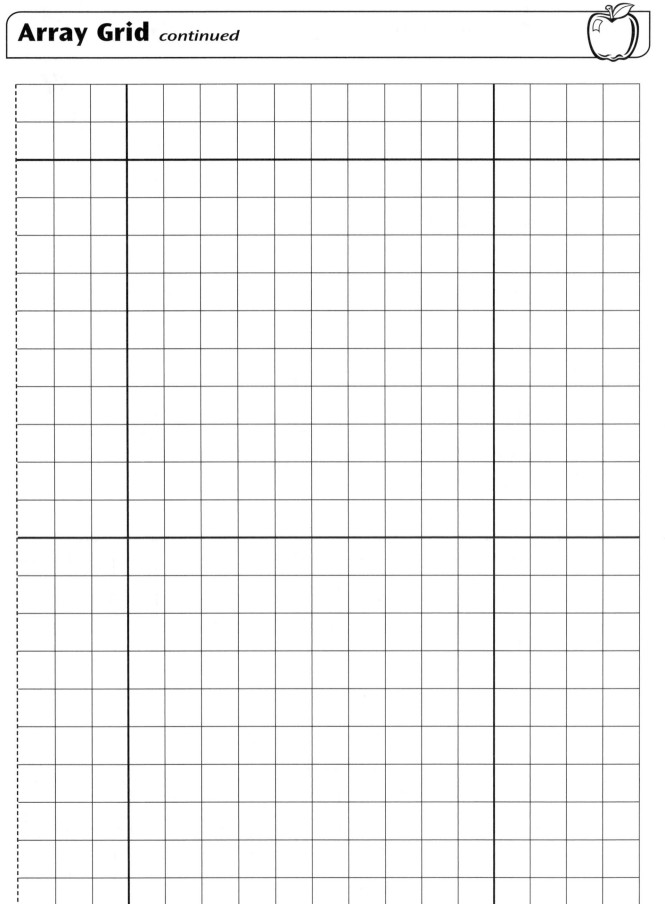

Lattice Multiplication Computation Grids

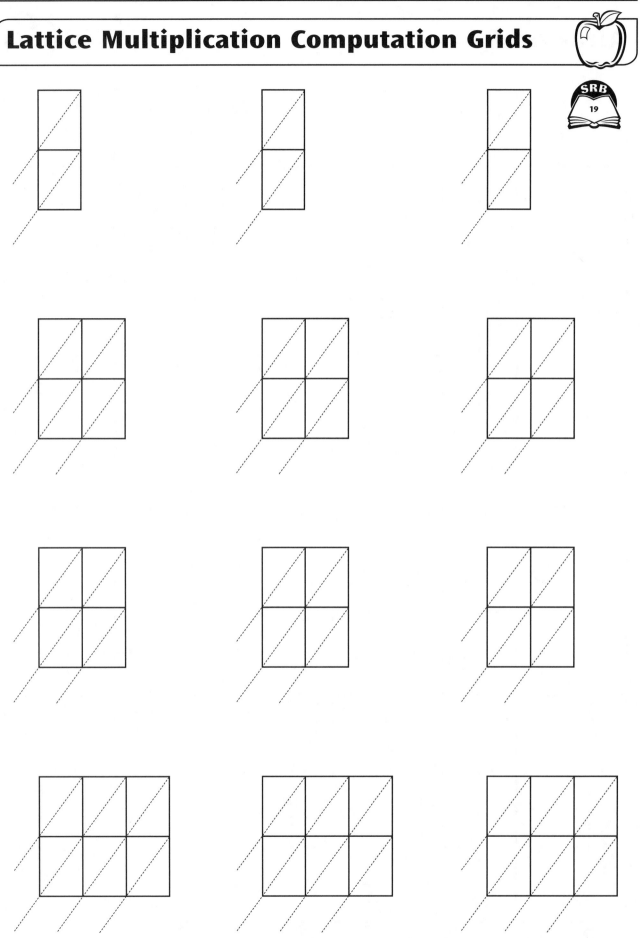

Fact Lattice

	9	8	7	6	5	4	3	2	1	0	
	0/0	0/0	0/0	0/0	0/0	0/0	0/0	0/0	0/0	0/0	**0**
	0/9	0/8	0/7	0/6	0/5	0/4	0/3	0/2	0/1	0/0	**1**
	1/8	1/6	1/4	1/2	1/0	0/8	0/6	0/4	0/2	0/0	**2**
	2/7	2/4	2/1	1/8	1/5	1/2	0/9	0/6	0/3	0/0	**3**
	3/6	3/2	2/8	2/4	2/0	1/6	1/2	0/8	0/4	0/0	**4**
	4/5	4/0	3/5	3/0	2/5	2/0	1/5	1/0	0/5	0/0	**5**
	5/4	4/8	4/2	3/6	3/0	2/4	1/8	1/2	0/6	0/0	**6**
	6/3	5/6	4/9	4/2	3/5	2/8	2/1	1/4	0/7	0/0	**7**
	7/2	6/4	5/6	4/8	4/0	3/2	2/4	1/6	0/8	0/0	**8**
	8/1	7/2	6/3	5/4	4/5	3/6	2/7	1/8	0/9	0/0	**9**

Multiplication/Division Diagrams

_____	_____ per _____	_____ in all

Number model: _____

Answer: _____

_____	_____ per _____	_____ in all

Number model: _____

Answer: _____

_____	_____ per _____	_____ in all

Number model: _____

Answer: _____

Dot Paper

Easy Multiples

100 * _____ = _____

50 * _____ = _____

20 * _____ = _____

10 * _____ = _____

5 * _____ = _____

2 * _____ = _____

1 * _____ = _____

100 * _____ = _____

50 * _____ = _____

20 * _____ = _____

10 * _____ = _____

5 * _____ = _____

2 * _____ = _____

1 * _____ = _____

100 * _____ = _____

50 * _____ = _____

20 * _____ = _____

10 * _____ = _____

5 * _____ = _____

2 * _____ = _____

1 * _____ = _____

100 * _____ = _____

50 * _____ = _____

20 * _____ = _____

10 * _____ = _____

5 * _____ = _____

2 * _____ = _____

1 * _____ = _____

Full-Circle Protractor

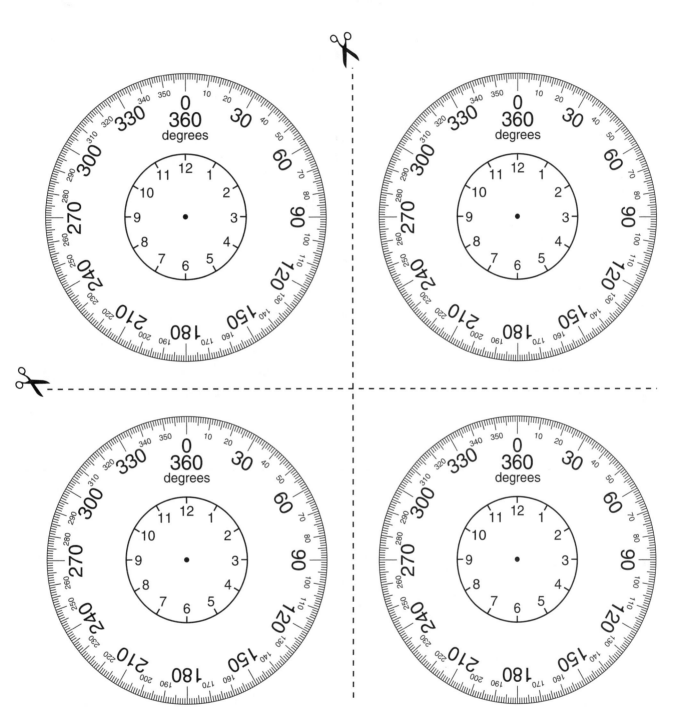

Coordinate Grids

1. Plot and label each point on the coordinate grid.

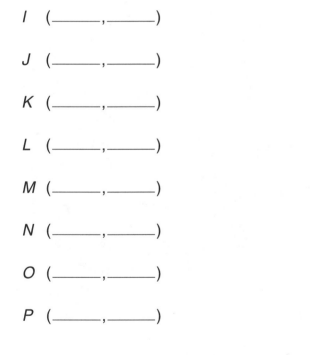

A (_____,_____)

B (_____,_____)

C (_____,_____)

D (_____,_____)

E (_____,_____)

F (_____,_____)

G (_____,_____)

H (_____,_____)

2. Write the ordered number pair for each point plotted on the coordinate grid.

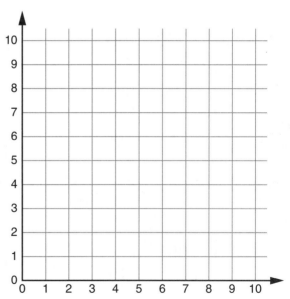

I (_____,_____)

J (_____,_____)

K (_____,_____)

L (_____,_____)

M (_____,_____)

N (_____,_____)

O (_____,_____)

P (_____,_____)

440

Tangram Puzzle

Base-10 Block Designs

Decimal: _____

Fraction: _____

Decimal: _____

Fraction: _____

Decimal: _____

Fraction: _____

Decimal: _____

Fraction: _____

Grid Paper ($\frac{1}{4}$ in.)

Grid Paper (1 in.)

Name _____   Date _____   Time _____

Fractions, Decimals, and Percents

Fill in the missing numbers. If the grid is not shaded, then shade the grid.

100%
large square

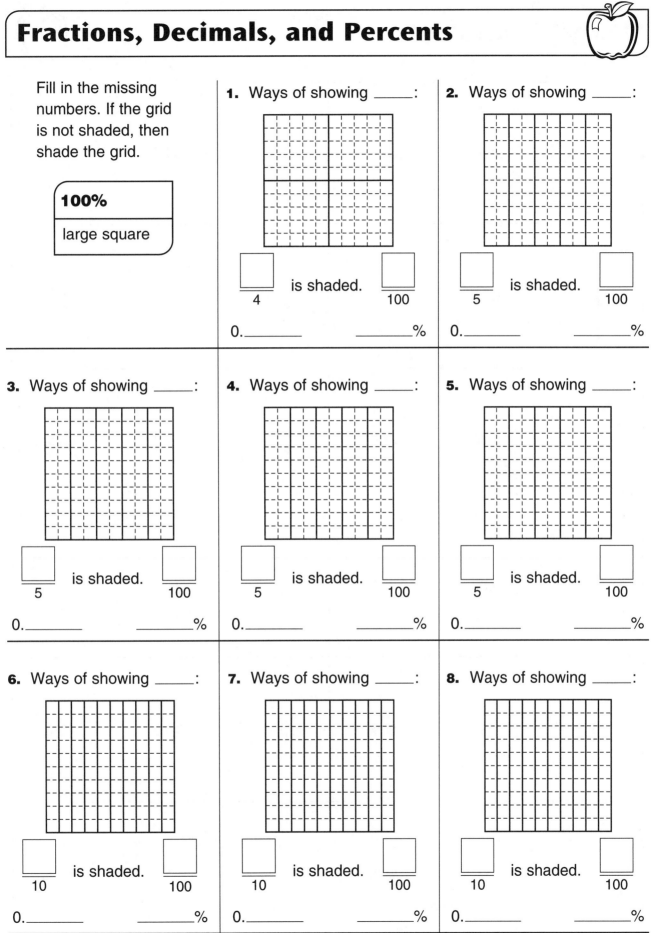

1. Ways of showing ____:

[□]/4 is shaded. [□]/100

0.____ ____%

2. Ways of showing ____:

[□]/5 is shaded. [□]/100

0.____ ____%

3. Ways of showing ____:

[□]/5 is shaded. [□]/100

0.____ ____%

4. Ways of showing ____:

[□]/5 is shaded. [□]/100

0.____ ____%

5. Ways of showing ____:

[□]/5 is shaded. [□]/100

0.____ ____%

6. Ways of showing ____:

[□]/10 is shaded. [□]/100

0.____ ____%

7. Ways of showing ____:

[□]/10 is shaded. [□]/100

0.____ ____%

8. Ways of showing ____:

[□]/10 is shaded. [□]/100

0.____ ____%

445

Name   Date   Time

"Easy" Equivalents

$\frac{1}{2}$	0.50	50%	$\frac{1}{4}$	0.25	25%
$\frac{3}{4}$	0.75	75%	$\frac{1}{5}$	0.20	20%
$\frac{2}{5}$	0.40	40%	$\frac{3}{5}$	0.60	60%
$\frac{4}{5}$	0.80	80%	$\frac{1}{10}$	0.10	10%
$\frac{3}{10}$	0.30	30%	$\frac{7}{10}$	0.70	70%
$\frac{9}{10}$	0.90	90%	$\frac{2}{2}$	1	100%

446

Isometric Dot Paper

Ounces and Grams

ounces

| 0 | 2 | 4 | 6 | 8 | 10 | 12 | 14 | 16 | 18 | 20 |

| 0 | 100 | 200 | 300 | 400 | 500 |

grams

Square Pyramid Template

Triangular Prism Template

450

Cone Template

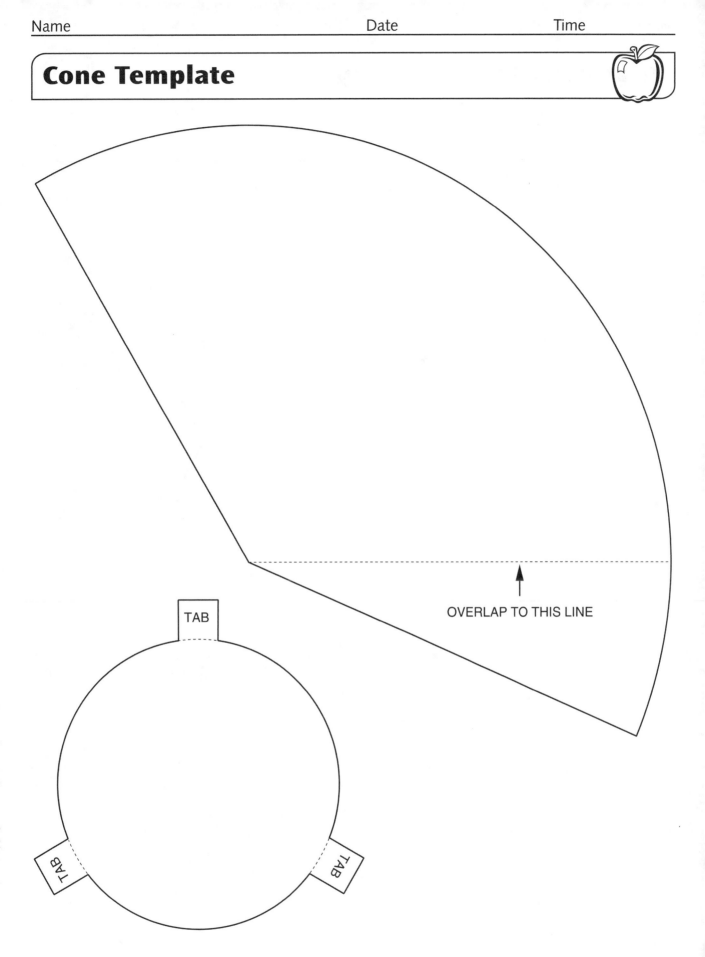

OVERLAP TO THIS LINE

TAB

TAB

TAB

451

Triangular Pyramid Template

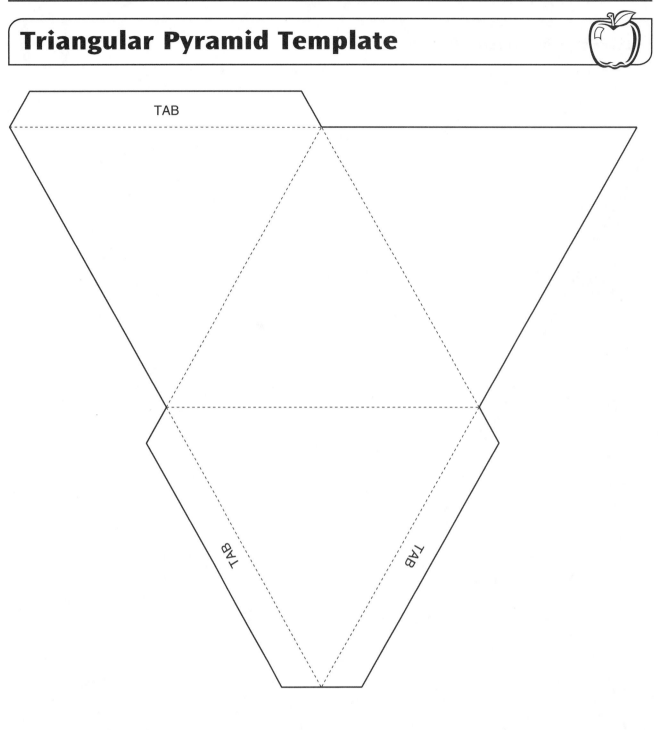

TAB

TAB

TAB

Cube Template

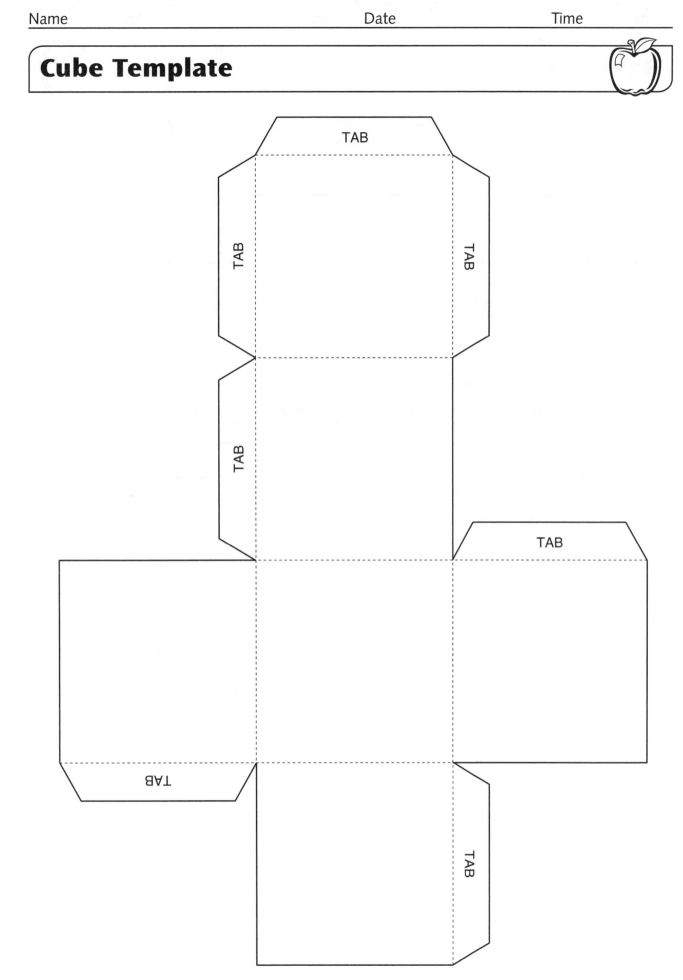

453

Rate Tables

For each problem, fill in the rate table. Then answer the question below the table.

1. _____

_____

_____ ? _____ _____
                                                                    (unit)

2. _____

_____

_____ ? _____ _____
                                                                    (unit)

3. _____

_____

_____ ? _____ _____
                                                                    (unit)

Game Masters

Angle Tangle Record Sheet

Copyright © Wright Group/McGraw-Hill

Name _____ Date _____ Time _____

Round	Angle	Estimated measure	Actual measure	Score
1		_____ °	_____ °	
2		_____ °	_____ °	
3		_____ °	_____ °	
4		_____ °	_____ °	
5		_____ °	_____ °	
			Total Score	

457

Multiplication Wrestling Record Sheet

Name _____ Date _____ Time _____

Round 1 Cards: _____ _____ _____ _____

Numbers formed: _____ * _____

Teams: (_____ + _____) * (_____ + _____)

Products: _____ * _____ = _____

_____ * _____ = _____

_____ * _____ = _____

_____ * _____ = _____

Total (add 4 products): _____

Round 2 Cards: _____ _____ _____ _____

Numbers formed: _____ * _____

Teams: (_____ + _____) * (_____ + _____)

Products: _____ * _____ = _____

_____ * _____ = _____

_____ * _____ = _____

_____ * _____ = _____

Total (add 4 products): _____

Round 3 Cards: _____ _____ _____ _____

Numbers formed: _____ * _____

Teams: (_____ + _____) * (_____ + _____)

Products: _____ * _____ = _____

_____ * _____ = _____

_____ * _____ = _____

_____ * _____ = _____

Total (add 4 products): _____

488

Copyright © Wright Group/McGraw-Hill

Alleyway **Game Mat**

SRB
311

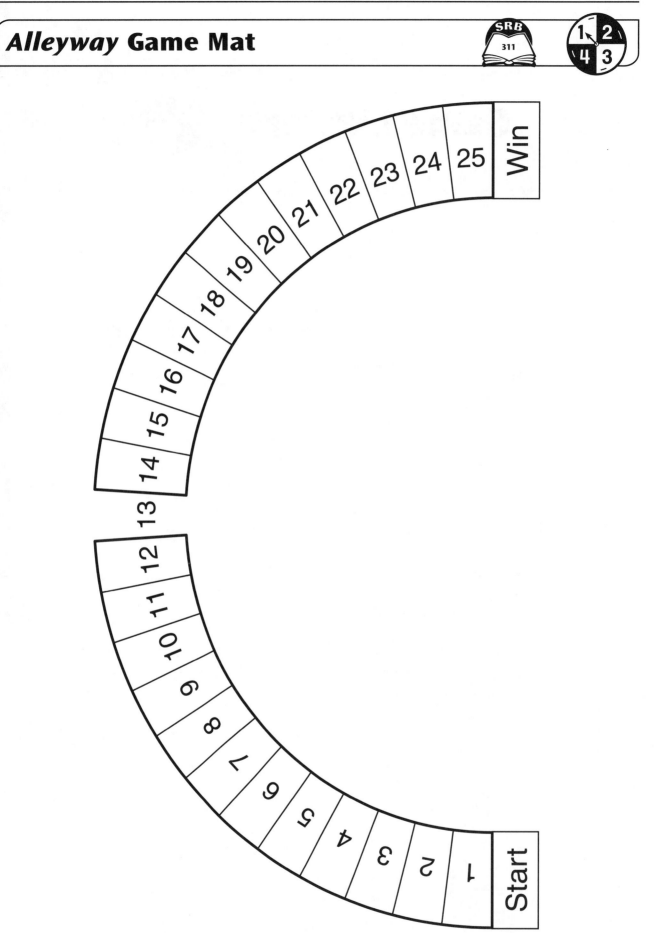

Name _____ Date _____ Time _____

Angle Tangle **Record Sheet**

Round	Angle	Estimated measure	Actual measure	Score
1		_____ °	_____ °	
2		_____ °	_____ °	
3		_____ °	_____ °	
4		_____ °	_____ °	
5		_____ °	_____ °	
			Total Score	

Copyright © Wright Group/McGraw-Hill

457

Base-10 Exchange (Hundredths)

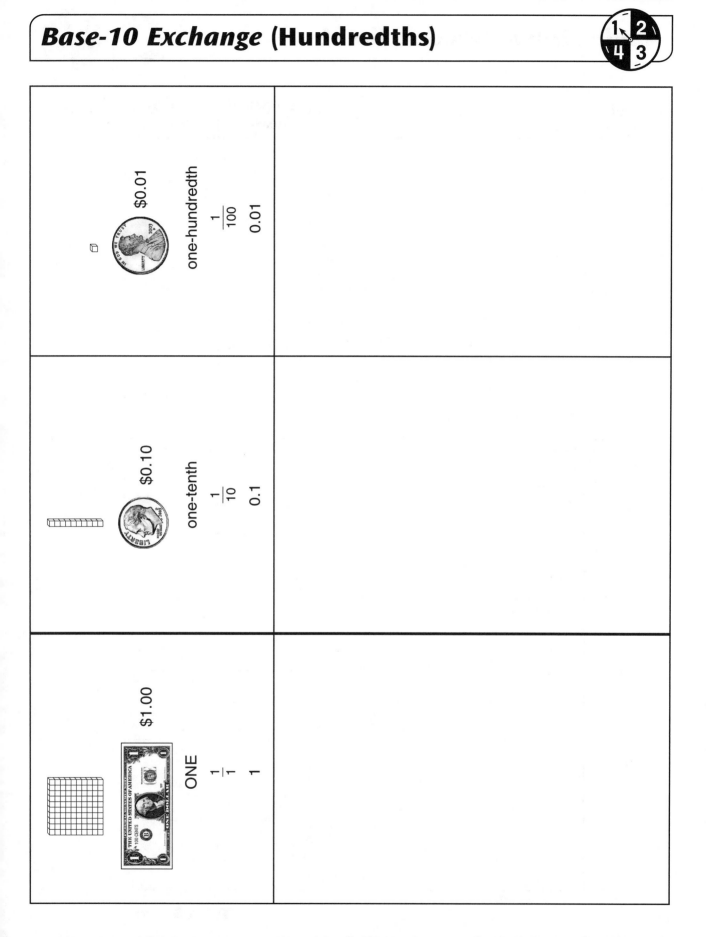

$0.01

one-hundredth

$\frac{1}{100}$

0.01

$0.10

one-tenth

$\frac{1}{10}$

0.1

$1.00

ONE

$\frac{1}{1}$

1

458

Base-10 Exchange (Thousandths)

one-thousandth $\frac{1}{1,000}$ 0.001	
one-hundredth $\frac{1}{100}$ 0.01	
one-tenth $\frac{1}{10}$ 0.1	
ONE $\frac{1}{1}$ 1	

Name _____ Date _____ Time _____

Baseball Multiplication Game Mat

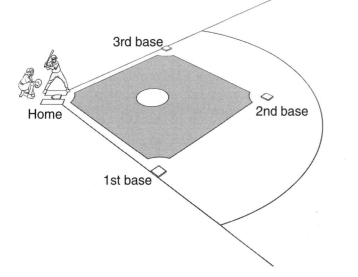

3rd base

2nd base

Home

1st base

Hitting Table 1-to-6 Facts		
1 to 9	Out	
10 to 19	Single (1 base)	
20 to 29	Double (2 bases)	
30 to 35	Triple (3 bases)	
36	Home Run (4 bases)	

Inning		1	2	3	Total
Team 1	Outs				
	Runs				
Team 2	Outs				
	Runs				

Inning		1	2	3	Total
Team 1	Outs				
	Runs				
Team 2	Outs				
	Runs				

Inning		1	2	3	Total
Team 1	Outs				
	Runs				
Team 2	Outs				
	Runs				

Beat the Calculator Gameboard

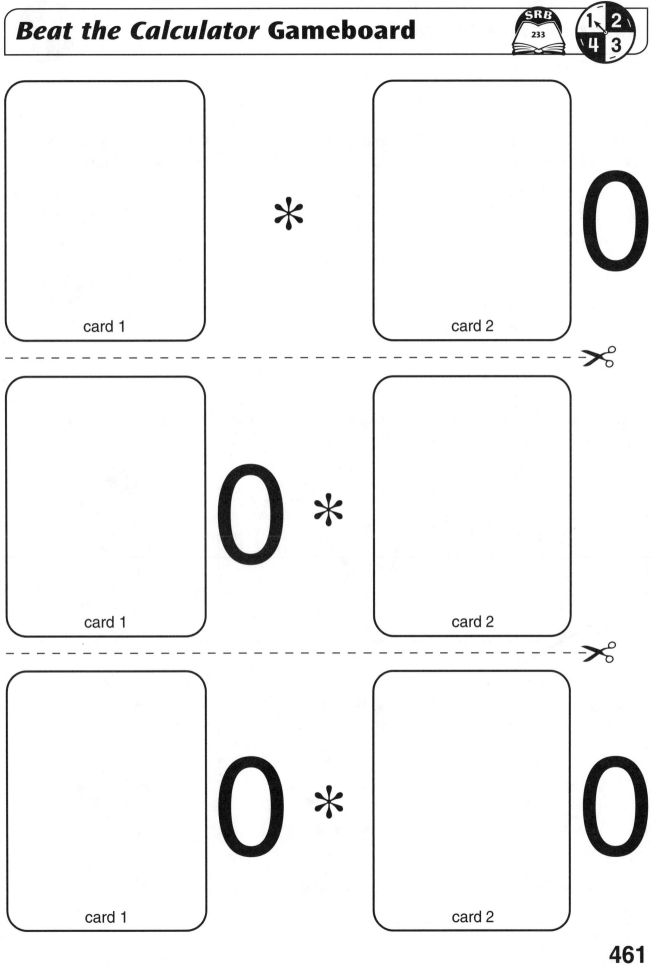

461

Chances Are Event Cards

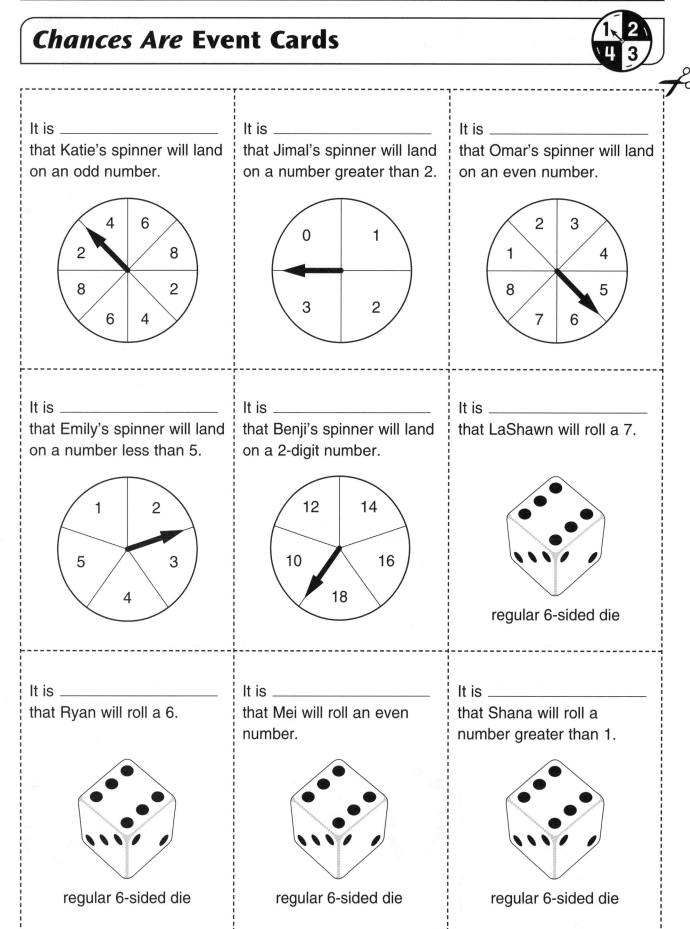

It is _____
that Katie's spinner will land
on an odd number.

It is _____
that Jimal's spinner will land
on a number greater than 2.

It is _____
that Omar's spinner will land
on an even number.

It is _____
that Emily's spinner will land
on a number less than 5.

It is _____
that Benji's spinner will land
on a 2-digit number.

It is _____
that LaShawn will roll a 7.

regular 6-sided die

It is _____
that Ryan will roll a 6.

regular 6-sided die

It is _____
that Mei will roll an even
number.

regular 6-sided die

It is _____
that Shana will roll a
number greater than 1.

regular 6-sided die

Chances Are **Event Cards** *continued*

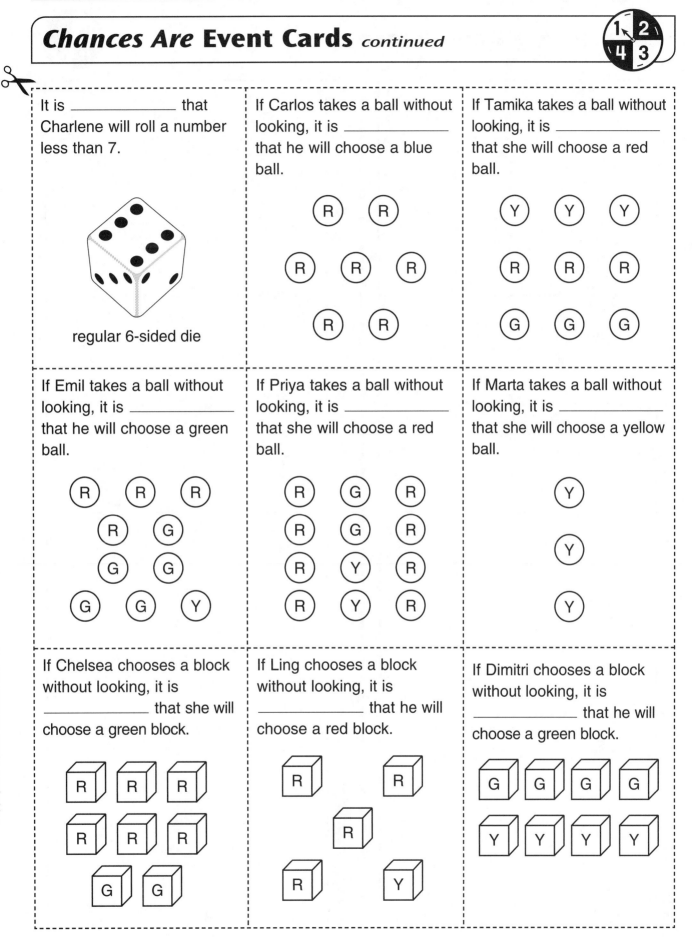

It is _____ that Charlene will roll a number less than 7.

regular 6-sided die

If Carlos takes a ball without looking, it is _____ that he will choose a blue ball.

R R
R R R
R R

If Tamika takes a ball without looking, it is _____ that she will choose a red ball.

Y Y Y
R R R
G G G

If Emil takes a ball without looking, it is _____ that he will choose a green ball.

R R R
R G
G G
G G Y

If Priya takes a ball without looking, it is _____ that she will choose a red ball.

R G R
R G R
R Y R
R Y R

If Marta takes a ball without looking, it is _____ that she will choose a yellow ball.

Y
Y
Y

If Chelsea chooses a block without looking, it is _____ that she will choose a green block.

R R R
R R R
G G

If Ling chooses a block without looking, it is _____ that he will choose a red block.

R R
R
R Y

If Dimitri chooses a block without looking, it is _____ that he will choose a green block.

G G G G
Y Y Y Y

463

Chances Are Gameboard

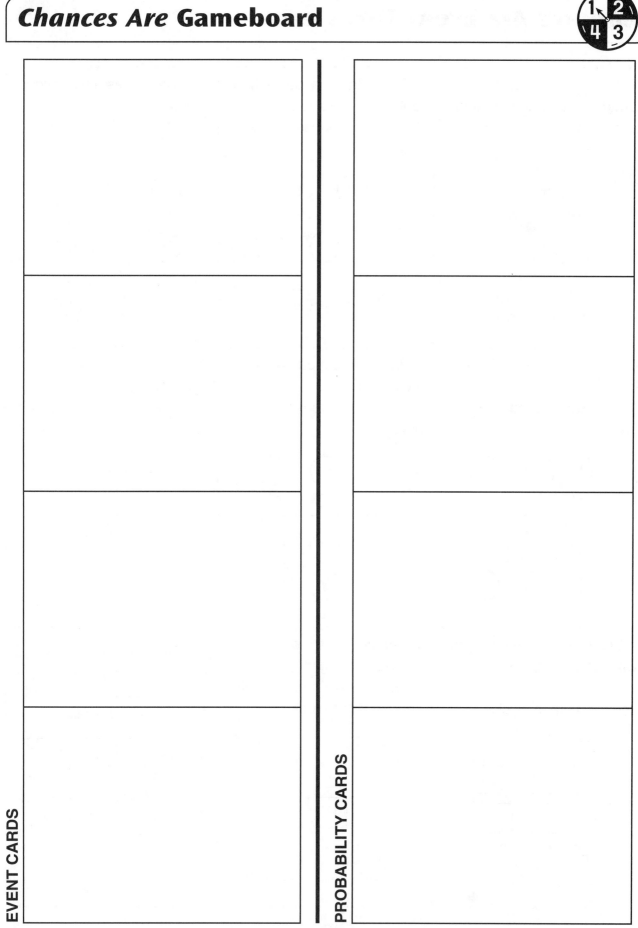

EVENT CARDS

PROBABILITY CARDS

Chances Are Probability Cards

Impossible No chance Can't happen No way	Impossible No chance Can't happen No way	Impossible No chance Can't happen No way
Unlikely Less than half Slight chance Not much	Unlikely Less than half Slight chance Not much	Unlikely Less than half Slight chance Not much
Unlikely Less than half Slight chance Not much	50-50 About half Even chance	50-50 About half Even chance

465

Chances Are Probability Cards *continued*

50-50 About half Even chance	50-50 About half Even chance	Likely More than half Good chance Probably
Likely More than half Good chance Probably	Likely More than half Good chance Probably	Likely More than half Good chance Probably
Certain Sure thing Positive Absolutely	Certain Sure thing Positive Absolutely	Certain Sure thing Positive Absolutely

Coin Cards

Credits/Debits Record Sheets

SRB 238

Game 1

Record Sheet

	Start	Change	End, and next start
1	+ $/0		
2			
3			
4			
5			
6			
7			
8			
9			
10			

Game 2

Record Sheet

	Start	Change	End, and next start
1	+ $/0		
2			
3			
4			
5			
6			
7			
8			
9			
10			

Number line: -22 to 22

Credits/Debits Game (Advanced Version) Record Sheets

Game 1

	Start	Change		End, and next start
		Addition or Subtraction	Credit or Debit	
1				
2				
3				
4				
5				
6				
7				
8				
9				
10				

Game 2

	Start	Change		End, and next start
		Addition or Subtraction	Credit or Debit	
1				
2				
3				
4				
5				
6				
7				
8				
9				
10				

Division Arrays **Record Sheet**

Your score is the number of counters per row. If there are 0 leftover counters, your score is double the number of counters per row.

Round	Rows	Counters per Row	Counters in All	Leftover Counters	Score
Sample	*3*	*5*	*15*	*0*	*10*
1					
2					
3					
4					
5					
				Total Score	

✂ -

Name   Date   Time

Division Arrays **Record Sheet**

Your score is the number of counters per row. If there are 0 leftover counters, your score is double the number of counters per row.

Round	Rows	Counters per Row	Counters in All	Leftover Counters	Score
Sample	*3*	*5*	*15*	*0*	*10*
1					
2					
3					
4					
5					
				Total Score	

Division Dash Record Sheet

	Division Problem	Quotient	Score
Sample	49 ÷ 4	12 R1	12
1			
2			
3			
4			
5			

✂ --

Name   Date   Time

Division Dash Record Sheet

	Division Problem	Quotient	Score
Sample	49 ÷ 4	12 R1	12
1			
2			
3			
4			
5			

Fishing for Digits Record Sheet

	Beginning Number	X						
1	New Number							
	New Number							
2	New Number							
	New Number							
3	New Number							
	New Number							
4	New Number							
	New Number							
5	New Number							
	Final Number							

✂ -

Name   Date   Time

Fishing for Digits Record Sheet

	Beginning Number	X						
1	New Number							
	New Number							
2	New Number							
	New Number							
3	New Number							
	New Number							
4	New Number							
	New Number							
5	New Number							
	Final Number							

Fraction Match Cards

$\frac{0}{2}$ $\qquad$ $\frac{0}{2}$	$\frac{1}{2}$ $\qquad$ $\frac{1}{2}$	$\frac{2}{2}$ $\qquad$ $\frac{2}{2}$	$\frac{0}{3}$ $\qquad$ $\frac{0}{3}$
$\dfrac{0}{2}$	$\dfrac{1}{2}$	$\dfrac{2}{2}$	$\dfrac{0}{3}$
$\frac{1}{3}$ $\qquad$ $\frac{1}{3}$	$\frac{2}{3}$ $\qquad$ $\frac{2}{3}$	$\frac{3}{3}$ $\qquad$ $\frac{3}{3}$	$\frac{0}{4}$ $\qquad$ $\frac{0}{4}$
$\dfrac{1}{3}$	$\dfrac{2}{3}$	$\dfrac{3}{3}$	$\dfrac{0}{4}$
$\frac{1}{4}$ $\qquad$ $\frac{1}{4}$	$\frac{2}{4}$ $\qquad$ $\frac{2}{4}$	$\frac{3}{4}$ $\qquad$ $\frac{3}{4}$	$\frac{4}{4}$ $\qquad$ $\frac{4}{4}$
$\dfrac{1}{4}$	$\dfrac{2}{4}$	$\dfrac{3}{4}$	$\dfrac{4}{4}$
$\frac{0}{5}$ $\qquad$ $\frac{0}{5}$	$\frac{1}{5}$ $\qquad$ $\frac{1}{5}$	$\frac{2}{5}$ $\qquad$ $\frac{2}{5}$	$\frac{3}{5}$ $\qquad$ $\frac{3}{5}$
$\dfrac{0}{5}$	$\dfrac{1}{5}$	$\dfrac{2}{5}$	$\dfrac{3}{5}$

Fraction Match Cards *continued*

Fraction Match Cards *continued*

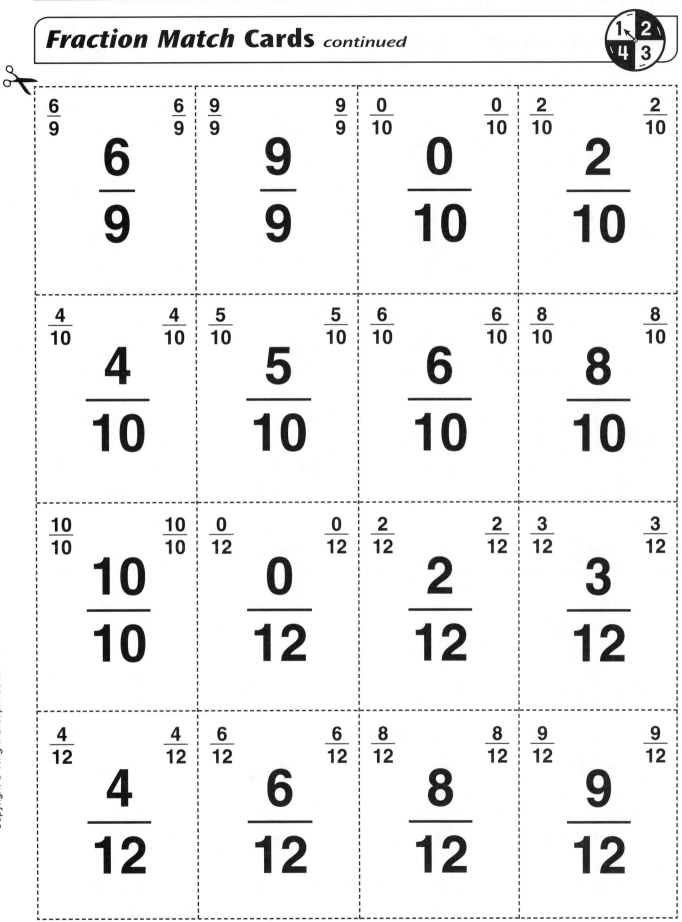

$\frac{6}{9}$ $\frac{6}{9}$ $\frac{6}{9}$	$\frac{9}{9}$ $\frac{9}{9}$ $\frac{9}{9}$	$\frac{0}{10}$ $\frac{0}{10}$ $\frac{0}{10}$	$\frac{2}{10}$ $\frac{2}{10}$ $\frac{2}{10}$
$\frac{4}{10}$ $\frac{4}{10}$ $\frac{4}{10}$	$\frac{5}{10}$ $\frac{5}{10}$ $\frac{5}{10}$	$\frac{6}{10}$ $\frac{6}{10}$ $\frac{6}{10}$	$\frac{8}{10}$ $\frac{8}{10}$ $\frac{8}{10}$
$\frac{10}{10}$ $\frac{10}{10}$ $\frac{10}{10}$	$\frac{0}{12}$ $\frac{0}{12}$ $\frac{0}{12}$	$\frac{2}{12}$ $\frac{2}{12}$ $\frac{2}{12}$	$\frac{3}{12}$ $\frac{3}{12}$ $\frac{3}{12}$
$\frac{4}{12}$ $\frac{4}{12}$ $\frac{4}{12}$	$\frac{6}{12}$ $\frac{6}{12}$ $\frac{6}{12}$	$\frac{8}{12}$ $\frac{8}{12}$ $\frac{8}{12}$	$\frac{9}{12}$ $\frac{9}{12}$ $\frac{9}{12}$

Fraction Match Cards *continued*

$\frac{10}{12}$ $\frac{10}{12}$ **$\dfrac{10}{12}$**	$\frac{12}{12}$ $\frac{12}{12}$ **$\dfrac{12}{12}$**	WILD WILD **WILD** Name an equivalent fraction with a denominator of 2, 3, 4, 5, 6, 8, 9, 10, or 12.	WILD WILD **WILD** Name an equivalent fraction with a denominator of 2, 3, 4, 5, 6, 8, 9, 10, or 12.
WILD WILD **WILD** Name an equivalent fraction with a denominator of 2, 3, 4, 5, 6, 8, 9, 10, or 12.	WILD WILD **WILD** Name an equivalent fraction with a denominator of 2, 3, 4, 5, 6, 8, 9, 10, or 12.	WILD WILD **WILD** Name an equivalent fraction with a denominator of 2, 3, 4, 5, 6, 8, 9, 10, or 12.	WILD WILD **WILD** Name an equivalent fraction with a denominator of 2, 3, 4, 5, 6, 8, 9, 10, or 12.
WILD WILD **WILD** Name an equivalent fraction with a denominator of 2, 3, 4, 5, 6, 8, 9, 10, or 12.	WILD WILD **WILD** Name an equivalent fraction with a denominator of 2, 3, 4, 5, 6, 8, 9, 10, or 12.	WILD WILD **WILD** Name an equivalent fraction with a denominator of 2, 3, 4, 5, 6, 8, 9, 10, or 12.	WILD WILD **WILD** Name an equivalent fraction with a denominator of 2, 3, 4, 5, 6, 8, 9, 10, or 12.
WILD WILD **WILD** Name an equivalent fraction with a denominator of 2, 3, 4, 5, 6, 8, 9, 10, or 12.	WILD WILD **WILD** Name an equivalent fraction with a denominator of 2, 3, 4, 5, 6, 8, 9, 10, or 12.	WILD WILD **WILD** Name an equivalent fraction with a denominator of 2, 3, 4, 5, 6, 8, 9, 10, or 12.	WILD WILD **WILD** Name an equivalent fraction with a denominator of 2, 3, 4, 5, 6, 8, 9, 10, or 12.

Fraction Of Fraction Cards

477

Fraction Of **Fraction Cards** *continued*

$\dfrac{0}{4}$	$\dfrac{3}{4}$	$\dfrac{4}{4}$	$\dfrac{0}{5}$
$\dfrac{2}{5}$	$\dfrac{3}{5}$	$\dfrac{4}{5}$	$\dfrac{5}{5}$
$\dfrac{0}{10}$	$\dfrac{2}{10}$	$\dfrac{3}{10}$	$\dfrac{4}{10}$
$\dfrac{6}{10}$	$\dfrac{7}{10}$	$\dfrac{8}{10}$	$\dfrac{9}{10}$

Fraction Of Gameboard and Record Sheet

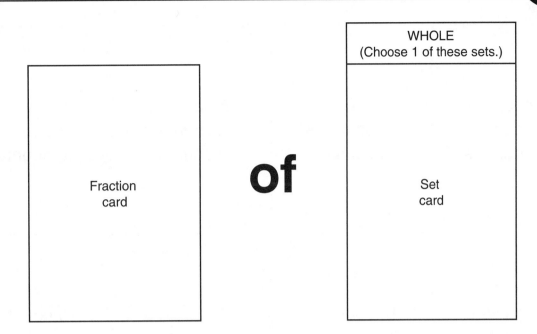

Round	"Fraction-of" Problem	Points
Sample	$\frac{1}{5}$ of 25	5
1		
2		
3		
4		
5		
6		
7		
8		
	Total Score	

Fraction Of Set Cards

3 counters 20 counters 15 counters	4 counters 21 counters 30 counters	5 counters 12 counters 20 counters	6 counters 28 counters 40 counters
8 counters 27 counters 20 counters	10 counters 32 counters 24 counters	12 counters 30 counters 25 counters	15 counters 36 counters 20 counters
18 counters 36 counters 10 counters	20 counters 4 counters 3 counters	21 counters 30 counters 24 counters	25 counters 6 counters 40 counters
28 counters 35 counters 30 counters	30 counters 32 counters 15 counters	36 counters 20 counters 24 counters	40 counters 18 counters 25 counters

Fraction/Percent Concentration

SRB 246

10%	20%	25%	30%
40%	50%	60%	70%
75%	80%	90%	100%
$\dfrac{1}{2}$	$\dfrac{1}{4}$	$\dfrac{3}{4}$	$\dfrac{1}{5}$
$\dfrac{2}{5}$	$\dfrac{3}{5}$	$\dfrac{4}{5}$	$\dfrac{1}{10}$
$\dfrac{3}{10}$	$\dfrac{7}{10}$	$\dfrac{9}{10}$	$\dfrac{2}{2}$

Fraction/Percent Concentration *continued*

0.10	0.20	0.25	0.30
0.40	0.50	0.60	0.70
0.80	0.75	0.90	1

0.10	0.20	0.25	0.30
0.40	0.50	0.60	0.70
0.80	0.75	0.90	1

Grab Bag Cards

Lina has a bag of ribbons. She has 2 red, 2 blue, *x* pink, and *y* green ribbons.

What are the chances she will pick a green ribbon without looking?

Mario has a bag of art pencils. He has 3 purple, 1 white, *x* violet, and *y* yellow pencils.

What are the chances he will pick a yellow pencil without looking?

Kenji has a bag of marbles. He has 6 striped, 1 clear, *x* solid, and *y* swirl marbles.

What are the chances he will pick a swirl marble without looking?

There are 2 red, 2 white, *x* black, and *y* brown beans in a bag.

Without looking, what are the chances of picking a brown bean?

There are 3 clear, 3 blue, *x* white, and *y* orange beads in a bag.

Without looking, what are the chances of picking an orange bead?

There are 5 lemon, 2 strawberry, *x* cherry, and *y* grape lollipops in a bag.

Without looking, what are the chances of picking a grape lollipop?

A bag of markers has 1 yellow, 2 green, *x* pink, and *y* blue markers.

Without looking, Kendra picks a blue marker and then returns it to the bag.

Without looking, what is the probability that Kendra will pick a blue marker again?

A bag of erasers has 3 pink, 3 white, *x* blue, and *y* red erasers.

Without looking, Cyrus picks a red eraser and returns it to the bag.

Without looking, what is the probability that Cyrus will pick a red eraser again?

ERASER

A bag of buttons has 2 green, 3 gray, *x* black, and *y* white.

Without looking, Amir picks a white button and returns it to the bag.

Without looking, what is the probability that Amir will pick a white button again?

483

Grab Bag Cards *continued*

Rosa has a bag of 2 red, 6 green, *x* white, and *y* blue centimeter cubes.

If she picks one out of the bag without looking, what is the probability that it will be a blue centimeter cube?

Ingrid has a bag of 3 red, 5 green, *x* blue, and *y* yellow flag stickers.

If she picks one out of the bag without looking, what is the probability that it will be a yellow flag sticker?

Boris has a bag of 1 red, 5 black, *x* orange, and *y* green toy cars.

If he picks one out of the bag without looking, what is the probability that it will be a green car?

Jesse has a bag of painted blocks: 2 with flowers, 3 with leaves, *x* with animals, and *y* with dots.

Without looking, what is the probability he will pull a block with dots from the bag?

Victor has a bag of family photos: 3 of his parents, 4 of his brothers, *x* of his cousins, and *y* of his grandma.

Without looking, what is the probability he will pull a picture of his grandma from the bag?

Simone has a bag of playing cards: 1 diamond, 4 hearts, *x* spades, and *y* clubs.

Without looking, what is the probability she will pull a club from the bag?

There are 1 green, 2 blue, *x* red, and *y* yellow paper clips in a bag.

Without looking, what are the chances of picking a yellow paper clip?

There are 3 orange, 2 blue, *x* green, and *y* pink dice in a bag.

Without looking, what are the chances of picking a pink die?

There are 2 green, 2 purple, *x* gold, and *y* silver crayons in a bag.

Without looking, what are the chances of picking a silver crayon?

Grab Bag **Record Sheet**

Round	Number of Items Shown on Card		x	y	Total Number of Items in Bag	Probability of Event Occurring	Score
Sample	2	2	1	6 + 4 = 10	15	$\frac{10}{15}$	30
1							
2							
3							
4							
5							
						Total Score	

- -

Name _____ Date _____ Time _____

Grab Bag **Record Sheet**

Round	Number of Items Shown on Card		x	y	Total Number of Items in Bag	Probability of Event Occurring	Score
Sample	2	2	1	6 + 4 = 10	15	$\frac{10}{15}$	30
1							
2							
3							
4							
5							
						Total Score	

Grid Search **Grids**

Use Grids 1 and 2 to play a game.

My Pieces

(Grid 1)

Opponent's Pieces

(Grid 2)

Use Grids 1 and 2 to play another game.

My Pieces

(Grid 1)

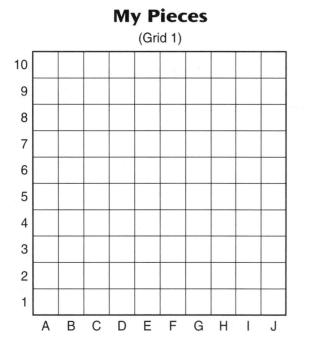

Opponent's Pieces

(Grid 2)

Name _____   Date _____   Time _____

High-Number Toss Record Sheet

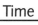

Hundred Millions	Ten Millions	Millions	,	Hundred Thousands	Ten Thousands	Thousands	,	Hundreds	Tens	Ones

Round	Player 1	>, <, =	Player 2
Sample	_1_ _3_ _2_, _6_ 132,000,000	>	_3_ _5_ _6_, _4_ 3,560,000
1	__ __ __ , __ _____		__ __ __ , __ _____
2	__ __ __ , __ _____		__ __ __ , __ _____
3	__ __ __ , __ _____		__ __ __ , __ _____
4	__ __ __ , __ _____		__ __ __ , __ _____
5	__ __ __ , __ _____		__ __ __ , __ _____

Copyright © Wright Group/McGraw-Hill

487

Multiplication Wrestling **Record Sheet**

Round 1   Cards: _____ _____ _____ _____

Numbers formed: _____ * _____

Teams: (_____ + _____) * (_____ + _____)

Products: _____ * _____ = _____

_____ * _____ = _____

_____ * _____ = _____

_____ * _____ = _____

Total (add 4 products): _____

Round 2   Cards: _____ _____ _____ _____

Numbers formed: _____ * _____

Teams: (_____ + _____) * (_____ + _____)

Products: _____ * _____ = _____

_____ * _____ = _____

_____ * _____ = _____

_____ * _____ = _____

Total (add 4 products): _____

Round 3   Cards: _____ _____ _____ _____

Numbers formed: _____ * _____

Teams: (_____ + _____) * (_____ + _____)

Products: _____ * _____ = _____

_____ * _____ = _____

_____ * _____ = _____

_____ * _____ = _____

Total (add 4 products): _____

488

Name That Number **Record Sheet**

Round 1

Target Number: _____ My Cards: _____ _____ _____ _____ _____ _____

My best solution (number sentence): _____

Number of cards used: _____

Round 2

Target Number: _____ My Cards: _____ _____ _____ _____ _____ _____

My best solution (number sentence): _____

Number of cards used: _____

✂ -

Name That Number **Record Sheet**

Round 1

Target Number: _____ My Cards: _____ _____ _____ _____ _____ _____

My best solution (number sentence): _____

Number of cards used: _____

Round 2

Target Number: _____ My Cards: _____ _____ _____ _____ _____ _____

My best solution (number sentence): _____

Number of cards used: _____

Number Top-It Mat (2-Place Decimals)

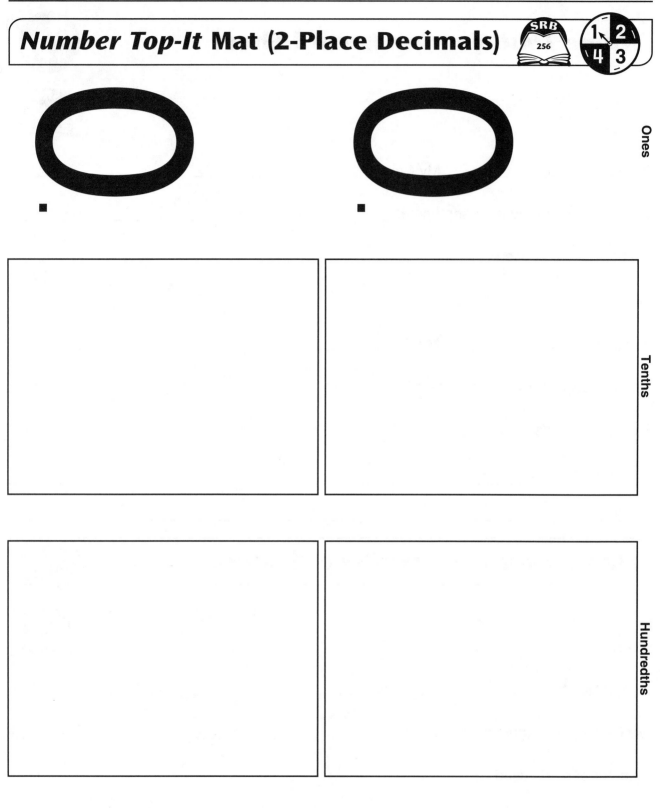

Ones

Tenths

Hundredths

Number Top-It Mat (3-Place Decimals)

SRB
256

Ones

Tenths

Hundredths

Thousandths

491

Number Top-It Mat (7-digits)

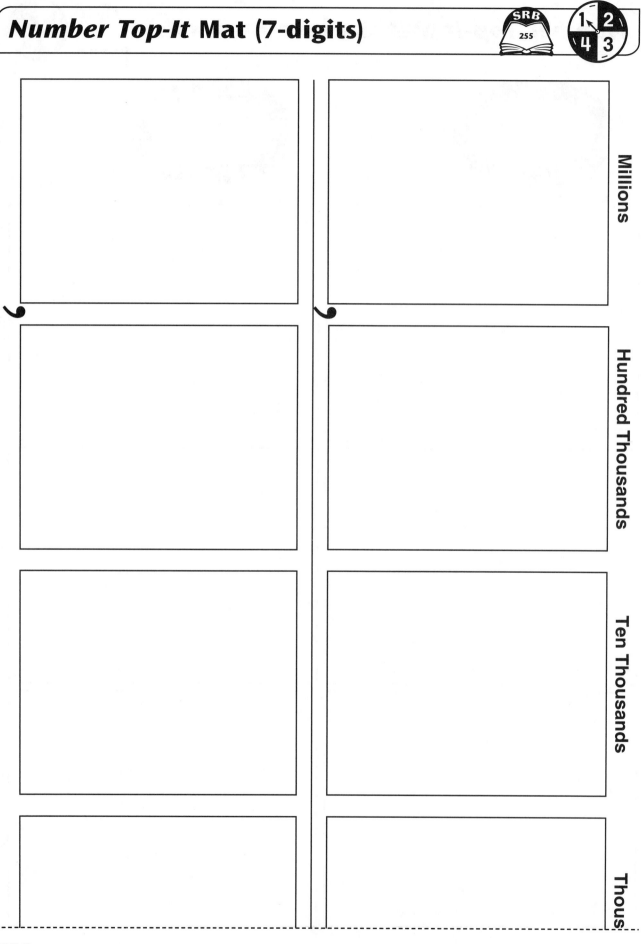

Millions

Hundred Thousands

Ten Thousands

Thous

Number Top-It Mat (7-digits) *continued*

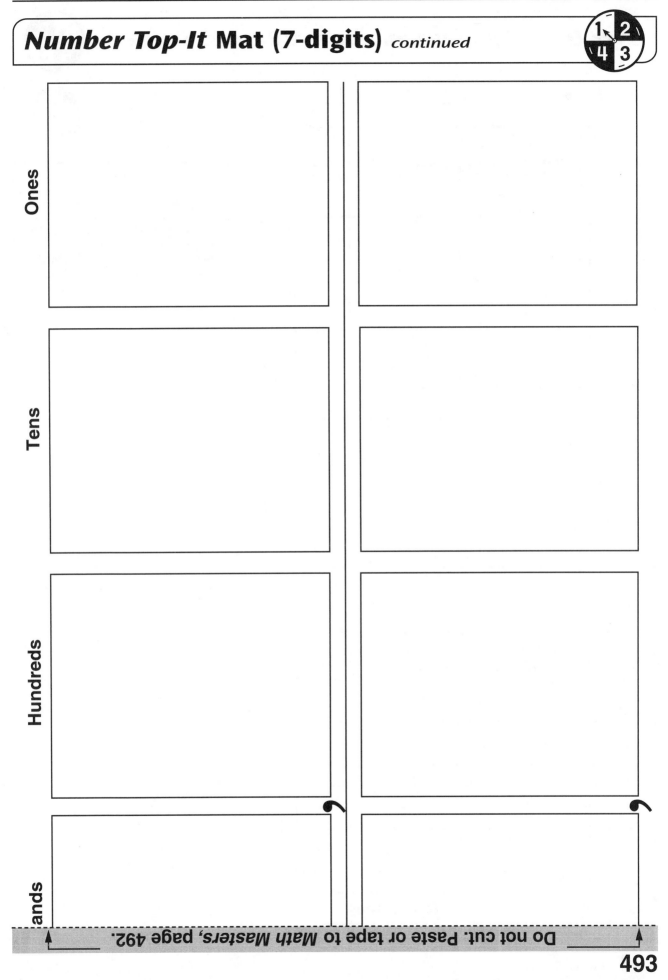

Ones

Tens

Hundreds

ands

Do not cut. Paste or tape to *Math Masters*, page 492.

493

Over & Up Squares Gameboard/Record Sheet

Player 1: _____

Round	Over x-coordinate	,	Up y-coordinate	Score
1		,		
2		,		
3		,		
4		,		
5		,		
6		,		
7		,		
8		,		
9		,		
10		,		
			Total Score	

Score	
Ordered pair	10 points
Line segment	10 points
Square	50 points

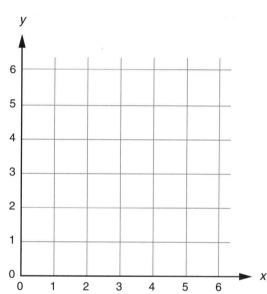

Player 2: _____

Round	Over x-coordinate	,	Up y-coordinate	Score
1		,		
2		,		
3		,		
4		,		
5		,		
6		,		
7		,		
8		,		
9		,		
10		,		
			Total Score	

Patolli Game Mat

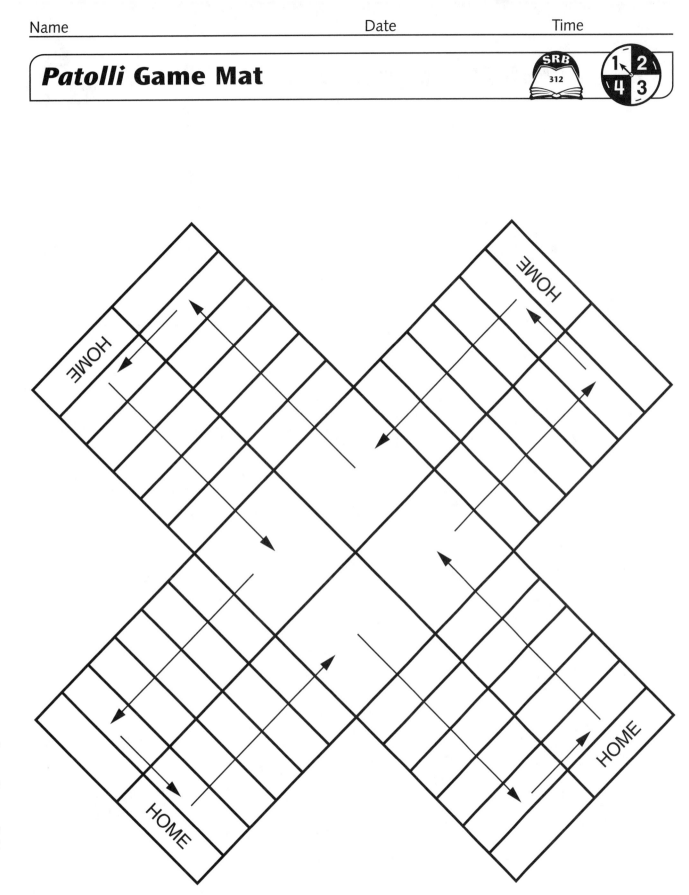

HOME

HOME

HOME

HOME

495

Polygon Pair-Up Polygon Deck

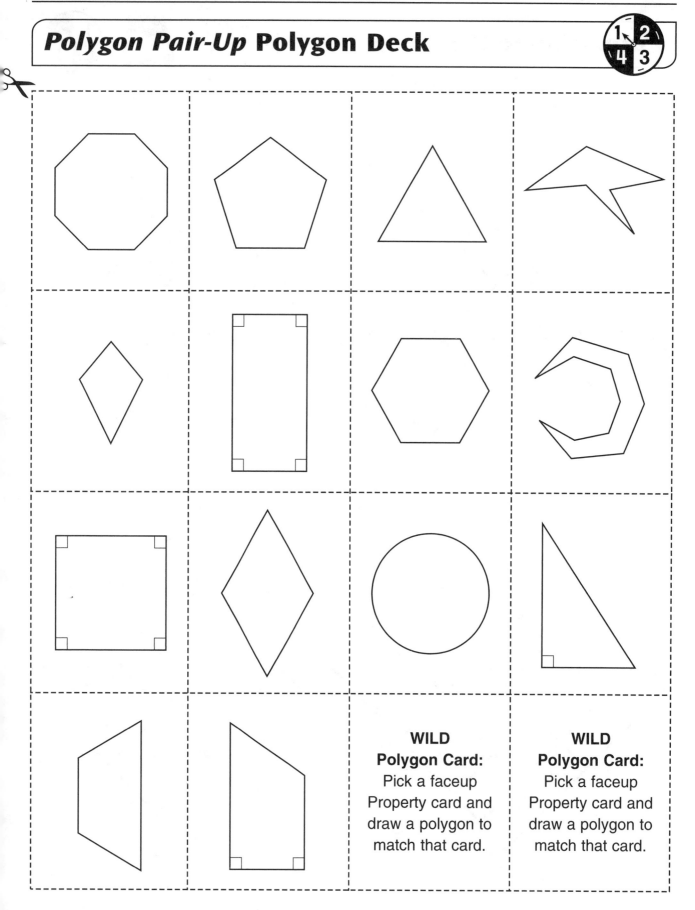

**WILD
Polygon Card:**
Pick a faceup
Property card and
draw a polygon to
match that card.

**WILD
Polygon Card:**
Pick a faceup
Property card and
draw a polygon to
match that card.

Polygon Pair-Up Property Deck

All sides are the same length.	All opposite sides are parallel.	All angles are right angles.	There are more than 4 sides.
There are 4 sides of equal length.	There is only 1 right angle.	There are 2 pairs of parallel sides.	This shape is NOT a polygon.
There are only 3 vertices.	There is only 1 pair of parallel sides.	There are only 4 sides.	This polygon is concave.
There are 4 equal sides and 4 equal angles.	Pairs of sides next to each other have the same length. There are no parallel sides.	**WILD Property Card:** Pick a faceup Polygon card and name a property to match that card.	**WILD Property Card:** Pick a faceup Polygon card and name a property to match that card.

497

Rugs and Fences Area and Perimeter Deck

A Find the area of the polygon.	**A** Find the area of the polygon.	**A** Find the area of the polygon.	**A** Find the area of the polygon.
P Find the perimeter of the polygon.	**P** Find the perimeter of the polygon.	**P** Find the perimeter of the polygon.	**P** Find the perimeter of the polygon.
A or P Opponent's Choice	**A or P** Opponent's Choice	**A or P** Opponent's Choice	**A or P** Opponent's Choice
A or P Player's Choice	**A or P** Player's Choice	**A or P** Player's Choice	**A or P** Player's Choice

Rugs and Fences **Polygon Deck A**

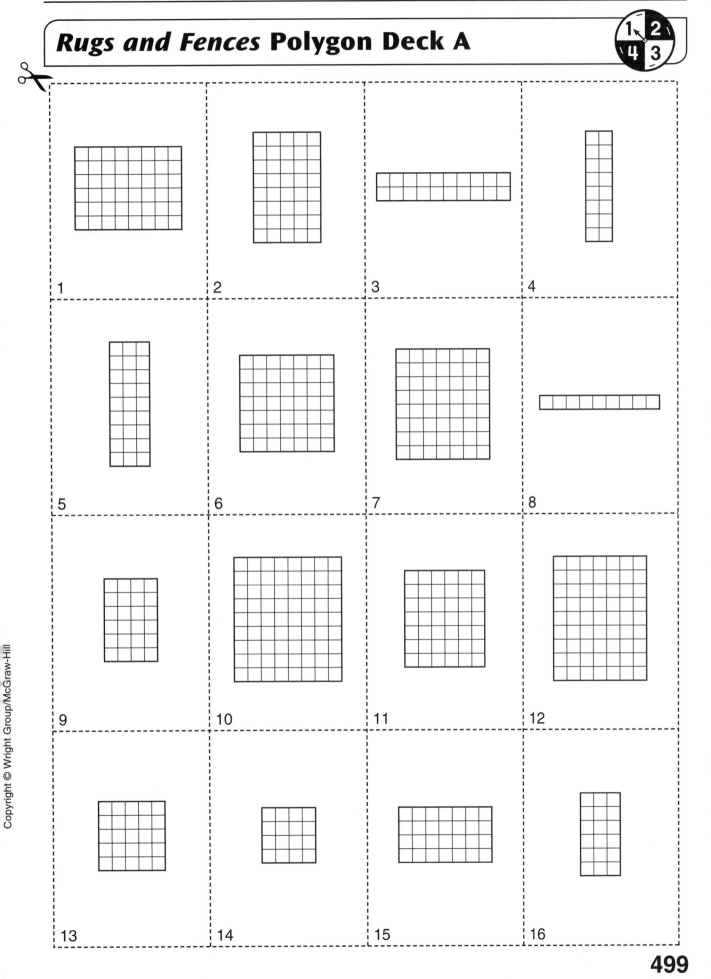

1

2

3

4

5

6

7

8

9

10

11

12

13

14

15

16

Rugs and Fences Polygon Deck B

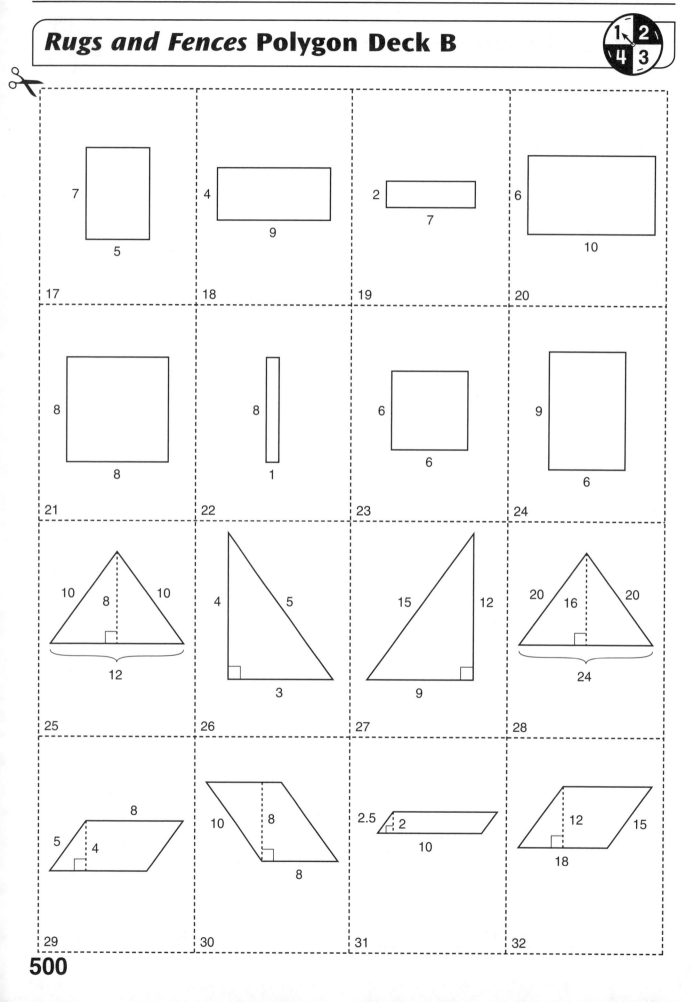

17   18   19   20

21   22   23   24

25   26   27   28

29   30   31   32

Rugs and Fences **Polygon Deck C**

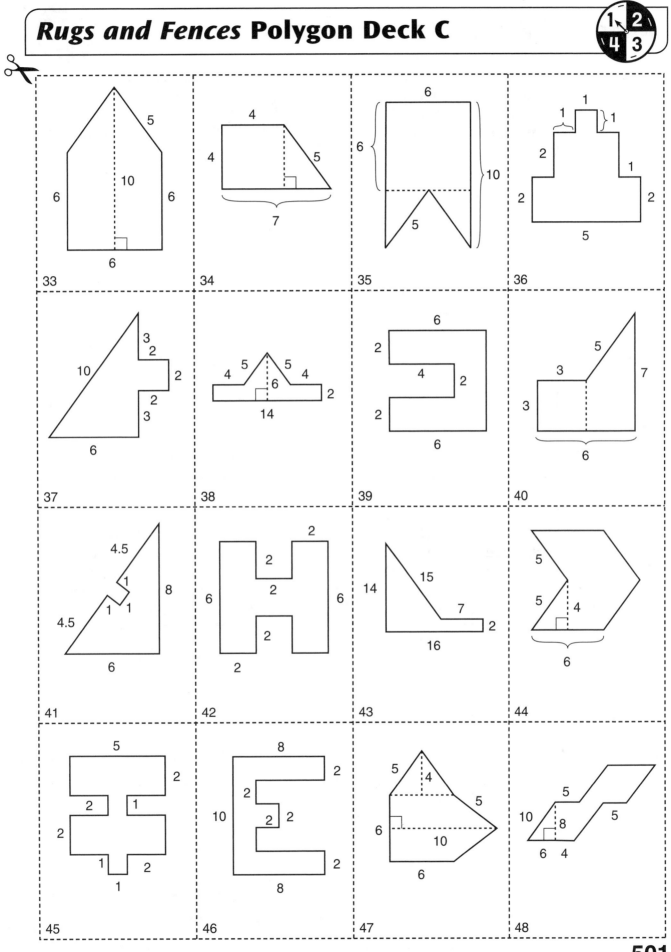

501

Rugs and Fences **Record Sheets**

Round	Record the card number	Circle A (area) or P (perimeter)	Write a number model	Record your score
Sample	3	A or Ⓟ	$10 + 10 + 2 + 2 = 24$	24
1		A or P		
2		A or P		
3		A or P		
4		A or P		
5		A or P		
6		A or P		
7		A or P		
8		A or P		
			Total Score	

Round	Record the card number	Circle A (area) or P (perimeter)	Write a number model	Record your score
Sample	3	A or Ⓟ	$10 + 10 + 2 + 2 = 24$	24
1		A or P		
2		A or P		
3		A or P		
4		A or P		
5		A or P		
6		A or P		
7		A or P		
8		A or P		
			Total Score	

502

Seega **Game Mat**

SRB
309

Player 1

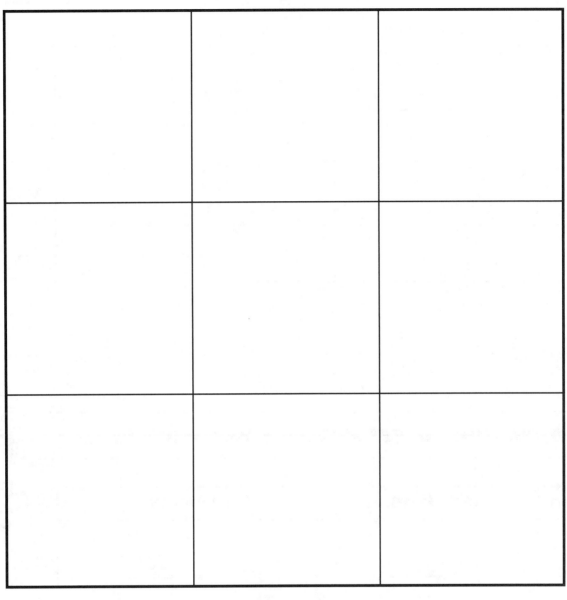

Player 2

Subtraction Target Practice **Record Sheet**

Turn	2-Digit Number	Subtraction
1		
2		
3		
4		
5		

Subtraction Target Practice **Record Sheet**

Turn	2-Digit Number	Subtraction
1		
2		
3		
4		
5		

Sz'kwa Game Mat

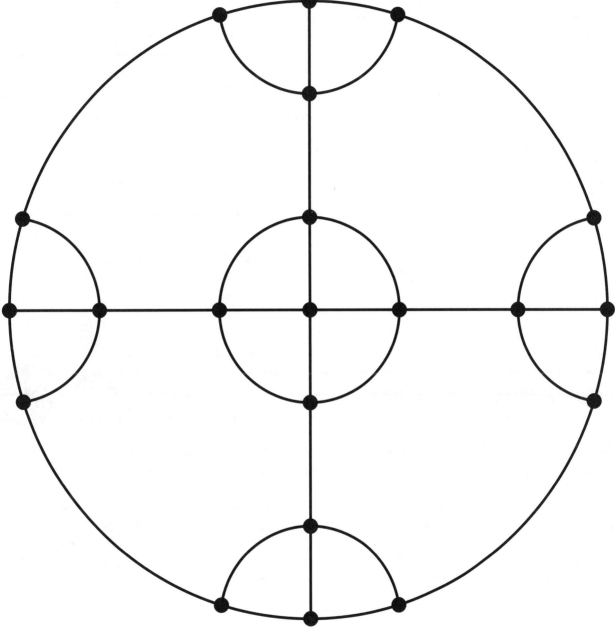

Name _____ Date _____ Time _____

Top-It Record Sheet

Play a round of *Top-It.* Record your number sentence and your opponent's
number sentence. Write >, <, or = to compare the number sentences.

Round	Player 1	>, <, =	Player 2
Sample	$4 + 6 = 10$	<	$8 + 3 = 11$
1			
2			
3			
4			
5			

Name _____ Date _____ Time _____

Top-It Record Sheet

Play a round of *Top-It.* Record your number sentence and your opponent's
number sentence. Write >, <, or = to compare the number sentences.

Round	Player 1	>, <, =	Player 2
Sample	$4 + 6 = 10$	<	$8 + 3 = 11$
1			
2			
3			
4			
5			